Christian Compassion

Christian Compassion

A Charitable History

MONTY L. LYNN

WIPF & STOCK · Eugene, Oregon

CHRISTIAN COMPASSION
A Charitable History

Wipf & Stock
An Imprint of Wipf and Stock Publishers
199 W. 8th Ave., Suite 3
Eugene, OR 97401

www.wipfandstock.com

PAPERBACK ISBN: 978-1-7252-5116-8
HARDCOVER ISBN: 978-1-7252-5117-5
EBOOK ISBN: 978-1-7252-5118-2

05/11/21

For Libby

Contents

Permissions

SACRED WORKS

Scripture quotations are from *New Revised Standard Version Bible: Catholic Edition* © 1989, 1993 National Council of the Churches of Christ in the United States of America. Used by permission. All rights reserved worldwide.

The Book of Mormon: Another Testament of Jesus Christ; The Doctrine and Covenants of the Church of Jesus Christ of Latter-day Saints; The Pearl of Great Price. Salt Lake City: The Church of Jesus Christ of Latter-day Saints, 1981.

IMAGES

AFSC Nurse Treating Palestinian Boy. Nurse Maire Halonon from Finland, a member of the Quaker unit in Khan Yunis, Gaza, treats a Palestinian boy while his older brother looks on. Used with permission by AFSC Archives, Philadelphia, Pennsylvania.

The Bridge of Saint-Bénézet, Avignon, France. E. Viollet-Le-Duc, *Dictionnaire raisonné de L'Architecture Française du XIe au XVIe Siècle*, Paris: Morel, 1867–1868. Public domain.

Bronze Slipper-Shaped Bread Stamp. Greek, Roman and Byzantine Objects from the Archbishop Iakovos Collection, Hellenic College and Holy Cross Greek Orthodox School of Theology © Very Rev. Joachim (John) Cotsonis and Maria Kouroumali, 2012. Used with permission.

Christ of the Breadlines, Fritz Eichenberg © 2019 Estate of Fritz Eichenberg. Licensed by VAGA at Artists Rights Society, NY. Used with permission.

Christian Herald. 1903. Public domain.

Clarence Jordan. Used with permission by Koinonia Farm, Americus, Georgia.

Columbian World Exposition. C. D. Arnold photographic collection, 1892–1901. Used with permission by the Avery Architectural and Fine Arts Library, Columbia University, New York, New York.

PERMISSIONS

David Lipscomb. Used with permission by Beaman Library Archives and Special Collections, Lipscomb University, Nashville, Tennessee.

Dirk Willems Saves the Life of his Captor Prior to his Execution, Jan Luyken, *Martyrs' Mirror,* 1685. Public domain.

Elizabeth Fry Entering Prison © Britain Yearly Meeting. Used with permission by the Library of the Society of Friends in Britain, Friends House, London, UK.

Ephraim United Order Mercantile, ca. 1880–1920. Courtesy of L. Tom Perry Special Collections, Harold B. Lee Library, Brigham Young University, Provo, Utah.

Family in Kavalla, Greece, Receiving a Heifer. Used with permission by the Brethren Historical Library and Archives, Elgin, Illinois.

A Farmer Who Set Aside an Acre of His Farm, 1961. Used with permission by Church World Service Archives, Elkhart, Indiana.

Fr. Georgy Gapon Leading Workers in St. Petersburg, 1905. Public domain.

Father Jack O'Malley Arrested During a UFW Demonstration. Used with permission by the United Farm Workers Photo Collection, Archives of Labor and Urban Affairs, Walter P. Reuther Library, Wayne State University, Detroit, Michigan.

Humility over Pride, Ars moriendi. Lessing J. Rosenwald Collection, Library of Congress, Washington, DC. Public domain.

The Ladder of Divine Ascent, Saint Catherine's Monastery, Mount Sinai, Egypt. Public domain.

The Martyrdom of Saint Lawrence, Pacino di Bonaguida, about 1340. Cutting from the *Laudario of Sant'Agnese.* Used with permission of the J. Paul Getty Museum, Los Angeles, California.

The Offering of the Poor Widow, S. Apollinare Nuovo, Ravenna, Italy. Photographed by Richard Stracke. Creative Commons license.

Pilgrim Flask of Saint Menas. The Walters Art Museum, Baltimore, Maryland. Public domain.

Saint Martin of Tours Dividing His Cloak with a Beggar, Ambrogio Lorenzetti, ca 1340. Yale University Art Gallery, New Haven, Connecticut. Public domain.

The Seven Works of Mercy: Refreshing the Thirsty, Master of Alkmaar. Purchased with the support of the Vereniging Rembrandt and the Commissie voor Fotoverkoop, Used with permission by Rijksmuseum, Amsterdam, Netherlands.

Tom Sinclair, Returned Home from the US Army to Finish the House he Started before World War Two. Manuscript Group 74, Series B, Subseries I, Box 5, Folder 7, Penn-Craft. Used with permission by the Indiana University of Pennsylvania Special Collections and University Archives.

Urine Analysis Chart, Ulrich Pinder. *Epiphanie medicorum,* 1506. Nuremberg, Germany, Folger Shakespeare Library, Washington, DC. Creative commons license.

Vincent de Paul Taking the Chains of a Prisoner. St. Vincent de Paul Image Archive, Vincentian Persons. Public domain.

Walter Rauschenbusch. Public domain.

William Booth. ca. 1907. Library of Congress, Washington, DC. Public domain.

TEXT

Catholic Social Teaching. Thomas Massaro, SJ, *Living Justice,* 2012. Used with permission by Littlefield and Rowman.

Christian Community Development Philosophy © Christian Community Development
  Association, Chicago, Illinois. Used with permission.

"Never Really." Published in Stanisław Barańczak, *The Weight of the Body*, Evanston, IL:
  Triquarterly/Northwestern University Press, 1989. © 1989 Stanislaw Baranczak.
  All rights reserved.

Acknowledgments

THIS WRITING JOURNEY WAS blessed by the compassion and companionship of many. Rob Gailey of Point Loma Nazarene University and Derran Reese of Abilene Christian University are gifted friends who supported and contributed to this effort throughout its development. Although the views and errors are mine, I am grateful for the insights provided by several accomplished scholars as they reviewed chapters; namely: Jeff Childers, Kelly Elliott, Doug Foster, Kent Smith, and Wendell Willis of Abilene Christian University; David Swartz of Asbury University; Warner Woodworth of Brigham Young University; Hugh Feiss, OSB of the Monastery of the Ascension; and Mike Naughton of the University of St. Thomas (MN). Elizabeth Miller and Kaitlin Barr Nadal improved the writing and Lydia Buchanan assisted with graphics.

I also am thankful for the assistance of several librarians, archivists, and communication specialists; specifically: Libby Adams and Lisa McQuillan with the Library of the Society of Friends at Friends House, London; Craig Churchill of the Brown Library at Abilene Christian University; Elizabeth Clemens of the Walter P. Reuther Library at Wayne State University; Bishop Joachim (Cotsonis) of Amissos of the Archbishop Iakovos Library at Hellenic College and Holy Cross Greek Orthodox School of Theology; Maria Kouroumali of the University of Oxford; Laura Curkendall of Church World Service; Don Davis of the American Friends Service Committee Archives; William Kostlevy with Brethren Historical Library and Archives; Katie Miles of Koinonia Farm; Katherine Prater of the Avery Architectural and Fine Arts Library at Columbia University; Elizabeth Rivera of the Beaman Library at Lipscomb University; Jeff Thompson of the Church History Library of The Church of Jesus Christ of Latter-day Saints; and Harrison Wick of Indiana University of Pennsylvania Libraries.

Unbeknownst to them, I have benefitted and learned from the compassion of family and friends who have taught me by their lives and thereby have nourished this project. These include: Mac and Marty Lynn, Vernon and Alice Boyd, Hilary and Mark Jurgens, Ryan and Valerie Lynn, Karen and David Morris, Kim Johnston, Matt Johnston, Richie and Buffy Lynn; Ali Alasaeed and Ezdehar Alsahow, Garry Bailey, Samo Bobek, Sam Brinkman, Jozell Brister, Zach Casey, Elisabeth and Barrett Danelski, Jack Griggs, Randy Harris, Savannah Hennig, LaClaire Hermann, Abigail Hunt, Mark and Nancy Johnson, John Kelly, Vince LaFrance, Rick Lytle, David Moberg, Andrej and Matjaž Mulej and Jelka Mulej-Grilc, Dan Norell, Larry Norsworthy, Gary and Debbie Oliver, Wilson C. "Dub" Orr, Bill Petty, Greg and Cynthia Powell, Tim Redmer, Lamar Reinsch, Tim Sensing, Charles Small, Ed Timmerman, Mel Williams, Steve and Bonnie Willingham, and Marge Wood. Finally, I am thankful to Libby for teaching me compassion by the minute and by the decade, and for her support during this project's long course.

I am grateful for the funding provided by Abilene Christian University that enabled this project and for my many colleagues who supported it through encouragement and friendship. Thanks as well go to Tom Harvey and the staff at the Oxford Centre for Mission Studies where this work delightfully began. Its start was blessed by the hospitality of scholars and students.

Spending time with each of these has made me, I hope, more compassionate. May this book do the same for others.

Opening

COMPASSION IS AN ENDURING motif in the history of Christianity. It is not unique among Christians, nor is it activated evenly across all believers. But when Christianity shines, it often does so because of compassion.[1] As Pope Francis wrote, "The Church's very credibility is seen in how she shows merciful and compassionate love."[2]

Compassion comes from the Latin *compassio* which means to "suffer with." This literal definition is accompanied by several kindred concepts and facets that enlarge its meaning.[3] If we collect some of these related notions and place them in a Christian light, we might say that *compassion is a divinely-inspired calling to charity, mercy, service, and justice that participates in the suffering, love, and hope of all humanity and thereby enables us to partake in God's healing of the world.* More simply, we might say that *Christian compassion is sensing and responding to brokenness because of the love of God.*[4]

For Christians, compassion is not merely a collection of kindnesses that create curb appeal for the faith or the faithful. Rather, compassion encapsulates an orientation to life wherein we see with charity beyond ourselves to others and to the common good (Phil 2:1–11). Surveilling this active virtue is important because we so often are tempted to limit our

1. The Charter for Compassion, a project launched by Karen Anderson in 2008, begins with the words, "The principle of compassion lies at the heart of all religious, ethical and spiritual traditions . . . ." See https://charterforcompassion.org/.

2. Francis, *Misericordiae Vultus*, para. 10. Also see Ireland, "Missionary Theology of Compassion."

3. There is no Greek term that precisely parallels the Latin, *compassio*. The Greek word *plagchnizomai* suggests an ache in one's stomach or heart when greatly troubled, such as in Phil 2:1 and Phlm 7, 12.

4. This is a modern, theological composite of compassion and its cognates. For historical insights into *compassio* and related terms, see Ruys, "Alternative History of Medieval Empathy," 192–5.

allegiances to ourselves, to our present interests, and to those with whom we identify. In an address on the fusing of politics and religion, Caleb Hutcherson counsels that

> By keeping people who are marginalized and oppressed prioritized in our thinking and practices, precisely as Christ teaches us to do, we neutralize the kinds of political ideologies in our midst that leave abuse and destruction in their wake.[5]

Compassion resides at the heart of the Christian gospel. It is a guardian against self-centered living. It nurtures life.

Although some may view compassion as innumerable, relatively undifferentiated acts of kindness, the views propelling compassion evolve, as do the contexts surrounding it, which leads to colorful and variegated practices across the centuries. What others have thought and done deepens and informs our understanding and practice of compassion today. History introduces us to a cloud of witnesses and beckons us to join them.

Thus, my aim in this work is to sketch this quick-moving flipbook of Christian compassion, noting prominent ideas and the individual and institutional actors who employed them. My primary focus is on making introductions rather than offering novel, in-depth analysis. We will see patterns and motifs appear, however, as we keep a quick pace. The time span is capacious—from the first century to the early twenty-first century. As Christianity divides, first East and West and later in the Protestant Reformation and around the U.S. Civil War, patterns become more complex. In the modern and contemporary eras, I will focus on introducing ideas and individual and institutional, allowing detailed patterns to relax into the background.[6]

HAZARDS

As we journey together, we can anticipate a few hazards, two of which loom large: *What* to address (and what to omit) in such a sweeping endeavor, and *how* to treat actors so we avoid hagiography and caricaturization.[7] On

---

5. Hutcherson, "Antidote."

6. Institutional diversity increased after the Reformation but it is a historical optical illusion to imagine that geographic and intellectual differences were not present in the past. Every era has diverse thinkers and heterodox actors. As much activity, ingenuity, and constructive synthesis occurred in antique and medieval times as occurs today. We simply have more historical data available the closer we get to our time, making the past merely appear, in contrast, to be more homogeneous and less detailed.

7. A more extensive discussion of hazards is offered by Leemans, *Reading Patristic Texts* and Tanner, *Politics of God*, 1–34. Tanner's book offers a Christian theology of

the first point, it is obvious that we cannot catalog every instance of kindness and clemency that, to Christians, encircles every moment of life (Eph 2:4–7).[8] My focus will be on describing how compassion is understood and practiced by groups of Christians. I occasionally draw on primary sources, but mostly my goal is to gather and condense extant historical scholarship. Merging these accounts into a single narrative allows us to consider how the river of charity bends through the ages.

Persons and organizations are candidates for inclusion in the compassion narrative by their mere identification as "Christian." I attempt to highlight actors who draw deeply from their Christian identity, despite their limitations and flaws. The searchlight frequently shines on the Mediterranean and on North America due to the accessibility of materials from these regions for the author. The Occident, however, represents only part of the story of world Christianity. I encourage the reader to expand the latitudes and longitudes of the story whenever possible, adding global witnesses.[9]

When you encounter persons or institutions of interest in a chapter, I hope you will track them beyond the pages of this primer, unveiling more of their contributions. Innumerable worthy mentions remain in the shadows. For these, I hope you will step into the story, recalling persons and institutions who fit happily in a chapter and perhaps noting them in the margins.

With actors and ideas circumscribed, a second and more pernicious hazard is how we avoid hagiography and caricaturization, painting an overly heroic or simplistic view of actors, particularly with a subject as saccharine as compassion. Paired with this challenge is how we keep ideas and practices moored to their cultural context, training ourselves to see them in their native habitat rather than uprooting and transplanting them to the unnatural backdrop of our own times. Both of these unrelenting challenges deal with context and *how* we consider compassion over time.[10]

We begin a response to these concerns by acknowledging that the victory column of history includes tragedies and triumphs; depictions of Christians sacrificing to aid others and of Christians furthering injustice

---

social justice that would be an appropriate theological scaffold for any study of compassion. An introductory Christian ethics perspective is provided by Outka in *Agape*.

8. Compassion is not only evidenced through the actions of individuals but through liturgy and formal and informal institutions. As an illustration of the weaving of compassion through daily, lived religion, see Morgan, *Ordinary Saints*.

9. Sources such as the *Dictionary of African Christian Biography* are reminders of numberless Christian leaders who lived compassionately.

10. Rather than arguing for a supersessionist view of history, where succeeding eras replace past ones, the history of compassion illustrates that historic actors and ideas cascade into present-day thinking and practice.

or ignoring need. At times, help and harm cohere in ideologies of injury.[11] Although my focus will be on compassion (thus the subtitle, *A Charitable History*), I will attempt to avoid casting an overly rosy tint on the motives or actions of actors. Likewise, I will attempt to provide a backdrop to each era to keep actors and ideas within their historic context. This is challenging given our quick pace, but appreciating the context is critical for truly understanding ideas and actions.

A related hazard is that lifting a single strand of Christian compassion from history inadvertently halos Christianity and shadows other developments, including the deep roots of Jewish justice, or Buddhist teachings on compassion that were present in Palestine during Jesus' day, or advancements in Islamic medicine and hospitals that informed medieval Christian pharmacology and medical care.[12] I will not develop these contributions but we would be uncharitable and inaccurate to not acknowledge that these and many other tributaries flow into the Christian stream.

Finally, we would commit a grave error if we domesticated our subject. Compassion is gritty and costly—the work of prophets as much as of pastors. It nearly always requires sacrifice and virtue. Christians believe that human compassion reflects the love of God as the dim moon reflects the brilliance of the sun. Thus, overly humanizing compassion diminishes its sources, just as romanticizing it diminishes its reality.

COMPASSION'S COMPOSITION

Before stepping into history, we want to set one more foundational stone in place, and that is to consider compassion's composition. Various disciplines have put compassion under the microscope. Although we do not wander far into these woods, we want to linger long enough to draw the boundaries around our topic.

Our first group of scholars is philosophers and moral ethicists who have interrogated compassion and its cousins. One of these was Max Scheler who studied *sympathy* and teased apart ten of its manifestations, one of which was compassion.[13] Although we will not explore Scheler's concepts, his list illustrates how a single word can contain an abundance of expressions.

---

11. For examples, see Gonzalez, "Flights of Fancy."

12. Sugirtharajah, *Jesus in Asia*, 168–75; Hartnell, *Medieval Bodies*, 17–18.

13. Scheler's ten expressions of sympathy were benevolence, commiseration/pity, community of feeling, compassion, emotional identification, emotional infection, empathy, fellow-feeling, love, and rejoicing. Scheler, *Nature of Sympathy*.

He credited love as the energizing force enlivening compassion and all of sympathy's expressions.[14]

While Scheler reasoned that sympathy and its cognates narrowed the space between persons, philosopher Hannah Arendt argued that this was never completely possible. Moral action requires constant effort to imagine the suffering of others. Arendt described this as *visiting* others. Lisa Jane Disch explains Arendt's notion as: "To visit . . . you must travel to new locations, leave behind what is familiar, and resist the temptation to make yourself at home where you are not."[15] Compassion requires that we see beyond ourselves and attempt to walk in another's shoes. But it also respectfully acknowledges that we cannot fully know another's experience. Both Scheler and Arendt help us see that compassion is multifaceted and that it requires *kenosis*, or emptying in Christian terms (Phil 2:7a). It stops short of assuming that we can fully know and feel another's pain and perspective.

Biologists contribute to our understanding of compassion, too. In contrast to the renown claim that "the fittest survive," Charles Darwin and Henry Drummond explained that species flourish when they cooperate and protect their weaker members.[16] Endowed with intellect and language, humans were specially equipped, they believed, to instinctively feel empathy.[17] In contrast with Scheler's love as the fount of sympathy and compassion, Darwin believed that *self-interest* was the animating impulse—a motive he may have borrowed from economist Adam Smith.[18] More recently, biological research has affirmed an altruistic impulse behind compassion.[19] Whether animated by self-interest or self-sacrifice, biologists help us see that compassion is widely distributed. They add to our wondering about its source and purpose.

Social scientists pick up the baton to help us see compassion's internal operation; specifically, that it engages how we *see, feel,* and *act.* Compassion involves *seeing* by taking the perspective of others; *feeling* sympathy and concern by experiencing what others feel; and *acting* or being motivated to

---

14. The *Catechism of the Catholic Church* (sec. 1827) similarly identifies charity as animating and inspiring all the virtues. For a review of contemporary philosophical insights, see Bein, *Compassion and Moral Guidance*, 2–10. For a perspective from Christian moral philosophy, see Pope, "Love in Contemporary Christian Ethics."

15. Disch, *Hannah Arendt*, 159.

16. Drummond, *Lowell Lectures*. For recent evolutionary arguments for compassion, see Goetz et al., "Compassion." For a response from Christian ethics, see Pope, *Human Evolution*, 214–49.

17. Segal, *Social Empathy*, 10.

18. Smith, *Theory of Moral Sentiments*. For analysis, see Kleer, "Final Causes."

19. Batson, "Empathy-Altruism Hypothesis."

alleviate suffering.[20] Acting without seeing can be intrusive; seeing without feeling can be detachment; and feeling without acting can be mere sentimentality. When combined, however, these facets deepen compassion.

Psychologists show us that compassion tends to snowball; empathy leads to charitable giving, prosocial behavior, and personal wellbeing.[21] Further, being compassionate toward oneself can spillover into compassion toward others because it lifts our chin above our own pain and isolation.[22] In sum, social scientists show us that compassion involves our entire selves and is good for us, collectively and individually.

Perspectives from philosophy and the natural and social sciences help fill in our understanding of compassion. Christian theology does so by intentionally bringing God in the frame.[23]

Compassion's Divine Nature

Scripture teaches that God is the fount of compassion. Jesus "emptied himself" and "humbled himself (Phil 2:7a, 8a) because it is God's nature to know and bless others.[24] Compassion comes from God.

A parable that is often cited regarding compassion is the good Samaritan (Luke 10:29–37). James Keenan says that the Samaritan parable is "first and foremost not a story about how we should treat others but rather the story of what Christ has done for us . . . . it is a retelling of the entire Gospel."[25] The Samaritan is a stand-in for God who aids the wounded. Indeed, "The Lord is good to all, and his compassion is over all that he has made" (Ps 145:9).

---

20. I chose the term *compassion* because it connotes action as well as seeing and feeling. *Empathy* is often the term used to address the latter two components. A variety of definitions and theories exist for these constructs. For additional detail, see Davis, "Measuring Individual Differences in Empathy"; Lam et al., "Empathy Training," 163; Stuber, "Empathy"; Wilhelm and Bekkers, "Helping Behavior." For a philosopher's view of seeing and feeling, see Nussbaum, "Compassion," 31.

21. Kim and Kou, "Not All Empathy is Equal"; McClure, "Go and Do Likewise"; Saarinen, "Relationship of Dispositional Compassion."

22. Self-compassion is defined as "kindness toward oneself when facing pain or failure; perceiving one's experiences as part of a larger human experience rather than feeling isolated; and holding painful thoughts and feelings in balanced awareness": Welp and Brown, "Self-Compassion," 54.

23. Lived compassion is impacted by culture, ritual, institutions, and other influences. Formal theology helps us frame the essence of our topic but it is not the only defining influence on historical actors.

24. Gorman, *Inhabiting the Cruciform God*, 9–39.

25. Keenan, "Radicalizing the Comprehensiveness of Mercy," 195.

Although the gifts of God cannot be repaid, one response is to pay them forward by extending compassion to others. In other words, rightly-formed compassion grows from thankfulness. As the Swiss theologian Karl Barth said, "The best and most pious works in the service of God, whatever they might be, would be nothing if in their whole root and significance they were not works of gratitude."[26] Compassion is not intended to proceed from guilt or force. Rather, it flows out of a deep thankfulness for God's abundant love. It is a *calling* as our definition states; a *conversion* that occurs as a thankful heart blooms into a charitable life.[27]

Barth described divine and human compassion as flowing through a circular relationship: God shows compassion to people who in turn witness to God's nature and gifts by responding compassionately to one another (1 John 4:11).[28] Similarly, David Augsburger used the term "tripolar spirituality" to describe this intimate relationship, this *sobornost*, as Russian mystics might say, among God, others, and oneself: we are led through "love of God to love of neighbor (who stands in for God in our daily encounters) . . . ultimately to becoming a loved and loving self." (cf.1 John 3:17, 4:20b).[29]

Compassion is not limited to discrete acts of individual agency. It can also be woven into a community or society, embedded in laws, cultures, and institutions that promote *shalom*. This was the vision of Israel's moral ethic wherein each person was charged with ensuring justice for the most vulnerable.[30] It is the vision of the church and kingdom of God as well, where relationships and institutions of charity, mercy, service, and justice glorify God.

When humans show compassion toward others, Scripture teaches that it is not a mere mustering of human virtue. Rather, compassion is animated and enabled by God. When you serve, it is "God at work in you, enabling you both to will and to work for his good pleasure" (Phil 2:13). As Paul wrote in the Ephesian letter, "For we are what he has made us, created in Christ Jesus for good works, which God prepared beforehand to be our way

---

26. Barth, *Church Dogmatics*, III.2, §43–44:170. Cf. I Cor 13:3.

27. Ivan Illich stressed this point in the parable of the Good Samaritan. Cayley (*Rivers North*, 31) writes of Illich's view: "The Samaritan, Jesus says, is moved by 'compassion.' He undergoes a conversion, an inward turning around which begins in his guts and ends in a unique and entirely personal relationship."

28. Matheny, *Dogmatics and Ethics*. Augustine offered a similar argument; see Stewart-Kroeker, *Pilgrimage*, 205–6. Thomas Aquinas wrote that charity toward God and others is unitary, "for its end is one, namely, the goodness of God." Aquinas, *Summa Theologica*, II–II, q. 23, a. 5.

29. Augsburger, *Dissident Discipleship*, 14.

30. Cohen, *Justice in the City*; Unterman, *Justice for All*, 83.

of life" (Eph 2:10). God created opportunities for compassion and helps us respond virtuously and resiliently to them. As the modern Coptic monk Matthew the Poor advised would-be disciples of Christ:

> If he seeks to please God by works, labor, vigil, tears, prayer or service, he is denied the spirit to do so. He has no strength to fulfill any work whatsoever. No sooner does he attempt to do so that he leaves it unfinished. This goes on until he understands that it is not by strength nor by power, but by the Spirit of God that man [sic] does the works of God, however simple.[31]

Finally, regarding compassion's divine nature, just as its source and enabling is divine, so is its end. Compassion's intended effect is to honor God. Jesus warned against reveling in honor received for compassionate deeds when compassion's aim is to incarnate goodness and spread gladness by glorifying God (Matt 6:3–4; 2 Cor 9:11–14).

Seeing, Feeling, and Acting in Christ

If we return to the *seeing, feeling,* and *acting* framework that social scientists introduced to us, and spy these through a Christian lens, we gain additional insight.

Desiring and Seeing

Generally speaking, *seeing* refers to perspective-taking: attempting to see from another person's view or walk in another person's shoes. A Christian perspective enhances this notion by nurturing a desire to see and a habitus in seeing, by finding God in others, and by avoiding pride.

Jon Sobrino observes that seeing begins with *desiring* to see. Jesus wants to liberate us to see brokenness—to heal us from being blind to injustice and inhumanity; to wake up to hunger, poverty, and injustice; and to repent from supplanting justice with religious tradition and unjust social structures (Mark 7:10–13).[32] To suddenly wake up to God and the needs of others can be life-changing, as Paul, Constantine I, Francis of Assisi, Martin Luther, August Hermann Francke, Óscar Romero, and millions of others

---

31. Matthew the Poor and Rubenson, *Sojourners*, 218. John Wesley taught a similar view. As summarized by Randy Maddox: "our love for God and others can awaken and grow only in response to experiencing God's gracious love for us, shed abroad in our hearts by the Holy Spirit." Maddox, "Visit the Poor," 74.

32. Sobrino, *Where Is God?*, 37–43.

can attest. Sometimes, desiring to see is a progressive healing, awakening us again and again to our and others's needs (cf. Rev. 3:2; Mark 20:22–26). Learning to see can be stimulated by spending time with others [**Visiting the Poor**], but it is transformed by being born again (see chapter 4).

Visiting the Poor

John Wesley's theology of compassion was grounded in experience. Wesley often visited the sick and the poor. Experiences with them transformed his views about illness and poverty. In one of his sermons, Wesley commented that "One great reason why the rich, in general, have so little sympathy for the poor, is, because they so seldom visit them."[33]

Two Wesleyan scholars, Randy Maddox and Ted Jennings, elaborate on Wesley's counsel and practice. Maddox wrote that:

> Authentic compassion can only take form through sincere encounters with those in need. This is why Wesley emphasized the need to *visit* the poor and sick even more than he did the need to offer them aid. He recognized that failure to visit was the major contributing cause of the lack of compassion that lay behind withholding aid.[34]

Jennings adds that:

> By seizing on something so apparently simple as visiting the sick, Wesley has provided . . . a practical grounding for what can become a radical praxis. In visiting the marginalized, we invite them to transform us, to transform our hearts, to transform our understanding, to transform us into instruments of the divine mercy and justice.[35]

Wesley reminds us that experiences with others can stimulate and sharpen our sight.[36] Following the language of Pope Francis, con-

---

33. Wesley, "On Visiting the Sick," II.3.

34. Maddox, "Visit the Poor," 77.

35. Jennings, *Good News*, 57–58.

36. Historians have argued that later visiting the poor may have been propelled by other motives, including quieting social unrest by reestablishing relationships between social classes, attracting the poor to the church, and determining the worthiness of the needy. See Shok, "Organized Almsgiving," 20–21.

temporary Catholics use the term "accompaniment" to emphasize that "visiting" is about growing in relationships.[37]

Over time, perspective-taking can become a trait and develop into the virtue of compassion.[38] Philosopher Iris Murdoch describes it this way:

> if we consider what the work of attention is like, how continuously it goes on, and how imperceptibly it builds up structures of value round about us, we shall not be surprised that at crucial moments of choice most of the business of choosing is already over . . . . The moral life, in this view, is something that goes on continually, not something that is switched off in between the occurrence of explicit moral choices. What happens in between such choices is indeed what is crucial.[39]

Murdock encourages us "to pierce the veil of selfish consciousness and join the world as it really is."[40] We do this by acknowledging, lamenting, and engaging brokenness, calamity, and injustice. We see this modeled in Jesus.[41] Although we cannot respond to every need, compassion doesn't occur if we are blind to the grace of God or the plight of others or of our own poverty.[42]

One thing seeing enables, with practice, is recognizing the divine in others [**Sheep and Goats**]. Maria Skobtsova, a twentieth-century Orthodox nun, used to say, "Each person is the very icon of God incarnate in the world."[43] Skobtsova pictured those she encountered on the streets of Paris as walking icons. If we have a pure heart, if we desire to see, Jesus promises that we will see God (Matt 5:8). This is similar to how Gregory of Nyssa interpreted the sixth beatitude: if we have a pure heart, we will witness the divine in others. Like Barnabas, we may appear and see the grace of God in the lives of others (Acts 11:23).[44]

---

37 Francis, *Evangelii Gaudium*; Lamberty, "Art of Accompaniment."

38. Cloninger et al., *Temperament and Character Inventory*.

39. Murdoch, *Sovereignty of Good*, 36.

40. Murdoch, *Sovereignty of Good*, 91. For elaboration, see Benbassat, "Reflective Function."

41. Rowe addresses this in his delightful, *Christianity's Surprise*.

42. Fikkert and Kapic, *Becoming Whole*.

43. Skobtsova, *Mother Maria Skobtsova*, 25, 57. Gregory of Nazianzus used similar language to link humans to Christ and to the Spirit's life-giving work at creation. See Thomas, "Human Icon."

44. Eklund, "Blessed Are the Image-Bearers," 739.

Sheep and Goats

In a seminal teaching near the end of his ministry, Jesus described himself as a king who gathered the nations, dividing people according to their acts of compassion (Matt 25:31–46). Although neither the righteous nor the wicked in the teaching saw Jesus among the hungry, thirsty, naked, sick, incarcerated, or displaced, Jesus assumed their identities: "Truly I tell you, just as you did it to one of the least of these who are members of my family, you did it to me" (Matt 25:40b).

This oft-cited passage emphasizes that we act compassionately, but it also prompts reflection on sight. First, as Maria Skobtsova proclaimed, Jesus goes by pseudonyms.[45] He invites us to look for him at the pantry and jail, at the border and brothel, in the womb and in war (see Fig. i.1). Second, I suspect that the wicked and the righteous did not see Jesus in others for different reasons. The wicked did not desire to see the needs of others and, therefore, did not respond. The righteous saw the need and extended charity. Jesus validated their acts, affirmed the interlaced relationship among God, self, and others, and assured the future compassionate to know that he was blessed by their care. Perhaps the passage also suggests that seeing God in others requires practice given that the divine is often in disguise.

45. Skobtsova, *Mother Maria Skobtsova*, 79–83.

Fig. i.1. *The Christ of the Breadlines* by Fritz Eichenberg.

Theologians affirm the importance of believing that the indelible image of God, the *imago Dei*, rests on persons (Gen 1:26, 27; 5:1; Acts 17:29).[46] Although Christians relinquish some rights as servants of the *kenotic* Christ (Phil 2:7), the rights accorded to divine identity are inalienable.[47] We cannot renounce them, nor would we want to—they represent the dignity of one created, loved, and redeemed by God. They serve as a warrant for compassion, and when they are cloaked, honor is all the more justified (1 Cor 12:22–25).

Endowed with a divine impression, human dignity endures, regardless of whether it is recognized or respected. Thomas Massaro draws out the implications of this teaching:

> There is nothing a person can do or undergo to forfeit this lofty status. Even those who commit heinous crimes, acquire debilitating diseases, or find themselves separated from their homelands or from gainful employment retain immense worth and

46. Visiting the sick or poor may require brief, minimal contact or it may conjure up romantic notions of benevolence. In actuality, caring can be demanding. The *imago Dei* offers a pastoral practice of the presence of God and an ethic of praxis. Vincent de Paul reminded the Daughters of Charity: "You will go and visit the poor ten times a day, and ten times a day you will find God there!" The divine identity may be cloaked, but one can learn to see Christ. Ivan Illich encouraged acting out of the belief "that he who knocks at the door, asking for hospitality, will be treated by me as Christ, not *as if* he were, but as Christ." Quoted in Cayley, *Rivers North*, 110.

47. Catholic theologians view human dignity and rights as grounded in the *imago Dei*.

are to be accorded the greatest of dignity. All people—whether they are languishing on death row in a prison, receiving treatment at an AIDS clinic in a hospital, or living in a refugee camp in the most remote corner of the world—deserve to be treated with inalienable respect as children of God.[48]

Finally, in regard to seeing, we have the consistent biblical injunction to eschew the pride that frequently stalks charitable acts (Matt 6:3–4; 2 Cor 9:11–14). We are susceptible of attributing gifts and good to ourselves. In the Gospels, however, Jesus regularly shocks his hearers when he announces that the guest list of heavenly parties is not composed of patrons but of sinners, the sick, the poor, the lame, and the blind who inevitably see, hear, and live good news (Matt 9:11–13; Luke 14:13).[49] This is not to say that poverty or disability is to be desired; rather, it reminds us that Jesus is among the poor and that often, those without eyes have the keenest vision (Matt 5:29). Compassion requires seeing the upside-down kingdom of God.[50]

Feeling

Let's advance to the *feeling* aspect of compassion, also known as "empathy." While caring can be born of reason, it often is quickened by affect.[51] The coming of Immanuel ("God with us") conveys to us divine participation and solidarity with humans. Similarly, the author of Hebrews says that Jesus can sympathize with our weaknesses because he lived as a human (Heb 4:14–15). This means experiencing suffering and death in addition to observing it. Suffering is not beyond God's knowledge (Exod 3:7) and God did not become human for self-enrichment. Jesus became poor for the sake of humanity; he participated and joined with us: "For you know the generous act of our Lord Jesus Christ, that though he was rich, yet for your sakes he became poor, so that by his poverty you might become rich" (2 Cor 8:9).[52]

48. Massaro, *Living Justice*, 81.

49. Louise J. Lawrence interprets gospel healing accounts to recognize the abilities of those who are blind, deaf, mute, epileptic, and leprous and how they exceed those of the righteous who seem unable to see or hear (Matt 13:13). See Lawrence, *Sense and Stigma*.

50. Kraybill, *Upside-Down Kingdom*.

51. Many antique and medieval theologians viewed affect as an inferior prompt to charity, preferring reasoning over passion. In modern times, affect has been critiqued if it is sentimentality without action or if it is given to manipulation by actors who prolong inequality or promote unhealthy pity or patronage: see Adams, *Markets of Sorrow*, 9–12; Lupton, *Toxic Aid*, 5. Our emphasis, however, is on responding holistically to need and to the ways affect contributes to compassion.

52. For a theology of God and pain see Kitamori, *Theology of the Pain of God*.

Followers of Christ join Jesus in death (Rom 6:3–4) and participate in
his sufferings and in his resurrection to new life (Luke 9:23; Rom 6:5; Col
1:24; 1 Pet 4:13). We imitate Jesus' (*imitatio Christi*) participation by moving
toward rather than away from sorrows, entanglements, and tragedies. Why?
Because in these engagements we yearn for and experience the kingdom of
God. To feel broken with others is to appreciate God's healing. As Randy
Maddox writes:

> We do not engage in works of mercy just because we "feel like
> it" or only when we feel like it, nor do we engage in them only
> because it is what God commands or because it helps others. We
> are encouraged to engage in works of mercy because God has
> graciously designed this engagement to have an empowering
> and formative impact on us.[53]

Compassion does not depend on affection. Rather, empathy prompts
us to care about and participate with others (Phil 2:4). Its *telos* exceeds pa-
thos or pity. Empathy causes us to reflect—to wrestle with injustice, idols,
and brokenness in society and in ourselves.[54] Ignacio Ellacuría and Jon Sobrino argue that this is formative—that the gospel cannot truly be realized
if one remains at arm's length from crucified people (Matt 19:23).[55] Michelle
Ferrigno Warren agrees:

> Seeing and sharing the pain and injustice surrounding the poor
> doesn't just change our perspective and social construct and
> force us to dig deeper into our faith; it also changes our per-
> ception of our own wholeness and our ability to confront the
> brokenness around us.[56]

Once again, we see the interlaced strands of God, others, and self in Christian discipleship.

Hearing

Before proceeding to acting, I will insert one additional element important
to compassion, and that is *hearing*. Hearing acknowledges the insight and
honors the dignity of those suffering. It elevates the vulnerable rather than

---

53. Maddox, "Visit the Poor," 75.

54. Fikkert and Kapic, *Becoming Whole*.

55. See Sobrino, *No Salvation Outside the Poor*. This is not to suggest that we are subsumed by pain, or that we are unable to separate ourselves from others who are in pain.
To be compassionate often requires a clear sense of ourselves and emotional regulation.

56. Warren, *Power of Proximity*, 44.

heroizing caregivers.[57] Listening is not perfunctory. A person who has experienced hardship knows a unique reality that can be approached by others, but never fully known. That person and their experience is worthy of special respect. Stanisław Barańczak recognized this in his poem, "Never Really," as he reflected on writing about the Nazi concentration camps of World War II:

> I never really felt the cold, never
> was devoured by lice, never knew
> true hunger, humiliation, fear for my life:
> at times I wonder whether I have any right to write.[58]

A posture of hearing affords the respect and deference due to others who are in or have passed through fire.[59]

Hearing also directly addresses issues of power. It affirms the agency and resources of those who are suffering, identifying and challenging beliefs and structures that further alienation, fatalism, and domination. Careful listening and true hearing can avert actions that are unhelpful and dehumanizing, and instead, promote a mutual acknowledgement and exchange of gifts.[60]

Acting

We arrive finally at *action*. For the Christian, action grows from hope. Jon Sobrino reminds us of this joyful reality:

> Fidelity to the real . . . includes hope—a hope made possible by reality itself. But this hope is an active one, and not only an expectant one. It helps concrete reality to come to be what it seeks to be. And that is love. Love and hope—in that order—are two sides of the same coin: the conviction, put in practice, that reality has possibilities. Love and hope mean helping to bring to light the better, the more humane, presently gestating in the womb of reality.[61]

Often, we do not know what to do. We rightly assess that others ask for more than we can give. Our efforts to assume the place of God in healing the world inevitably ends in disillusionment, burnout, oppression, and

---

57. For the role of conversation and contemplation in listening, see Goulding, "Celebrating Grace."

58. Barańczak, *Weight of the Body*, 30.

59. Matthiesen and Klitmøller, "Encountering the Stranger."

60. Paolo Freire discusses power extensively in *Pedagogy of the Oppressed*.

61. Sobrino, "Spirituality," 684.

idolatry.[62] It is a delicate balance to recognize what we can do and to do it. As Jesus asked his disciples in the feeding of the four thousand, "How many loaves have you?" (Matt 15:34).

Joan Chittister emboldens us to act when we are able:

> God provides us with everything we need in life to come to wholeness by living well the lives we have, however paltry they may be. If there are those who lack the goods of life, it is not because God does not provide them. It is because we do not provide them. God is not a ringmaster whose function it is to save us either from the learnings of life or from the darkest, weakest parts of ourselves. To hope otherwise, I am convinced, belies the very notion both of life and of the nature of God. Life, if we allow it, is what grooms us to the point of godliness. God is what waits to fulfill us when we have finally filled ourselves to the ready point.[63]

These are strong words and we are quick to apply the salve of God's grace to relieve the sting. But Chittister is not shortening the activity of God in healing; she begins and ends the passage with divine action. Neither is she attempting to strong-arm compassion with guilt or advance neo-colonial paternalism. She simply is entreating us to serve and respond cheerfully to the grace of God, who "by the power at work within us is able to accomplish abundantly far more than all we can ask or imagine" (Eph 3:20).[64] As the apostle John wrote, "Little children, let us love, not in word or speech, but in truth and action" (1 John 3:18).

It is important, however, that we not make action the ultimate and definitive expression of compassion. A façade of good works can be motivated by self-interest rather than compassion (1 Cor 13:3).[65] Compassionate

---

62. For one take on this see Wigg-Stevenson, *World Is Not Ours to Save.*

63. Chittister, *In Search of Belief*, 34.

64. Announcing the Year of Jubilee in *Misericordiae Vultus*, para. 9, Pope Francis wrote:

> As we can see in Sacred Scripture, mercy is a key word that indicates God's action towards us. He does not limit himself merely to affirming his love, but makes it visible and tangible. Love, after all, can never be just an abstraction. By its very nature, it indicates something concrete: intentions, attitudes, and behaviours that are shown in daily living. The mercy of God is his loving concern for each one of us. He feels responsible; that is, he desires our wellbeing and he wants to see us happy, full of joy, and peaceful. This is the path which the merciful love of Christians must also travel. As the Father loves, so do his children. Just as he is merciful, so we are called to be merciful to each other.

65. In "Understanding Compassion," Ukeachusim informally describes good works

action may entail lament and prayer. It may involve direct aid or advocacy. It may require the sharing of time or money, stopping a habit, or shifting a lifestyle. It is impacted by *how* we give: a response of gratitude to the gifts of God; a witness. Action is concerned with how we act also: ideally, out of gratitude for the gifts of God and with love for neighbor, witnessing to hope in pain, wealth in poverty, and joy in caring [**Indifference and Renewal**].

Action is a natural response to desiring, seeing, feeling, and hearing; without these, care is distorted; with these, care is perfected. As the parable of the Good Samaritan (Luke 10:25–37) reminds us, the priest and the Levite *saw* but the Samaritan *saw* and *acted*.[66] As affirmed by God's circulating gifts, action turns givers into receivers and receivers into givers.

Indifference and Renewal

Well-formed compassion requires indifference as well as passion. Rather than an absence of concern or interest, as the English word suggests, Vincent de Paul used the French word *indifférence* to mean relaxing into God's will. *Kenosis*, mentioned earlier, is a similar idea. As Sung Hae Kim summarizes, Vincent's indifference allows "people to free themselves from their own desires and attachments and helps them to 'love all things from the eyes of God.'"[67] Indifference invites us to trust God. It liberates Christians from focusing on ambition, greed, fear, and self-centeredness, freeing them to serve with simplicity, humility, gentleness, and courage. The compassionate pray that they will see, feel, and act as God does and that God's will will be evinced on earth as it is in heaven (Matt 6:10b).[68]

Although the primary storyline of the history of compassion focuses on action rather than renewal, honest diaries and biographies

---

in Nigeria—schools, hospitals, fund-raising for causes—that enhance the social status of church leaders and marginalize the poor (p. 386).

66. For insights into this and other biblical passages that contrast seeing with acting, see Donahue, "Companions on a Journey," 8–9.

67. Kim, "Virtue of Holy Indifference," 1.

68. Ignatius of Loyola introduced the virtue of indifference in his "Spiritual Exercises" (article 179). Antonio Rosmini (1797–1855) expounded upon this virtue in *Constitutions of the Institute of Charity*. Rosmini encouraged six tests of indifference, each lasting one month: spiritual exercises; serving the sick in hospitals or hospices; making a month's pilgrimage, without money; carrying out humble and lowly duties with great care; "teaching Christian doctrine to children and uneducated people"; and "preaching or hearing confessions (priests) or assisting the poor." See Belsito, *Constitutions*, 22–23.

reveal that discouragement and compassion fatigue visit all engaged in charitable service, just as it visits those suffering. On several occasions, the Gospels record Jesus retreating to pray alone (Mark 1:35; Lk 5:15–16; 22:39–41). Although we only have a record of one of these prayers, many surmise that Jesus was seeking to align himself with God's will and be renewed in God's presence. Spiritual disciplines, the Eucharist, and other actions of renewal can be vehicles of the love of God, just as acts of compassion can be.

Figure i.2 illustrates the five facets of Spirit-enabled, Christian compassion that we have discussed. These facets need not follow in sequence and they may not all be present on each occasion, but compassion tends to be energized when multiple facets are present. In sum, because of God's mercy, we desire to see. We put on the shoes of others and we see in people, human dignity and Christ himself. We empathize with and listen to others, and love and hope enable us to act. When we extend a hand (or receive one), we see ourselves and life, anew. We love God and we taste the kingdom of heaven.

Although the five facets of compassion are described at the level of a single person, it is important to recognize the strong communitarian nature of Christian compassion. As Deuteronomic and New Testament moral codes suggest, *communities* see, feel, and act. Israel and Christians were called to live in such a way that the society met the needs of the most vulnerable.[69] Concepts such as the common good, the body of Christ, and the kingdom of God remind us that Christian charity and mercy are woven into the fabric of the community.

69. Hare, *Moral Gap*, 168–9; Unterman, *Justice for All*, 83.

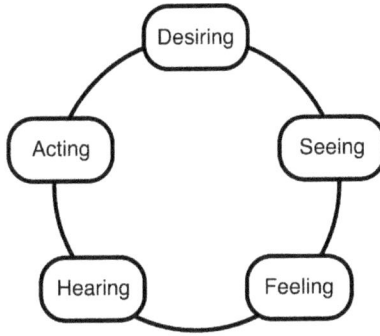

Fig. i.2. Facets of compassion.

LOOKING AHEAD

We are now ready to open the pages of history and to follow the Christian church and her members as they attempt to live out Christian compassion. Our journey begins in chapter 1 with the vulnerability of the ancient church wherein the nascent Christian community shared a common purse and took significant risks to share God's gifts with others. They imitated Jesus, experienced shame and threats, and trusted in God's ultimate justice. An eschatological vision shaped and equipped the Christian community for compassion as they offered their bodies as living sacrifices (Rom 12:1).

In chapter 2, we explore the third and fourth centuries wherein the tables are turned on shame and persecution. The burgeoning church was challenged by ascetics and Byzantine bishops to live simply and give alms. Virtue was emphasized in both almsgiving and suffering, and innovations were sparked in small-scale institutionalized care. Church fathers who occupied imperial roles pacified some, irritated others, and stirred a few to action. The church became the patron of the poor and occupied a role in society's wellbeing.

In chapter 3, we consider the medieval era—a diverse period stretching across a thousand years. In it, compassion is balkanized, sanctified, bureaucratized, democratized, and chastised in an undulating ribbon of developments. People lived in a sacralized world, attempting to discern God's will and defend their own salvation through works of mercy. An industry of distributed, institutionalized care emerged as Christendom mushroomed. Compassion found a home in parishes and monasteries and, on occasion, was professionalized and specialized. Toward the end of the era and into the next (chapter 4), church structures came under critique for pouring funds into ecclesial and monastic coffers while the poor suffered. Reform in compassion's delivery is demanded and the state provided a suitable partner for social care.

The modern era of the sixteenth to nineteenth centuries (chapters 5 and 6) mirrored the diversity and innovation emerging from the Reformation and produced a marketplace of ideas about wealth, aid, and church-state relations. A global missions race between Catholics and Protestants pitted compassion against conquering, with some missionaries resisting and others, abdicating. In chapter 6, we see civil society blooming in the eighteenth century as institutions such as the International Red Cross and the Salvation Army expanded along with other initiatives, including the *diakonia* movement, Quaker reforms, the social gospel, and thousands of other activist lights, often glowing with a paternalistic hue.

Twentieth-century developments continued the widening spectrum of Christian charity that I organize in three streams. The first is liberation and justice (chapter 7) shaped by Catholic social teaching and liberation and black theology. We explore their operation in the domain of labor and commerce. The second theme is peace and humanitarianism (chapter 8). Parachurch agencies were established and grew, peace churches became pioneers in international relief, and evangelicals made a late but rousing return to the holistic gospel. Mutual aid and community development are the theme in chapter 9. These include ecclesial expressions among Anabaptists and Latter-day Saints, in economic cooperatives, auxiliary, fraternal, and mission organizations, intentional communities, and in community development. In the conclusion, I tie together unique contributions from each era that have or could be explored.

Through the journey, I hope you will gather a deeper and more intimate appreciation of the development of ideas, individuals, and institutions that give expression to Christian compassion and to the suffering that prompts it. Although not perfected in any age, we catch glimpses of the Spirit and kingdom of God. All these predecessors remind us that we are but the latest invitees to a path where all are encouraged to "abound in love for one another and for all" (1 Thess 3:12).

ANTIQUE AND MEDIEVAL

IN THE FIRST THREE chapters, we explore compassion from the patristic through the medieval eras: a period of fifteen centuries of dramatic change. During this time, Christian compassion shifts from individual care to church-, philanthropic-, and empire-funded efforts in dramatically dynamic surroundings of considerable need. Each era cascades into the next echoing past motifs and introducing new responses. Some of the themes and actors we will encounter are given in the table that follows.

Chapter	Century	Era	Themes	Actors
1	First to Third	Formation and Sacrifice	God's gift economy, sharing and serving, formation, eschatological justice, persecution, pandemics	Jesus, Paul, deacons, widows, Tabitha, Lawrence, Cyprian, Dionysius the Great
2	Fourth to Fifth	Contentment and Simplicity	Asceticism, almsgiving, virtue, sparing and sharing, *Basileias, xenodochia*, Bishop's court, *caritas*	Constantine 1, desert fathers and mothers, John Climacus, Chrysostom, Gregory of Nazianzus, Gregory of Nyssa, Ambrose, Basil, Jerome, Pelagius, Augustine
3	Sixth to Fifteenth	Mobilization and Participation	Sacralization, pilgrimage, tithes, institutions of care, corporal works of mercy, parish care, reformers, mendicants	Gregory I, Benedict, Robert of Arbrissel, Norbert of Xanten, Peter Waldo, Humiliati, Peter the Chanter, Francis, Dominic

Compassion themes and actors in the antique and medieval eras.

1

Formation and Sacrifice

THE FIRST THREE CENTURIES of the Christian church set in motion enduring patterns of compassion that continue to shape our thinking and practice. Within them, we find a group of formed and tested disciples who take
Paul's pleading to heart:

> I appeal to you therefore, brothers and sisters, by the mercies
> of God, to present your bodies as a living sacrifice, holy and
> acceptable to God, which is your spiritual worship. Do not be
> conformed to this world, but be transformed by the renewing of
> your minds, so that you may discern what is the will of God—
> what is good and acceptable and perfect. (Rom 12:1 2)[1]

This era includes the imprimatur of Christian compassion—Jesus—
and his earliest followers in Israel and throughout the Roman Empire. We
arrive on the scene at a time of considerable vulnerability.

---

1. The Greek word *leitourgia*, literally means "work of the people" and in the non-
Christian world of the first centuries referred to benefits or services the wealthy did for
their city or province. Paul uses it in 2 Corinthians 9:12 to refer for the collection he
is raising for the poor and in Philippians 2:17and 2:30 for financial aid sent to him in
prison. See Holman, *Hungry Are Dying*, 48–54.

VULNERABILITY AND THE POOR

Although Roman occupation brought some degree of order and prosperity, existence was precarious for nearly everyone during the first three centuries of Christianity. Most people (some scholars estimate around 90 percent) lived at or near subsistence, with minimal food or money reserves.[2] For a person, or an entire region, the scales could tip toward a crisis if one experienced a loss of income, food, health, or—worst of all—social approval.[3]

Frequently, agriculture—the largest economic sector—yielded harvests, food prices, and incomes that were as erratic as the rains that refreshed the land. The rich and those with animals and fields could smooth their dietary supply by growing and storing food, but many lived in a state of food insecurity, making Jesus' claims of being "the bread of life" (John 6:35) poignant to ancient ears.[4]

More menacing than most agricultural fluctuations, however, were the waves of parasitic and infectious diseases that voyaged and traveled along trade routes. With limited understanding of disease contagion, malaria and smallpox devastated populations.[5] Even the wealthy could not avoid these invaders. Estimates vary, but many place life expectancy in Jesus' time in the mid-twenties. Half of the population did not survive to adulthood. Although many who survived childhood lived into their sixties and seventies, at thirty-three, Jesus exceeded the average life span.[6]

In terms of housing, Palestine was fortunate to have plentiful rock and stone which made for dusty roads but secure homes. Other cities were not so lucky. Rome was packed with wood-framed, plaster-covered dwellings that were susceptible to accidental fires or the arson of agitated rioters or

2. Friesen, "Injustice or God's Will?" 21.

3. Although Morley addresses Rome, some of his observations are relevant to other parts of the Roman Empire. See Morley, "Poor in the City of Rome."

4. Food insecurity is hinted at by the thousands seeking a second day of bread and fish from Jesus in John 6:22–31.

5. Jonathan Reed describes ancient disease and demography: "Chronic and seasonal disease, especially malaria, cut down significant segments of the population and left even the healthy quite often ill. The age structure was youthful, women bore many children, random death made family and household patterns ephemeral, young men were often mobile, and elderly women especially vulnerable. Survival depended on extended family networks, especially for the most vulnerable: old women and young children" (Reed, "Instability in Jesus' Galilee," 345). For a detailed description of malaria in the medieval era, see Newfield, "Malaria and Malaria-like Disease." During epidemics, elites escaped to rural estates in an effort to enhance their survival: Watts, *Final Pagan Generation*, 29.

6. Reed, "Mortality, Morbidity, and Economics," 242–43.

marauders.[7] And then, of course, there was the latest of many occupying forces: the Roman Empire, which bridled, taxed, and governed those who made their home in Israel.

In addition to the vulnerability of food, income, health, shelter, and governance, Jews (as all societies do) stigmatized and marginalized certain individuals. Jewish social distinctions were based on Levitical purity laws and a variety of other factors, most of which were beyond a person's control and could mark one for life. One might be born to a slave, or be female, ill, or of a despised religion; one might be of a shunned ethnicity or work in a despised occupation; or one might confess that Jesus was the Messiah which was a sufficient cause for shunning (John 9:22).[8]

Being a social pariah was a harsh blow considering that family, friends, and the synagogue provided the only significant social safety nets. In some Roman-occupied cities, a ration of grain (*annona*) was distributed but it did not reach every person and the ration was insufficient for survival.[9] Begging yielded some monetary benefit as well as an opportunity for pity (*misericordia*), but flanked as they were by slaves and servants when stepping beyond their gates, the rich generally avoided the poor.[10] There was no public welfare system or any system of organized charity for the poor, nor any compelling reason to develop one.[11] Slaves and the laboring classes were viewed as predestined for their roles by the gods or they may have arrived at their state through fate, chance, or vice.[12] Why show pity and allow emotions to guide reason when people were merely playing the roles they were

7. Roth et al., "Wood Economy"; Stark, *Rise of Christianity*, 159.

8. For the treatment of leprosy, see Shinall, "Social Condition of Lepers." For shame in the New Testament, see deSilva, *Honor, Patronage, Kinship and Purity*, 43–93.

9. The *annona* was managed by Rome and delivered to select groups in particular cities. It functioned more as a political tool to forestall food riots than an attempt at poverty alleviation. Paul may have been a passenger on one of these private vessels carrying grain. See Acts 27:38; Hands, *Charities and Social Aid*, 54; Jongman, "Early Roman Empire." Unterman documents that the Jewish Bible is the first to legislate food for the poor. See *Justice for All*, 83.

10. Wolfe, "Writing Poverty in Rome."

11. Philanthropy existed—Greek and Roman cities were awash with inscriptions recognizing generous gifts (sometimes pried free from the estates of elites by social pressure). But most philanthropy (*euergetism*) circulated among elites or brought praise on the entire municipality by subsidizing banquets, libraries, schools, or roads, or by providing revolving loan funds from which a person of means might dip occasionally, repaying the lender with money and praise. Occasionally, a banquet invitation might be extended to the enslaved and free to honor local gods, but most philanthropy did not trickle down to the impoverished because their standing, assets, and praise were insufficient counter-gifts for benefactors. See Hands, *Charities and Social Aid*.

12. Armitage, *Theories of Poverty*, 49–75.

assigned or due? And who would want to challenge the divine ordering of society anyway, especially among an aristocracy that benefitted from the system?[13] For Stoics, poverty or wealth was irrelevant: a wise person adapted and did not let external conditions or emotions rule the day.[14]

Greek philosophers such as Plato and Aristotle did ponder the poor (*aporoi*), but not through a lens of compassion; rather, the poor were merely the clockworks inside an idealized polis.[15] When Greek and Roman authors addressed poverty, they often did so rhetorically, as a *persona* in a tragedy, exorcising the anxieties of impoverishment and social expulsion that haunted the well-to-do.[16] Other than these political and social projections, Greek and Roman writers left relatively little systematic thought regarding compassion and the poor.[17] Pragmatic Romans valued the "virtuous hardworking citizen, who had no time for anything except earning his living on his farm and doing his civic duty."[18] But this was a romanticized view of the poor, and it did not mature into a moral warrant for compassion.

The poor might attempt to enhance their assets by competing for Roman land grants in new, distant colonies, or they might reduce expenses if destitute, such as through infant exposure to reduce the number of mouths to feed. But beyond the informal safety net of family and friends and the support of the synagogue, provisions for the poor were nonexistent. People lived on the edge of poverty with little ability to mitigate their fate. This was the setting in which Jesus and his companions lived.

13. Some of the destitute (*ptochoi*) bullied and extorted funds from shopkeepers or were suspected of feigning disability or exploiting maimed children to heighten donations. See Parkin, "'You Do Him No Service.'"

14. Armitage, *Theories of Poverty*, 109.

15. Plato's *Laws* banned beggars but also restricted inequality, preventing citizens from owning more than five times the smallest land allotment. Aristotle provided for the poor by supplying public lands. Neither Plato nor Aristotle commented at length on economic or social policy and the poor: Hands, *Charities and Social Aid*, 65–66.

16. For the distinctive and subtle use of tragedy in ancient to post-Constantinian Christian writing, see Blowers, *Visions and Faces of the Tragic*. Christian writers emphasized the salvific response to lived tragedy that Greek and Roman writers could not.

17. Wolfe, "Writing Poverty in Rome." Advocacy for compassion among Greek and Roman writers is sparse but not nonexistent. Elios was the Greek personification of mercy and Clementia was the Roman goddess of clemency; fragments refer to Zeus as the champion of beggars and strangers; and Cicero supported limited almsgiving to the deserving poor. See Armitage, *Theories of Poverty*, 54, 69–70.

18. Osborne, "Introduction," 13.

JESUS

We begin with Jesus because, for Christians, he is the pattern to emulate (Heb 12:2). Jesus is described as a suffering savior (cf. Isa 53:3–11; Matt 8:17; Acts 8:32–35); one who identifies and participates with the oppressed.[19] Jesus experienced a number of social and physical challenges that would be considered significant during nearly any time.[20] He lived in a country under foreign occupation, he and his family fled as political refugees (Matt 2:13–15), he was itinerant as an adult (Luke 9:58), he was subject to social exclusion and violence (Mark 3:6; Luke 4:28–29), and his life ended in an unjust conviction and execution. Jesus was encircled by poverty, war, disease, famine, natural disaster, and conflict. He experienced all of the conditions described in the judgment scene of Matthew 25:31–46. Through his lived experience, he identifies with those who are suffering, and they with him (Heb 2:18).

As God incarnate, Jesus not only suffered, but also set a pattern for compassionate and just living, calling people to a high social ethic in caring for others—including enemies (Matt 5:43–48)—and resisting unjust structures. Jesus began and ended his public ministry by calling attention to the poor, ill, incarcerated, alienated, and oppressed (Luke 4:16–20; Matt 25:31–46). In the three years between, he lived that call, healing the sick (Matt 11:4–5; 20:30–34), releasing the captive (Mark 5:1–20), feeding the hungry (Matt 15:32), welcoming outcasts (Mark 1:40–41; Luke 7:36–50; 18:16), and bringing good news to the poor (Matt 11:5).

Jesus empathized (Matt 9:36; 14:14; 15:32; 20:34). He blessed the poor in spirit, the mourning, and the persecuted (Matt 5:3–4, 10–11), and ultimately, he offered conquering liberation through his death. In his teaching, Jesus portrayed God as a compassionate father (Luke 15:20), welcoming "the poor, the crippled, the blind, and the lame" (Luke 14:21b). One on one, in small gatherings, and in crowds, Jesus extended mercy.[21] According to Jon Sobrino, "Mercy is not the sole content of Jesus' practice, but it . . . stands

---

19. McClure, "Introducing Jesus's Social Network."

20. Julian of Norwich and other medieval writers asserted that Jesus suffered more than any other human due to his divine and human nature. Suffering is central as well in the life of Mary, the mother of Jesus. "Our Lady of Sorrows" recalls seven specific sorrows in her life where her soul was pierced by a sword (Luke 2:34–35) because of her empathy for Jesus.

21. In the New Testament, Jesus most often heals and raises individuals (twenty-nine occasions, e.g., John 4:46–54; Mark 1:21–27; 2:1–12). Occasionally, he heals individuals in twos or tens (Matt 9:27–31; Luke 17:11–19) or in unspecified numbers (Matt 8:16–17; Mark 6:53–56). He feeds large groups (Matt 14:13–21; 15:32–39). His redemption on the cross was for all humanity (1 Tim 2:56).

at the origin of all that he practices; it is mercy that shapes and molds his entire life, mission, and fate."[22]

Jesus' moral teaching was not completely new—the Hebrew Bible emphasized a moral ethic of protection, provision, and inclusion for the vulnerable.[23] His emphases were orthodox and authentic. He brought the vulnerable center stage, upending social convention for Greeks and Romans as well as for Jews who sometimes viewed sin as calamity's cause.

Jesus taught his followers to follow an ethic of compassion—to love rather than curse enemies (Matt 5:43–48) and to "do to others as you would have them do to you" (Luke 6:31). The suffering and compassion he shares is intended to circulate (Rom 8:16–17; 2 Cor 11:20–28; 1 Pet 2:21). As Paul wrote,

> Blessed be the God and Father of our Lord Jesus Christ, the Father of mercies and the God of all consolation, who consoles us in all our affliction, so that we may be able to console those who are in any affliction with the consolation with which we ourselves are consoled by God. For just as the sufferings of Christ are abundant for us, so also our consolation is abundant through Christ. (2 Cor 1:3–5)

As the Gospels and epistles were carried from one house church to another, the example and teachings of Jesus leavened the early Christians. The church's sacraments reinforced joining Christ in dying to self (Rom 6:3–4) while attending to the interests of others (Phil 2:3–4).

In a time of vulnerability, Jesus affirmed and advanced a just, pro-poor social ethic that is marbled through Scripture [**A Scripture Sampler on Compassion**]. Given his example and teachings, and their practice and reinforcement in the Christian community, it is not surprising that Jesus brought comfort. But, perhaps ironically, he also brought angst, ushering his disciples into centuries of struggles and debates over wealth, power, and war.

---

22. Sobrino, *Principle of Mercy*, 19–20. Gregory of Nazianzus argued similarly that mercy was central in God's healing. See Daley, "Oration 14." Ukeachusim describes compassion as a central virtue of Jesus: "As preserved in the gospels, Jesus demonstrated genuine compassion by preaching the good news of the kingdom, forgiving sins, healing the sick, feeding the hungry, casting out demons, raising the dead, and giving his life as a ransom for the remission of the sings of others": "Understanding Compassion," 373.

23. Hussain, "Participating in Godliness."

A Scripture Sampler on Compassion

The Hebrew Bible and the New Testament are filled with moral teachings related to compassion, pity, mercy, kindness, and justice. Here are just a few selections:

- You shall not oppress a resident alien; you know the heart of an alien, for you were aliens in the land of Egypt. (Exod 23:9)
- To do righteousness and justice is more acceptable to the Lord than sacrifice. (Prov 21:3)
- The righteous know the rights of the poor; the wicked have no such understanding. (Prov 29:7)
- Speak out for those who cannot speak, for the rights of all the destitute. (Prov 31:8)
- Learn to do good; seek justice, rescue the oppressed, defend the orphan, plead for the widow. (Isa 1:17)
- He has told you, O mortal, what is good; and what does the Lord require of you but to do justice, and to love kindness, and to walk humbly with your God? (Mic 6:8)
- Thus says the Lord of hosts: Render true judgments, show kindness and mercy to one another; do not oppress the widow, the orphan, the alien, or the poor; and do not devise evil in your hearts against one another. (Zech 7:9–10)
- Blessed are the merciful, for they will receive mercy. (Matt 5:7)
- So whenever you give alms, do not sound a trumpet before you, as the hypocrites do in the synagogues and in the streets, so that they may be praised by others. Truly I tell you, they have received their reward. But when you give alms, do not let your left hand know what your right hand is doing, so that your alms may be done in secret; and your Father who sees in secret will reward you. (Matt 6:2–4)
- For I was hungry and you gave me food, I was thirsty and you gave me something to drink, I was a stranger

and you welcomed me, I was naked and you gave me clothing, I was sick and you took care of me, I was in prison and you visited me. (Matt 25:35–36)

- Do to others as you would have them do to you. (Luke 6:31)

- Give, and it will be given to you. A good measure, pressed down, shaken together, running over, will be put into your lap; for the measure you give will be the measure you get back. (Luke 6:38)

- He answered, "You shall love the Lord your God with all your heart, and with all your soul, and with all your strength, and with all your mind; and your neighbor as yourself." (Luke 10:27)

- But a Samaritan while traveling came near him; and when he saw him, he was moved with pity. He went to him and bandaged his wounds, having poured oil and wine on them. Then he put him on his own animal, brought him to an inn, and took care of him. (Luke 10:33–34)

- So he set off and went to his father. But while he was still far off, his father saw him and was filled with compassion; he ran and put his arms around him and kissed him. (Luke 15:20)

- By this everyone will know that you are my disciples, if you have love for one another. (John 13:35)

- Contribute to the needs of the saints; extend hospitality to strangers. (Rom 12:13)

- As God's chosen ones, holy and beloved, clothe yourselves with compassion, kindness, humility, meekness, and patience. (Col 3:12)

- For you had compassion for those who were in prison, and you cheerfully accepted the plundering of your possessions, knowing that you yourselves possessed something better and more lasting. (Heb 10:34)

- Let mutual love continue. Do not neglect to show hospitality to strangers, for by doing that some have entertained angels without knowing it. Remember those who are in prison, as though you were in prison with them; those who are being tortured, as though you yourselves were being tortured. (Heb 13:1–3)

- For judgment will be without mercy to anyone who has shown no mercy; mercy triumphs over judgment. (Jas 2:13)

- We know love by this, that he laid down his life for us—and we ought to lay down our lives for one another. How does God's love abide in anyone who has the world's goods and sees a brother or sister in need and yet refuses help? Little children, let us love, not in word or speech, but in truth and action. (1 John 3:16–18)

- Whoever does not love does not know God, for God is love. (1 John 4:8)

SHARING GIFTS

Turning to the earliest Christians, we witness their desire to identify with and emulate Jesus. They lived out the compassion of Christ through two primary expressions: sharing and serving. Both were expressions of charity that circulated the gifts of God and became a distinctive group norm, supported by apostolic teaching.[24]

Although some retained personal property, early Christians pooled many of their material and spiritual assets to meet the needs of the poor and achieve a more equitable distribution among the community (Acts 2:44–45; 4:32–37). This pattern followed the example of Jesus and the early disciples (John 12:5–6) and is a pattern that many have argued through the centuries is worthy of emulating.[25] As Bruce Longenecker suggests, asset sharing was an expression of community rather than charity or the start of a political system:

> The poor were to be welcomed into the very heart of those communities of fellowship and "gifted" as contributing members within it. No different from anyone else, the economically poor were expected to contribute their own "gifts" and to participate in the nurturing of a group of fictive kin who supported each other in various ways, not all of which were economic.[26]

24. Kim, "Explaining Early Christian Charity."

25. A thread of having all things in common in a small community runs through Christian history and is prominent in monastic rules. Chapter 8 offers modern expressions of communal sharing. For a biblical argument see Beed and Beed, "Biblical Basis."

26. Longenecker, *Remember the Poor*, 290.

In other words, they smoothed abundance and need (2 Cor 8:12–15), sharing material as well as nonmaterial goods, such as healing and encouragement (Acts 3:1–10; 5:14–16; 8:4–8), giving to any in need.[27]

The pooling of goods was not new. It occurred to a lesser degree in elite Greek and Roman associations and may have been influenced by Jewish moral teaching and the gift economy [**Gifts and Favors**]. Indeed, pooling has occurred throughout history, most often when people experience wide-spread calamity.[28] Distinct in the early Christian case was voluntary sharing among different classes of people, propelled by Jesus' teachings and the anticipation of his return.

Gifts and Favors

Economies can be created around three allocation tools, frequently called gift, hierarchy, or market. Although the latter were present in the ancient world, relying on gifts and favors was common, particularly in allocating services unavailable in the marketplace or to bestow grants as a patron. In gift economies, individuals are bound together in ongoing relationships of reciprocal exchange and mutual benefit. The goal is not to merely to repay debts, but to show honor and join networks of mutual benefit.

Typically, gifts were exchanged in the ancient world among people of equal or near-equal status, creating a safety net of friendships within socio-economic strata for services akin to those provided by today's banking, legal, hospitality, and insurance industries.[29] A person in need might inquire with a friend who could provide direct assistance or refer one to another able friend. The recipient would then acknowledge the gift with gratitude, honor, and reciprocated giving in the future. Substantial historical evidence documents a robust gift economy among wealthy patrons but scholars suspect that hospitality and reciprocity existed among all strata of society.

---

27. Twelftree, *In the Name of Jesus*, 77; Richardson, *Early Christian Care*.

28. Olson, *Logic of Collective Action*.

29. Hands, *Charities and Social Aid*, 26–33. Aristotle argued that friendships could not exist between people of unequal status because friendship required the possibility of mutual exchange. Public benefaction was a form of gift, and it crossed economic strata, but it was acknowledged by civic gratitude.

Early Christians viewed the spiritual economy through the lens of gift, yet Jesus modified and Paul reinforced new social customs in gift-giving.[30] Material and spiritual goods were given by God and circulated among people across all economic strata within a broad network of humanity (a concept acknowledged in the Hebrew Bible in passages such as Ps 116:12).[31] The exchange between Christians in Jerusalem and Asia Minor provides an example of gift-giving across nationalities, socio-economic strata, and spiritual-material benefit:

> For Macedonia and Achaia have been pleased to share their resources with the poor among the saints at Jerusalem. They were pleased to do this, and indeed they owe it to them; for if the Gentiles have come to share in their spiritual blessings, they ought also to be of service to them in material things. (Rom 15:26–27)

While a gift economy might be viewed as a complex ledger of debits and credits among an extensive list of parties, in gift economies, it generally functions as a safety net. Sharing among the early Christians was not merely a system of mutual benefit; it made visible the gifts of God.

Jesus' teaching transformed the exchange of friendship among people of near-equal status in Greek and Roman society and affirmed that all we are and have is gifted by a loving God and intended for sharing among rich and poor (Matt 18:21–35.[32] In the Christian view, some reciprocity would occur in life (Mark 10:29–30; 2 Cor 9:6–8), but many exchanges would be credited in the next age (Matt 6:1–4).[33] As Jesus said:

> When you give a luncheon or a dinner, do not invite your friends or your brothers or your relatives or rich neighbors, in case they may invite you in return, and you would be repaid. But when you give a banquet, invite the poor, the crippled, the lame, and the blind. And you will be blessed, because they cannot repay

---

30. John M. G. Barclay details six perfections of grace which characterize complete ancient and divine gifts. They require explanation but, for convenience, are: superabundance, singularity, priority, incongruity, efficacy, and non-circularity. See Barclay, *Paul and the Gift*, 70–75.

31. Blanton, *Spiritual Economy*; deSilva, *Honor, Patronage, Kinship and Purity*, 95–119.

32. This in itself was a transformational notion given that Roman gods generally were incapable of loving.

33. For a historical and theological treatment of gift see Barclay, *Paul and the Gift*.

you, for you will be repaid at the resurrection of the righteous. (Luke 14:12b–14)

We see Christian gift-giving played out in the early church. Paul portrayed the provision of material aid as an exchange of gifts: Greek Christians received spiritual benefit from the Jewish Christians in Jerusalem, and in turn, the Greeks should help the Jerusalem church, materially; in the process, God would be glorified and would bless all (2 Cor 9:5–15; Rom 15:27).[34] Paul encouraged the Hellenistic Christians to see their giving as cheerful and voluntary, not as extortion or social compulsion, as Roman patrons might be wont to feel.

Over time, funds collected by house churches were distributed widely in "feeding and burying the poor, and on boys and girls who do not have parents, on aged domestic slaves, shipwrecked persons, and any who are in the mines, on islands, or in prisons," all for the sake of the faith.[35] The circulation of gifts among impoverished friends and strangers beyond the local city (Rom 15:26) and among disputed ethnic and national groups represented a prominent social innovation, although it echoed Jewish moral teachings regarding the stranger.[36] It asserted the reality that the Christian church was global and multicultural from its infancy.[37]

Paul shamed the Corinthian Christians, whose communal sharing slipped back into Greek and Roman patronage rather than nurturing equality (1 Cor 11:17–34). Further, Christian gift exchange does not seek praise or special treatment but elevates the vulnerable (Matt 6:1–4; Jas 2:1–10). Rather than contradicting the concept of God's freely-given grace, a gift calculus unites people and compels them to share God's abundant resources (Eph 2:4–10).

---

34. The amount given was individually decided but was suggested to come from "whatever extra you earn" (2 Cor 9:7; 1 Cor 16:2b). Christoph Stenschke observes that Paul had several obstacles to overcome in asking the Gentile Christians to financially support the Jewish Christians in Jerusalem: the gift economy customarily was local; Jewish prejudice existed against Greeks; Paul's relationship was strained with the Corinthians; and detractors challenged his credibility (Stenschke, "Obstacles on All Sides").

35. Tertullian of Carthage, Apology (Apologeticus), quoted in Ascough, Associations in the Greco-Roman World, 249.

36. Regarding ethnic attitudes, see Balch, "Attitudes toward Foreigners." See also the Hebrew Bible treatment in Gardner, "Care for the Poor."

37. Bantu, Multitude of All Peoples.

The generosity of Joseph and others in the early Jerusalem church (Acts 4:32–37) did not completely eliminate economic inequality. Ananias and Sapphira (Acts 5:1–11) lied about their holdings, Philemon was a slave-holder, and the rich and poor, slave and free, remained in the church (Gal 3:28), posing the dilemma of how to relate to one another in the Christian community. Added to this diversity were many Christians who carried the name of Christ but less so his ethics.[38]

When Jesus did not immediately return as expected, early Christians did not abandon their ethic of sharing, but widened their circle into an even more inclusive economy that enveloped strangers and enemies in need, as Jesus had taught (Matt 5:43–48; Luke 10:25–37). As Paul wrote, "So then, whenever we have an opportunity, let us work for the good of all, and especially for those of the family of faith" (Gal 6:10).[39] As economic needs arose in the early church, Paul reminded Christians to "remember the poor" (Gal 2:10), and he praised them for their generosity to all (2 Cor 9:13; Gal 6:9–10). He attempted to emulate Christ's compassion personally and encouraged young Christians to follow his example (Acts 20:35).[40] Irenaeus (c. 130–c. 202)[41], a Christian bishop in today's France, taught similarly:

> Instead of the tithes which the law commanded, the Lord said
> to divide everything we have with the poor. And he said to love
> not only our neighbors but also our enemies, and to be givers
> and sharers not only with the good but also to be liberal givers
> toward those who take away our possessions.[42]

Remembering the poor was unifying. It affirmed the reality that the church was "one body"—a common metaphor in the early church—and

38. Not all Christians shared their wealth. The first- or second-century *Shepherd of Hermas* chides wealthy disciples who aligned more with pagans than with the Christian community, engaging in extravagance while the poor suffered: Herm.Sim.1,10.1 in Ehrman, *Apostolic Fathers*; Lampe, *Paul to Valentinus*, 90–103.

39. Montero argues that communal sharing was an enduring characteristic of the Christians in Roman society: Montero, *All Things in Common*. Augustine would later write, "You should think of everyone as your neighbor, even before he or she is a Christian, for you do not know what that person is in God's sight, or what God's foreknowledge of him or her might be": Augustine of Hippo, *Expositions of the Psalms*, 25.2.2.

40. Longenecker highlights several passages in Pauline writing where early Christians were encouraged to show compassion to the poor. Additionally, Longenecker and Lim interpret Gal 2:10 as referring to the poor everywhere, not just in Jerusalem: Lim, "Generosity from Pauline Perspective"; Longenecker, *Remember the Poor*. Also see Collins, *Diakonia Studies*, 78–100.

41. All dates are CE unless otherwise noted. Parenthetical dates are provided, when known, at the first mention of an actor of notoriety in the history of compassion.

42. Irenaeus, *Against Heresies*, 4.14.3, quoted in Ferguson, *Early Christians Speak*, 205.

that members help one another, even beyond one's city, which was novel in Roman philanthropy: "If one member suffers, all suffer together with it; if one member is honored, all rejoice together with it" (1 Cor 12:26). As the church grew throughout Asia Minor, Paul called upon Greek Christians to save and collect relief funds for believers in Jerusalem who were experiencing a famine, representing yet another transformation of the common purse—sharing beyond one's immediate community.

At some point, resources would reach their end, but Clement (c. 35–99), an early bishop of Rome, enjoined disciples to avoid identifying who was deserving or undeserving of aid:

> Do not judge who is worthy and who unworthy, for it is possible for you to be mistaken in your opinion. In the uncertainty of ignorance, it is better to do good to the unworthy for the sake of the worthy than by guarding against those who are less good not to encounter the good. For by being sparing and trying to test those who are well deserving or not, it is possible for you to neglect some who are loved by God.[43]

Although Acts 2 and 4 are remembered for their embrace of mutual aid, individuals (Acts 5:1–5) and groups of believers struggled to relinquish assets and abandon prejudices. At times, Jews neglected non-Jews (Acts 6:1), and Greeks—possibly lacking familiarity with Jewish ethics—were reminded to care for the poor (Gal 2:10).[44] Despite their imperfect practice, sharing widely from the abundance of God's gifts was a distinctive characteristic of the early church.

SERVING OTHERS

Serving was a second compassionate habitus of early Christians. Initially, service took the form of distributing food among widows, but it expanded in serving the ill, those imprisoned, and others as Jesus instructed in Matthew 25:31–46.[45]

---

43. Clement of Alexandria, "Who Is the Rich Man that Is Saved?," 33–34, quoted in *Ferguson, Early Christians Speak*, 205.

44. Longenecker argues that remembering the poor was not an add-on to the apostolic council in Jerusalem, but a primary injunction: Longenecker, *Remember the Poor*, 199–202.

45. A chain of moral responsibility appears in ancient law wherein the divine expected the powerful to protect the vulnerable. This is true in many societies, and not always kept, but John J. Collins affirms that "For the Hebrew Bible, no value is more central or fundamental than the demand for social justice." Collins, *What are Biblical Values*, 177.

As the early community of believers grew in Jerusalem, some Greek widows were overlooked in the serving of communion and in the distribution of food. The church responded by appointing seven Greek men to serve as deacons (*diakonoi*) (Acts 6:1–6), possibly with Stephen as the lead deacon. These servants were specifically not to be "greedy for money" (1 Tim 3:8), seeing that they would be managing the community's resources.[46]

The deacon role in Acts 6 traditionally has been viewed as pattern-setting, novel, and limited to temporal service. In actuality, it may have been ad hoc; mimetic of communal Jewish soup kitchens (*tamhui*), charity funds (*quppa*), and Essene practices; indicative of a general calling to service rather than being attached to a narrow definition of caring for physical needs.[47]

By the third century, deacons were caring for more than fifteen hundred widows in Rome [**St. Lawrence**]. The churches divided the city into seven administrative districts, each administered by a lead deacon. The Council of Neocaesarea (315) limited the number of deacons to seven in any city, regardless of the population, in deference to those originally called to service. In a formal capacity, deacons have continued through much of church history to serve needs.

St. Lawrence

Pope Sixtus II appointed twenty-seven-year-old Lawrence (225–258) as archdeacon for the church in Rome. One year later, in 258, the Roman emperor Valerian declared that all Christian bishops, priests, and deacons should be executed and their property surrendered to the Empire. As chief bishop, Pope Sixtus was killed first. Officials then approached Lawrence and demanded that he surrender the church's abundant assets. Lawrence, the story goes, asked for several carts to

---

46. Some deacons apparently dipped into the till for widows and orphans: Ehrman, *Apostolic Fathers*, 2:Similitude 9.26.2.

47. Gardner suggests that Jewish rabbis encouraged all to contribute to a community chest to avoid the ethical and social challenges inherent in almsgiving. This intermediary structure provided for beggars, protected the dignity of the poor, and benefitted the entire community (Gardner, *Origins of Organized Charity*); cf. Seccombe, "Was There Organized Charity?" *Diakon-* words are used in Acts 6:1–6 to refer to the distribution of food, serving food at tables, and the ministry of the word, but not as a title for the seven. Scholars debate whether these indeed were the first deacons and whether the deaconate was limited to social assistance: Collins, *Deacons and the Church*, 43–56. Finally, Collins and others have carefully studied the use of *diakon-* words in the New Testament, and they suggest it has been overly limited in popular understanding: Collins, *Diakonia Studies*; Nordstokke, "Study of Diakonia," 57–58.

use in transporting the wealth to the officials. Lawrence filled the carts with gold and silver and dispersed the church's financial wealth among the poor. Lawrence then asked the indigent to climb into the carts. He returned to the officials with the carts in tow, announcing that "These are the treasures of the church." Lawrence was summarily tortured and killed. Applying his story in a sermon preached in 401, Augustine said:

> The needs of the needy are the great wealth and treasure of Christians. . . . If we deposit our savings with them, we won't lose them. We aren't afraid of anybody making off with them; the one who gave them to us, you see, is keeping them safe; nor could we find a better guardian, nor a more trustworthy maker and keeper of promises.[48]

Fig. 1.1. *The Martyrdom of St. Lawrence.*

---

48. Augustine of Hippo, *Works of Saint Augustine*, Sermons (273–305A) on the Saints, sec. 304.

Another group that served was the widows. Bonnie Bowman Thurston describes how, in the second and third centuries, widows formed a church order that engaged in prayer and serving others. According to Paul, the qualifications for a "real widow" included that "she must be well attested for her good works, as one who has brought up children, shown hospitality, washed the saints' feet, helped the afflicted, and devoted herself to doing good in every way" (1 Tim 5:10). One of these was Tabitha or Dorcas, known for her acts of charity and sewing garments for others (Acts 9:36–42).[49]

More foundational than the function or office of the deacon or widow, however, was the affirmation that all Christians should serve others. According to John Collins, when service (*diakonia*) words appear in the New Testament, they typically apply to how the Christian community cared for one another and for others, rather than the ecclesial office.[50] Service characterized all Christ-followers, not just those called to a task.

Early Christian sharing and serving may have been influenced by Jewish ethics and, to a lesser degree, Greek and Roman organizations (such as funerary associations), but we have to look more deeply into Christian community to understand why they pursued compassion with such vigor.[51] What we find pulsing in their minds and hearts are their Christ-inspired formation and view of the future.

FORMATION AND FUTURE

Ancient Christians were inspired by Jesus' cruciform life and teaching. Becoming a Christian meant being like him, being clothed in his life and death and united with other disciples (Gal 3:27–28; Phil 3:10–11; Col 3:9–11). The gospel occupied their lives; *they* were the good news of Jesus.[52]

The catechetical process leading to baptism could take up to three years. Catechumens learned and practiced and ultimately were baptized into Jesus' death, arising to new life in him (Rom 6:3–4).[53] Living compassionately was part of the formation process. It served to reorient disciples in

49. Thurston, *Widows*.

50. Collins, *Diakonia Studies*, 58.

51. Regarding the influence of funerary associations on Christians, see Rebillard, *Care of the Dead*.

52. The apostles, it was believed, were charged with the "great commission" (Matt 28:18–20; Mark 13:10). The diminutive Christian community was inadequate to imagine changing the overshadowing Roman Empire. See Davidson, "Church Growth in the Early Church"; Gorman, *Becoming the Gospel*; Thompson, *Church According to Paul*.

53. In *Rule of St. Benedict*, the formation of monks was called "winning souls": Benedict, *Rule of St. Benedict*, chap. 58:6.

the way of Jesus while benefitting those receiving care and building up the entire community (1 Pet 2:5).[54]

According to Paul Blowers, "For the early churches, Christian morality was neither merely dictated by experts nor reduced to an exclusive, exhaustive list of behavioral axioms. Rather, it was inculcated over the course of time as believers were admonished to imitate paragons of moral excellence."[55] Disciples did what their Lord did and were inspired by the examples of others. Challenges "tested the solidarity and viability of whole communities and not just the religious identity or fidelity of their individual members," Blowers writes.[56]

Although the early church struggled to align with the Christian moral vision at times, the calling to compassion was distinctive and visible in the lives of believers. Ivor Davidson underscores the way disciples became the gospel:

> To see that witness close up, to live and work alongside those who professed faith, would be to learn, in practical ways, what the gospel had to offer. And so it was that people surely came to faith, a very great deal of the time, through their social networks, in encounter with living examples of Christian behavior, worship, prayer and piety and first-hand contact with the seriousness with which believers pursued their everyday spiritual and moral duties.[57]

As Cyprian is believed to have said in 256, "We do not speak great things but we live them."[58] Christians spoke, but it was their entire lives that served as a recommendation letter for Jesus (2 Cor 3:2).

The second transformative element that propelled compassion among the early Christians was their eschatological vision: a vision of the future that allowed them to see the present afresh.[59] A vision of a great reversal where mercy and justice come to the poor and oppressed (1 Sam 2:1–10;

---

54. Peterson, "Being the Church in Philippi." Donna Geernaert clarifies that "although 'koinonia' is never equated with 'church' in the New Testament, it is the term that most aptly expresses the mystery underlying the various New Testament images of the church." See her "Church as Koinonia/Church as Sacrament."

55. Blowers, *Moral Formation*, 4.

56. Blowers, *Moral Formation*, 2.

57. Davidson, "Church Growth in the Early Church," 162.

58. Cyprian had much to say, too: See Cyprian, Pat. 3, FC 36, quoted in Kreider, *Patient Ferment*, 13.

59. Regarding eschatology and compassion, see Armitage, *Theories of Poverty*, 215–226; Daley, *Hope of the Early Church*; Kreider, *Patient Ferment*; Rhee, "Wealth, Poverty, and Eschatology."

Luke 1:46–55, 6:20–26). Alister McGrath describes this view as trusting God with the long lens on life—not allowing present anxieties to be privileged but placing trust in God's ultimate justice:

> The Christian hope is about longing for and hoping for this coming reality, which, in the meantime, we try to display and enact in our individual lives, in the church, and in the world. The church is called on to realise what might otherwise only be imagined—not something that is *imaginary*, a product of our hopeless longing, but something that is *imagined*, seen in the light of the gospel promises and the actions of a creating and recreating God.[60]

An eschatological vision resulted in a reordering of life in at least two ways: it allowed disciples to relax the terminative primacy of their own lives—to see themselves as secure and merely transitioning to a fuller reality; and it gave meaning to compassion and suffering. A secure future settled an uncertain present. This is evident in the way early Christians viewed violence and disease, which provides a final illustration of sharing and service.

PERSECUTION AND PANDEMICS

The Roman Empire of the first three centuries was multiethnic and tolerated differences as long as insurrection or disloyalty was avoided.[61] Indeed, maintaining the *Pax Romania* was one of Rome's contributions to population growth and trade in the lands radiating out from the Mediterranean. Despite their spotty presence, Christians generated sufficient attention for laws to be passed banning their worship, on the grounds that it was an affront to local deities. Christians were watched with suspicion as they delivered food and comforted the sick and imprisoned.[62] "They could never feel completely safe," Timothy Barnes concludes.[63]

Most persecution did not reach the point of death but consisted of "maligning, reproach, beatings, imprisonments and financial ruin"—attempts in

---

60. McGrath, "Theology, Eschatology and Church Growth," 101.

61. Markus, "Secular in Late Antiquity," 354.

62. Watts argues that the absence of Christians in public or family celebrations might not be as stark an absence given that people excused themselves for a variety of reasons: *Final Pagan Generation*, 33, 39.

63. Romans expressed fear, hatred, and pity for Christians, making confessing to being a Christian (thus, "martyr," which means "witness") sufficient cause for conviction (Barnes, *Tertullian*, 161). Persecution is recorded among the earliest Christians. For a New Testament record, see Schnabel, "Persecution in the Early Christian Mission."

an honor-shame culture to reclaim Christians who had deviated from Greek, Roman, and Jewish norms.[64] The most intense eruptions of persecution occurred in an uneven patchwork. Under some emperors, Christians served in government, bishops were recognized, and houses of worship were constructed. Under others—such as Nero (in 64) and Valerian (in 253–260)—Christians suffered.[65] Religious fanaticism by non-Christians stirred regional flare-ups that dispersed believers. Hundreds of Christians were martyred in localized outbreaks; they had their property confiscated, were fined, and were humiliated in legal trials. A list of martyrs was kept in individual house churches and later collected, combined, and ratified by the church.

Ignatius of Antioch (d. 108/140) considered heretics to "have no regard for love; no care for the widow, or the orphan, or the oppressed; of the bond, or of the free; of the hungry, or of the thirsty."[66] According to historian John Behr, "Demanding a great deal from the Christians, both in terms of commitment and charity, the churches were also able to offer much to both the spirit and the flesh."[67]

An especially devastating pandemic (whom some believe was caused by smallpox) ravaged the Roman Empire from 249 to 262. Christian bishops encouraged disciples to render aid rather than abandon ailing family and neighbors. Christians were blamed for the disease (again, due to insulting local deities), but faith brought meaning and assurance. With stirring resolve, Cyprian, bishop of Carthage, wrote in 252:

> Our brethren who have been freed from the world by the summons of the Lord should not be mourned, since we know that they are not lost but sent before; that in departing they led the way; that as travelers, as voyagers are wont to be, they should be longed for, not lamented.[68]

Although death by torture or disease was not necessarily sought, neither was it wholly feared.[69] As Dionysius the Great, wrote of the Christian community's response to the plague in Alexandria in 262:

---

64. DiSilva, *Honor, Patronage, Kinship and Purity*, 45.

65. Tabernee, "Eusebius' 'Theology of Persecution'" 319–34.

66. Roberts et al., *Epistle of Ignatius*, vol. 1, chap. 6.

67. Behr, "Social and Historical Setting," 61.

68. Saint Cyprian, "Morality," 215.

69. Generally, the question was whether one was *willing* to be martyred. Some taught that one should avoid it if at all possible. Others recommended standing firm rather than fleeing: Heine, "Articulating Identity," 211.

Visiting the sick without thought of the danger to themselves, resolutely caring for them, tending them in Christ, they readily left this life with them, after contracting the disease from others, drawing the sickness onto themselves from their neighbours, and willingly partaking of their sufferings. The best of our brethren departed life this way—some presbyters and deacons and some of the laity, greatly esteemed, so that, on account of the great devotion and strong faith it entails, this kind of death does not seem inferior to martyrdom.[70]

Around the same time, the Emperor Decius (reigned 249–251) gave an edict for all citizens to offer a sacrifice to Roman gods—a sacrifice that would be certified by local magistrates. Although likely intended as an endorsement of unity across the empire, Decius's edict became a test for Christians. Most believers complied with the edict, not seeing or caring about a conflict of loyalties. Some feared torture. Some attempted to evade the edict by bribing officials, sending a proxy to sacrifice on their behalf, or by hiding or fleeing. A minority refused and were tried, imprisoned, and tortured. Many of those who lapsed later returned to the church, seeking a spiritual harbor.[71]

To die for Christ was to become the Eucharist, a chrysalis emerging as truly and completely human in the next life.[72] In illness, they were healed, and with each blow, Satan was defeated.[73] A passage in Wisdom (3:1–9) offers a glimpse of this image:[74]

But the souls of the righteous are in the hand of God,
and no torment will ever touch them.
In the eyes of the foolish they seemed to have died,
and their departure was thought to be a disaster,
and their going from us to be their destruction;
but they are at peace.
For though in the sight of others they were punished,
their hope is full of immortality.
Having been disciplined a little, they will receive great good,

70. Eusebius, *Church History*, 6.22.7, 9–10, quoted in Lee, *Pagans and Christians*, 139.

71. Later, these diverse responses led to conflict between those who lapsed and those who did not. For a description of Decius's edict, see Rebillard, *Christians and Their Many Identities*, 47–55; Torjesen, "Social and Historical Setting."

72. Behr, "Learning through Experience"; Gavrilyuk, "Overview of Patristic Theodicies"; Moss, *Other Christs*.

73. Rebillard, *Christians and Their Many Identities*, 14–15.

74. Wisdom is a Jewish book written in the first century BCE. It is considered canonical by Catholics and Orthodox, and deuterocanonical by Protestants. Wisdom provided encouragement for early Christians: McGlynn, *Divine Judgement*.

because God tested them and found them worthy of himself;
like gold in the furnace he tried them,
and like a sacrificial burnt offering he accepted them.
In the time of their visitation they will shine forth,
and will run like sparks through the stubble.
They will govern nations and rule over peoples,
and the Lord will reign over them forever.
Those who trust in him will understand truth,
and the faithful will abide with him in love,
because grace and mercy are upon his holy ones,
and he watches over his elect.

Christians were called to see persecution and pandemics with spiritual eyes, as proving their faith (1 Pet 1:7). Christians followed Jesus by extending compassion, confident of his faithfulness (Rom 6:5; 8:17; Phil 3:8–10; 1 Pet 4:12–14) and encouraged by the community's (1 Thess 1:6–7; 2:14; 1 Cor 4:16–17; 11:1). It was not merely holding fast to belief or faith that enabled these Christians to endure, but joyful allegiance—as Matthew Bates describes it, the "embodied participation in the new creation."[75]

Some modern scholars have critiqued the early Christian example as an incomplete expression of compassion due to their focus on charity rather than structural change, possibly because of their small size [**Size**]. But Helen Rhee argues that they were intently committed to social justice, trusting God with the final retribution of their own lives and the actions of others.[76] Further, the actions of these early Christians were radical in their equality, reach, and nonviolent resistance to an oppressive political and economic system.[77]

Size

The throngs of Pentecost and Paul's far-flung missionary journeys may give a mistaken impression that the Christian movement instantly catapulted to prominence. Most research suggests that it did not. Although estimates of adherents are speculative, Keith Hopkins concludes that in the first two centuries, "Christians were statistically insignificant."[78]

75. Bates, *Salvation by Allegiance Alone*, 13.

76. Rhee, "Wealth, Poverty, and Eschatology," 77.

77. For a brief review, see Elliott, "Political Theology."

78. Hopkins estimates that about seven thousand Christians existed in 100 AD and two hundred thousand in 200 AD. This represents fast growth but translates into 0.01 percent and 0.35 percent, respectively, of the Roman Empire's population; see Hopkins, "Christian Number and Its Implications." Rodney Stark offers a slightly more

What is striking about this for our purposes is that early Christians cared for the sick, the dying, and those in prison without any vision of things changing. They cared without any assurance that the need would come to an end or that their efforts would make a measurable difference. Despite this, they cared at significant risk, being blamed at times for the very illnesses they tended. They joyfully followed the example of Christ and believed that ultimate justice would occur in the afterlife.

Several reasons are suggested for this exponential growth, including Christians developing herd immunity in serving the ill and non-believers losing social ties due to death that may have otherwise held them back from becoming Christian.[79] But Henry Chadwick contends that the primary driver of conversion was compassion: "The practical application of charity was probably the most potent single cause of Christian success."[80]

FROM THEN TO NOW

From the earliest Christians, we see the importance of beginning with and returning to Jesus. This reality frames everything: how we see people, how we hold or share resources, how we view suffering and status, how we live in community and society, and how we endure.[81] These early disciples introduce us to God's overwhelming favor—a common purse from which all humanity draws and can share in mutual aid and service. We see as well a reframing of insurmountable odds in a hostile culture as a temporary waypoint on a path toward an inevitable and glorious reality (Matt 5:10–12).[82]

---

optimistic estimate of 4.2 percent of the population of Rome; see Stark, *Triumph of Christianity*, 163.

79. Stark, *Rise of Christianity*, 73–94.

80. Chadwick, *Early Church*, 56.

81. For a succinct and fresh view of the transformative Christ, see Rowe, *Christianity's Surprise*.

82. Similarly overwhelming settings include Christians enduring war, urban blight and crime, economic depression, catastrophe, racism, and outnumbering. For documentary evidence, see Ferguson, *Early Church*. When the Friends were poised similarly, Henry Cadbury wrote, "I believe it may still be said that the world has yet to see the great things God can do through a small denomination wholly devoted to his will. May it be the aim of Quakerism, by the grace of God, to show the world what he can do through us" ("Quakerism as an Experiment Station," quoted in Bacon, *Let This Life Speak*, 29).

Ever looking to Jesus and confidence in God's judgment freed these disciples to prioritize the needs of others and channel the gifts of God toward them.

We also see humanity in these earliest Christians as they held on to their possessions, slipped back into stratification, and lapsed before shame and sword. As we will see in centuries to come, it often is the minority who labor in the sickrooms, the arena, and the fire; we tend to remember and memorialize these. Others, sometimes the majority of lay and clergy, retreat. Even these tell a story about moral choices and divine and human grace. But if we return to the ideal, we might hear the early Christians reciting and encouraging one another with the words of Wisdom 12:13a, 19:

> For neither is there any god besides you,
> whose care is for all people;
> Through such works you have taught your people
> that the righteous must be kind,
> and you have filled your children with good hope,
> because you give repentance for sins.

None could have imagined the era to follow when the unbelievable occured: the Roman emperor converted to Christianity, and Constantine's Edict of Milan in 313 restored property and freedom to Christians. The acceptance of Christianity and the gradual shifting of the empire to the east, portended a fundamental reshaping of Christian compassion.

2

Contentment and Simplicity

WITH THE EDICT OF Milan in 313, Constantine I (c. 272–337) halted the persecution of Christians. Seven decades later, in 381, Christianity became the official religion of the Roman Empire. Desiring to replace a frayed and flagging Rome, Constantine moved the capital to Byzantium and renamed it Constantinople (today's Istanbul, Turkey). As a successful military general, Constantine chose this centrally located isthmus that hinged the Roman Empire's massive landholdings to the east in Asia with those to the west in North Africa and Europe. From Constantinople, the Byzantine Empire held back invaders for seven centuries.[1]

Constantine favored Christianity and welcomed it into the halls of government and jurisprudence. His actions mingled political and social power with Christian teachings, provoking conflict between Christians and pagans and generally disrupting centuries of Roman society.[2] Confiscated land was restored to believers and to the church, and frenzied new church construction began.[3] The local bishop became a valued counselor, second only to the bishop of Rome. He served as God's prophetic guardian and spokesman for Christians. Novitiates applied to the church because of belief, strategy, or

---

1. Laiou's background on Constantinople and the Byzantine Empire informs this section and is available at "Political History."

2. Considerable conflict occurred as Christians and pagans clashed over sacred sites, funding, and policy: Watts, *Final Pagan Generation*.

3. Emperor Gratian (359–383) advanced Christianization by appropriating pagan land and shrines and limiting privileges previously enjoyed by pagan priests.

being caught up in the social current. The number of Christians–a few rich and many poor–dramatically increased.[4] Aristocrats and bureaucrats joined as well, bringing their influence and status with them and receiving the embrace of the church. Some seasoned leaders—such as Ambrose (337–397)—were selected as bishops. Most of the new Christians were young, breaking from their families and rejecting their traditional upbringing and Roman deities. Many of the old guard remained pagan.[5]

With fresh acceptance for Christianity and a flood of believers, many Christians faced an identity crisis. Their vision had been that Jesus would return and bring justice to Rome. But now the church was allied with the empire, and that was an incomprehensible thought. What does it mean now to follow Jesus? Constantine's rise to the role of emperor and his Christian conversion surprised everyone, and none knew quite what it meant for the future.[6] How might the empire—its laws and its very foundation—be Christianized, and what would that mean in terms of loving one's neighbor?[7]

The emperor's Christian conversion did not mean that social ills evaporated. Constantine oversaw an empire in disarray, morally and economically. Winds of famine, economic crisis, and disease swept the empire, and poverty kept life expectancy low—at twenty-two years if all births were counted or forty-seven years among those who survived the first five years of life.[8]

In this new world where former prosecutors befriended and joined Christians, and bishops no longer marched to their deaths in chains, teaching and practice was needed to maintain the high calling of the faith, especially with most believers being young in faith and age. What should Christians believe? How should they live? These became primary questions for bishops and seekers.[9]

---

4. The church grew rapidly in the latter decades of the third century, welcoming a cross-section of Roman society. Its growth continued under new circumstances in the fourth century: Behr, "Social and Historical Setting," 399.

5. Of the older generation, Watts writes, "Beginning in the 370s . . . men who had once served as teachers, advocates, and even imperial governors entered into bishoprics, a trend that accelerated as the fifth century approached": *Final Pagan Generation*, 151.

6. Watts, *Final Pagan Generation*, 39–40.

7. With Constantine, Christianity begins shaping social reality, as Max Weber saw it, and the negotiation of influence by religious and imperial powers begins. As an example of the Christianization of law and policy, accompanied by enduring ethical and legal concerns, Constantine placed restrictions on infant exposure, yet he allowed rescuers to raise an *expositus* as they saw fit (e.g., as a slave) and allowed the selling of children in cases of extreme poverty: Evans Grubbs, "Infant Exposure and Infanticide." For an extended treatment, see Koskenniemi, *Exposure of Infants*.

8. Laiou, "Human Resources."

9. Moral life as a Christian included more than compassion—marriage, diet, and

Although during the first three centuries, many believers joined Jesus by finding meaning in suffering, in the late antique era, a young and diverse church focused on growing in Christian virtue through asceticism and almsgiving. Although much of this era's activity occurred below deck amid abundant need, the spotlight is on the upper deck, where prominent leaders and regional bishops were attempting to manage their institutions and perhaps live their lives in light of Christian teaching.[10] We begin by considering desert and urban asceticism—a proxy for persecution and a path toward holiness—and the almsgiving that followed it.

ASCETICISM

Asceticism comes from a word meaning "exercise" or "practice"—actions soldiers, athletes, or artisans might undertake to perfect their skills. Greek Stoic philosophers advocated asceticism as a means of overcoming one's passions. Likewise, some Roman elites wore simple dress, abstained from sex, slept on a hard bed, and engaged in disciplines that produced a virtuous lifestyle.[11]

Ascetic ideals and practices were as old as the Christian movement itself. But in the fourth century, Christians adapted asceticism as an antidote to the incursion of the worldly distractions and attachments that seemed to be flooding into the church. It could be extreme or mild, but it meant avoiding attachments that might hold one back from ascending toward God with singular desire.[12]

The true ascetics were the "holy poor"—the desert fathers and mothers who deprived themselves and sometimes radically renounced attachments to purify their passions. They gave up sleep, food, sex, family, career, honors, wealth, oppression, slaves—anything that could keep them from unifying

---

other issues were debated: Heine, "Articulating Identity," 200.

10. Constantinople was located on the eastern edge of civilization, and it had a reputation to develop. The fifth and sixth centuries brought growth and development, spurred in part by responses to fires, earthquakes, and the bubonic plague, which created food and water shortages and stimulated contrite and charitable responses. Plagues did not calm until around 747. See Magdalino, "Medieval Constantinople"; Morrisson and Sodini, "Sixth-Century Economy."

11. Torjesen, "Social and Historical Setting," 193–95.

12. Although varying in expression, the divestment of goods was not new to this age. According to 1 Clement, "We know that many among ourselves have given themselves up to chains in order to redeem others. Many have surrendered themselves to slavery and provided food for others with the price they received for themselves": Walsh and Glimm, *Fathers of the Church. 1 Clement*, chap. 55.2, 51. Burchill-Limb argues that for Augustine, asceticism was more nuanced than a physical-spiritual polarity: Burchill-Limb, "Actuality of Augustine's Distinction," 196–97.

their will with God's.[13] Asceticism achieved intentionally what persecution brought naturally: purification for the believer. It also served as something of a protest or reform movement critiquing undisciplined discipleship.

With the desert fathers and mothers, poverty became linked with virtue. Although theologians of the day advanced differing views on the nature of materiality (good, neutral, bad), the corruptibility of wealth was clear, as the story of Lazarus and the rich man so clearly illustrated (Luke 16:19–31). The act of giving and detaching was virtuous. Amassing and holding was corrosive. Yet one needn't give all. The voluntary relinquishment of attachments for the good of oneself or others existed in the early church (Acts 2:44–47; 4:32–37) and it is reasserted as a path to virtue in this era in the form of simplicity and almsgiving.[14]

SPARING, SHARING, AND VIRTUE

Like disciples gathering to hear John the Baptist, curious devotees trekked to deserts in Asia Minor, Syria, Palestine, and especially Egypt in search of learning from male and female hermit teachers and fellowship with like-minded disciples.[15] Others heard these desert teachings second-hand.[16] Some of these disciples eventually became church leaders, scattered in bishoprics across the empire. They included Gregory of Nazianzus (329–390), Basil of Caesarea (c. 329–379), Gregory of Nyssa (c. 335–c. 395), Ambrose, Jerome (345–420), John Chrysostom (c. 349–407), Augustine of Hippo (354–430), and Theodoret of Cyrrhus (c. 393–458/466).[17]

13. Ramelli, *Social Justice*, 235.235. Ascetics in eastern Christianity continue until the present-day, such as Father Paisios of Mount Athos (1924–1994) who received and prayed for thousands of sick and suffering visitors.

14. Brown, *Treasure in Heaven*; Holmes, *Life Pleasing to God*, 107–14. For an introduction to asceticism, see Rhee, *Early Christian Literature*, 106–8.

15. Some of these monasteries remain in operation today, such as the Monastery of St. Macarius the Great in Egypt. On desert monasticism, see Hartney, *John Chrysostom*, 23; Swan, *Forgotten Desert Mothers*. Among the ascetic notables are St. Melania the Younger (c. 383–439) and her husband, Valerius Pinianus. At Augustine's encouragement, they abandoned considerable wealth and became ascetics in Palestine. Some desert communities were quite large; the White Monastery in southern Egypt had four thousand residents at its height. Eventually, leading ascetics attracted sizable communities, creating small cities of sorts in the desert: Chitty, *Desert a City*. Desert asceticism migrated to urban areas as well. Constantinople had a monastic presence from 350 forward: Hatlie, *Monks and Monasteries*.

16. Augmenting the desert teachers were the martyrs who continued to teach by example.

17. Bishops and ascetics radiating out in surrounding areas were active in compassion as well. Examples include Achillius of Larisa (d. c. 330) of Greece, known for his

The desert teachers and the church leaders they inspired were united but not uniform. Each contributed nuance and influence in the forging of Christian doctrine.[18] Some taught that private ownership was sinful, and some relinquished all of their personal wealth to the poor. Most, however, viewed possessions as neutral but suspect, often becoming baggage on the spiritual journey. In place of acquisition, many advocated a graduated asceticism accompanied by almsgiving.[19]

One of those disciples drawn to the desert was the well-to-do young lawyer from Syrian Antioch, John Chrysostom (c. 349–407).[20] After spending two years with a desert teacher, Chrysostom returned to Antioch and became a deacon and then a priest, pastoring the poor as part of his duties. Eventually, Chrysostom became bishop of Constantinople. Despite being a priest in an affluent Antioch parish and then serving as bishop of the empire's capital city, Chrysostom never forgot his time in the desert—his formation in the way of Christ.

Chrysostom taught by example and by well-crafted homilies. Many described him later as "golden-mouthed."[21] He lived relatively simply in one of the world's largest and most affluent cities, and he encouraged parishioners to follow his example by denying themselves luxuries and giving alms to the poor. Chrysostom was not against art and beauty but argued that by forgoing luxuries and living simply, one increasingly would be shaped by Christian rather than worldly virtues. According to Jaclyn Maxwell,

> His ideal was not for all Christians to become ascetics. He insisted that people could live in the city, with jobs and families, and lead perfectly acceptable Christian lives. In order to do this, however, catechumens and baptized Christians required a great

---

healings; and Nerses I the Great (d. 373) of Armenia, remembered for his construction of charitable institutions, including schools and hospitals. Also of note is St. Theosebia (d. 385) a charitable deaconess and sister to Basil and Gregory of Nyssa who voluntarily accompanied Gregory during his three years in exile.

18. Differences in teachings were a product of the individuals and their experiences, their setting, the church working out ideas, and the diversity of voices in Scripture regarding wealth and poverty. On the diversity of the patristic church fathers, see Hays, "Resumptions of Radicalism"; Holman, *Hungry Are Dying*; Mayer, "John Chrysostom on Poverty."

19. Interest in asceticism brought concerns that a two-story, sacred-secular church would develop between ascetics and ordinary Christians: Behr, "Social and Historical Setting," 409.

20. Basil and Chrysostom were classmates. After completing their studies, Basil journeyed to the desert to become an ascetic while Chrysostom began practicing law. They maintained a friendship but later conflicted. One of many overviews of Chrysostom is Sterk, *Renouncing the World*. Also see Watts, *Final Pagan Generation*, 157–61.

21. "Chrysostom" was John's nickname. In Greek it means "golden mouth."

deal of instruction before they could sort out the non-Christian and/or sinful habits from their daily lives.[22]

Chrysostom and his contemporaries emphasized that Christian virtue was accessible to all. Many envisioned the process of virtue formation as ascending a ladder [**Ascending the Ladder**], wherein a monk or disciple took successive steps to renounce their own will and embrace God's. To be compassionate like Christ required inner development as well as outward actions, so wealth and possessions were a common concern. Navigating wealth and poverty amounted to an obstacle course for those committed to learning the way of Christ.[23]

Ascending the Ladder

John Climacus (c. 579–649) was a monk in the Egyptian desert. In *The Ladder of Divine Ascent*, Climacus's guide for the formation of monks, he describes thirty steps wherein one renounced and detached from the world (steps 1 and 2), broke from avarice through poverty (steps 16 and 17), abandoned vainglory and pride (steps 22 and 23), accepted simplicity and humility (steps 24 and 25), and is subsumed by love (step 30). His view was popular among church leaders. It was easy to teach and challenging to achieve.

---

22. Maxwell, *Christianization and Communication*, 144. Later, Symeon the Theologian (949–1022) wrote similarly: "Provided they live a worthy life, both those who choose to dwell in the midst of noise and hubbub and those who dwell in monasteries, mountains and caves can achieve salvation": Symeon the Theologian, *Philokalia*, 4:20.

23. Dunn, "Why Care for the Poor?"

Fig. 2.1. *The Ladder of Divine Ascent.*

Some, such as Augustine, treated wealth as an asset that could be employed for good or ill. Augustine asked, "What does gold say to me? 'Love me.' But what does God tell me to reply? 'Let me use you, and so use you so that you don't possess me, and that you part me from you.'"[24] Still, Augustine acknowledged that wealth was fraught with hazards.[25] Riches provided "an occasion for sin," in Jerome's view, in how they are obtained, in how they possessed their owners, and because of the cares associated with managing them (Matt 13:22).[26] Others (including Chrysostom) believed that wealth equated to robbery, reasoning that the only way one could gain riches was by impoverishing others.

An antidote for the poison of excess was to spare and share—to deny accumulating inessentials and share one's excess with those in need. This was the advice of the bishops for urban Christians. Giving was a moral imperative, as passages from the widely circulated *Sentences of Sextus* affirmed:

24. Sermon 65A.1; NBA 30/1, 324–326, quoted in Allen and Morgan, "Augustine on Poverty," 144.

25. Allen and Morgan, "Augustine on Poverty." Abandoning wealth was rooted in passages such as Matthew 19:21, 24; Luke 6:24, 14:33; and Acts 20:35.

26. Jerome's discussion occurs in *On Riches!* (sect. 6, para. 1), quoted in Rees, *Pelagius*, 179.

"It is impious for those who have God in common, indeed as father, not to have possessions in common." Additionally, "Do not judge something to be good that you cannot share with others and still have yourself. Nothing is good that is unshared." Or, more simply, "Things that you freely receive from God, freely give as well."[27]

Almsgiving was necessary for the rich and poor alike, as modeled by the widow whom Jesus praised for contributing more than the wealthy (see Fig. 2.2)—for "she out of her poverty has put in all she had to live on" (Luke 21:1–4).[28] The temptation of wealth could usher in spiritual poverty, regardless of whether one had much or little, as "greed is clever at asking for more than it needs," wrote Chrysostom.[29]

Fig. 2.2. *The Offering of the Poor Widow, Luke 21:1–4.*

Church fathers taught that giving alms aided the destitute with material goods, affirming the early church's emulation of the faithful in Matthew 25:31–46. But exceeding the material value of the gift was the *virtue development* that occurred as the giver was generous and the receiver was grateful.[30]

27. The *Sentences of Sextus* was a fourth-century document written in the style of Christian wisdom literature, resembling the biblical book of Proverbs. It shows hints of Greek philosophy (especially that of Pythagoras) but is Christian in content: Wilson, *Sentences of Sextus*, secs. 228, 242, 295, 296.

28. David Downs distinguishes between meritorious and atoning almsgiving, with the former resulting in reward for the donor and the latter relieving one from sin: Downs, *Alms*, 6–17.

29. Chrysostom, "Homily 7" in *Homilies on Paul's Letter to the Philippians*, 133.

30. Chrysostom addressed slavery similarly. His focus was not on ending slavery but on becoming truly free as a slave to Jesus. Chris L. de Wet says, "Unfortunately the more the metaphor of slavery was developed and spread in Christian theology, the more insouciant and blasé Christian attitudes became toward institutional slavery." See de Wet,

How one suffered, *how* one gave, and *how* one received were paramount. The controversial monk Pelagius (c. 355–c. 420) offered a picture of how open-hearted virtue and open-handed care were woven together in the faithful disciple:

> *He* is a Christian who shows compassion to all, who is not at all provoked by wrong done to him, who does not allow the poor to be oppressed in his presence, who helps the wretched, who succors the needy, who mourns with the mourners, who feels another's pain as if it were his own, who is moved to tears by the tears of others, whose house is common to all, whose door is closed to no one, whose table no poor man does not know, whose food is offered to all, whose goodness all know and at whose hands no one experiences injury, who serves God all day and night, who ponders and meditates upon his command- ments unceasingly, who is made poor in the eyes of the world so that he may become rich before God, who is held to be without fame among men so that he may appear renowned before God and his angels, who is seen to have no feigning or pretense in his heart, whose soul is open and unspotted, whose conscience is faithful and pure, whose whole mind is on God, whose whole hope is in Christ, who desires heavenly things rather than earthly, who spurns human possessions so that he may be able to possess those that are divine.[31]

Almsgiving offered several social benefits beyond individual virtue de- velopment. It smoothed the lost wages of poor agriculturalists during winter months when physical needs increased and opportunities for employment dried up, salved suspicion and disdain between the rich and poor, and gener- ally sensitized people to social injustice.[32] Additionally, "rich" and "poor" were

---

Preaching Bondage, 272. Cf. Mayer, "John Chrysostom on Poverty."

31. Rees, *Pelagius*, 124.

32. According to Aideen Hartney, "While Chrysostom worries about town houses reaching lavish proportions, and commercial activities driving the lifestyles of the citi- zens, the likes of Basil of Caesarea and Gregory Nazianzus are concerned about the large estates that exist in the countryside, on which the poor are forced to labour for their very survival: 'One of us oppressed the poor, taking his lands and moving the boundaries . . . as if he alone were to inhabit the earth. Another polluted the earth with interests and rents, reaping where he did not sow . . . not tilling the soil, but exploiting the sufferings of the needy. . . . Another had no mercy for the widow and the orphan, and did not feed the hungry. . . . It is for these reasons that God's wrath is unleased upon the children of unbelief.'" Gregory of Nazianzus, *Oration* XVI.18, quoted by Hartney, John Chrysostom.

transitory statuses for many. Today's giver might be tomorrow's receiver.[33] Thus, sparing and sharing oiled the social gears of church and society.[34]

Chrysostom encouraged giving more during times of increased need: "Let us substitute for the employers' hands the hands of the almsgivers."[35] He advised keeping an alms box in the house and making daily deposits prior to praying. Periodically, the donor distributed these funds among the destitute or transfered them to the alms box at the church.[36] Gregory of Nyssa encouraged responding to nearby needs: "Let everyone take care of his neighbors. Don't let someone else treat those in your neighborhood. Don't let another rob you of the treasure laid up for you."[37] Gifts were not limited to money. Augustine taught that giving counsel or forgiveness was of equal, if not greater, value than sharing money or food.

At least with church funds, Chrysostom advocated against haphazard giving. Discrimination was needed in the disbursement of aid, as indicated in his chastening letter to Olympias, a deaconess lent support to an unfit beggar:

> I applaud your intentions; but would have you know that those who aspire to the perfection of virtue according to God, ought to distribute their wealth with economy. . . . You ought, therefore, to regard your wealth as belonging to your Master, and to remember that you have to account for its distribution. If you will be persuaded by me, you will in the future regulate your donations according to the wants of those who solicit relief. You will thus be enabled to extend the sphere of your benevolence.[38]

Likely, some degree of discernment was needed from the beginning as evidenced by a lack of full disclosure by Ananias and Saphira in Acts 5:1–11, the need for deacons to rectify perceived inequity in the distribution of goods, and the finite funds available to sustain all needs over the long term.

---

33. Buell, "Be Not One Who Stretches."

34. To quote Jerome again, "We know that we are 'one body', in the words of the apostle (1 Cor. 12.13); if we are truly one, then we should act as one. There is no room for such [economic] variety in the same people." Jerome, *On Riches!*, sect. 6, para. 5.

35. Chrysostom, "Homily 10: A Sermon on Almsgiving," 132.

36. House churches had cash boxes as early as the second century: Liebeschuetz, *Ambrose and John Chrysostom*, 196.

37. Gregory of Nyssa, *On the Love of the Poor*, in Holman, *Hungry Are Dying*, 195. Augustine argued as well that because it is impossible to help everyone, a pragmatic response is to aid those "more closely connected with you": Augustine of Hippo, *St. Augustine's City of God*, vol. 2, sec. 1.28.29.

38. Constantelos, "Origins of Christian Diakonia," 19.

Setting discernment aside, however, and pausing at the cathedral door, we can hear Chrysostom, Basil, Ambrose, and Gregory of Nazianzus entreat Christ-followers to spare and share and grow in character:

> What's the meaning of the golden roof? Surely it has the same usefulness as a roof does to the person whose house is modest? "No, it brings with it a great deal of pleasure." Yes, for one or two days, but no more after that: it simply stands there. I mean, if the sun doesn't amaze us by customarily being there, how much more so is it with works of art? Rather, we pay attention to them just like objects of clay. Tell me, what do lots of pillars and beautiful images and gold inlaid in walls contribute to an upmarket house? Nothing, except that it's a sign of indolence, and hubris, and excessive pretension, and stupidity. I mean that everywhere there should be what's necessary and useful, not superfluous.[39]

+++

> For if what you say is true, that you have kept from your youth the commandment of love and have given to everyone the same as to yourself, then how did you come by this abundance of wealth? Care for the needy requires the expenditure of wealth: when all share alike, disbursing their possessions among themselves, they each receive a small portion for their individual needs. Thus, those who love their neighbor as themselves possess nothing more than their neighbor; yet surely, you seem to have great possessions! How else can this be, but that you have preferred your own enjoyment to the consolation of the many? ... Now your possessions are more a part of you than the members of your own body, and separation from them is as painful as the amputation of one of your limbs.[40]

+++

> When someone steals a man's clothes we call him a thief. Should we not give the same name to one who could clothe the naked and does not? The bread in your cupboard belongs to the hungry man; the coat hanging unused in your closet belongs to the man who needs it; the shoes rotting in your closet belong to the man who has no shoes; the money which you hoard up belongs to the poor.[41]

---

39. Chrysostom, "Homily 11" in *Homilies on Paul's Letter to the Philippians*, 225.
40. Basil, *On Social Justice*, 43.
41. Basil, "Homily on Luke."

+++

The person who gives alms is taught not to admire money or gold. When they have been instructed about this as far as disposition goes, they have made the greatest beginning in the ascent to heaven and have cut out myriad occasions for fighting, strife, envy, and despondency. . . . No longer do they fear punishment, for almsgiving has taught them this. No longer do they covet their neighbor's goods—how could they when they have given them up and given away their own? No longer are they jealous of the rich—how could they be when they wanted to become poor? The eye of the soul has purged them through and through.[42]

+++

Do you see that it's not poverty or wealth either that's good but our disposition? Let's train it; let's teach it to do philosophy. If it's properly disposed, wealth won't be able to exclude us from the kingdom, nor will poverty cause us to have less. No, let's bear poverty gently, being collaterally damaged with regard to the enjoyment neither of the good things to come nor of those in this life.[43]

+++

Yet you say, "I will enjoy all these things during my life, but after my death I will leave my goods to the poor, making them beneficiaries of my will and granting them all my possessions." When you are no longer among your fellow human beings, then you will become a philanthropist! . . . Tell me, however, from what period you intend to seek your reward: the time of your life, or that which comes after your departure? When you were still alive, squandering your years in luxury and wasting them on frivolous pursuits, you never bothered to consider the plight of the needy. What exchange is possible now that you are dead? . . . No one transacts business after the end of the festival, nor is anyone who arrives after the close of the games crowned, nor does anyone who comes after the war perform deeds of valor. It is thus apparent that no one can perform good works after the conclusion of this life. . . . Dead offerings are not accepted at the altar; you must rather present a living sacrifice.[44]

42. Chrysostom, "Homily 1" in *Homilies on Paul's Letter to the Philippians*, 13.
43. Chrysostom, "Homily 3" in *Homilies on Paul's Letter to the Philippians*, 57.
44. Basil, *On Social Justice*, 55, 57.

+++

Why do you reject nature's partnership of goods, and claim possession of nature for yourselves? The earth was established to be in common for all, rich and poor; why do you rich alone arrogate it to yourselves as your rightful property? Nature knows no rich, since she brings forth all men poor.[45]

+++

Do you think your great halls exalt you—when they ought rather to cause you remorse because, though they are big enough to take in multitudes, they shut out the voice of the poor? Though, indeed, nothing is gained by your hearing their voice if, when you hear it, you do nothing about it. In fine, does not your very dwelling-place admonish you of your shame, in that in building it you wished to show that your riches surpass [those of others]—and yet you do not succeed? You cover walls, but you leave men bare. Naked they cry out before your house, and you heed them not: a naked man cries out, but you are busy considering what sort of marbles you will have to cover your floors. A poor man asks for money, and does not get it; a human being begs for bread, and your horse champs a golden bit. You gratify yourself with costly ornaments, while other men go without food. How great a judgment, O rich man, do you draw down upon yourself! The people go hungry, and you close your granaries; the people weep, and you turn your finger-ring about. Unhappy man, who have the power but not the will to save so many souls from death: the cost of the jewel in your ring would have sufficed to save the lives of a whole people.[46]

+++

When wealth is scattered in the manner which our Lord directed, it naturally returns, but when it is gathered, it naturally disperses. If you try to keep it, you will not have it; if you scatter it, you will not lose it.[47]

---

45. *On Naboth*, Ch. I, 2, Ch. II, 4, Ch. III, 11, Ch. V, 20 (*MPL*, XIV, 767–772), quoted in Lovejoy, "Communism of Saint Ambrose," 460.

46. *De Nabuthe*, XIII, 56 (*MPL*, XIV, 784), quoted in Lovejoy, "Communism of Saint Ambrose," 461–62.

47. Basil the Great, *On Social Justice*, 44.

+++

If, then, I am at all persuasive, fellow servants of Christ, brothers and sisters and joint heirs (cf. Rom 8:17; Eph 3:6), let us, while the time is ripe, visit Christ. Let us care for Christ. Let us feed Christ. Let us clothe Christ. Let us welcome Christ in (Matt 25:35). Let us honor Christ, not simply with food, as some do (Luke 7:36); nor with ointments, like Mary (John 12:3); nor only with a tomb, like Joseph of Arimathea (Matt 27:57–60); nor merely with items needed for burial, like the half-hearted friend of Christ, Nicodemus (John 19:38–39); nor with gold, frankincense, and myrrh, like the Magi (Matt 2:11) who were there before all the others. Rather, since the Lord of all "desires mercy, and not sacrifice" (Hos 6:6; Matt 9:13), and since "visceral mercy is worth more than a myriad of fat rams" (Dan 3:40, Old Greek), let us bring this gift to Christ through the poor who today are cast to the ground, so that when we are set free from this world they may welcome us into the "eternal tabernacle" (Luke 16:9) in Christ himself, our Lord to whom be glory for all the ages. Amen.[48]

Stirring words, indeed! Many were struck by teachings such as these, including Martin of Tours [**Martin of Tours**]. Yet, as poignant as these orations are, we must consider their audience and their impact. While these sermons plead for sympathy, simplicity, and alms, some call for radical and socially challenging action, including ending usury and oppressive and enslaving debt. As Susan Holman puts it, the poor were pressed into "earthly and heavenly coinage," hounded by debt and forced to beg from the rich.[49] These preachers walked a fine line in prophetically calling for social justice while maintaining the church, and some—even "golden-mouthed" Chrysostom—were banished at the end of their lives for crossing that threshold.

Martin of Tours

Martin of Tours (c. 316–397) was a young man who converted shortly after Christianity was legalized. He declared his faith at age ten and was baptized at age eighteen. He moved with his family from his birthplace in modern-day Hungary to Italy and then on to France, where he was conscripted into the Roman army.

48. Gregory of Nazianzus, "On the Love of the Poor." Cited in Blowers, *Moral Formation*, 162.

49. Holman, *Hungry Are Dying*, 133, 161.

According to his hagiographer, Sulpicius Severus, Martin was on military duty one cold day in Amiens when he encountered a beggar. Being taken by his lack of clothing in the cold, Martin stopped his horse and cut his cape in half with his sword. Martin gave one half of the cape to the beggar and covered himself with the remainder. That night, Martin had a vision that Jesus himself was the beggar whom he had met on the road.[50]

Around the age of twenty, Martin announced to his military superiors that as a Christian, his conscience would no longer allow him to fight. He was accused of cowardice and ordered to be jailed. Martin offered to go into battle unarmed instead. His superiors accepted the arrangement, but before the battle, the opposing Germanic army agreed to a truce, and afterward, Martin was released from military service.

Later, Martin became a hermit and took vows to serve as a bishop and monk. Today, Martin is known as the patron saint of beggars, wool-weavers, and tailors. Martin Luther was named after St. Martin, and the church in Tours, France, that bears his name is a popular stop on the *Via Turonensis* pilgrimage route from Paris to Santiago de Compostela, Spain.[51]

---

50. Martin's half cape was preserved as a relic and regularly was carried into battle. The priest who cared for the cape (*capa*) was given a special title—a title that eventually was given to all priests who ministered to the military (*chaplain* is our word today). Shrines built to display the cape were called "capelles," from which we take the word *chapel*.

51. Accounts of the saints' lives frequently are written to inspire readers and heroize the saint. Some accounts meld history with legend and sometimes it is difficult to separate the two.

Fig. 2.3. *Charity of St. Martin.* Martin of Tours dividing his cloak with a beggar.

Alms Exchange

Although almsgiving cultivated virtue, some viewed giving in more mechanistic terms: the giver gave alms and kindnesses and the poor prayed for benefactors. The poor were, in essence, "porters" in Augustine's language, changing gifts of grain and coin into righteousness, carrying charity credits to God.[52] The poor were equipped to do this because they were unencumbered by attachments and, thus, on average, closer to God while the rich tended to be blinded by possessions.[53] As Paul advised Timothy, a young minister:

> As for those who in the present age are rich, command them not
> to be haughty, or to set their hopes on the uncertainty of riches,
> but rather on God who richly provides us with everything for

52. Shuler, "Almsgiving," 85–86.

53. This teaching found biblical accompaniment in John's revelation to the Laodicean church angel (Rev 3:17), "For you say, 'I am rich, I have prospered, and I need nothing.' You do not realize that you are wretched, pitiable, poor, blind, and naked"; in the words of James, "Has not God chosen the poor in the world to be rich in faith and to be heirs of the kingdom that he has promised to those who love him?" (Jas 2:5b); and in the angel's declaration to Cornelius that "your prayers and your alms have ascended as a memorial before God" (Acts 10:4b).

our enjoyment. They are to do good, to be rich in good works, generous, and ready to share, thus storing up for themselves the treasure of a good foundation for the future, so that they may take hold of the life that really is life. (1 Tim 6:17–19)[54]

Tobit counsels more plainly: "For almsgiving saves from death and purges away every sin" (Tobit 12:8b).[55]

Whether given for virtue or merit, Christian giving in the early Byzantine era eclipsed considerably the occasional coin tossed to a beggar in Roman society. Energized by spiritual teaching, almsgiving continued for centuries. According to Peter Brown, "The incommensurability between the gift and its heavenly reward fostered an attitude that favored regular, small donations. Each gift, however small, was charged with a magic all of its own."[56]

EARLY CHARITABLE INSTITUTIONS

Christian philanthropy included sizable gifts similar to those of Greek and Roman elites. A notable distinction, however, was that the former were directed toward the poor rather than circulated among persons of near-equal status. These established some of the first independent Christian institutions (xenodochia) designed to serve the vulnerable.

The Cappadocian fathers (Basil, Gregory of Nazianzus, and Gregory of Nyssa) differed in how they thought about suffering. Basil of Caesarea (c. 329–379) saw a causal connection between the immoral behavior of Christians and a severe famine that swept Cappadocia in 368. Gregory of Nazianzus, on the other hand, viewed famine as an opportunity to respond to need.[57] Basil is most prominently remembered for acting, organizing a

54. Similar teaching is offered by Ambrose (c. 340–397): "It is money that you distribute, but for him [the pauper], it is life that he receives; you give silver, but he considers it his means of survival; your coin is his estate. In this exchange, you gain more, for he is your debtor in the order of salvation: if you clothe the naked, you clothe yourself in justice. If you take a stranger under your roof, if you receive a needy person, he acquires for you the friendship of the saints and the eternal tabernacle. This grace is not balanced: you sow the corporal and reap the spiritual. . . . On the day of Judgement he will hold his salvation from the Lord whom he will hold as the debtor of his mercy." Ambrose, *Les Devoirs. Tome II, Livres II–III*, 1:113 quoted in Firey, "'For I Was Hungry,'" 337–38.

55. Also see Luke 11:41; Tobit 12:8–9; Sirach 3:30; 29:7–13.

56. Brown, *Through the Eye of a Needle*, 365.

57. According to Susan Wessel, "While Basil thought adversity brought to light the sins of the community, Gregory thought it tested the human capacity for sympathy and compassion. Unlike Basil, who had asked the community to trace every action along the casual chain of its moral implications, Gregory asked them to examine the sincerity

large agriculturally-based ministry to provide food and jobs during and after the famine [**Basil of Caesarea's Basileias**].

Basil of Caesarea's Basileias

In 368, a poor harvest resulted in an extreme food shortage, which drove prices up in Caesarea and other areas of Cappadocia (today's central Turkey). Observing his fellow Christians, Basil reflected that "in everyone love has grown cold. Unanimity among brothers has disappeared, and even the name of accord has become unknown."[58]

As bishop of Caesarea, Basil responded by devoting a portion of his family's land for the building of a hospital (some say the first ever), traveler residences, leper facilities, a nursing home, a food program, and workshops for learning a trade. Basil got the ball rolling, the clergy organized it, and the wealthy financed it.[59] The *Basileias*, as it was called, employed "brothers in disciplined service" and constituted an urban mission with hints of desert monasticism.[60]

The *Basileias* was one of several monasteries that Basil established, each emphasizing community and service in contrast to eremitic life. Basil viewed an isolated existence as vulnerable to hubris, but "by living in a community, the gifts given by the Spirit to one will also be given to the others."[61] Communal living smoothed the residents' rough edges and provided an opportunity to practice love.[62] Basil's early designs of community and his short and long community rule (constituted by 45 and 311 instructions, respectively) later inspired Benedict to develop a rule for Christian communal living.

Basil was an active letter writer, appealing on the behalf of poor people to military leaders, governors, treasury officials, physicians,

---

and depth of their emotional responses." See Wessel, *Passion and Compassion*, 38.

58. Florovsky, *Eastern Fathers*, 7:76–77.

59. Heyne, "Reconstructing the World's First Hospital." Ancient and medieval references to "hospital" often differ from their modern use. A "hospital" might provide care for the ill or infirm or a secure place of rest for travelers, like today's hostels. Basil's hospital was the former. Some inns in the ancient world provided both rest and care, such as in the story of the Good Samaritan (Luke 10:34).

60. For more on the *Basileias*, see Holmes, *Life Pleasing to God*, 39; Karayannopoulos, "St. Basil's Social Activity."

61. Florovsky, *Eastern Fathers*, 7:76.

62. Louth, "Cappadocians," 293.

mayors, and others. Because of Basil's appeals, the government granted tax exemptions to clergy and provided financing for humanitarian
efforts. He sometimes ruffled feathers, however, in the government
and church. "What have I to lose," he retorted to a threatening official,
"my life? But I will then go sooner to my God. My fortune? But I have
only the tunic I wear. My residence? But man is a wanderer and his
residence can be anywhere."[63]

The *Basileias* was just the start of institution-building Christian philanthropy.[64] Beginning in the fifth century, wealthy benefactors contributed to church construction and founded specialized charitable institutions
(*ptōchotropheion*) to benefit the ill, aged, and orphaned of poor and mid-
dling classes.[65] These institutions generally served a single demographic
and were located near large cities so they could be supervised by bishops
and benefactors, and accessible to relatively large populations of potential
clients. In some cases, estates were designed so they eventually could be
converted to charitable use.[66]

Most of these institutions were founded by Christian imperial family members, noblemen, and wealthy benefactors. Helena—Constantine's
mother—founded what is believed to be the first nursing home. Scholars
have counted ten nursing homes and twenty-two homes for the needy operating by the end of the fifth century, and hundreds by the close of the sixth.
Institutions operated in the Balkans, Cyprus, Asia Minor, Syria, Palestine,
and Egypt.[67]

Facilities were staffed with physicians, nurses, aides, cleaners, and
cooks and were commonly supervised by deacons and deaconesses. Churches were constructed in urban areas in a frenzy of building, but "no church
was simply an isolated hall of worship," Paul Magdalino writes.[68] Churches

63. Recounted by Gregory of Nazianzus (Oration 43, page 36: 560b-c) and cited in
Karayannopoulos, "St. Basil's Social Activity," 384.

64. As church wealth grew, stories of massive aid efforts occurred elsewhere as well.
In southern Egypt, St. Shenoute of Atripe (c. 347–c. 465) built a church and monastery
from which he claimed to feed twenty thousand refugees for three months and the
hungry poor at one hundred tables a day: López, "Shenoute of Atripe ," 46–72.

65. For-profit inns had existed for some time—recall the inn appealed to by Joseph
and Mary (Luke 2:7) or the one utilized by the good Samaritan (Luke 10:34–35).

66. Brown, *Poverty and Leadership*, 79.

67. Lascaratos et al., "Nursing Homes for the Old." Cf. Constantelos, "Origins of
Christian Diakonia."

68. Magdalino, "Medieval Constantinople," 530.

served needs, and hospitals were attached to monasteries to nurse infirm monks and visitors.[69] These efforts represented a considerable innovation from past practice, and one that will endure through time in faith-based nonprofit institutions.

Peter Brown suggests that the church fathers were attempting to entice the wealthy to direct a portion of their giving away from civil luxuries in Roman tradition and toward the church and the poor: "They had to break with their background as civic benefactors and learn to give to the church instead," and it appears to have been successful.[70] Civil giving continued, but a new stream of donations flowed to the church and the poor. The legitimation of Christianity and the growing number of Christians with assets allowed compassion to be expressed through nascent institutionalization.[71]

One other fourth-century innovation to introduce before drawing this chapter to a close was the bishop's court (*episcopalis audientia*). Constantine empowered bishops to arbitrate civil cases, reducing the caseload burden of the governor's court. Over time, this role was formalized into "the bishop's court." Augustine served as a judge in such a court and devoted considerable time to the task.[72] These courts followed Roman law and appeared to operate with more dispatch than imperial courts.

According to Brown, "the poor" had not coalesced as an economic group and were recognized more by their lack but power than their little wealth. Bishops were seen as providing justice and protection to any, regardless of assets.[73] The bishop's court and the availability of church funds to care for the poor established the church and her bishops as guardians for the poor. The court heard cases and delivered justice and aid.

CRITIQUE AND CONTRIBUTION

To draw this era to a close, let's step back from homilies and laudatory institutions and apply a more critical or, at least, wide-angle perspective. Some contemporary scholars have argued that by focusing on virtue, the church fathers objectified people in poverty, treating almsgiving as theatre and turning its benefit largely toward the giver.[74] Holman, for example, argues that "in most early Christian texts, the poor exist primarily as a passive tool

69. Gilleard, "Old Age in Byzantine Society," 634–35.

70. Brown, *Through the Eye of a Needle*, 356.

71. Anderson, "Mistranslations of Josephus," 159.

72. Brown, *Poverty and Leadership*, 67–70.

73. Brown, *Poverty and Leadership*, 69–70.

74. Cardman, "Poverty and Wealth as Theater," 174.

for redemption. . . . The poor are thus rendered with a profound, if inert, liturgical identity."[75] If this critique is true, it might have been supported, in part, by a biblical translation [**Caritas**].

Caritas

By the fourth century, knowledge of the Greek language was fading in the West, and several scholars set out to translate various works into Latin to keep them alive. Jerome chose the Bible, translating its use of *agapē* (such as in 1 Cor 13) into the Latin word *caritas*.[76] Church fathers understood *caritas* as the love between God and people rather than as compassion expressed by one human toward another human. Thus, the first commandment, to love (*agapē*) God, superseded the second, to love (*caritas*) others (Matt 22:36–40). The implication was that spiritual formation (loving God) was more important than alms-giving (loving others).[77] Augustine (354–430), among others, affirmed this view, developing a two-story version of love for God and people.[78]

Some modern critics have further argued that the Byzantine fathers fell short in advocating for social change. Theodoret of Cyrrhus held the Roman view that the rich and poor occupied God-given roles, needed for a functioning society. Pope Leo I agreed, stating that God gave the wealthy paternalistic responsibilities over the poor.[79] Most authorities supported slavery.[80] A focus on the act and process of giving and the acceptance of relatively fixed social strata weakened any desire to relieve poverty in the long term or work for just structures. Some bishops were willing to preach about sparing and sharing but did not find asceticism personally attractive.[81]

75. Holman, *Hungry Are Dying*, 54.

76. Buhrer, "From Caritas to Charity," 115–16.

77. Buhrer, "From Caritas to Charity," 117–18.

78. It is possible that the translation of *agapē* as *caritas* affected the western church more than the eastern church, given the latter's enduring familiarity with Greek.

79. Salzman, "From a Classical to a Christian City," 74.

80. Church fathers were multivocal regarding slavery. Some saw slavery as God-ordained (Theodoret), while others viewed it as a necessary evil (Chrysostom). A few (Gregory of Nazianzus and Gregory of Nyssa) spoke out against it as unjust on the grounds of the *imago Dei*: Ramelli, *Social Justice*.

81. McKinley, "First Two Centuries," 175.

Many bishops and ascetics fanned the flames of anti-pagan attacks.[82] And if it is not sarcasm, Ambrose's calling of the poor to gratitude seems to go a bit too far: "You don't have golden lamps or ivory beds, but you have something much greater—the moon for illumination and grass on which to sleep."[83] A final critique is that the needle on basic social and economic inequality does not appear to have moved. Perhaps the need was too great or the reach of the church was too short or the emphasis on virtue was too strong, but institutions and orations do not appear to have altered the social strata.[84]

To their credit, deacons, priests, and bishops spent countless hours extending aid toward the poor. Many lived the words they taught, receiving praise from the poor and occasional ire from the powerful. They mobilized massive amounts of aid and left a legacy of charitable institutions.[85] Early Byzantine fathers brought the elites and the indigent masses closer together than they had been in Greek or Roman society, and they attempted to adapt the ascetic life for the everyday, urban Christian. The church amassed and distributed considerable resources to the poor, bishops delivered stirring ovations, and charitable institutions spread.

Virtue development may be this era's most unique contribution to compassion. The desert fathers and mothers entreat us to see the formative effects of material abundance and of generosity and to consider how detachment and contentment enhance life.[86] They encouraged voluntary simplicity when persecution no longer demanded it. Everyone was called to grow in virtue—the wealthy and powerful, the pauper, and the slave. Learning compassion was a life-long journey. In its ideal form, it was not

82. Bieringer, "Texts That Create a Future," 26; Brown, *Poverty and Leadership*, 61–63; Watts, *Final Pagan Generation*.

83. A portion of this text reads, "But you, perhaps, take it ill that you have no gold-plated lamps to give you light; yet the moon spreads abroad for you a far more resplendent illumination. You complain, it may be, of the cold, because not for you are there any sweating-chambers filled with steam from roaring fires; but you have the heat of the sun, which warms the whole earth for you and in the winter protects you from the cold. . . . You consider it a luxury to lie on ivory beds, and do not consider how much greater a luxury is the earth, that spreads for the poor man beds of grass whereupon there is sweet repose and gentle slumber, which he who stretches himself out in a golden bedstead seeks the whole night through and does not find." From *Hexaemeron*, VI, 8, 52 (*MPL*, XIV, 279–80), quoted in Lovejoy, "Communism of Saint Ambrose," 467.

84. MacMullen, "What Difference Did Christianity Make?"

85. Speaking truth to power can be a delicate endeavor. Some view Chrysostom and others as placating the powerful. At the end of his life, Chrysostom had religious and imperial enemies. He was banished to exile and died *en route*.

86. In the early medieval period, Pope Gregory I will argue for a three-step process to compassion: stop wanting what others have and stop wanting what you have, and you will find contentment enables giving to others: Demacopoulos, *Gregory the Great*.

forced from the hands of patrons or a salvific exchange; it demanded introspection—an awareness of one's heart and action. Compassion emphasized temperance (self-mastery) as well as justice, and it illumined Jesus' words, "'If you wish to be perfect, go, sell your possessions, and give the money to the poor, and you will have treasure in heaven; then come, follow me'" (Matt 19:21)—emphasizing completeness in virtue rather than merely fulfilling a command. Byzantine church fathers also help us appreciate that compassion is a two-way street where both give and receive. In sum, we have these early Byzantines to thank for bringing simple living, virtue development, and transformational giving to compassion.

One final related angle should be offered, largely from historian Peter Brown: during this era, the church was offered and accepted responsibility for the poor. This role can be viewed commendably, accentuating the values of a compassionate church. Brown highlights it more as an administrative achievement for a religious institution garnering social influence:

> Traditional Christian charity to fellow believers within the Christian community came to be regarded as a public service, as a more general "care of the poor" performed in return for public privileges. . . . [Bishops] were to know their place—closer to the poor than to the top of society.[87]

The bishop was central in benefaction and justice. He presented the clemency of God and was accountable for the administration of church funds and for the welfare of the flock. He was, in essence, a patron as well as a pastor, which included not merely placating to the imperial government but advocating for the poor and at times, challenging civil authorities.[88]

Brown casts those stirring sermons in a somewhat different light, too—as evidence of accountability that the bishops were executing their roles in relief and advocacy. Brown writes:

> It is easy to be blinded by the urgency and brilliance of fourth-century Christian preaching on "love of the poor." We tend to look always to the bishops as the organizers and facilitators of what were, at times, impressive ventures of poor relief. As a result, we have overlooked the constant, mute pressure exerted upon the Church itself by the expectations of lay persons—of lawyers, bureaucrats, and the advisers of the emperors—who needed to be reassured, in terms of the classical, "civic" model

87. Brown, *Poverty and Leadership*, 31.

88. Corke-Webster, "Emperors, Bishops, Art and Jurisprudence"; Rhee, *Loving the Poor*, 156.

with which they were familiar, that the privileges of the clergy were being used for the public good.[89]

In sum, the welfare of Christians and the vulnerable was shouldered on the Christian church. While this was true of the earliest church, the scale and centrality of this reality increased considerably in the late antique era.

LOOKING AHEAD

At the close of the fifth century, inflation and taxes skyrocketed due to unfunded fiscal expenditures, expensive Germanic incursions in western Europe, sporadic labor shortages, and government corruption. According to historian Rondo Cameron, "The economy reverted to a primitive sub-sistence basis as population declined, towns and cities were deserted, and the villas of the greatest estates came more and more to resemble fortified castles. By the end of the fourth century the empire in the west was a hol-low shell that gradually collapsed under its own weight."[90] The seeds of a large-scale institutional response to poverty established in the Byzantine era would go dormant but sprout again in the centuries to come.[91]

Toward the end of the era, a bishop may have recalled the words of Gregory of Nyssa in his sermon "On the Love of the Poor"—words that seem faded in a bygone era:

> Insofar as you sail on tranquil waters, hold the hand of the un-fortunate who have suffered shipwreck. You all sail on the same sea, prone to waves and tempests: and reefs, underwater break-waters and other dangers of the ocean evoke the same apprehen-sion in all sailors. Insofar as you are floating, healthy and safe, on the calm sea of life, do not arrogantly pass by those who have shipwrecked their vessel on the reefs. . . . Let us all go forward to attain the port of our rest and desire that the Holy Spirit grant us a serene haven at the end of our journey![92]

Whatever calm that had existed was gone; all were headed into choppy waters once again.

---

89. Brown, *Poverty and Leadership*, 32–33. A similar argument is made by López about Egypt: "Shenoute of Atripe."

90. Cameron, *Concise Economic History*, 41.

91. MacMullen, "What Difference Did Christianity Make?" 343.

92. Gregory of Nyssa, "On the Love of the Poor": Holman, *Hungry Are Dying*, 206.

3

Mobilization and Participation

THE MEDIEVAL ERA STRETCHED across a long millennium from 476 to 1453 when Constantinople fell to the Ottoman Empire. Contained within this span are previous themes, bubbling and swirling in a cauldron as they develop a richer, deeper flavor. New developments emerged as well. Life centered around feudal estates and became sacralized; Byzantine *xenodochia* expanded into networks of parish and monastic care; and a strong desire fomented to break free of feudal life and abandon or reform ecclesial caregiving.[1]

Rather than a flat expanse, the medieval millennium is characterized by valleys and peaks. Modern scholars often divide the epoch into multiple segments. I will simplify these by referring to the early Middle Ages (fifth to tenth centuries), characterized by European balkanization and Christian continental expansion; the high Middle Ages (eleventh to thirteenth centuries), characterized as a golden age of church flourishing; and the late Middle Ages (fourteenth and fifteenth centuries), characterized by plague, economic stagnation, the Renaissance, and growing desires for reform. I reference these divisions occasionally as we consider tripartite themes of sacralized life, institutional innovation, and participative poverty.

As in previous epochs, the medieval era was a time of clashes, contrasts, and ironies. The empire was fractured, yet boundaries periodically widened. Western rulers no longer oppressed Christianity but Christianized

---

1. This chapter is written largely from the perspective of the western rather than Byzantine church. Our quick stride through time hints at but also bypasses a great deal of diversity and change in this colorful millennium.

others, sometimes compelling submission to the faith. As the wealth of the church increased, reformers blazed with fresh convictions about gospel poverty. Mobilization, participation, and poignant contrasts marked the medieval era.

CHANGE AND UNCERTAINTY

By the fifth century, the western half of the Roman Empire was crumbling. The City of Rome had been conquered in 410, and many of its residents were scattered. Waves of Germanic invaders circulated through the West, disrupting the economy and society. In 476, the last western emperor stepped down.[2] Contests ensued over sections of Italy, with some conquerors being peaceable and others oppressive. Life in western, rural parts of the empire centered around feudal estates. Some balkanized into kingdoms that appeared and fell in regional conquests. In the Byzantine East, invasion, plague, and earthquakes seemed to herald the end of the world. Battles with invaders were constant.

Plagues traveled along land and sea trade routes, decimating populations in their way. A particularly catastrophic pestilence from 541 to 544 reduced Constantinople's population by 40 percent. Pandemics continued to flare up until around 747.[3] Toward the end of the medieval era, the Bubonic plague, or "black death," erupted with a vengeance around 1348, spreading from Asia to Europe [**Dying Well**]. It reduced the European population by a third. When plagues scattered or ravaged peasants, labor shortages occurred and famines followed, exacerbating the specter of hunger. Plagues disrupted trade patterns and culture, just as they altered demography, leaving families without children and parents.[4]

2. The remnant of the Roman Empire—the Byzantine Empire—fell to Ottoman marauders in 1453.

3. Laiou, Human Resources.

4. Although the time of her life is unknown, according to tradition, history tells of a woman named Sophia who lost her husband and six children to a plague. Surrounded by others in a similar state, Sophia dedicated her house to orphans and others in need. Supposedly, she adopted over one hundred children. Today, St. Sophia of Ainos is known as the "Mother of Orphans."

Dying Well

The *Artes moriendi* ("art of dying well") were treatises written in the wake of the black death to aid the dying and the caregivers attending them. Complete with questions, confessions, prayers, and illustrations, an *Ars moriendi* served as a pastoral care guidebook. Assisting the dying was viewed as a compassionate act. "If assisting a sick person to recover bodily health is thought to express true friendship," writes Jared Wicks, "how much more conformed to charity is assisting a dying person to attain his or her soul's salvation and eternal life."[5] Consistent with medieval views on illness, the *Artes* encouraged seeing through one's imminent demise to embrace transcendent reality and entrust oneself to God.

Fig. 3.1. Humility over pride in an *Ars moriendi*.

---

5. Wicks, "Applied Theology at the Deathbed," 346–47.

Although naturalistic explanations existed for plagues and disease, becoming ill or remaining healthy fell within the scope of God's will. Plagues regularly fueled fear and faith, encouraging confession, penitence, scapegoating, church construction, prayers to saints and pilgrimages to their relics, and eschatological fever.[6] Plague tracts attempted to educate and often began by encouraging confession. As Michel Mollat writes, "Every scourge and affliction was regarded as a trial leading to possible redemption or as a punishment, and suffering was always interpreted in terms of sin."[7]

LORDS AND PRIESTS

In the early Middle Ages, popes in Rome were busy with administrative duties, handling negotiations with tribal rulers and bishops over lands and teachings, while lords, monks, and ecclesial leaders carried Christianity to the edges of Europe. Wealthy landowners attempted to "Christianize" and "depaganize" the heathen by means of religious instruction, social pressure, and threats of damnation.[8] Although some landowners were missionaries at heart, many also believed that moral development would aid a well-functioning fiefdom. Catechesis became a continuous endeavor for parish priests living among people of diverse pagan and superstitious beliefs and practices. Priestly education was uneven and teaching did not always accord with official doctrine.[9] Churches and chapels nevertheless became known as places of worship, prayer, and aid.[10]

Basic ideas about society from the late antique era blended with regional cultural influences. Eventually, much of Europe practiced some form of Christianity. The eschatological judgment of the earliest Christians

6. Gary Ferngren convincingly argues that many ancient and medieval Christians subscribed to naturalistic disease etiologies but considered them to fall within the power and will of God: Ferngren, *Medicine and Health Care*. Also see Gecser, "Doctors and Preachers." Regarding the conditions of priests remaining or fleeing pestilence, see Gecser, "Giovanni of Capestrano," 40. For eschatology, see Meier, "Justinianic Plague," 284.

7. Mollat, *Poor in the Middle Ages*, 26.

8. Considerable efforts were required by the bishop to acculturate people to Christian ways. Some people refused to work on Thursdays in honor of Jupiter; many venerated sacred trees: Klingshirn, *Caesarius of Arles*, 213, 226–43. Christianization was an elongated and constant effort. Occasionally, Christians reverted to paganism: Meier, "Justinianic Plague."

9. As an example, accounts exist of the baptismal formula being announced, "*in nomine patria et filia et spiritus sancti*" ("in the name of the fatherland, the daughter, and the holy spirit"): Tellenbach, *Church in Western Europe*, 25.

10. Klingshirn, *Caesarius of Arles*, 236.

remained but was augmented by a moment-by-moment sense of God's shifting pleasure and judgment. As with the ancient church, few felt completely safe, but now it was because one lived under a watchful, judging God.

The Byzantine emperor retained ultimate civil authority in the East and bishops retained their centralized pastoral role with the poor. In the West, innovations in jurisprudence allowed wealthy landowners to offer protection and land for loyalty and rent, providing work and a modicum of order and protection. Clergy provided for spiritual and physical needs, and peasants and slaves [**Slavery**] supported landowners and clergy through taxes, rents, and tithes.[11]

Slavery

For centuries, enslaved people represented the most profitable trading commodity.[12] Many slaves were young—age twenty or younger. Some were captured from military campaigns or kidnapped by traders. Others were sold by their parents to pay for debts. Still others were the children of slaves. Boys increased in value when they were castrated.[13] Some Christian teachers railed against the institution; others saw it as a necessary evil. Some supported it as consistent with divine order.[14]

During the high Middle Ages, slavery declined in many areas as serfdom and indenture filled the need for labor. When cities and the economy began to flourish in late medieval Europe, the feudal system began declining. The trade of workers shifted to the Americas where forced labor and, eventually, slave trade, revitalized. Some argued that conscripting non-Christians into forced labor was the only way to eradicate superstition and instill Christian character in indigenous peoples.[15] Slavery rose and fell with supply and demand. It predated the medieval age and continued through and after it, even to today.

---

11. Klingshirn, *Caesarius of Arles*, 207.

12. Fletcher, *Barbarian Conversion*, 113.

13. Balkan "Slavs" were among these. Some evidence suggests a linguistic connection between "Slavs" and "slaves": McCormick, *Origins of the European Economy*, 244–54.

14. The Bible does not condemn the institution of slavery but addresses how slaves are treated and proffers values which oppose it. For a brief analysis, see Collins, *What are Biblical Values*, 126–46.

15. Blackburn, *Making of New World Slavery*, 61–64.

In the early medieval period, cities declined, and populations gathered around manors. Agriculture was overwhelmingly the dominant economic sector. Peasants cultivated and harvested the landowner's crops and planted some of their own in a checkerboard of open fields scattered around the lord's holdings. Peasants lived meager lives and handed over most surpluses to landowners and the church.[16] William Manchester describes the scene:

> Typically, three years of harvests could be expected for one year of famine. The years of hunger were terrible. The peasants might be forced to sell all they owned, including their pitifully inadequate clothing, and be reduced to nudity in all seasons. In the hardest times they devoured bark, roots, grass; even white clay. Cannibalism was not unknown.[17]

Agricultural innovation was modest, especially in the early Middle Ages, because slaves and peasants provided sufficient, low-cost labor in relatively small fields. Despite three-field crop rotation, misuse sometimes resulted in infertile soils and food shortages. Peasant households often resorted to asking for alms from neighbors and pious travelers, especially between harvests.[18]

Attacks and wars provided another threat. Peasants were captured as slaves. Rulers and bishops redeemed some, including those who were considered to be enemies.[19] Every vulnerable group in Scripture was in plentiful supply: the hungry, thirsty, stranger, naked, sick, and imprisoned, plus widows and orphans. The church and Christians faced endemic need and suffering, affording daily opportunities to support family and neighbors and to share goods [**Bread Stamps**].

Bread Stamps

In the early Middle Ages, eucharistic bread commonly was prepared, blessed, and stamped with a cross or with words such as *Phos* ("Light"), *Zoe* ("Life"), *Hygeia* ("Health"), or *IC XC NIKA* ("Jesus Christ Conquers"). *Eulogia* (blessings) bread, was imprinted with

16. Shuler, "Almsgiving," 274.

17. Manchester, *World Lit Only by Fire*, 54.

18. Shuler, "Almsgiving," 276. Land tenure differed, however, place to place.

19. Bishop Caesarius of Arles (c. 468–542) ransomed captured peasants from his southern Gaul (France) as well as enemies on the basis that both were human and both in need of salvation.

similar words and shared with worshippers on Sundays and feast days, and with pilgrims or the poor. *Eulogia* was a means of sharing food among the hungry.

Terra cotta or bronze stamps were crafted to imprint the dough before rising. Typically, the words were written backwards on the stamp so they would read correctly on the bread, but, sometimes, illiterate craftsmen produced backward-worded stamps.[20] The receivers likewise were mostly illiterate. Lettered loaves may have reminded some of Jesus' words after feeding the five thousand: "Do not work for the food that perishes, but for the food that endures for eternal life, which the Son of Man will give you. For it is on him that God the Father has set his seal" (John 6:27).

Fig. 3.2. Bronze slipper bread stamp with "grace" in reverse.

GREGORY I AND OTHER GUARDIANS

Surrounded by threat and crisis, the last imperial Roman pope, Gregory I (Gregory the Great; c. 540–604), sought to awaken Christians to the needs of others. Gregory departed from most of the late antique writers in asserting that one had to forgo contemplative peace for active care and ministry. As George Demacopoulos writes, Gregory believed that "one had to be willing to suspend those spiritual joys for the sake of others, even if doing so meant

20. Patrich, "Four Christian Objects."

losing some measure of contemplative progress."[21] Gregory's pragmatic approach seemed appropriate for the times.

With violent Germanic Lombards advancing through northern Italy, Rome was overflowing with refugees. Gregory appealed to Constantinople for aid, but the East was occupied with battles of its own. Receiving no word from the imperial capital, Gregory borrowed from various formal and informal institutions—the imperial *annona*, Byzantine *xenodochium*, the early church's collection, and Greco-Roman *euergetism*—and organized them into a comprehensive system.[22]

He turned to local elites, who donated considerable sums of land, food, money, and art. Gregory liquidated material assets of the church and dispersed food and money through a network administered by deacons and monks, expecting them not only to serve but also to seek out the poor. Gregory utilized a careful inventory and distribution record-keeping system and directed the crops from productive land back to the church for distributing among the indigent. Although they differed, Gregory's estate management was essentially Basil's *Basileias* on a massive, decentralized scale. Tradition suggests that Gregory led by example, practicing generosity and regularly hosting twelve destitute persons (after the twelve apostles) as dinner guests.[23] While a deacon, he called himself a "servant of the servants of God," and he kept that title the rest of his life, even when serving as pope.[24]

Through the Middle Ages, some Christian civil rulers would be heralded in comparable light for their personal generosity. John the Almsgiver (560–619), archbishop of Alexandria, built a network of hospitals, poorhouses, and hostels. He is remembered for redeeming boys in Alexandria, Egypt, who worked as agricultural and sex slaves. In addition to freeing the boys, he assigned priests to teach the abusers.[25] Saxon noblewoman Matilda (c. 892–968) is another example. She is praised by her hagiographer for regularly sharing food from the royal table with peasants.[26] Wenceslaus I (c. 911–935) is remembered for personally aiding the Czech people, as the "Good King Wenceslas" Christmas carol recounts.[27] Charlemagne

---

21. Demacopoulos, *Gregory the Great*, 29.

22. Doleac, "Triclinium Pauperum."

23. Doleac, "Triclinium Pauperum."

24. Richards, *Consul of God*, 48.

25. Baynes, "Life of St. John the Almsgiver."

26. Shuler, "Almsgiving," 158.

27. Written in 1853 by John Mason Neale, a portion of the "Good King Wenceslas" lyrics read, "'Hither, page, and stand by me, / If thou know'st it, telling / Yonder peasant, who is he? / Where and what his dwelling?' / . . . / 'Bring me flesh and bring me wine, / Bring me pine logs hither, / Thou and I will see him dine / When we bear them thither

(748–814) and other emperors are remembered for their beneficence and liberality in material and spiritual gifts. Elizabeth of Hungary (1207–1231), a princess, resonated as a young woman with Franciscan teaching. She engaged in many charitable acts and built a hospital, personally caring for patients before she died at age twenty-four.

While not whitewashing acts of violence or harshness by civil or religious leaders, or sliding into hagiography, we may wonder what nudged these and other leaders to such largesse? One possible answer lies in their closeness to God and their sacralized view of life.

SACRALIZATION

Life had long taught that fortunes could reverse, as if one were rotating on a wheel. Given the unpredictability of life, theologians encouraged believers to transcend their external circumstances by submitting to God and growing in virtue and holiness.[28] In the medieval age, a parallel development occurred whereby the material world became increasingly sacralized. Spirituality became earthier, and physical existence more mystical. While church teachers differentiated between a sacralized world and superstition and magic (which were condemned), not everyone discerned a difference.[29] A broken lamp, a wandering ox, the withholding of rain, the arrival of plague—every event was a sign, imbued with significance. Diseases, such as leprosy, carried moral stigma. God was the ultimate ruler of spiritual and physical realms but the world was subject to Satan's machinations. "Life was dominated by a longing for aid and for rescue from death," Gerd Tellenbach writes.[30]

While disease and weather might have natural causes, both were viewed as operating within the will of God.[31] With all of life reflecting

/ . . . / Therefore, Christian men, be sure / Wealth or rank possessing, / Ye who now will bless the poor / Shall yourselves find blessing."

28. Early in the medieval era, Severinus Boethius (480–524) wrote *The Consolation of Philosophy,* wherein he described the ancient wheel of fortune and the Christian's escape by looking toward an unchanging God at center of the wheel. Later, in *The Book of Divine Consolation,* Meister Eckhart (1260–1328) offered thirty arguments to support sufferers. Eckhart asserted that: "For a man to have a peaceful life is good, but for man to have a life of pain in patience is better; but that man should have peace in a life of pain is best" (Eckhart, *Meister Eckhart,* p. 167). These and other popular works advocated for Christians to reframe, detach, or transcend the vicissitudes of life.

29. Straw, *Gregory the Great,* 48.

30. Tellenbach, *Church in Western Europe,* 97.

31. While they may seem extraordinary today, Scripture records more than 150 miracles, including occasions where God controlled climate, insects, animal health (Exod 8:1–24; 9:8–12; 10:1–23; Josh 10:12–14; 1 Sam 12:18; 1 Kgs 17:1; Matt 8:26), plague, disease

spiritual realities of an ongoing battle between good and evil, one's salvation was precarious. Motives mattered. Actions mattered. Compassion counted. One's acts in this world would be judged in the next. Several texts, including *The Life of Basil, The Life of Andrew*, and *The Life of Niphon*, dramatized the last judgment of souls who had lived charitably and virtuously or who reveled in selfish debauchery. Mosaics and frescos visualized the division of people in the end times into righteous and wicked groups (Matt 25: 31–46) following the reading and weighing of one's thoughts, motives, and deeds (Rev 21:12).[32] In exceptional cases of physical, social, or spiritual need, a perilous pilgrimage to a holy site afforded an outlet for penance as well as possible intervention from God into the struggles of life [**On Pilgrimage**].

Saints were available to support the faithful. Fourteen saints associated with ailments were depicted as available for those in need during times of illness. Called the "fourteen holy helpers," they included St. George and St. Christopher, among others.[33] Veneration of Mary, the mother of Jesus, raised the status of medieval women and provided a special advocate, helper, and intercessor who, moved by pity, initiated the miracles of Jesus (John 2:1–12).[34]

On Pilgrimage

Pilgrimages generally began from one's home and ultimately converged on well-traveled paths to a sacred site—often, a tomb or a church with relics, or a local grotto. Although commonly associated with penance and healing, pilgrimages also were a medium for divine compassion through healing. Pilgrimages terminated at sacred sites where one might appeal for a spouse, the blessing of children, physical healing, the protection of crops, or a speedy release from purgatory. Stories circulated widely, and not always consistently, regarding the miracles that occurred. Local grottos as well as distant sites developed their own rituals to enhance the desired outcome.[35]

(Exod 9:8–12; 4:6–7; Num 12:10–16; 16:41–50; 2 Kgs 5:10–14; Matt 8:3, 13, 15, 32), and death (Acts 5:5, 10; 12:23), and where the prayer of the righteous could alter their course.

32. Marinis, *Death and the Afterlife*, 59–73.

33. The group was modified in different areas to include St. Roch, St. Apollonia, and other favored saints who aided in this life and the next.

34. A description of women in the Middle Ages (and throughout Christian history) is provided by Tucker and Lyfeld, *Daughters of the Church*, 130–2. For a sampling of prayers to Mary, see Roten, "Prayers of Saints to Mary."

35. For a review of purgatory, see Delaney, "Purgatory."

Particularly popular pilgrimages led to the Church of the Holy Sepulcher in Jerusalem, the seven pilgrim churches in Rome, Canterbury Cathedral in England, and the cathedral in Santiago de Compostela in northwestern Spain. Latin guidebooks (*itineraria*), modeled after those used by Roman soldiers, provided land and sea routes for religious tourists, complete with distances and places of respite along the way.[36]

Many goods were sold by merchants along pilgrimage routes. One was ampulla for retrieving holy water or oil at home for healing and bless (see Fig. 3.3).[37] One might also purchase an amulet at a pilgrimage site, bringing material healing, protection, and a reminder of God's presence.[38] The words of Scripture carried a similar power to ward off the evil forces.[39]

Fig. 3.3. Pilgrim's ampulla.

36. Avramea, "Land and Sea Communications," 63.

37. Bell and Dale, "The Medieval Pilgrimage Business."

38. Peter Murry Jones offers a description of the potency of amulets: "Once the amulet has been sacralized, whether it be by containing a relic, touching it to a shrine, or even simply by inscribing sacred characters upon it, the wearer of the amulet has constant physical contact with an object that is a kind of material sediment left behind by that flow of divine power. The amulet also acts as a focus of devotion, for both the theological and medical perspectives on amulets stressed the importance of the state of mind of the wearer. The object is therefore also a reminder of the devotion owing to God and the saints, without whose intervention no protection will avail: Jones, "Amulets and Charms," 197.

39. Childers, *Divining Gospel*.

The pilgrimage journey was as meaningful as the destination. Israel wandered in the wilderness and in exile. Jesus traveled with his family, and he and church martyrs walked to their deaths. Ascetics and their disciples journeyed to the desert and missionary monks traveled to distant locales.[40] A pilgrimage was a performative act of walking and crawling that signaled submission, renunciation, transformation, and trust.

Pilgrimages also were communal. Pilgrims frequently traveled together for safety. Upon arriving at the site, pilgrims would ask the appropriate saint to appeal to God on their behalf for mercy and healing.

Generally, as a penance, pilgrimages were assigned only to those who had sinned badly and were able to do it. Not all pilgrimages were penitential and most penances were not pilgrimages. Confession and private penance served as an alternative to pilgrimage. But pilgrimage and fasting retained penitential potency, especially in preparation for Easter, Pentecost, and Christmas celebrations, agricultural seasons, and in times of crisis.[41]

Pilgrimages never became a sacrament for Christians, but they were meaningful in many ways, including as a metaphor. Perhaps most famously, Augustine, and later John Bunyan in *The Pilgrim's Progress* (1678), allegorized the robust nature of the journey. Modern-day ascetics have continued the metaphor and encouragement, as Matthew the Poor (1919–2006) did in a letter posthumously titled "Christ Is Enough":

> When the pilgrim covers a long distance in his journey, he never finds comfort except in doubling the speed of his progress. He relinquishes much of his previous sensitivity toward his flesh and the concern about his health or illness. A mystical power seizes him and takes the place of physical life. It equips him secretly with hope, so much so that his body actually becomes stronger even as he increases in poverty or illness. The joy with which he strives for the clear goal day after day causes him to ignore the labors, hardships and tribulations that the strongest man on earth could not endure.[42]

---

40. Fletcher, *The Barbarian Conversion*, 94.

41. Shuler, "Almsgiving," 88, 104, 114, 124.

42. Matthew the Poor and Rubenson, *Sojourners*, 215.

Life often reflected a reverse mirror image of spiritual realities: pleasure would end in pride, tears brought joy, prosperity yielded adversity, and suffering taught endurance ['lhomas à Kempis]. As well as a state to be transcended or salved, suffering yielded insight and an opportunity for the wealthy to exercise benefaction.[43] As Ernst Troeltsch (1865–1923) observes,

> . . . the Church simply exhorted mankind to submit to the sufferings of this sinful world and except all the trials of this "our earthly pilgrimage." The Church was also careful to point out that the "minimum" was not even a right or claim, but a gift of love, to be received in love and humility. The main point was the creation of loving relationships in the spirit of love, not the giving of material help.[44]

Thomas à Kempis

Thomas à Kempis (c. 1380–1471) authored *The Imitation of Christ*, a devotional work that has inspired many through the centuries. It emerged from the Devotio Moderna reform movement which spread through the Low Countries and Germany in the late fourteenth century. à Kempis reminds readers that the poor are blessed:

> Therefore, O Lord God, I consider it a great blessing not to have many things which human judgment holds praiseworthy and glorious, for one who realizes his own poverty and vileness should not be sad or downcast at it, but rather consoled and happy because You, O God, have chosen the poor, the humble, and the despised in this world to be Your friends and servants. The truth of this is witnessed by Your Apostles, whom You made princes over all the world. Yet they lived in this world without complaining, so humble and simple, so free from malice and deceit, that they were

43. See 13–42, for suffering and the body-soul, and 61–80 for pain as a restorative power in Mowbray, *Pain and Suffering*.

44. Troeltsch, *Social Teaching*, 137. Some observers suggest that the Catholic Church's otherworldly orientation continued until the twentieth century when Latin American theologians flavored the church with a greater emphasis on the preferential option for the poor. See Neal, "Faith and Social Ministry: A Catholic Perspective."

happy even to suffer reproach for Your name and to embrace with great affection that which the world abhors.[45]

Monks and priests mediated between God and people, and petitioning the saints for aid was a daily activity for all. But an act of grace extended from one person to another remained a social salve among people. As Gregory I taught: "The way to prove holiness is not to perform miracles, but to love every man as one's self. . . . It is not miracles but charity alone that proves the true servants of God."[46]

In sum, a sacralized view of life, combined with significant medieval need and the coming weighing of moral acts, afforded abundant opportunities for one to request, extend, and experience the compassion of God.

INSTITUTIONAL INNOVATION

A second contribution of the medieval era to compassion was the significant growth of institutionalized charity that mushroomed under monasticism, becoming increasingly professionalized, and eventually undergoing significant grassroots reform.

Tithes and Endowments

Tithes and endowments constituted significant catalysts to institution building in the medieval era. Dating back to the writing of Caesarius of Arles in 779, one-tenth of one's income or produce was required from rich and poor. Tithes did not have the same spiritual potency as almsgiving (which was also encouraged) but was treated as a divine expectation. In some regions, such as the Carolingian Empire of western Europe (800–888), tithing was mandated by law.[47] Originally, tithes supported the local parish priest, but priests often went underfunded, having to farm their own land and charge for church services to survive. Increasingly, tithes were diverted to support monastic houses.[48]

Adding to ecclesial wealth were laws from the Byzantine Empire which allowed estates to be willed to the church. This legal innovation provided

---

45. à Kempis, *The Imitation of Christ*, chap. 22.

46. Gregory the Great, *Moralia in Iob*, vol. 2, Book 20, sec. 17.

47. Shuler, "Almsgiving," 227; Shuler, "Caesarius of Arles," 59.

48. Snyder, "Anabaptist Spirituality and Economics," 4–5.

substantial resources for monastic orders and limited wealth accumulation in families. Intercession for oneself or for others to be released from purgatory provided a strong motivation for bequeathing charitable endowments.[49] Substantial monetary flows continued until the eleventh century when elites began bequeathing larger sums to their heirs.[50]

In the late Middle Ages, wealthy traders provided an additional source of funding for the construction and operation of charitable facilities.[51] Benefactors frequently stipulated that in exchange for their sizable donations, prayers be offered on their behalf, sometimes by all caregivers and beneficiaries at a specified time during the day.[52] Beneficiaries also might be charged a portion of the cost of service to provide additional revenue and to emphasize responsibility on the part of the recipient.

Monastic Communities

Tithes and bequeathed estates catalyzed the growth of monastic communities—a type of institutionalized asceticism. Monks took personal vows of poverty, chastity, and obedience, and communities followed rules or guides of community life. One early guide was *The Rule of St. Benedict*. It informed Benedictine and Cistercian communities in the proper way to model Christian community, welcome guests, balance prayer and work, and share goods and tasks within the monastery.[53]

Although most religious communities were male, scattered convents formed as well. In the antique era, desert mothers attracted followers to remote locations to learn from these women of deep spiritual insight. In the fourth century, some holy women attracted communities of followers. Convents were modest and tended to attract the daughters of the well-to-do. Medieval notions of women's roles influenced their activities. Marilyn Oliva writes:

49. Delaney, "Purgatory."

50. Brodman, *Charity and Religion*, 9–10; Gilleard, "Old Age in Byzantine Society," 629. Echoing the exchange relationship of the church fathers, St. Eligius (588–660) wrote, "God could have made all mankind rich, but in fact he wanted there to be poor in this world so that the rich would have by that means a way of remedying their sins." Quoted in Buhrer, "From Caritas to Charity," 113.

51. Davis, *Medieval Economy*.

52. Sneider, "Bonds of Charity," 141. Also see Buhrer, "From Caritas to Charity."

53. Benedict also specified that they care for infirm brothers: "Before all things and above all things care is to be had of the sick"; see Benedict, *Rule of St. Benedict*, chap. 36.

Medieval society and culture assessed women's contribution to society solely by their roles as wives and mothers. Religious women incorporated these criteria into their vocation which, if anything, stressed their roles as carers and nurturers, as prescribed by St Benedict's injunctions to care for the poor and needy.[54]

Women religious mostly fed the hungry, nursed the sick, and taught youth; a few recorded sermons and copied books as well.[55]

Most spiritually-called women in the early Middle Ages were limited to dedicating themselves to God at home and in their parish, especially after the Vikings destroyed many convents in the ninth and tenth centuries. Some religious seekers attached themselves to a male monastery.[56] Convents and orders slowly rebuilt, but they remained small in number compared with the abundance of male monasteries.[57] In 1298, convents were required to be cloistered, supposedly for their own protection and (so it was said) to prevent men from being tempted by the nuns. Once cloistered, nuns had limited opportunities to extend compassion beyond their daily prayers, but some found ways to continue extending compassion [**Foundling Wheels**].

Foundling Wheels

Cloistered nuns lived behind walls and grails, devoting themselves to prayer and contemplation. During times of plague, famine, and poverty, families sometimes could not adequately care for infants. One option was to leave newborns at convents. Turntables were built into the wall of the convent to allow children to be passed to the nuns while maintaining separation. Parents would lay the child on the wheel, ring a bell, and rotate the turntable.

Although these tables sometimes received gifts of food or other tokens of blessing, foundling wheels were made specially to accommodate infants. Thousands of babies rotated to a new life.[58] Sadly,

---

54. Oliva, *Convent and the Community*, 147.

55. Cyrus, *Scribes*; Stoop, "Fifteenth-Century Vernacular Sermons." Examples abound of medieval women serving with devotion. One example from the eastern church is Juliana of Lazarevo (1530–1604).

56. McGuinness, *Called to Serve*, 2–6.

57. Following St. Francis, for example, Clare of Assisi (1194–1253) founded the Order of Saint Clare (the Poor Clares) in 1212.

58. Although illegal in some countries, some hospitals have revived foundling wheels by installing "baby boxes" where a parent can leave an infant. Advocates assert that the

many did not survive as convents often did not have the necessary food and medical supplies to provide for infants. Although they never knew the parents, nuns inside the convent shared the burden of grief felt by individuals who were forced to give up their children..

Hospitals, Pharmacies, and Bridge Societies

Building on the tradition of the Byzantine *xenodochia*, churches and monasteries were designed with the assumption that they would accommodate the needs of travelers and the poor. Even St. Peter's Basilica in Rome incorporated an overnight shelter.[59] While some were symbolic or strategic additions, many became a focal enterprise for priests or monks.

Church and monastery services were directed toward the "seven corporal works of mercy" [**Seven Corporal Works of Mercy**].[60] Where needed, confraternities and parish councils filled gaps in service.[61]

Seven Corporal Works of Mercy

Well known in the medieval age were seven corporal works of mercy which included the six mentioned in Matthew 25:31–46 (feed the hungry, provide drink to the thirsty, clothe the naked, shelter travelers and the homeless, visit the sick, and visit and ransom prisoners) plus a seventh, bury the dead, especially needed during times of

---

practice saves the lives of children, and others (including the United Nations) argue that child relinquishment violates the rights of children and is the result of inadequate public policy and financing: UN Human Rights, *Rights of Vulnerable Children*, 37–39.

59. Late antique popes Gelasius I (d. 496) and Symmachus (d. 514) were known for their charity. The latter attached a shelter for the poor to Old St. Peter's Basilica in Rome. Richards points out that papal attention to the poor may in part be motivated by a political strategy of ingratiating the masses: *Popes and the Papacy*, 63, 83. Also see Dey, "Diaconiae."

60. Decker, "Civic Charity, Civic Virtue."

61. James William Brodman offers two insightful surveys: Brodman, *Charity and Religion*; Brodman, *Charity and Welfare*. See also, Scott, *Experiences of Charity*. Brown notes that charity tended to be gendered: "Men's charity was frequently monetarily based, while women's charity was expressed in the locus of the home and through the allocation of household resources such as food, drink, and clothing to the needy." See "That Peace Shall Always Dwell" 16.

plague.[62] These seven works were commonly presented as necessities in a healthy, Christian society. Paintings depicting these seven works adorned medieval churches, affirming the Church's mission and inspiring parishioners to grassroots charity.[63]

A Dutch painter known as the Master of Alkmaar depicted the works of mercy in a seven-panel painting in 1504 (Fig. 3.4).[64] Although social and economic problems abounded in Alkmaar, the painter depicted a thriving and well-functioning city with residents working through the Confraternity of the Holy Spirit to meet the needs of the hungry, thirsty, and unsheltered. The painting shows that the confraternity discriminated between the deserving and the undeserving poor and pooled funds so allocations would be both efficient and effective. A depiction of Jesus appears in each image as one of the persons in need. The regional prince is portrayed as a divinely appointed overseer.[65] Created at the end of the medieval era, the Master of Alkmaar's painting does not include monks, who were widely believed to have diverted funds intended for the poor to fund their orders.[66]

62. Paralleling these were the post-Tridentine seven sacraments, seven deacons, seven pilgrimage churches in Rome, and the seven spiritual works of mercy: instructing the ignorant, counseling the doubtful, admonishing sinners, bearing wrongs patiently, forgiving offenses, comforting the afflicted, and praying for the living and dead. These remain represented in the Catechism of the Catholic Church, sec. 2447. Of course, other works of mercy were practiced too, such as providing dowries so poor girls could marry, plus innumerable other charitable acts.

63. In twenty-two British counties, historian Katherine French documented thirty-nine wall paintings of the works of mercy in British churches: French, *Good Women*, 189.

64. A renowned painting with a similar name was painted by Caravaggio in 1607.

65. Although the precise purpose of the painting remains hidden, art historian John Decker has speculated that the painter was making an appeal to Prince Philip the Fair, who ruled over the area and had placed a hearth tax on the well-to-do. The painting illustrates that the Alkmaar elite could care effectively for the poor, the city would flourish, and the prince would be blessed if he relaxed the tax burden and allowed parishioners to mobilize an orderly distribution of mercy. Whether the painting was seen by the prince is unknown, but the tax was not lifted, and the city languished for another thirteen years before the prince was deposed. Decker, "Civic Charity, Civic Virtue."

66. For a description of internal monastic reform, see Beach, *Trauma of Monastic Reform*.

Fig. 3.4. Refreshing the thirsty, from *The Seven Works of Mercy*.

A variety of specialized facilities emerged to deliver services to the sick and to travelers and strangers. At times, first-class and second-class accommodations catered to the rich and the poor. Care homes were built for children and for the aged.[67] Almshouses served food and distributed money and clothing. Monasteries or churches provided wet nursing for abandoned babies. Trade apprenticeships were provided for orphaned boys and girls as young as age five. Reformed prostitutes were extended opportunities to become nuns or be cared for if they were aged.[68] Many service models were similar but innovations appeared as well [**Repenties**].

67. Priories and convents were active as well but provided local charity more informally in food, money, clothing, and other services: Oliva, *Convent and the Community*, 139–47. Also see Dey, "Diaconiae," 407.

68. Patients with psychiatric ailments generally were cared for at home. Prostitutes

Repenties

In medieval society, women received most of the blame for sexual indiscretions. Women were viewed as weaker than men in avoiding temptation, and their beauty and enticements could debilitate the righteous. Although prostitution was unquestionably sinful, it provided an outlet for the male libido, and, thus, it performed a social function. Prostitution simultaneously was viewed as the fault of women, a sign of human frailty worthy of grace, an unfortunate but beneficial social service, and sin.

Prostitution had long been present in Avignon (southern France) but the move of the papacy to the city from 1309 to 1377 expanded the number of males. The sex industry flourished. Prostitutes were segregated from others by what they wore and where they lived.[69] If they touched food in the market, they were required to buy it. As a regulated industry, sexual services were provided throughout the city in brothels, taverns, and other locales.

When the curia began its migration back to Rome in 1376, it left more supply than demand for sexual services in Avignon. Prostitution faced continued legal restrictions along with occasional attempts at reform through marriage or the convent. Marriage, it was thought, would help avert the poverty of women and the necessity of selling oneself. To prevent a life of prostitution, confraternities of laypersons distributed dowries to poor girls and prostitutes. Marrying a prostitute was considered an act of piety.

The other redemptive path was a convent of repentance (*Repenties*), commonly dedicated to Mary Magdalene. More like halfway houses or third orders, women residents were not true religious, and some were encouraged to marry after they were rehabilitated. Many of these efforts at reform failed, however. Some were convents by day and brothels by night.

---

were differentiated and not always treated equally as others in need: Brodman, *Charity and Welfare*, 105. Pagans had a tradition of wet nursing as well. They were known for their ability to tell stories that would quiet children, which often were about the gods: Watts, *Final Pagan Generation*, 33.

69. The law stipulated that prostitutes wear a veil and single-colored clothing and that they, and all Jews, live outside the city.

In Avignon, a structure was built and attached to the Chapel of Our Lady of Miracles to provide housing for *Repenties*. But rather than operate as a halfway house, the women in this convent followed an Augustinian rule. They were cloistered, took vows of stability, did penance, labored, worshipped, and attracted benefactors. Generally indistinguishable from traditional nuns, the women were allowed to study the Bible. The women did penance to become spiritually virginal, and many sisters took the ecclesiastical name Sister Magdalene. The only distinction between this convent and others was the exceptional beauty of the residents—a constant reminder to the women about their need for penance and conversion.

After two hundred years of operation, a cardinal evicted the *Repenties* of Avignon from their convent on the edge of the city to serve in a city-center hospital. Their house became the residence of a more respectable order of sisters. No longer cloistered, the Repenties were exposed to the city. They lost their spiritually-focused rhythms, and their new house eventually became a women's prison. According to Jo-elle Rollo-Koster, "Medieval penitential solitude was thus abandoned after the mid-sixteenth century and was replaced by penitentiary enclosure." Poignantly, punishment rather than penitence became society's customary response to sex work.[70]

While many people did not venture far from home, some were forced to flee from war, disease, or poverty. Others were missionaries or traders. Some were worshippers, trekking to church or to a pilgrimage site. Open spaces could be unregulated and unpoliced, making travel dangerous.[71] Religious orders responded to the needs of travelers by attaching a "hospital" to monasteries along pilgrimage routes. Closer to today's hostel than a medical facility, hospitals offered food and lodging for rich and poor who were traveling or on pilgrimage.[72] Monks welcomed travelers to the safety and rest of

---

70. This retelling benefits exclusively from Rollo-Koster, "From Prostitutes to Brides of Christ," 113, 132.

71. Kleinschmidt, *People on the Move*, 77.

72. The hospitable provision of rooms for the protection and comfort of travelers was common in the ancient world. Consider the angels's stay with Lot in Sodom (Gen 19:1–4) and Mary and Joseph's stay in a *kataluma*—a private room in a home. *Kataluma* is also the word used in the parable of the Good Samaritan (Luke 10:34). See Carson, "Accommodation."

a nighttime shelter with a greeting, foot washing, and food, and presented them with a farewell gift at morning's departure. Sermons were sometimes preached affirming the penitential value of serving and suffering.[73] Some guests were invited to join in *lusma*, a bathing and singing ritual intended to cleanse participants physically and spiritually.[74] Hundreds of these small hospitals were established during the twelfth and thirteenth centuries.

Long-distance pilgrimages were risky and dangerous. In locales where fording rivers and ravines was perilous, bridge societies raised money to construct and maintain roads and wooden and stone bridges to provide for the safe crossing. One of these, still partially standing today, is the Bridge of Saint-Bénézet which crosses the Rhône River in Avignon, France (see Fig. 3.5). Bridge building was difficult and hazardous, and bridges required regular maintenance to remain safe.[75]

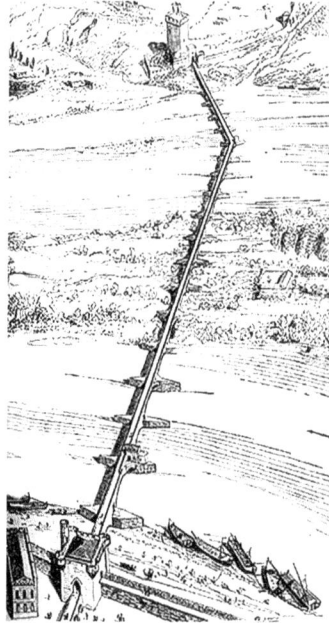

Fig. 3.5. The Bridge of Saint-Bénézet.

73. Davis, "Preaching in Thirteenth-Century Hospitals."

74. Dey, "Diaconiae," 405.

75. St Bénézet is appropriately the patron saint of bridge builders. Over time, monasteries sought exemptions from the responsibility of bridge building. Some charity-built bridges had no clear line of responsibility for maintenance and fell into disrepair. Road maintenance also included policing it for thieves. In some cases, civil rulers took on bridge building and maintenance responsibilities: Cooper, *Bridges, Law and Power*, 4.

Ill pilgrims descending on a pilgrimage site often required medical support. Orders such as the Hospital Brothers of Saint Anthony (Antonines) and Hospitallers of Saint John built and staffed medical facilities and defended pilgrim routes.[76] Increasingly, these orders assumed militant roles during the crusades, defending cities, building watchtowers, and redeeming Christians captured in wars with Muslims through monetary payment.[77] In more peaceful times and regions, selected monasteries aided healthcare by specializing in medicinals [**Monastic Pharmacies**].

Monastic Pharmacies

Western Christian monastic medicine and pharmacology were influenced by Islamic and Greek thought, the latter of which dates back to the second century BCE. Monastic medical texts can be traced to Alphanus I (c. 1015–1085), a physician and archbishop of Salerno, who translated two Greek texts into Latin. Alphanus invited Constantine the African (d. c. 1097), a young physician from Carthage (in today's Tunisia), to join him in Salerno, Italy, become a Benedictine monk, and assist Alphanus in translating and preserving Greek and Arabic medical texts. Over time, several other monks joined the effort to translate medical texts, which detailed conditions such as fever, freckles, fatigue, infection, nutrition, and insect stings.

By the late Middle Ages, monasteries on the Balkan peninsula, in Cyprus, Egypt, and elsewhere, operated pharmacies where monks researched and dispensed medicines.[78] Many of the formulations were plant-based, using stems, roots, berries, and leaves. Some included animal and inorganic substances.[79] Incense was used as well, possibly

---

76. The Antonines were themselves established from an endowment by Gaston of Valloire in 1095 out of gratitude for his son being healed from Saint Anthony's Fire, a disease caused by fungal poisoning from grain.

77. Two of these orders were the Trinitarians, or Order of the Most Holy Trinity for the Redemption of Captives, and the Mercedarians, or Order of Our Lady of Mercy for the Redemption of Captives, who took a fourth vow to die if necessary for others: Brodman, *Charity and Religion*, 150–72.

78. Lardos and Heinrich, "Continuity and Change"; Lev and Chipman, *Medical Prescriptions*; Watts, *Final Pagan Generation*, 25–28.

79. Jarić et al., "Phytotherapy in Medieval Serbian Medicine"; Počivavšek, "Tradition of the Pharmacies."

replacing the stench of disease with the aroma of Christ, or aiding healing with the presence of the sacramental.[80]

Medicinal monasteries often maintained verdant gardens in which they grew plants for the kitchen and the pharmacy. When necessary, monks purchased exotic ingredients and relied on traded goods outside of growing seasons.[81] complete formulary of ingredients was quite large, but a sampling includes parsnip, gall, honey, horehound, rose, camphor, celery, saffron, aloe, orchid, nettle, poppy, garlic, and catnip.[82]

Monks had to diagnose medical conditions so they could prescribe an appropriate pharmacological treatment. The look, smell, and taste of urine was one of the diagnostic tools they utilized (see Fig. 3.6).

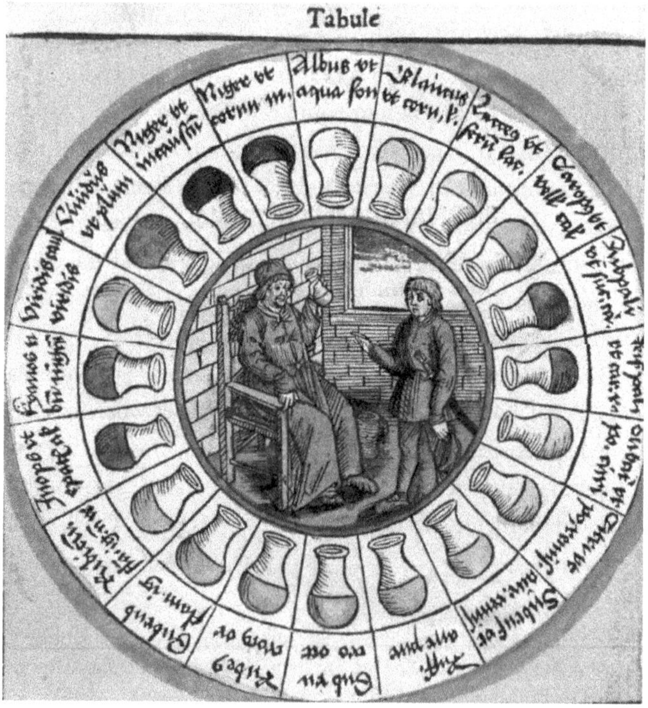

Fig. 3.6. Urine chart.

80. Burridge, "Incense in Medicine."

81. Montford, *Health, Sickness, Medicine and the Friars*, 55.

82. Arsdall, *Medieval Herbal Remedies*; Burridge, "Incense in Medicine."

Professionalization

In the high Middle Ages, monks began transitioning back to contemplative life, transferring service roles to deacons and lay professionals.[83] Although *The Rule of St. Benedict* stipulated that monks were to show hospitality, monastic houses were intended to be separate and ordered communities rather than guesthouses offering perpetual social services. Monastic houses had grown quite wealthy through the accumulation of tithes and bequests. Sacramental service provided a more appropriate and attractive role for literate monks and many followed that call.

RETURNING TO GOSPEL POVERTY

Beginning in the late eleventh century, popular dissatisfaction began growing among the laity regarding monasteries and the church. Although monks had taken vows of personal poverty they were living sumptuously off the tithes of the poor. The church had become the largest landowner in Europe yet many people were destitute. Increasingly, voices called for reform.[84] Shared among many reformers was the notion that the material simplicity of Jesus was a hallmark of authentic Christian discipleship, and that monastics had drifted from that reality.[85]

Parish Care

Supporting the feasibility of reform was the confidence that parishes and confraternities could effectively and faithfully deliver local aid. One way parishes managed their benevolence was by maintaining a poor list (*matricula*) of their most deserving parishioners. Lists customarily were fixed at twelve recipients but the number could grow as high as forty. These designated individuals (many were widows) received food and financial support from lay members and church coffers.

Church teachings underscored the importance of mutual aid. Pope Innocent III (c. 1160–1216), for example, issued three treatises on the works of mercy and encouraged an "activist spirituality" where parishioners where challenged to best monastics in caregiving: "It is good to pray," Innocent wrote, "but it is better to give alms because alms do both, descend toward

---

83. Dey, "Diaconiae," 421–22; Fehler, *Poor Relief*, 11.

84. For insight into these reforms, see Tellenbach, *Church in Western Europe*.

85. Grundmann, *Religious Movements*.

one's neighbor and ascend toward God . . . . It is better to pray with works than with words."[86]

Parish priests likewise emphasized charity and compassion in their homilies, teaching that uncharitable souls partaking of the Eucharist would be damned.[87] Avoiding immediate or eternal punishment was a potent motivator of compassion. Priests personified charity as a woman serving quietly and humbly. They warned men about vainglory in serving. Works of mercy frequently were underscored in religious dramas.[88]

Churchwardens's accounts record compassion-related parish activities and expenditures consisting of monetary benevolence, hospitality, care for the sick, and spiritual works of charity, including catechesis in plays and art and maintaining lights at altars for the living and the dead. Additionally, guilds provided opportunities to extend mutual aid.[89] Parishes pulsated with local acts of charity. Despite the historical interest in monastic activities, and finely pointed moral arguments [**Canon Law**], a substantial amount of care was delivered within the parish, making monastic services less necessary and reform more appealing.

Canon Law

Scholastic theologians took up the topics of charity, labor, aid, and the public square. Mostly focused on moral theology, their arguments bled into canon and secular law. Peter the Chanter (d. 1197) and his circle explored the rights of the poor and society's responsibility toward them, as well as the lines separating the authentically poor from those who were masquerading.[90]

---

86. Brodman, *Charity and Religion*, 23.

87. Powell, *John Mirk's Festial*.

88. Although McNamer sees the female representation of compassion as valorizing women, Ruys views the treatment as pejorative. See: McNamer, *Affective Meditation*; Ruys, "Alternative History."

89. Brown, "'That Peace Shall Always Dwell,'" 104, 109, 146–51, 159–60, 188–89, 221–24.

90. Peter's *Verbum abbreviatum* was a popular manual on ethics that contained entries on the poor, including "false beggars" who faked disabilities and indigence. Peter and his student Thomas of Chobham (c. 1160–c. 1233) chastised beggars who changed their clothing and expressions to look poor, and prostitutes who used makeup to look attractive, just as they chastised people for coming to church to extort money rather than hear sermons: Farmer, *Surviving Poverty*, 65–67.

Fields of questions such as these were well plowed: Were alms efficacious for the donor if they were acquired illicitly? (Generally, no.) Could a destitute person steal food from the well fed? (Yes.) Could doctors who charged a healthy patient for their services, or lawyers who charged exorbitant fees, or bankers who charged usurious interest redeem themselves through almsgiving? (Generally, no—restitution was required.) Should the poor be greeted with sumptuous food? (No; staples were sufficient.) Could one give alms without a heart of charity? (It yields no merit; indeed, it is simony.) Did one owe a greater responsibility to a Christian nonrelative or an infidel father? (Hmmm.)[91]

Although the tendrils of scholastic arguments curled into fine details, the general image that forms, as summarized by Brian Tierney, is that money should be justly acquired and shared with virtue and charitable intent, rather than out of pressure or pride—consistent with the Apostle Paul's encouragement.[92] Juanita Feros Ruys adds that scholastics viewed virtue as developing from *habitus*, or the habit of showing charity; that virtues were the result of reason and the will, not passion. In other words, sympathy or pity were not the wisest origins of charity. Ruys sums up antique and medieval theologians by saying: "The return of so many great thinkers to a similar conclusion over numerous centuries is cautionary: perhaps if we wish to do good for others, we should think before we feel."[93]

Early Reformers

Robert of Arbrissel (c. 1045–1116) was an early medieval reformer who called people to return to the basics of the faith. He taught by example, living simply and preaching to prostitutes. Wherever he wandered in France, he attracted crowds, eventually assembling a community of men who served women.[94] Around the same time, another reformer, Norbert of Xanten (c.

---

91. Almsgiving was not mere technique. Canonists also affirmed the importance of intent and virtue in giving: Tierney, *Medieval Poor Law*, 49–54, 57.

92. Tierney, *Medieval Poor Law*, 53.

93. Ruys, "Alternative History," 213.

94. Griffiths, "Cross and the Cura Monialium."

1075–1134), preached barefoot in Germanic lands. Norbert's asceticism was so extreme that his first three disciples died of exposure in the cold of winter. Norbert established the Canons Regular of Prémontré (Norbertines), who were among those who took a simple gospel to Scandinavia and Eastern Europe.

Robert, Norbert, and other barefoot preachers were unlicensed street evangelists, preaching repentance and warning about avarice. But radical as they appeared, they depended on a bishop or lay brothers for support.[95] Others were not so favored. A wealthy French merchant named Peter Waldo (or Waldes; c. 1140–c. 1205) heard the gospel and felt convicted that he was not following it.[96] He abandoned his wealth and encouraged others to do the same. Waldo alienated clerics, and Waldensian teachings were declared heretical. His followers continued underground for five hundred years and suffered massacres and atrocities at the hands of other Christians.

The Humiliati, or "humble ones," constituted yet another persecuted movement. From their motherhouse in Milan, Italy, they were operating two hundred houses by the mid-thirteenth century. They structured themselves into three orders: clerics following a structured rule, lay men and women living in community, and lay men and women living in their homes. They shared property in common (rather than renouncing it) and viewed work as a source of charity, in contrast to begging or depending on the church for financing. They brought woolen manufacturing techniques from Germany to Italy, enlarging textile production in the northern Italian states, employing the poor and dispersing earnings to those in need.[97] Over time, the Humiliati too attracted significant wealth and offended the church and the public. They were censured and dissolved in 1571.

Mendicants and Confraternities

The most lasting reforms of compassion were brought by two priests— Dominic of Caleruega (1170–1221) and Francis of Assisi (1181–1226),

---

95. Thompson, "Origins of Religious Mendicancy," 7–8.

96. Hoose thinks the readings may have been from around Pentecost and included "the reading from St. Luke in which Christ, sending out the twelve disciples to preach, commanded them to carry nothing for their journey. Second . . . a gospel reading from St. Matthew in which a rich young man, who asked Jesus what to do to attain eternal life, refused to renounce his great wealth. . . . Third . . . the parable of Lazarus and Dives from the gospel of St. Luke . . . and finally . . . the reading from St. Luke in which Christ instructed his disciples not to be anxious about tomorrow, to sell their possessions, and to place their treasure in heaven": Hoose, "Orthopraxy," 36.

97. Andrews, *Early Humiliati*.

founders of the Friars Preachers (Dominicans) and Friars Minor (Franciscan) orders, respectively. These reformers wanted to share life with the poor more than eviscerate those living in wealth.[98] They led wandering bands of fraternal preaching monks who lived simply and today are called "mendicants" (which means "beggars") [**Skete Monasticism**], although they did not always beg for alms.

Skete Monasticism

Thus far, we have encountered three types of monks: eremitic hermits in the antique era, cenobitic monks who typically lived in cloistered communities, and mendicants who wandered through villages and across the countryside. In Orthodox Russia, a fourth type of monasticism emerged: Skete monasticism, characterized by small bands of three missionaries living together in a hut among peasants at the edges of civilization. They focused on teaching and providing pastoral care to local peasants.[99]

Elsewhere in Russia, large monastic houses grew in wealth, funded by secular rulers and supporting Russian princes in return. Yosif of Volokalamsk (1439–1515) advanced a strict orthodoxy among these state-supporting monasteries. Eventually, he imprisoned Skete monastics as heretics. The alignment of the Russian Orthodox Church with Ivan the Great and the czars to follow, discouraged revolutionary impulses. In many ways, the church became absorbed into the state. Although seminaries, missionaries, and churches continued to engage in pastoral care, most civil reform attempts were quelled. (For an exception, see [**An Orthodox Flare**] in chapter 6.)[100]

98. Mollat, *Poor in the Middle Ages*, 119.

99. Skete monasticism is an updated expression of a late antique Egyptian style.

100. According to Benz, *Eastern Orthodox Church*, 94–96, 152: "as time went on, the state Church put itself more at the service of political absolutism, which was anchored in the principle of divine right. Gradually the Church withdrew from all but purely charitable social activity. It became a principle of Orthodoxy to remain aloof from politics, so that even in the eventful nineteenth century, the Russian Orthodox Church—and this was one of its tragedies—made scarcely any significant contribution toward a solution of the social injustices."

Dominic and his Friars Preachers were focused on evangelism and lived simply to that end. Eventually, they added begging to their means of sustenance.[101] Francis and his Friars Minor were more focused on joining the poor than alleviating poverty.[102] Francis preferred that his friars work, begging only if necessary.[103] A third mendicant order, Augustinians, originally lived as isolated hermits. They joined together in 1244, united under an Augustinian rule and focused on evangelism. They took on trades that allowed them to support themselves and others in the communities in which they lived. They buried the dead, worked in hospitals, and served as carpenters, teachers, and farmers.[104]

Mendicants stirred the charitable spirit in parishes.[105] Especially in Italy, some confraternities of laypersons honored a saint or engaged in a pious practice such as flagellation while others took on the challenge of feeding the hungry, comforting the condemned, and tending the ill.[106] These were spiritual communities (*compagnie spirituali*), paralleling artisanal (guilds) and armed (militias) companies, and they operated separately from parishes and religious orders. Like other voluntary groups, they provided a sense of community and surrogate family in urban locales and represented ongoing growth of the civil society sector.[107]

Dominic and Francis did not invent the itinerant model, but it took hold under their lead. Unlike the Waldensians and Humiliati, the Dominicans, Franciscans, and Augustinians were accepted by the church and welcomed widely.[108] Francis was the first person in history known to receive the stigmata, drawing further acclaim. Pope Innocent III and the Fourth Lateran Council sanctioned the Friars Minor (Franciscans) in 1215, and the

---

101. Prudlo, "Mendicancy."

102. Doyno, *Lay Saint*, 49.

103. Thompson, "Origins of Religious Mendicancy," 17.

104. Living simply became a delicate balance for mendicants when donations of land and money began coming their way and they found themselves headed down the same path as the Benedictines and Cistercians before them. The church also pressed mendicant orders to protect their institutional holdings.

105. Brown, "'That Peace Shall Always Dwell.'"

106. Black, *Italian Confraternities*; Doyno, *Lay Saint*. In Japan, Justa of Nagasaki founded a confraternity and consorority that taught children, nursed the sick, operated reformatories, and visited prisoners. See Ward, *Women Religious*, 297–323.

107. Barnes, *Social Dimension of Piety*; Black and Gravestock, *Early Modern Confraternities*; Terpstra, *Lay Confraternities*.

108. In Hoose's view, "Both the Waldensians and Franciscans sought to break the connection between greed and labor. The former did so by forbidding labor and the latter by encouraging labor as a way to avoid sinfulness": "Orthopraxy," 178.

Friars Preachers (Dominicans) were licensed by Pope Honorius III in 1216. The Augustinians were united in 1255.

Some have argued that the mendicant orders deepened poverty by pitting friars against other beggars in competing for alms, but little evidence supports this assertion.[109] Still, mendicant orders were not centered on ameliorating poverty or even caring for the ailing.[110] Their primary focus was on preaching and joining others in poverty. The mendicant call to simple living, however, spurred the church to expand services to poor people through parishes and even monasteries, and it encouraged compassion among the laity. Ironically, they also may have slowed institutional reforms because the church could point to them as evidence that monastics were not all living sumptuously.[111]

Laypersons sometimes felt a stirring to a more devoted life, and this too was an innovation of traditional understanding and practice. Perhaps best known among these were the Beguines, confraternities of women who chose to live celibate lives of service, often working in hospitals. They developed a spirituality that refreshed them as they cared for the poor, ill, and infirm. Many Beguines were women from wealthy families in Germany and the Low Countries who served during young adulthood.[112] The Beguines built and operated several convent-hospitals.

By the fifteenth century, urban centers and learning were flowering in the Renaissance. Compassion for human suffering was increasingly practiced, including assisting those condemned to death.[113] Reforms in care-giving were being called for in most religious orders. The Observant Movement attempted to steer monastic houses back to the basics of poverty,

109. Wolf, *Poverty of Riches*; Andrews, *Other Friars*. Also see Brodman, *Charity and Religion*, 270–71. Later, Bonaventure and other Franciscan and Dominican leaders rebalanced the importance of caring for poor people, emphasizing the need for both contemplation and action. Aquinas, Albert the Great, and Pope Innocent III emphasized that action should accompany contemplation. See Brodman, 272–75.

110. For a narrow and legal (canon law) discussion of Franciscan ownership, see Robinson, "Innocent IV."

111. As the Middle Ages ended, mendicant friars served as diplomat-missionaries, gathering intelligence, striking military agreements, and baptizing. This involved missionaries traveling to Asia and preaching in Mongol-controlled lands. Over time, Dominicans and Franciscans became embroiled in the Inquisition: Grieco, "Pastoral Care"; Ryan, *Spiritual Expansion*, xxvii.

112. Beguines were not always accepted by members of canonical orders or by the public—they were seen as too pietistic by some of the latter and unsanctioned by some of the former.

113. Zika, "Compassion in Punishment."

chastity, and obedience, but the effort fell short, readying Christian lands for additional reforms.[114]

SUMMING UP

The medieval age adds a millennium of activity and contrast to our charitable journey. It began with economic collapse, was beleaguered by wars and plague, and ended in social and religious upheaval. As in earlier times, Christians continued to await eschatological justice and grow in virtue, but they also had a keen sense of God's involvement in daily life, invoking divine protection and healing. The church's social role in caring for the poor, established in the early Byzantine era, plus the mobilization of tithes, bequests, and teaching, flowered into a considerable network of parish, monastery, and lay care that ended in institutional aggrandizement.

Although some served a loving God, compassion for many forestalled punishment. The reformer Ulrich Zwingli (1484–1531) would soon lament (although perhaps to excess) that "no one gives gladly solely to honor God and the good of his neighbor, but out of fear of the devil and of hell or of God as a tyrant, or in order to purchase time or eternity."[115] Although mendicants stirred empathy for the most vulnerable, the church seemed to have lost or at least tarnished its public trust as the primary guardian for the poor.

Reform efforts had fermented for over two centuries and would intensify in coming years. They reflected unique circumstances at the time but also the repeating motif through Christian history of returning to the ideals of the faith.

114. Mixson, "Observant."
115. Quoted in Pullan, "Catholics, Protestants, and the Poor," 446.

MODERN

IN THE MODERN ERA, from the sixteenth to the nineteenth century, we encounter revolutionary Protestant and Catholic ideas and institutions and the state assuming a more central role in social welfare. Compassionate care is attached to missionary excursions, nonprofit and secularized compassion mushrooms, and need comes under increased scrutiny. Some of the themes and actors we will encounter are given in the table that follows.

Chapter	Century	Era	Themes	Actors
4	Sixteenth to Seventeenth	Reform and Expansion	Increased role of the state, martyrs, Protestant and Catholic Reformations, Mounts of Piety, poor laws, scholastic theology, exploration and missions, *Misericórdias*	Juan Luis Vives, Martin Luther, John Calvin, Menno Simons, Conrad Grebel, Ignatius of Loyola, Vincent de Paul, Bartolomé de las Casas, Francis Xavier
5	Eighteenth to Nineteenth	Salvation and Service	Humanitarian missions, *diakonia*, Quaker reformers, Victorians, Red Cross, Salvation Army, Christian socialism, health care, holiness and the social gospel, scientific charity	Peter Parker, F. D. Maurice, Henry Dunant, Samuel Barnett, Thomas Chalmers, William and Clara Booth, Elizabeth Fry, Johannes Falk, John Woolman, Ursulines, Walter Rauschenbusch, Oscar McCulloch

Compassion themes and actors in the modern era.

4

Reform and Expansion

For nearly five hundred years, critics had burned with a sense that the church had drifted from its ancient calling and identity. The Renaissance accelerated church critiques, global exploration, and attention to humanity [**Deaf Education**], underscoring the kinship of the poor with Christ. By the sixteenth century, theologians and clerics were calling for reform of doctrine and practice. Reformers regularly accused clerics and monastics of impersonating poor people. Monks had taken a vow of personal poverty but enjoyed lifestyles of status and the abundant wealth of their monastic orders.[1] Although reformers agreed that the church had not been faithful in its care for the poor, their theology and practical remedies diverged. Most advocated a greater role for the individual believer and the state in caring for the vulnerable. The inability to resolve theological, political, social, and economic differences led to a fracturing of the church. Those differences also influenced diverse understandings and practices in compassion and care-giving.[2]

---

1. Nuns were not as frequently accused of kingdom building in their orders. It was the men who were accused of alms fraud. For a contrast of reformers remaining within the Catholic Church and those separating, see Congar, *True and False Reform*, 199–340.

2. For surveys of reformers, see Eire, *Reformations*; Ozment, *Age of Reform*.

Deaf Education

A Benedictine monk named Pedro Ponce de León (c. 1510–1584) is remembered as an early leader in deaf education. Possibly influenced by the Renaissance's more inclusive views of deafness, Fray Ponce desired to teach the gospel to those who had been denied an opportunity to physically hear. Ponce began teaching deaf children in his Spanish monastery. Some of the children came from wealthy families that had intermarried—a possible cause of their children's deafness.[3]

Ponce was accustomed to hand signs because they were commonly used in monasteries to communicate during periods of silence. He employed *Solace for the Sick*, a text published in 1593 by Franciscan monk, Melchor Sánchez de Yebra (1526–1586). The text included drawings of a hand alphabet with each letter being accompanied by an aphorism of Christian conduct given by St. Bonaventure. Reports exist of a book Ponce wrote on his teaching methods, but no copies of the book have been discovered.[4] Instruction continued under the tutelage of other Spanish educators, such as Juan Pablo Bonet (1579–1633) who authored the influential, *Simplification of the Letters of the Alphabet and Method of Teaching Deaf Mutes to Speak.*

ARCHITECTS AND REFORMERS

Juan Luis Vives (1493–1540) was one of the first reformers to focus on a fresh approach to poverty alleviation. For Vives, it was time for the state to play a larger role. Magisterial reformers, such as Martin Luther (1483–1546) and John Calvin (1509–1564), supported an increased role for civil authority in poor care as well, but also fully empowered believers through callings and stewardship.[5] They affirmed private property, arguing that abandoning all goods led to sloth and begging. Christians had an obligation, as an overseer and not an owner of goods, to steward their possessions and

---

3. Daniels, *Benedictine Roots*, 11–16.

4. Daniels, *Benedictine Roots*, 14–15.

5. For additional insights into religious and political reform, see Voltmer, "Political Preaching," 75–76.

contribute to the common good.[6] Radical reformers such as Menno Simons (1496–1561) and Conrad Grebel (1498–1526) emphasized congregation-based mutual aid and nonviolence. Catholic reformers, such as Ignatius of Loyola (1491–1556) and Vincent de Paul (1581–1660), affirmed traditional approaches. With followers attached to each, Christian compassion separated into a diverse spectrum of theological and practical responses.

Vives

A widely read early proposal addressing a new response to poverty was Juan Luis Vives's, *On Assistance to the Poor* (*De subventione pauperum*), published in 1526. Vives was not focused on theological disputation but on offering a practical remedy to poverty, decreasing the role of the church and affording the state a larger role. Vives wrote that "care should be taken that the priests, under cover of their divine office and the mass, do not turn the money into their own pockets. They are well enough provided for; they do not need any more."[7]

Vives was a Spanish-born scholar who lived most of his life in Bruges, France (modern Belgium). He offered innovative, practical proposals on poor relief, including treating the poor with respect; taking a census of the poor; holding the state responsible for poor relief (with supplements from private sources); providing training and job creation for the unemployed, blind, and elderly; and extending welfare to those under the poverty line. Vives recommended caring for the mentally ill in hospitals—something typically done at home—and he advocated for social censors who would monitor the behavior of impoverished youth and old men.[8] In that regard, Vives echoed the Apostle Paul who wrote that, "Anyone unwilling to work should not eat" (2 Thess 3:10b).[9]

Vives advised that wealthy hospitals should follow the example of the earliest Christians, redistributing their excess capital to poorer institutions in near and distant locales. He recommended that orphans's homes teach trades, and that the state senate serve as a watchdog over charitable

---

6. The *Book of Concord* read: "The poverty of the Gospel (Mt 5:3) does not consist in the abandonment of property, but in the absence of greed and of trust in riches." From Tappert, *Book of Concord*, 277, cited in Galler, "A Sham, Pretense, and Hypocrisy?" 71. For a review of the reformers on poverty and charity, see Pattison, *Poverty in the Theology of John Calvin*, 81–122.

7. Vives, *Concerning the Relief of the Poor*, 29.

8. Henry Ford experimented with a similar policy for his highly paid assembly workers.

9. Safley, *Reformation of Charity*.

institutions. For the wealthy, a better use of money than to spend it on funerary pomp would be to provide vouchers for the poor to purchase meat
and bread. To supplement public funds, alms boxes could be placed in the
largest parishes to collect donations from passers-by. Vives advocated for
spending and disbursing funds rather than amassing endowments that in-
centivized empire building.

Vives continued to advocate for reliance upon God among those in
poverty and "not to make much provision for the distant future, for this
increases their sense of security and diminishes their reliance on God." He
encouraged the rich to look to God and not depend upon their wealth or
planning:

> By how many examples has it been shown to men that, when a
> holy work has been undertaken by a certain group, with some
> anxiety and even despair on their part lest the funds provided
> for it should not be sufficient, as the work progressed it has been
> so blessed that even those who have charge of it are forced to
> wonder by what hidden ways the additional resources have been
> forthcoming! . . . Surely it is by the universal bounty of God that
> they are maintained, are fed, live and grow, and not by riches,
> nor their own strength, nor by human counsels. Wherefore,
> in pious undertakings it is sacrilegious to consider how much
> you can do; consider rather how much faith you have in Him to
> whom all things are possible.[10]

Martin Luther

Celebrating God's abundant grace, Martin Luther believed that salvation was
the beginning rather than the end of discipleship. In asserting this ordering,
he was challenging the popular belief that good works save.[11] Some feared
that Luther's teaching would neutralize good works because one was saved
by faith alone. But Luther emphasized that gratitude for God's grace would
flow into service for others in the "liturgy after the liturgy;" a life of compassion and service after communal worship.[12] Compassion was necessary, but
it occurred after salvation rather than as a requirement to receive it.

Luther advocated equality among works of charity extended in faith:
"One is like the other; all distinctions between works fall away, whether they

---

10. Vives, *Concerning the Relief of the Poor*, 27, 30, 31.

11. Ozment, *Age of Reform*, 22–42.

12. Lindberg, "No Greater Service," 51.

be great, small, short, long, few or many. For the works are acceptable not for their own sake, but because of the faith which alone is, works and lives in each and every work."[13] It was faith, rather than the virtue of the late antique era, that made compassion shine.

Luther believed that good works were within everyone's reach and were embedded in everyday activities. One merely needed faith, and one would see, feel, and act compassionately:

> On this is based the wonderful and righteous judgment of God, that at times a poor man, in whom no one can see many great works, in the privacy of his home joyfully praises God when he fares well, or with entire confidence calls upon Him when he fares ill, and thereby does a greater and more acceptable work than another, who fasts much, prays much, endows churches, makes pilgrimages, and burdens himself with great deeds in this place and in that.[14]

Good works exceeded acts of piety and included ordinary tasks within one's vocation and daily life. People improved the collective social welfare "when they work at their trade, walk, stand, eat, drink, sleep, and do all kinds of works for the nourishment of the body or for the common welfare."[15] Luther wrote that religious works, such as "singing, reading, organ-playing, reading the mass, saying matins and vespers and the other hours, the founding and decorating of churches, altars, and monastic houses, the gathering of bells, jewels, vestments, trinkets and treasures, running to Rome and to the saints," were not as meaningful as fulfilling one's obligations in daily life.[16] In essence, Luther re-emphasized a view of the sacredness of life in a way that recalled Francis. Everyday activities could be engaged with a heart of joy and freedom because they contributed to the common good, in contrast to their adding weight to the ever-precarious balance of salvation.

Diffusing service throughout the priesthood of all believers sparked innovations in mutual aid. It represented, in essence, the real presence of Jesus Christ living and active in the body of believers. Followers of Luther picked up the responsibility for care, joyously pursuing their vocations and establishing common chest funds in parishes, and providing interest-free loans, vocational training for children, dowries for needy women, and consolidation loans to replace those with high interest.[17]

13. Luther, "Treatise on Good Works," 190.
14. Luther, "Treatise on Good Works," 206.
15. Luther, "Treatise on Good Works," 188.
16. Luther, "Treatise on Good Works," 196–97.
17. Lindberg, "No Greater Service," 57.

Luther was comfortable with the civil authorities overseeing structural aspects of justice and compassion because they too were under God's sovereignty. In what has been termed Luther's "two-kingdom" view of the world, a spiritual kingdom is constituted by the church and a temporal kingdom by government, commerce, families, and other institutions. The temporal kingdom was established to battle the destructive forces of Satan through structures informed by the spiritual kingdom. Luther opposed the Catholic hierarchy but also opposed those who would abolish law and government. Both could be tools for justice and peace.[18]

With government and other institutions operating under the sovereignty of God, Luther drafted poverty alleviation schemes for communities in northeast Germany and Scandinavia that included municipal and regional legal and civil reforms.[19] Luther railed against capitalist profiteers who manipulated market prices by dumping goods, charging high interest rates for loans, or advertising falsely. He called for their excommunication and appealed to local and state government on behalf of the vulnerable.[20] Thus, Luther freed Christians for joyful and compassionate service, and he called upon public and private institutions to be faithful to their callings.

John Calvin

John Calvin's theology differed from Luther's in several ways that affected how compassion was viewed and practiced. Calvin emphasized that all humans were poor and destitute, and that God alone determined who was saved. For Calvin, one could not earn salvation through good works, but faithful stewards responded appropriately to God by denying themselves, living sparingly, and directing accumulated wealth toward social benefit. Just as God bestowed blessings on Jesus, "not for private use, but to enrich the poor and needy," so we must use wealth for others.[21] Calvin asserted that "whatever the Church possessed, either in lands or in money, was the patrimony of the poor."[22]

Calvin believed that wealth and poverty fell under the sovereignty of God and that it was possible to be rich both spiritually and materially. Poverty plagued so many, however, because the church diverted funds toward opulent cathedrals and vestments that the church mistakenly argued

18. Nygren, "Luther's Doctrine of the Two Kingdoms."
19. Pullan, "Catholics, Protestants, and the Poor," 449–51.
20. Lindberg, "No Greater Service," 60–61.
21. Calvin, *Institutes*, chap. 1, sect. 1.
22. Calvin, *Institutes*, chap. 5, sect. 6.

displayed the splendor of the kingdom of God. Bishops and priests had violated the people's trust, living opulently and building religious empires in which "the daily alms are swallowed up in this abyss."[23] The same could be said for the wealthy trader or even the pauper. Calvin wrote:

> For there is scarcely any one whose means allow him to live sumptuously, who does not delight in feasting, and dress, and the luxurious grandeur of his house, who wishes not to surpass his neighbor in every kind of delicacy, and does not plume himself amazingly on his splendor. And all these things are defended under the pretext of Christian liberty. . . . but when the means are supplied, to roll and wallow in luxury, to intoxicate the mind and soul with present and be always hunting after new pleasures, is very far from a legitimate use of the gifts of God. Let them, therefore, suppress immoderate desire, immoderate profusion, vanity, and arrogance, that they may use the gifts of God purely with a pure conscience. . . . Let every one then live in his own station, poorly or moderately, or in splendor; but let all remember that the nourishment which God gives is for life, not luxury, and let them regard it as the law of Christian liberty, to learn with Paul in whatever state they are, "therewith to be content," to know "both how to be abased," and "how to abound," "to be full and to be hungry, both to abound and to suffer need."[24]

Calvin warned that poverty opened the eyes to truths while luxury blind one's spiritual sight. Yet, whatever their economic or social state, Christians were called to be productive and charitable as an expression of worship and as contribution to the kingdom of God.[25]

Calvin recognized the importance of individual lifestyles and of social structures in poor relief. (Calvin advocated the building of a closed sewer system in his home city of Geneva.[26]) They distinguished between deserving and undeserving poor, and the faithful and unfaithful steward [**Stewardship**]. One should rise to one's calling, using one's sphere of influence justly in response to God's love and sovereignty, not out of fear of damnation.

23. Calvin, *Institutes*, chap. 5, sect. 18.

24. Calvin, *Institutes*, chap. 19, sect. 9.

25. Pattison, *Poverty in the Theology of John Calvin*, 117. In seventeenth-century Dutch colonies in today's New York, Reformed Church in America deacons stewarded funds and provisions for the elderly, orphans, and the poor. See Venema, "Poverty and Charity."

26. Rigby, "Christian Life."

Stewardship

The concept of stewardship has a long and rich history in Christian tradition, being rooted in the Hebrew Bible and New Testament, expounded upon by patristic writings, and emphasized in reformation theology, particularly by John Calvin. In his *Institutes of the Christian Religion*, Calvin wrote of the commandment, "Thou shalt not steal":

> If an agent or an indolent steward wastes the substance of his employer, or does not give due heed to the management of his property; if he unjustly squanders or luxuriously wastes the means entrusted to him; if a servant holds his master in derision, divulges his secrets, or in any way is treacherous to his life or his goods; if, on the other hand, a master cruelly torments his household, he is guilty of theft before God; since every one who, in the exercise of his calling, performs not what he owes to others, keeps back, or makes away with what does not belong to him.[27]

Stewardship began with the belief that all creation is owned by God and that Christians had a fiduciary responsibility to steward God's gifts (Gen 1:26–30; Matt 25:14–30). In the years hence, concept has been applied narrowly to sharing money with the poor, and broadly such as stewarding all of one's "time, talent, and treasure."[28] Over time, stewardship came to convey maximizing asset growth, enhancing investment efficacy, and preserving one's estate. Christopher Hays, and Calvin, however, argue that Scripture emphasizes that the steward's primary role is distribution. Hays writes:

> Contemporary Christian discourse about stewardship. . .often creates an implicit justification for preserving the goods entrusted to one by the Master. Quite to the contrary, however, Luke always refers to stewards in their capacities as giving away the goods of the Master.[29]

---

27. Calvin, *Institutes*, 346.
28. For a review, see Reumann, *Stewardship and the Economy of God*.
29. Hays, "Slaughtering Stewards and Incarcerating Debtors," 50.

Radical Reformers

Radical reformers such as Menno Simons and Conrad Grebel viewed the church as independent and countercultural to the state. Persecuted by other reformers, Anabaptists embraced a first-century model of mutual aid among like-minded members. These practices included a common purse and charitable provisions of lodging, food, clothing, and employment, when needed.[30]

Congregations employed a first-century model of appointing deacons to provide relief to people in need and to support orphans and refugees. Many Anabaptists became refugees themselves when the Swiss Brethren were forced out of Switzerland because of their refusal to swear an oath to their canton.[31] Persecuted from without, they relied upon one another for shelter and aid.

Anabaptists debated whether society or only the church could be reformed. The failed German Peasants's War (1524–1525) discouraged many from confidence in the former, and an attempt to create a Christian society in Münster—complete with common property and polygamy—lasted a year and a half and met a terrible end in 1535. Soon thereafter, Anabaptists focused their efforts on separating from a world operating under the reign of Satan.[32] Anabaptists viewed mutual aid—whether individual or communal—as the primary mechanism for compassion. These views were not merely a pattern of life among Anabaptists, but also a critique of other Christians who would not share their possessions with the poor.[33]

Anabaptist teachers promoted diverse views. Menno Simons railed against the fraud, usury, and self-interest of profit-making within most professions. Pieter Pietersz (1575–1651), argued against opulent clothes, feasting, and architectural ornamentation, advocating simplicity so goods could be shared and used appropriately.[34] Pietersz viewed tithes as training wheels for the Christian who had not yet discovered the law of love. Tithes got one started toward the robust compassion of giving one's all. Possibly to avoid an association with Münster communitarianism, many Anabaptists chose to practice congregation-based voluntary donation and redistribution to the worthy poor, tolerating economic inequality within the congregation.

---

30. Umble, "Mutual Aid."

31. Roth, "Mutual Aid."

32. Snyder, "Anabaptist Spirituality and Economics," 5–6.

33. Klassen, *Economics of Anabaptism*, 28–49; Snyder, "Anabaptist Spirituality and Economics," 7.

34. Sprunger, "Dutch Mennonites," 27.

Anabaptists also emphasized nonviolent action as an expression of compassion and justice, even when it meant risking one's life, as Dirk Willems did [**Foxe's Book of Martyrs and the Martyrs' Mirror**].

Book of Martyrs and the Martyrs' Mirror

Christians have had a long practice of honoring and drawing inspiration from martyrs. The early church kept a running list of those who had died for the faith. Occasionally, the faithful would visit the coffins of martyrs in the catacombs to draw inspiration and give thanks for their lives. In the medieval age, the cult of the saints memorialized martyrs and other saints, drawing spiritual power from their relics and inviting their prayers for the supplicant. In the early modern age, it was books that memorialized martyrs, and two of them became best sellers.

John Foxe's *Acts and Monuments* (known popularly as Foxe's *Book of Martyrs*) was first published in 1563 in England. At the time, it was the most illustrated and longest or second-longest book ever printed in English. It begins with the first century and recounts, one by one, the stories of martyrs through time, including Protestants martyred by Queen Mary I. Published a century later in 1660, *Bloody Theatre* (widely known as the *Martyrs' Mirror*) offered a similar account of tracing ancient and medieval martyrs. It included through Anabaptists whose lives were extinguished by Catholics and Protestants.

These books insert Protestants and Anabaptists into the lineage of Christian saints and martyrs, and offer a witness of how to live faithfully, non-violently, and compassionately. In essence, martyrologues became the reliquaries of Protestants.[35][36]

Entries demonstrate the compassionate response of martyrs toward their persecutors, perhaps most famously illustrated in an engraving of Dirk Willems (d. 1569) in *Martyrs' Mirror*. A Dutch Anabaptist imprisoned for his faith, Willems escaped from jail and was on the run across an icy lake. His pursuer fell through ice and Willems turned back to rescue his captor. Willems was summarily recaptured and, shortly thereafter, burned at the stake.

---

35. King, *Foxe's Book of Martyrs.*

36. Weaver-Zercher, *Martyrs Mirror*. Gruesome as its entries are, *Martyrs' Mirror* has been a treasured book among Anabaptists, who have passed copies down through families, given them as wedding gifts, and used them to teach adolescents about the faith.

Fig. 4.1. Dirk Willems rescuing his persecutor.

Ignatius and the Jesuits

Some reformers advocated for renewal while defending the church, limiting the Protestant exodus, and winning new converts. Two of these were Ignatius of Loyola (1491–1556), a Spaniard who cofounded the Jesuit order, and Vincent de Paul (1581–1660), a Frenchman who served slaves and inspired many to compassionate service. Both supported traditional approaches to mendicancy and mercy.

As a young man, Ignatius of Loyola was enamored with military life. But at age twenty-six, with leg bones shattered by a cannon ball, he nearly died. Recovering from surgery, he asked for a romance to read, but all that was available were two books on Christ and the saints. He began wondering if the calling of Francis and Dominic was his as well. As he read, he noticed that some of his thoughts led to sadness and others to joy.

When he had recovered well enough to travel, Ignatius set out on a pilgrimage from Spain to Jerusalem, first on horseback and then on foot. Along the way, he confessed his sin, begged for food, slept rough, abandoned his fine clothing, disregarded his hygiene, was manhandled by guards, and was humiliated. In his mistreatment and asceticism, Ignatius learned to shed pride, security, and self-dependence. He returned to Spain with ten companions and began studying and preaching in the streets.

Ignatius and his companions remained close to the poor. As a religious order, Ignatius's Jesuits (Society of Jesus) focused on education as an expression of compassion. They taught in colleges without a salary so the poor could study and learn, especially at young ages.[37] They fed starving people during winter months, freed inmates from debtors's prisons, and founded orphanages, hospitals, and homes to reform prostitutes. Abel Alves writes of Ignatius that "poor relief and the reform of personal morals were never far from his mind as proper activities for the Christian in the world."[38]

Jesuits were leaders in mission work, and their efforts commonly included charitable care. Frequently, charity provided an opportunity for religious and moral teaching, although it was not always charitably received.[39] According to historian Louis Châtellier,

> The distributions of alms were accompanied by inspection of bedrooms (to see the boys and girls were separated) and preparation of the sick for death, as well as care for young widows burdened with children, or orphan girls who were alone in the world, so as to save them from falling into prostitution.[40]

Vincent, Vincentians, and the Daughters of Charity

Late arriving among the reformers of this era was Vincent de Paul, known by some as the Apostle of Charity. Stirring but likely apocryphal accounts have him captured by pirates as a youth and sold as a slave. As a priest, he took a role as a teacher and confessor for the French family that managed the flotilla protecting France from seafaring attackers. The flotilla galleys were rowed by convicts and, eventually, Vincent was appointed chaplain to them.[41] Comparable to life in a modern-day concentration camp, galley service was punishing. With shaved heads and tattooed shoulders, clinking as they walked, heavily chained prisoners in groups of up to one hundred

---

37. Demoustier, "First Companions."

38. Alves, "Christian Social Organism," 15–16.

39. Châtellier, *Religion of the Poor*, 132–34.

40. Châtellier, *Religion of the Poor*, 134.

41. Among the prisoners were East European Orthodox and Protestant Huguenots convicted for heresy.

walked nearly three hundred miles from Paris to Marseilles to board the ships. As many as five hundred oarsmen powered the largest vessels.

Vincent endorsed imprisonment as a punishment for crime (including the jailing of Huguenot and Orthodox Christians), but he worked tirelessly in ministering to convicts. He advocated for humane confinement facilities for prisoners, recruited priests to provide sacraments, and facilitated visitation for the families of convicts. When convicts became too ill to work on sea or shore, they were taken to local hospitals that Vincent and his followers operated.[42] It was as if he helped carry the chains of the prisoners, as hagiographic images depict (see Fig. 4.2).

Fig. 4.2. Vincent de Paul taking the chains of a prisoner.

Vincent was quite skilled at organizing. During a homily, he mentioned a destitute family. That afternoon, the family was overwhelmed with parishioners bringing food. Vincent recommended that, in the future, a system of coordination be put in place so parishioners could care for others without

42. Rybolt, "Vincent de Paul."

wasting food.[43] Fortuitously, an Augustinian leprosarium in Paris was in decline and was offered to Vincent. It was the largest ecclesial structure in the city. From it, Vincent and his volunteers organized and served hundreds of hungry Parisians, daily.[44]

Two religious orders inspired by Vincent were the Congregation of the Mission (the Vincentians) and the Daughters of Charity. Founded in France by Vincent and Louise de Marillac (1591–1660) in 1633, the Daughters of Charity was a voluntary confraternity. Two hundred years later, Frédéric Ozanam (1813–1853) continued Vincent's efforts by founding the Society of Saint Vincent de Paul. Ozanam collaborated with Daughter of Charity sister, Rosalie Rendu (1786–1856).[45]

Whether Catholic or Protestant, reformers were bringing new ideas, energy, and organization to compassion, and many organized the laity beyond the parish level. Reforms were pursued on many fronts, including generating new financial services for the poor [**Mounts of Piety**].

Mounts of Piety

Pawnbroking was an effort to extend financial services to the poor. With minimal capital available to the moderately poor, small businesses, or even nobles, pawn brokers provided liquid funds in exchange for material goods placed on hold with the broker. Poor borrowers might place a cup or tool on loan, while wealthy, cash-poor borrowers might deposit jewelry. A 5 percent interest rate was common but rates increased for items of higher value on the assumption that their owner could pay more. After the passage of one year, unredeemed goods could be sold. Pawn brokers added deposit accounts to expand their lending capital, and they also managed dowry funds.

Jewish bankers had offered these services previously, but in Perugia, Italy, two Franciscans, one of whom was the colorful Girolamo Savonarola (1452–1498), adjusted the model. They gathered alms and launched a pawnbroking shop for the poor in 1462. Called a *Monte di*

---

43. Among Vincent's organizational designs were that ministry leaders have term limits, participation be encouraged, minutes be kept in meetings, and a mission guide all activities. See Fuechtmann, "There Is Great Charity."

44. Saint-Lazare was the first property sacked in the French revolution of 1789. It became a prison until it was designated for destruction, which occurred in 1940: Udovic, "Pictures from the Past."

45. Sullivan, *Sister Rosalie Rendu.*

Pietà or "Mount of Piety," these institutions grew in popularity and expanded throughout Italy, Germany, and beyond.[46] Initially, they were condemned by the Roman Catholic Church because they charged interest, but mounts of piety were eventually approved in the Fifth Lateran Council (1515). Maria Giuseppina Muzzarelli described how the Friars Minor opened a new branch:

> At the request of the city and with permission of his order's superiors, an Observant Franciscan preacher would arrive and begin a cycle of preaching. In the course of his sermons, the friar would propose the idea of a mount and suggest how to put words into action. Often he would bring with him a model statute to which the rules of the new mount were to conform. The preacher would then sponsor a great procession in the presence of the religious and civil authorities, and would participate in the procession himself, bearing the banner of the mount he helped to establish. The procession also served as the starting point for a fundraising campaign. The collection of funds took place in many ways, including charitable competitions between the city's guilds. Once the friar had collected the required amount of money, selected the location, defined the rules, and chosen the personnel for the new mount, the only thing left to do was to obtain a license from the civic authorities.[47]

Monti di Pietà join other cooperative financial institutions—including friendly societies, mutual aid, producer cooperatives, and microfinance—which have been advocated by Christians in recent decades (see chapter 6).[48]

Misericórdias

While new ideas and institutions were emerging, monastic care-giving enterprises continued to operate and innovate. Deacons and lay leaders kept endowed and funded operations whirring, while confraternities and lay volunteers supplemented care. In populated regions, some hospitals were consolidated and continued to be staffed by religious orders and laypersons.

---

46. Menning, *Charity and State*; Oeltjen, "Pawnbroking."

47. Muzzarelli, "Pawn Broking," 205.

48. Tracy, "Insurance and Theology."

Church-sponsored and laity-delivered health care continued to represent the majority of the medical care delivery system.[49]

The Portuguese *Misericórdias* became a modified model of Catholic care-giving in Europe and in Portuguese colonies. *Misericórdias* were established during a time of domestic peace. The influx of great wealth from overseas conquests and the Catholic Church's central role in Portuguese society enabled the new form to flourish. Established in 1498, the *Misericórdias* (which were lay confraternities) provided all fourteen works of mercy—the seven corporal works of mercy plus seven spiritual works: "instructing the ignorant, counselling those requiring it, admonishing those who err, comforting the afflicted, forgiving offences, suffering wrongs patiently, and praying for the living and the dead."[50] This innovation in compassion combined physical care and pastoral care that mostly focused on uprooting heresies. Because these were lay confraternities, they resulted in the continued "laicization," or secularization, of formerly clerically orchestrated functions.

POOR LAWS

With Protestant and some Catholic reformers suggesting an expanded role for the state in social welfare, one development during the early sixteenth century was the adoption of poor laws at the regional and municipal levels. Legal innovations reflected Enlightenment rationalization and economic growth, but also a Protestant emphasis on fulfilling one's calling and personal responsibility. Traced back to the Statute of Laborers of 1349–1351, their original intent was to deal with vagrancy, labor shortages, and wage inflation, but they also addressed the rights of the poor, restitution, and society's responsibilities toward those in need.[51] Family responsibilities remained, however. Adults were responsible for the well-being and behavior of their children and the sustenance of their parents.

Laws were passed in several locales to prohibit begging, including by mendicant monks in Protestant lands. Those who were legitimately poor could obtain a license to beg in select locales. The able-bodied were required to supplement the labor pool. Employers issued annual labor contracts to prevent day-laborers from pitting one employer against another and thus, creating wage inflation.[52] (Labor shortages remained from the Bubonic plague of 1347–1351, enabling workers to demand increasingly higher

49. Jones, "Perspectives on Poor Relief," 234–35.
50. Mendes Drumond Braga, "Poor Relief," 203.
51. Taliadoros, "Law, Theology, and Morality."
52. Arrizabalaga, "Poor Relief."

wages.) Workers were bound to abide by any employment contract offered. In England, laborers were jailed if they separated early from a contract unless they received the approval of two justices of the peace.[53]

To limit rural to urban migration (except at harvesttime), the Poor Relief Act of 1662 (the Act of Settlement) allowed justices of the peace to return newly arrived migrants to their birthplace if they had not found work in forty days. Until the law was relaxed three decades later, this resulted in thousands of people in poverty being shuttled around Britain annually.

Violation of poor laws could result in a person being jailed or whipped, or—for second offenses—having an ear severed. Included among those who were not to beg were "scholars from the Universities of Oxford and Cambridge" and fortunetellers. The law also prohibited giving shelter or money to able-bodied beggars, and it required "idle vagrants to be branded with the letter V, sent to the place of their birth and then compelled to labor as virtual slaves on bread and water for two years."[54]

To ensure accountability, those receiving aid in England were required to wear a letter "P" in red or blue cloth on their clothing.[55] William Quigley underscores the Calvinistic flavor of poor relief:

> Badging or stigmatizing the poor was a legislative reflection of common moral assumptions about the poor: poverty was the fault of the individual who was poor; if people remained poor it was because of their own bad decisions, laziness or drunkenness; poor people are sinful because they are squandering God-given opportunity; assisting the poor must be limited and punitive; and, therefore, relief of poverty must be very carefully restricted and monitored so it does not go to the wrong people.[56]

Dividing the deserving and the undeserving poor (those working and those unemployed) became commonplace, with categories such as the able-bodied, the idle poor, those prevented from work by age or health, and other groups. In England, unenviable destinations such as orphanages and workhouses were created to deal with vagrancy and homelessness. Taxes were gathered to provide for these institutions, rudimentary and even harsh as they were.

Poor laws prevented almsgiving to the able-bodied unemployed, to pressure them back into the workforce.[57] In some regions, Protestants pressed

---

53. Quigley, "Five Hundred Years," 96, 99.

54. Tierney, *Medieval Poor Law*, 50–51; Quigley, "Five Hundred Years," 94–95, 106.

55. Quigley, "Five Hundred Years," 103–8.

56. Quigley, "Five Hundred Years," 106.

57. Quigley, "Five Hundred Years," 87.

for laws that would place charitable institutions under a single administrator's direction so services could be specialized and avoid duplication.[58]

Mendicant orders resisted many of these poor laws, advocating a traditional approach with the right to beg and travel freely, and asserting personal rather than bureaucratic responses to relief.[59] In contrast, Protestant reformers pressed for social legislation that could standardize treatment of the poor and emphasize an individual's calling to work. Some Catholic reformers advocated for policies similar to those of the Protestants. With increasing pressure on separating the worthy poor from the unworthy, reformatory institutions in Spain taught work values and trade skills to prostitutes, orphans, and the able unemployed.[60]

This wave of legal changes was not as revolutionary as it may appear at first blush. Many laws were modified or only partially implemented or enforced. However, with the salvific potency of mendicancy and almsgiving removed, and the emphasis on fulfilling one's calling, begging and vagrancy were met with increased contempt in many Protestant regions. Christians continued to be exhorted to provide for the validly needy, but they placed more weight on stewarding funds responsibly, and they had more funds at their disposal to manage.

EXPLORATION

In the late fifteenth century, geographic discoveries and advances in shipbuilding fueled a race for commercial exploration and missionary outreach. Pope Gregory XV (1554–1623) founded the Congregation for the Evangelization of Peoples (originally, the Sacred Congregation for the Propagation of the Faith) in 1622, which pursued missions in non-Catholic countries in a proselytization race with Protestants.

Jesuits were active in the New World, but also in China and India, following their cofounder, Francis Xavier (1506–1552), who had been the first Christian missionary to reach Japan and Indonesia.[61] As the gospel was

58. Safley, *Reformation of Charity*.

59. Pullan, "Catholics, Protestants, and the Poor," 449–51.

60. Arrizabalaga, "Poor Relief."

61. Catholic missions began to slow in the late eighteenth century over papal concerns with Jesuits and the near-home distraction of Napoleon. Catholic missionary activities revived during the nineteenth century, paralleling the growth of Protestant missions, and produced several new missionary religious orders with a focus on the poor masses impoverished by industrialization. Orders were established to minister to the poor at home and abroad, such as the Marists and the Salesians of Don Bosco (Salesians), who cared for impoverished children during the Industrial Revolution. See

communicated in local languages, it took on local flavors as it conveyed the import of Christian doctrine, including charity.[62] Exploration exposed the leaven of power as well as charity in mission—and it did so for Protestants as well as Catholics.

Critical views would reach their peak in the twentieth century, but they existed at the time as well. One of the most memorable voices for justice was the Spanish explorer Bartolomé de las Casas (1484–1566).[63] Las Casas sailed to Hispaniola with his father. He became a Dominican friar and was the first priest ordained in the Americas. Yet, while in his twenties, he joined in slave raids and atrocities against "Indians." Complaints against him by Christopher Columbus's son led to his being relocated by the king of Spain to Cuba. There, he continued participating in oppressive acts, but his conscience was weighing heavily.

It is said that he reached a turning point when, at the age of twenty-nine, he was preparing for a sermon that included the text of Ecclesiasticus 34:21–26:

> If one sacrifices ill-gotten goods, the offering is blemished;
>> the gifts of the lawless are not acceptable.
> The Most High is not pleased with the offerings of the ungodly,
>> nor for a multitude of sacrifices does he forgive sins.
> Like one who kills a son before his father's eyes is the person
>> who offers a sacrifice from the property of the poor.
> The bread of the needy is the life of the poor;
>> whoever deprives them of it is a murderer.
> To take away a neighbor's living is to commit murder;
>> to deprive an employee of wages is to shed blood.

This passage struck his heart. Nations were becoming rich through the enslavement he supported, and las Casas could no longer abide it.

From this point forward, he turned his energies to defending native peoples. In Cuba and in Chiapas, Mexico, where las Casas briefly served as bishop, he withheld absolution and last rites from incalcitrant slaveholders. He wrote stinging missives and gave speeches to Pope Paul III and Charles V, the Holy Roman Emperor, appealing for the church to protect and defend native peoples, to evangelize in native languages, and to make restitution for

---

Endres, "American Crusade," 1–2.

62. As an example, see the Christian-inspired teachings in Wang Zheng's (1571–1644) *Benevolent Society Regulations* also reflect the high Confucian regard for benevolence. See Starr, *Chinese Theology*, 15–16.

63. Romero argues that las Casas begins a 500-year legacy of advocacy for justice in brown theology: *Brown Church*.

crimes and property.[64] Felipe Guamán Poma de Ayala (ca. 1535–ca. 1616) was a Quechua nobleman and Catholic who described and denounced colonial rule in an illustrated work of over eleven hundred pages. Unfortunately, *El primer nueva corónica y buen gobierno (The First New Chronicle and Good Government)* never reached King Philip III of Spain. Around the same time, Frs. Alonso de Sandoval (1576–1652) and Peter Claver (1580–1654) furthered the cause, working tirelessly to minister to enslaved Africans in today's Colombia, advocating for their rights as humans and as fellow Christians.[65] Around the same time, Martín de Porres (1579–1639), the son of a freed slave, healed physical and social wounds in Peru. He served humbly and compassionately, bearing the name today, the "Saint of the Broom."

GERMAN PIETISM

Back on the Continent, a movement gathered steam among Protestants encouraging a deeper commitment to the way of Christ. Starting in Germany and spreading through central and northern Europe, Lutherans were invited to a new birth in the faith. They studied the Scriptures and were inspired to live a moral life as they awaited the return of Christ. Philipp Jakob Spener (1635–1705), who influenced the founding of the University of Halle, and August H. Francke (1663–1727), who served on its faculty, were leaders in pietism. They taught that the Holy Spirit created a new person who, through baptism, was enlivened for priestly service: prepared for "faith working in love" (Gal 5:6).[66]

For Spener and Francke, poverty was a stain on the church. Its eradication was possible. Francke established more than two dozen institutions including an apothecary and an infirmary, and the renown Halle Orphan Home. He inspired a network of schools, called Francke Institutes, that provided religious instruction for thousands of children. He educated the poor, provided a bed for each child, and sheltered children in beautiful

---

64. As an alternative to native slavery, las Casas advocated importing African slaves and attracting Spanish peasants to migrate to the Indies to farm the land. Rivera-Pagán, "Political Praxis," 139.

65. In the future, others would continue advocating for the liberation of the enslaved, including Anne-Marie Javouhey (1779–1851) in French Guiana.

66. Clifton-Soderstrom, "Convergence Model of Pietist Ethics"; Kuenning, *Rise and Fall*, 13–17. A new birth in Christ did not mean that human volition was unnecessary. Pietists recognized that Christians could choose not to be compassionate. To that end, they taught on biblical passages such as the rich man and Lazarus (Lk 16:19–31) and James 2:13a: "For judgment will be without mercy to anyone who has shown no mercy": Waldenström, "Lord Jesus, Make us Merciful," 201.

architecture. Francke founded the first Bible society for translating and publishing the Bible and inspired many to follow his example of serving others as Christian joy.[67]

SUMMING UP

The Reformation generated an overflow of new ideas regarding compassion and social care. Given the diversity of thought and practice in various regions, it is easy to overlook the patterns forming in Christian compassion. Among the numerous tributaries of change and constancy, at least two significantly impact future eras.

The first change was that monastic orders and the institutional church were widely believed to have failed in their fiduciary responsibilities for the poor: they had diverted resources from and for the poor to institution-building. The people and civil society (confraternities and organizers of small-scale initiatives) believed that they could do better. Lords and other regional governors had a poor performance record as well but the ability of professional civil authorities to coordinate services and address large portions of society posed an alternative for civil oversight. In short, institutional actors other than the church were taking on a larger share of responsibility for care-giving.

A second change was that Protestant leaders altered care-giving by considering it the fruit rather than the seed of salvation. In the monastic era, individual responsibility for compassion had been accentuated. But now, as stewards of callings, secular work increased in meaning and import and individuals played a greater role in adjudicating when, how, and how much to share with others. The implication was clear and far reaching: do not do as the monastics do; work hard, live modestly, and expect the same of others; help each other when needed and deserved.[68] Anabaptists took a more collectivist view, but than many Protestants, but these values are

---

67. Yoder, *Pietism and the Sacraments*. Two individuals inspired by Spener and Francke were Hans Nielsen Hauge (1771–1824), who was imprisoned for nearly ten years for his faith and who brought literacy to Norway's peasants, and George Müller (1805–1898) who emigrated from Germany to England and established Ashley Down Orphanage. See Haukland, "Hans Nielsen Hauge"; Shaw, "This Way of Living." In the centuries to follow, Pietist influences cascaded into the Moravians, Wesleyans, and British evangelicalism, inspiring living faith in action.

68. Some argue that it was not the reformers who inculcated hard work, but the Cistercians. This is just one of several contests against Max Weber's famous thesis that the Reformation created an economic revolution in the Protestant work ethic; see Andersen et al., "Pre-Reformation Roots"; Becker et al., "Causes and Consequences."

present among them as well. This theological reinterpretation liberated some to freely and compassionately give, but it also increased judgment on those who were seen as derelict in executing their callings.

"By breaking the ancient bond between almsgiving and religious merit," writes historian Brian Pullen, "the reformers made it possible to reconsider poor relief as 'a civil obligation to the Christian commonwealth' that concentrated not on the hereafter but on the living poor and their social problems."[69] A second round of the Bubonic plague in 1575–1577 further advanced the state's coordinating role in addressing public health and welfare.[70]

Several of the themes we encountered in this chapter appeared in earlier eras: the state took a role in social care during the Byzantine Empire; modest living harkens back to the ascetics; in the early church, Christians aided one another; Ignatius reaffirms that joining the poor was not pleasant, but was transformational. We also see the irony of las Casas defending native populations but supporting African slave trade; Jesuit participation in education but also in the Inquisition and colonialization; Vincent's ministry to the incarcerated but his support of imprisoning non-Catholics; and Protestant strictures on the able poor. Catholics and Protestants of many varieties were now set on an increasingly divergent course in how they viewed and responded to human need.

---

69. Pullan, "Catholics, Protestants, and the Poor," 449.

70. Cohn, *Cultures of Plague.*

5

Salvation and Service

REFORM AND OTHER INFLUENCES prepared leaders of states, Christian denominations (several now existed), and commercial enterprises to fan out within countries and across the globe, responding to human need. The nineteenth century represented a blossoming—even a race—toward humanitarianism.

We begin with the missionary work of Catholics and Protestants before discussing the *diakonia* movement, Quaker reforms, Victorian charity, and the launch of global humanitarianism with the Red Cross. The Salvation Army and hundreds of church-led humanitarian and justice initiatives were founded during the nineteenth century. Modern hospitals were established and progressive Protestants carried the torch of the social gospel. Finally, scientific charity attempted clinically to separate the worthy from the unworthy poor. This rush of effort attempted to shine the light of Christ, albeit, at times, with paternal and colonial hues [**Paternalism, Colonialism, and Humanitarianism**].

Paternalism, Colonialism, and Humanitarianism

Generally, paternalism denotes usurping a person's choice in an effort to advance their wellbeing: "I know best and I'm doing this for your own good!" Paternalism is commonly viewed critically, asserting that the benefactor may not know what is best; rather, the recipient does. But paternalism can be a neutral descriptor. It can also be cultural and welcome.

In medieval societies, the church, monarchies, and land owners had responsibilities in governing. Property was viewed as sacred, giving landowners rights, and maintaining order was a quality and expectation of the divine. In the early nineteenth century, the church and local authorities discerned and directed much of society's needs. As the century progressed, benevolent individuals and organizations increasingly took the reins although their actions were salted by social Darwinism and laissez-faire economic thinking, both of which warned against excessive aid and promoted self-reliance, and to some degree, distanced benefactors from the needs of others.[1]

Similar to paternalism, colonialism carries strong negative overtones. Wolfgang Reinhard defines it as "one people's control over another people through the economic, political and ideological exploitation of a development gap between the two."[2] (We might add, *religious*, as well.) Colonialism—and its kindred term, *imperialism*—is often used to achieve political or economic ends but colonialism also can occur as templates of language and culture are pressed on others. Rather than excoriate missionaries, scholars increasingly depict them and indigenous people as engaged in two-way relationships where each influenced the other and accepted, integrated, resisted, and enacted cultural blending.[3] Nineteenth-century government intervention, on the other hand, typically had less sensitivity to local cultures and more self-interest as they attempted to extract resources and modernize the developing world.[4]

Humanitarianism can overlap with paternalism or colonialism, but it also can differ from both. Humanitarianism simply means being concerned about human welfare; desiring to help others and alleviate suffering. Generally today, it suggests being impartial in who is aided

---

1. Roberts, *Social Conscience*, 2; also, 44–71. Roberts identifies five notions that influenced nineteenth-century oversight and amended medieval paternalism: the sacredness of property; providential order; the economic idea of an invisible hand that benefits all; the morality of self-reliance; and voluntarism drawn from the wealthy and others.

2. Reinhard, *Short History of Colonialism*, 1.

3. Robert, "Introduction," 1–6.

4. Decker and McMahon, *Idea of Development*, 106–10. For Post-WWII development, see Grubbs, *Secular Missionaries*.

and respectful in how they are aided, but it too can occur without consulting the wishes or interests of the recipient.[5]

HUMANITARIAN MISSIONS

The eighteenth and nineteenth centuries represented a golden age of missions and service. Just as the printing press spread the Reformation, so the railway, telegraph, steamship, and eventually radio scattered the seeds of Christianity abroad.[6] Missionary societies were established in Britain to further the missions cause, including the Society for Promoting Christian Knowledge (SPCK), founded in 1698, and the London Missionary Society, launched in 1795. Mission societies burgeoned elsewhere too—the Netherlands Missionary Society (1797), the South African Mission Society (1799), the American Board of Commissioners for Foreign Mission (ABCFM) (1810), the Basel Mission (1835), and others.[7] Protestants were racing to catch up with Catholic mission excursion, which had an earlier start [The Sisters Arrive].

The Sisters Arrive

Catholic sisters were some of the earliest providers of organized compassion in the New World.[8] The first to be freed from monastery cloisters were French Ursulines. They built a convent in Quebec City, Quebec, in 1639, educated First Nation girls and boys and opened a hospital, Hôtel Dieu. For a century and a half, Catholics administered most of the institutionalized education, health care, and social services in Quebec.[9]

5. For a discussion of paternalism and humanitarianism, see Barrett, *Empire of Humanity*, 33–37.

6. Becker et al., "Causes and Consequences"; Clark and Ledger-Lomas, "Protestant International"; Rubin, "Printing and Protestants."

7. Cornick, *Letting God Be God*, 50.

8. Franciscans operated a school in today's St. Augustine, Florida around 1606.

9. Elson, "Short History of Voluntary." Throughout the world, Catholic religious orders flowered, serving in missions, teaching, health care, and other ministries with each following a charism and leaving a legacy.

In 1727, Ursuline sisters arrived in New Orleans.[10] They started schools and a hospital and catechized African Americans, enslaved and free.[11] This early effort was followed by many others, including the first U.S.-founded congregation of religious sisters, the Vincentian-inspired Sisters of Charity of St. Joseph, launched by Elizabeth Ann Seton (1774–1821) in Maryland in 1809. These sisters eventually would develop one of the largest Catholic health care systems in the U.S.[12] Henriette Delille (1813–1862) followed, founding the Sisters of the Holy Family in 1836. A descendant of slaves and of Creole descent, Delille and her sisters operated orphanages and schools, cared for the ill during yellow fever epidemics in New Orleans, and founded the first U.S. nursing home. Katharine Drexel (1858–1955) followed later, noteworthy for the many schools she and her Sisters of the Blessed Sacrament founded for native and African Americans.

Sisters in North America served the Catholic community in a number of ways: educating children, caring for victims of illness and epidemics, raising orphans, tending the wounded, easing the way of immigrants, and founding and operating hospitals and settlement houses. Although they served beyond the convent, their lives were generally quite regimented. Their hours of service cannot be numbered.

Protestant missions typically emphasized evangelism and schooling, but Protestant physicians joined up too, feeling called to treat the body as well as the soul in distant lands, imitating the Great Physician.[13] German Moravian missionary-surgeons were some of the earliest to serve, landing in Newfoundland and Labrador in the 1770s and providing medical care and medicinal treatments made from native plants.[14] English physician John Thomas (1757–1801) journeyed to India in 1783, John Scudder (1793–1855) served in Ceylon as the first medical missionary sponsored by the ABCFM, and American Peter Parker (1804–1888) traveled to China in

10. Other early schools included a Jesuit preparatory school in Newtown, Maryland in 1677 and a Franciscan school in New Orleans in 1727.

11. Most Catholic leaders at the time disliked but did not excoriate slavery.

12. For an introduction to Elizabeth Ann Seton, see McNeil, "Daughters of Charity"; Metz, "Sister Anthony O'Connell"; O'Donnell, "Many Customs and Manners."

13. Grundmann, "Christ as Physician." Jesus is seen the gospels as extending healing and deliverance more than financial aid. See Armitage, *Theories of Poverty*, 228.

14. Rollmann, *Labrador through Moravian Eyes*, 42.

1834. Parker introduced anesthesia to China and is sometimes called the father of medical missions.[15] Scores of other medical practitioners followed, including Albert Schweitzer (1875–1965), who was inspired to go to medical school after reading a French mission journal.[16]

Medical discoveries further encouraged practitioners to carry the latest developments to the new frontiers.[17] Frequently, tensions developed between the medical practitioners, driven to treat patients compassionately, and the mission society's desire for spiritual conversion. Medical work was dangerous, and many physicians and nurses died due to epidemics and the limited availability of medical care for themselves.[18] Still, clinics, hospitals, public health work, and medical training expanded.[19] While some have critiqued missionary work as entangled with colonial power and ethnocentrism, many of the British East India Company actively worked against missionaries whom they saw as dangerous to the colonial project.[20] Abundant examples exist of beloved missionaries who served compassionately from deep conviction: among them, John Woolman [**John Woolman**] and Fr. Damien of Molokai [**Fr. Damien of Molokai**].[21]

John Woolman

A Quaker from New Jersey, John Woolman (1720–1752) was known for his deep empathy for others and for his principled life. Woolman

15. Chesterman, *Service of Suffering*, 15.

16. Schweitzer, *Out of My Life*, 85.

17. Adventists had a largely distinctive take on medical missions, incorporating a "gospel of health" in their missionary teaching. Nutrition, exercise, and temperance were included in church teachings and provided a path to additional instruction. Founder Ellen G. White wrote extensively on the subject, publishing *Counsels on Health and Instructions to Medical Missionary Workers*, *The Ministry of Healing*, and *Medical Ministry*, and calling "every member of the church to take hold of medical missions." See White, *Call to Medical Evangelism*, 10. The Latter-day Saint Word of Wisdom represented an evolving practice of abstinence from alcohol, tobacco, tea, and coffee, but it was more a message for Saints than sinners. See Peterson and Walker, "Brigham Young's Word of Wisdom."

18. Risk in medical missions continued to be witnessed over time, such as in Bridges, *Moganga Paul*, and other accounts.

19. For a history of medical missions beyond the eighteenth century, see Browne et al., *Heralds of Health*; Grundmann, *Sent to Heal!*

20. Frey and Wood, *Come Shouting to Zion*; Potts, *British Baptist Missionaries in India*.

21. For a critique, see Clossey, *Salvation and Globalization*, 120.

apprenticed as a merchant but decided that a busy lifestyle focused on material gain represented a temporal and material imbalance that would distract him from a quiet and simple life focused on God. He chose tailoring (and a few other occupations) and allowed the light of Christ to influence his vocation. Woolman discouraged poor customers from purchasing beyond their means and he avoided tailoring luxuries.

While in his twenties, he began traveling as an unpaid itinerant minister and missionary, making thirty excursions in New England and the Carolinas within a decade. Woolman was disturbed by slavery long before abolitionist sentiment caught fire. He attempted to separate himself as much as possible from benefitting from slavery. When he stayed with Quaker slaveholders in the Carolinas, he insisted on paying for his lodging rather than accepting their hospitality. He avoided eating sugar or molasses (as did others) because they were grown and harvested with slave labor in the West Indies. He befriended native Americans to preempt conflict. He refused to pay war taxes.

On a voyage to England, Woolman sailed in steerage so as to share the life of sailors. He walked long distances rather than accept rides in stagecoaches to put himself on the level of slaves and avoid contributing to the misery of post-boys who drove stagecoach teams. Describing Woolman, David Shi writes that

> The consistency and the humility with which Woolman lived his simple life were a source of enormous inspiration to those around him. He did not have the vehemence of an agitator, but rather moved among men as an embodied conscience, demonstrating that religion was something to be lived as well as felt.[22]

Fr. Damien of Molokai

Native Hawaiians were subject to various contagious diseases brought to the islands by traders. One of these diseases was leprosy (Hansen's Disease). Viewed as incurable and contagious, and exuding an unbearable stench, individuals with leprosy were identified and transferred to the isolated island of Molokai, never to return to family or society. Belgian/Flemish missionary priest, Fr. Damien De Veuster

---

22. Shi, *Simple Life*, 47. Also see Moulton, "John Woolman"; Moulton, *Journal and Major Essays*.

(1840–1889), was assigned as pastor to the Molokai colony in 1873. Damien cared for 500 residents, daily attending the sick and burying deceased children and adults.

Living with a death sentence, many succumbed to fatalism, neglected self-care and abused alcohol and drugs. Damien chided parishioners, sometimes in anger, but attempted to restore dignity by encouraging the formation of musical bands, making regular rounds visiting and teaching residents, and caring for the dying. Damien improved conditions for the living by constructing adequate shelter, improving the water supply, and arranging for clothing to be delivered.

Toward the end of his sixteen years in the settlement, in 1888, Damien contracted the disease himself. According to tradition, he announced this by adjusting his weekly homily opening statement slightly from "You lepers know that God loves you" to "We lepers know that God loves us."[23]

Some Protestant missionaries advanced the dual interests of "Christianizing" and "civilizing." According to Jonathan Barnes, "Because of the Enlightenment and the idea of progress, many Global Christians believed that social transformation was part of their Christian duty. However . . . this also involved an inherent paternalism as they sought to remake them, 'the other,' in their image."[24] But others, such as William Carey, resisted imprinting a British stamp on others.[25] Whether civilizing or not, many missionaries, abolitionists, and reformers of prisons, schools, and public sanitation attempted to relieve human suffering and advance the human race.[26]

The writings of Presbyterian missionary James Dennis (1842–1914) illustrate the ethical challenge these missionaries faced. In his book *Christian Missions and Social Progress* (1897), Dennis acknowledged that "good sense and prudence should restrain any unnecessary invasion of society with demands for changes which are merely concessions to foreign tastes, uncalled for by the requirements of moral principle."[27] Dennis catalogued mission-

23. Volder, *Spirit of Father Damien.*

24. Barnes, *Power and Partnership,* 44. Over time, missionary societies shifted the weight distributed between these two goals.

25. Potts, *British Baptist Missionaries in India*; Stanley, "Christian Missions and the Enlightenment."

26. Calhoun, "Imperative to Reduce Suffering," 77–78.

27. Dennis, *Christian Missions and Social Progress,* 8.

ary initiatives in the late nineteenth century. These illustrate the challenge of discerning between "unnecessary invasion" and Christian compassion. Missionary initiatives included:

> temperance reform . . . deliverance from the opium habit . . . restraint upon gambling . . . higher standards of personal purity . . . discrediting self-inflicted torture or mutilation . . . arresting pessimistic and suicidal tendencies . . . cultivating habits of industry and frugality . . . substituting Christian humility and proper self-respect for barbaric pride in foolish conceit . . . the elevation of women . . . restraining polygamy . . . checking adultery and divorce . . . the abolishment of child marriage . . . alleviating the social miseries of widowhood . . . mitigating the enforced seclusion of women . . . improving the condition of domestic life and family training . . . rendering aid and protection to children . . . diminishing infanticide . . . hastening the suppression of slave trade and labor traffic . . . aiding in the overthrow of slavery . . . abolishing cannibalism and inhuman sports . . . arresting human sacrifices . . . initiating the crusade against foot binding . . . prison reform and mitigating brutal punishments . . . famine relief . . . modern medical science . . . conducting dispensaries, infirmaries, and hospitals . . . founding leper asylums and colonies . . . establishing orphan asylums . . . promoting cleanliness and sanitation . . . mitigating the brutalities of war . . . and instilling a peaceable and law-abiding spirit.

Missionary performance on these fronts is certainly open to critique.[28] Despite criticisms, positive impacts on health care, literacy, and gender attitudes still can be detected.[29]

ACTIVISM

Several eighteenth- and nineteenth-century movements reflected what David Bebbington calls, *activism*: the sense that one is duty-bound to work

---

28. For the intriguing history of nineteenth-century Christian mission, see Barnes, *Power and Partnership*; Bevans and Schroeder, *Constants in Context*, 206–80; Robert, *Christian Mission*, 53–113.

29. Research links historic mission efforts and positive outcomes: Calvi et al., "Protestant Legacy"; Calvi and Mantovanelli, "Long-term Effects"; Castelló-Climent et al., "Higher Education." We can also see the enduring influences of individuals such as William Carey (1761–1834), David Livingstone (1813–1873), Hudson Taylor (1832–1905), Charles Stewart Thompson (1851–1900), C. F. Andrews (1871–1940), and countless others.

for the Lord in response to God's work of salvation and presence [**Reform of the Heart**].[30] After picking up the story of deaf education, we will consider several movements and institutions including the Lutheran *diakonia* movement, Quaker reformers, and Victorian mobilization along with some notable institutions.

Reform of the Heart

John Wesley (1703-1791) was an early influence in evangelical activism. Numbered among his contributions was his economic ethic for the everyday Christian.[31] Randy Maddox describes Wesley's ethic as characterized by four points:

1. Ultimately, everything belongs to God.

2. Resources are placed in our care to use as God sees fit.

3. God desires that we use these resources to meet our necessities . . . and then to help others in need.

4. Spending resources on luxuries for ourselves while others remain in need is robbing God![32]

Wesley viewed spiritual formation and works of mercy as intertwined. He warned that accumulating wealth rather than sharing it would retard spiritual growth. Caring, on the other hand, shaped the one extending aid perhaps more than the one receiving it. He taught a holistic, integral view of spiritual and physical salvation and advocated for subsidized boarding schools for children of the poor, free health clinics, and inexpensive medical remedies in his *Primitive Physick*. For Wesley, compassion was the fruit of the love of God and the duty of disciples.

---

30. In *Evangelicalism in Modern Britain* (pp. 2–3), Bebbington identifies *activism* as one of four defining characteristics that emerged from the Second Great Awakening and broadly influenced Christianity in Britain, the continent, and elsewhere. The other three characteristics were *conversionism*, *biblicism*, and *crucicentrism*.

31. Jennings, *Good News to the Poor*, 71–96.

32. Maddox, "Visit the Poor," 62; the remainder of this section draws heavily on Maddox's analysis.

Modern Deaf Education

Picking up the efforts of Spanish deaf educators in the seventeenth century, Charles Michael de l'Epée (1712–1789), a Parisian deacon, was moved to teach two deaf siblings the gospel. Knowing nothing about deaf education, he experimented and learned from the work of Juan Pablo Bonet (chapter 4). De l'Epée authored instruction manuals and a dictionary useful to teaching the deaf. In 1755, he founded and operated the world's first public school for deaf children. Upon his death, the school was renamed The French National Institute for the Deaf.[33]

In North America, the young minister, Thomas Hopkins Gallaudet (1787–1851), met a deaf girl and determined to bring deaf education to the United States. (Previously, deaf children of means, traveled to Europe to be educated.) Gallaudet traveled to Europe to learn more and was received warmly by the National Institute for the Deaf in Paris where he received several months of instruction.

Gallaudet returned to the United States and with the aid of Laurent Clerc (1785–1869), established a school for the deaf in Connecticut in 1817. Eventually, the school attracted students from across the United States and was renamed the American School for the Education of the Deaf and Dumb. Among many other contributions, the American School developed and popularized American Sign Language.

Thomas's son, Edward Miner Gallaudet, took up leadership of the Columbia Institute for the Deaf and Dumb and Blind in Washington, DC. Under the young Gallaudet's leadership, the school was granted permission to offer collegiate education in 1864. It was renamed Gallaudet College in 1894.[34]

---

33. Daniels, *Benedictine Roots*, 29–39.

34. Daniels, *Benedictine Roots*, 65–95. Dozens of deaf schools were established by Christian leaders and missionaries across multiple countries. Established near Detroit, Michigan in 1874, the Evangelical Lutheran Institute for the Deaf utilized an oral method of instruction and inspired multiple missionaries and educators. In time, schools and programs for children with a variety of disabilities were founded. One example is Elim, a Chicago school for children with disabilities, founded in Chicago in 1948 by members of the Reformed Church in America. See Swierenga, *Elim*.

The *Diakonia* Movement

The *diakonia* movement was a primarily Lutheran, lay-led effort in central and northern Europe offering care to those in need. It traces its origins to a desire to care for children orphaned in the Napoleonic wars. *Diakonia* (from which we get *deacon*) is a Greek word meaning "servant" or "service." As an expression of Christian activism, Johannes Falk (1768–1826) of Weimar, Germany, and his wife, Caroline, took thirty orphans into their house and started a "Sunday school" consisting of vocational training programs. Similarly, Adalbert von der Recke-Volmerstein (1791–1878) and his wife, Countess Mathilde, added forty-four orphaned children to their own, housing the family in a Trappist abbey they purchased. To feed and train the children, Recke-Volmerstein added a farm along with vocational training in printing and bookbinding, shoemaking, tailoring, carpentry, blacksmithing, locksmithing, baking, milling, farming, and livestock husbandry.[35]

Johann Hinrich Wichern (1808–1881) added a communal dimension to the movement. Wichern focused on young men in poverty, inviting them into a fellowship of brothers who served the poor and aiding them in shunning "sin and destruction." Wichern focused on the "inner mission" and limited the number of youth he could mentor to an apostolic twelve.[36] Also reminiscent of lay communities from the past, Amalie Sieveking (1794–1859) of Hamburg, Germany, founded a benevolent society of a dozen women who worked in the schools, poorhouses, and hospital, which she also founded.[37]

Through the nineteenth century, the *diakonia* movement spread to the Nordic countries, primarily within Lutheran, Reformed, and Methodist churches and agencies. Trained deacons and deaconesses taught and delivered medical and social work services and served prisoners, the sick, and those disenfranchised by industrialization and social change. Health care and social service training occurred in special *diakonia* institutions that were sometimes attached to universities and at other times were freestanding. Over time, increasing numbers of graduates went to work in governmental agencies. Rifts occurred in the movement between those who leaned into more liberal theology and those (such as Wichern) who emphasized individual conversion and spirituality as the focus of social service and reform.[38]

35. Hauff, *Frauen Gestalten Diakonie.*

36. Nordstokke, "Study of Diakonia," 50.

37. Lutheran minister Theodor Fliedner (1800–1864) was another pioneer in Germany around 1830, as was Johann Konrad Wilhelm Löhe, (1808–1872) who founded a Lutheran school for girls in Neuendettelsau in 1850 and is sometimes credited with founding the *diakonia* movement.

38. Nordstokke, "Study of Diakonia," 51. In the early twenty-first century, the World

Quaker Reformers

A second activist effort occurred within the Religious Society of Friends, or Quakers. Believing God indwells all—"that of God in everyone," as George Fox put it—and perhaps feeling tension with their own worldly success, Quakers in England (and later in the United States) actively advocated for social reforms as evangelicalism spread through Britain. William Allen (1770–1843), an English pharmacist and pharmacologist helped lead several reform efforts including supporting the Society for the Abolition of the Slave Trade and promoting the African Institution which worked to recolonize freed slaves in Sierra Leone. He founded the Society for Diffusing Information on the Death Penalty in 1808 and established a Soup Society in the east London district of Spitalfields where he attempted to create self-sufficient colonies of people growing nutritious food. Allen gathered research on how best to grow nutritious foods and he promoted colonies of self-sustaining micro-farms for the poor as an alternative to migrating to the Americas.

Allen and his fellow Quaker, Elizabeth Fry (1780–1845), regularly visited London's Newgate Prison. Appalled by the conditions and treatment, Fry preached to the inmates and advocated for reform. Londoners flocked to hear her preach and see its effects on prisoners. Rather than incarceration focusing on punishment, Allen and Fry advocated rehabilitation achieved through kindness, silence, order, and friendships, mostly orchestrated by volunteers.[39]

The Quaker-led Society for the Improvement of Prison Discipline (1816) focused on architectural and bureaucratic reforms and it ultimately eclipsed some of softer elements advocated by Allen and Fry.[40] Fry continued her activism by founding a nursing school that contributed to English nursing reform, established savings societies for the poor, and set up libraries for the coastguard; considerable efforts, despite being plagued by dyslexia, ill health, possible alcoholism, and family bankruptcy during her life.[41]

Federation of Diaconal Associations and Communities reported that the formal *diakonia* movement was in decline. Training and research institutions continued, however, including the Diakoniewissenschaftliches Institut at the University of Heidelberg. For a modern view of *diakonia* see Church of Sweden, *Bishops' Letter*.

39. In the United States, Frances Joseph-Gaudet (1861–1934) was a notable activist with the Prison Reform Association. She boldly and sacrificially advocated for young African Americans.

40. McGowen, "Well-Ordered Prison," 95–97.

41. Huntsman et al., "Twixt Candle and Lamp."

Fig 5.1. Elizabeth Fry entering a prison.

Another social institution that attracted reform by Friends was the mental asylum. William Tuke (1732–1822) founded the York Retreat in England in 1792 as an alternative approach to traditional psychiatric care. Families generally cared for relatives with mental illnesses as long as they could but the mentally ill also could be found in British workhouses and poorhouses and in hospitals and asylums. In contrast to bleeding, emetics, fear tactics, and chains, a "moral approach" to therapy emphasized order, charity, self-restraint, and conversation.[42]

Revolutionizing institutionalized mental health in the United States was Quaker Thomas S. Kirkbride (1809–1883), a physician and founder of the American Psychiatric Association. Kirkbride is remembered for the "Kirkbride Plan," an architectural design for asylums that specified large, cheerful structures filled with light and ventilation and located in bucolic settings. Constraints were minimized. Kindness, labor, and entertainment were prescribed.

Victorian Mobilization

A third movement stirred by activism was the Victorian era (1837–1901), a period of intense humanitarian mobilization. Victorian Anglicans, Christians in free church traditions, and independent Christians such as Josephine Butler (1828–1906) felt compelled to be benevolent toward their

42. Grob, *Mad Among Us*, 26–27.

neighbor, seeing poverty abound while the nation's wealth and power were increasing.[43] For most, charity was a matter of paternalism and self-help.

Through a plethora of voluntary organizations, Christians organized and provided a broad array of social services. London was the epicenter of organizing societies and fraternities that targeted a variety of social and spiritual needs. According to Frank Proshanka,

> In the mid-Victorian years most communities would have boasted various schools for the poor, visiting societies, working parties, mothers' meetings, and temperance societies, which met in homes, churches, or chapels, or in mission rooms rented for the occasion. Soup kitchens, maternity charities, crèches, blanket clubs, coal clubs, clothing clubs, boot clubs, medical clubs, lending libraries, and holiday funds expanded the expression of Christian service. . . . Meanwhile, innumerable penny banks, savings banks, Provident clubs, goose clubs, slate clubs, and pension societies, often attached to city missions, mothers' meetings, and other charities, reflected the Victorian obsession with thrift and mutual aid. They were part of the makeshift economy in poor neighbourhoods, where strategies for survival were all too often touched by desperation.[44]

Individuals and churches set up societies to reform slaves, chimney sweeps, slums, and education. Women mobilized into Dorcas Societies to sew clothing for the poor, and formed mothers's meetings to teach sewing and parenting skills.[45] Female attendees made a nominal payment for materials and practiced sewing while readers regaled them with wholesome instruction and literature. Up to a million women attended these gatherings in the nineteenth century. Some attendees bristled at the paternalistic approach leaders often took. One attendee commented,

> I . . . attended Mother's Meetings, where ladies came and lectured on the domestic affairs in the workers' homes that it was impossible for them to understand. I have boiled over many times at some of the things I have been obliged to listen to, without the chance of asking a question.[46]

In addition to voluntary organizations, owners of commercial organizations took up a call to bring justice and aid others as well. Industrialists

---

43. For a history of free church initiatives, see Husselbee and Ballard, *Free Churches and Society.*

44. Prochaska, *Christianity and Social Service,* 19.

45. Richmond, *Clothing the Poor,* 215.

46. Richmond, *Clothing the Poor,* 219.

such as Titus Salt (1803–1876) and W. H. Lever (1851–1925) envisioned and built model villages in England, devoting considerable sums to paternalistic social experiments in Saltaire and Port Sunlight.

Despite these abundant and valiant efforts, poverty persisted for several reasons; one, being the paternalistic governance that often misdiagnosed poverty's cause and cure as rooted in personal failing. Organizations also represented a diverse, cottage industry of social care, duplicating efforts and leaving other needs unmet. Efforts were made to enhance social care methods and improve coordination so charity could continue complementing governmental services supported by poor laws.

Charity was viewed as uniquely capable of remediating need caused by moral lapses.[47] Some recognized failings in the approach, however. Anglican historian Arnold Toynbee confessed in his last public lecture in 1884:

> We—the middle classes, I mean, not merely the very rich—
> we have neglected you; instead of justice we have offered you
> charity, and instead of sympathy, we have offered you hard and
> unreal advice; but I think we are changing. If you would only
> believe it and trust us, I think that many of us would spend our
> lives in your service.[48]

Toynbee encouraged spiritual growth to accompany material flourishing:

> We will ask you to remember this—that we work for you in the
> hope and trust that if you get material civilization, if you get a
> better life, if you have opened up to you the possibility of a better
> life, you will really lead a better life. If, that is, you get material
> civilization, remember that it is not an end in itself. Remember
> that man [sic], like trees and plants, has his roots in the earth;
> but like the trees and plants, he must grow upwards towards the
> heavens. If you will only keep to the love of your fellow-men and
> to great ideals, then we shall find our happiness in helping you,
> but if you do not, then our reparation will be in vain.[49]

---

47. The welfare state of postwar Britain remained a long way off and would have been considered anathema by many who actively distinguished between the "deserving and undeserving poor" and encouraged people toward self-reliance, rather than dependence on government. Fraser, *Evolution of the British Welfare State*, 155–59.

48. Toynbee, *"Progress and Poverty,"* 53.

49. Toynbee's aspirational yet unfulfilled words were: "And last of all, you must remember that if you will join hands us with, we do intend that we shall as a nation accomplish great things, and seek to redeem what is evil in our past. We shall try to rule India justly. We shall try to obtain forgiveness from Ireland. We shall try to prevent subject races being oppressed by our commerce, and we shall try to spread to every clime the love of man" (Toynbee, *"Progress and Poverty,"* 54).

Confidence in a bootstrap approach to poverty alleviation was challenged by an economic depression that began in the 1870s and lasted until near the turn of the century. Many who had enjoyed wealth were now impoverished through no fault of their own. As a new century approached, first-hand witnesses to poverty began breaking down walls as well.[50]

The Red Cross

While voluntarism was flourishing in Britain, emergency response was about to take root on the continent. In June 1859, Swiss businessman Henry Dunant (1828–1920) was traveling south when he came across a fresh battlefield in Solferino, Italy. The fighting between France and Austria had barely ended, and the scene was horrendous. In total, 3 field marshals, 9 generals, 1,566 officers, and 40,000 noncommissioned officers had been killed. An additional 40,000 deaths would occur over the next two weeks as the wounded died.

From the battlefield, 1,000 wounded arrived nightly in Milan. The city was not prepared but people and institutions mobilized as best as they could. Makeshift field hospitals were set up. Businesspeople, merchants, women, and religious volunteered as nurses, mailing letters home and providing water, food, medical care, transport, burial, clothing, and tobacco. Supplies ran short and soldiers of different languages did not always trust the medical care being provided.[51]

Dunant wrote down a record of the battle as he imagined it, along with the care that he and others provided. He called for societies to spring up to care for the wounded in times of war or natural disaster. His book, *Un Souvenir de Solferino* (*A Memory of Solferino*), took Europe by storm and led to the founding of the International Committee of the Red Cross. Dunant was also instrumental in the writing of the Geneva Convention to include protections for medical personnel.[52] For inspiring the Red Cross, Dunant

---

50. These diverse contributions included settlement houses, social gospelers, Charles Booth's (not to be confused with William Booth of the Salvation Army) seventeen-volume survey—complete with maps—documenting London's 35 percent poverty rate and titled *Inquiry into Life and Labour of the People of London* (1903), plus others.

51. Dunant, of course, was not the first to treat the wounded in battle. St. Camillus de Lellis (1550–1614) generally is credited with organizing a military field ambulance and hospital more than two hundred years earlier, in 1595.

52. Dunant's attention to humanitarian needs led to his neglecting his business interests. He soon went bankrupt, defaulting on the loans friends had made to his business. Pained by this loss, Dunant disappeared as a pauper on the streets of Paris. After fifteen years on the streets, he was discovered by a Swiss teacher and his family, who

was awarded the first Nobel Peace Prize, in 1901. Many tag the beginning of modern humanitarianism to the Red Cross and Dunant's efforts.

The Salvation Army

Another institution of note launched during the nineteenth century was the Salvation Army. Leaving the Christian Methodist Episcopal Church after being sanctioned for holding revivals, William Booth (1865–1912) and his wife, Catherine (1829–1890), lived simply while William began preaching in a tent in east London. He emphasized social action, believing it would encourage personal sanctification.[53] In 1878, William founded the Salvation Army.

Fig 5.2. William Booth, Founder of the Salvation Army.

Early Salvationists advocated for and supported formerly trafficked women and girls; established soup kitchens, a missing persons bureau, and farm colonies (most of which struggled); and hired trash collectors, who removed refuse in exchange for food and shelter and resold usable items. Booth opened an immigration agency to assist men and women seeking

invited Dunant to live out his life with them.

53. Gariepy, *Christianity in Action*, 9.

a new life in Canada, Australia, New Zealand, and the United States. Salvationists established a match factory in 1891 that avoided using the commonly employed but dangerous phosphorus, which poisoned workers.[54]
Booth acknowledged the impact of social structures on poverty but stressed
internal agency and personal holiness. He emphasized self-reliance over
charity and, when possible, prevention over rescue.

Booth placed the church and individual redemption at the heart of his
efforts, as did others before and after him [Thomas Chalmers].

Thomas Chalmers

Church of Scotland minister and economist Thomas Chalmers (1780–
1847) is remembered in part for placing the church at the heart of
social reform. He argued that mandatory tithes and taxes should be
commuted so people could more effectively direct their funds where
they wished. Instead of aid flowing from the rich to the poor, the poor
should be equipped to help themselves through moral formation and
education. Chalmers argued that: "An educated peasant, familiarized
to his Bible, and observing a close and weekly attendance on the weekly instructions of his minister [will yield] a fineness of moral com-
plexion which would be revolted by the humiliations of pauperism."[55]

In Chalmers's view, the minister was responsible to provide moral instruction and mentoring, and this would be sufficient to rectify
pauperism. In cities where populations were too large for a minister
to manage and mentor, a collection could be taken up for churches to
be planted. Given an adequate number of small parishes, parishioners
could be mentored. Chalmers dealt differently with illness and old age,
however:

> Open a door of admission for the indigent, and we shall behold
> a crowd of applicants increasing every year, because lured hith-
> erward by the inviting path of indolence or dissipation. Open a
> door for the admission of the diseased, and we shall only have a
> definite number of applicants. Men will become voluntarily poor,
> but they will not become voluntarily blind or deaf, or maimed
> or lunatic. It is thus that while an asylum for want creates more
> objects than it can satisfy; an asylum for disease creates none,

---

54. Gariepy, *Christianity in Action*, 54–58.
55. Chalmers, *Political Economy*, 1:309–35, 400–420, 2:284.

but may meet all and satisfy all. Public charity has been profuse where it ought not, and niggardly where it ought not.[56]

Years later, another economist, Edward Thomas Devine (1867–1948) of Columbia University, argued that churches were only part of the solution. Social institutions were necessary as well. Devine asks:

> How far may the church in the performance of its great spiritual mission in the world engage in the work of relieving distress? How far shall it devote its energies to the building of hospitals, the rescue of neglected and ill-treated children, the distribution of food to the hungry and clothing to the naked? And if these things are to be undertaken what mechanism for these purposes shall it devise and put into operation? . . . Shall we expect this church to supply their needs, or to aid in supplying them, or is the problem, in the individual case, to be regarded as an economic and secular problem which interests the community at large. . . ? . . . [H]ow far is the church a natural source of relief?[57]

The debate continues and differs in different settings. Echoes of Chalmers's and Devine's views are heard whenever personal responsibility are spiritual regeneration are asserted as paths to self-reliance.

CHRISTIAN SOCIALISM, SETTLEMENTS, AND THE INSTITUTIONAL CHURCH MOVEMENT

On the political, intellectual front, Anglican critics, such as F. D. Maurice, advocated for a more humane, Christian approach to political economy than either capitalism or Marxism offered. Maurice and his students and friends appealed for a society and economy based on cooperation rather than competition, and for unity instead of division. Their ideas faced head-winds, but they inspired passionate followers.[58]

Their efforts were not all speculative. Christian socialists inspired the founding of the Christian Social Union in 1889; a movement that spread through British cities, assembling members dedicated to applying gospel

---

56. Chalmers, *Political Economy*, 1:419.

57. Devine, *Practice of Charity*, 84–85.

58. For a sampling of Christian socialist ideas, see Norman, *Victorian Christian Socialists*.

teachings to social conditions, paralleling the social gospel in the United States. More lasting perhaps were the efforts of a handful of students inspired by Maurice's lectures and writings who determined to move into the working-class East End of London to establish an outpost of education and culture. A "settlement house," as it was called, was envisioned as a training ground for ministers and reformers and an opportunity for the well-to-do and the poor to form relationships and join in mutual learning.[59]

Samuel Barnett (1844–1913), an Anglican clergyman, established the first settlement house in the East End around 1884. Named "Toynbee House" in honor of the recently deceased Arnold Toynbee, Barnett and his wife welcomed Oxbridge and other university students to live together and offer a type of university extension program with courses, discussions, and lectures in languages, the arts, sciences, and skills such as bookkeeping and swimming. According to Gertrude Himmelfarb,

> It was Barnett's intention that the young men living among the poor would become better acquainted with them, move more easily among them, understand and sympathize with them, and serve them in whatever way they could—but not that they would live the life of the poor or lose themselves in the service of the poor. They were not to be latter-day St. Francises. On the contrary, they were to show the poor the possibility of a more elevated, more gracious, more fulfilling life, a life that the poor could not hope to emulate but that could, by its example, enrich and enlarge them.[60]

Jane Addams (1860–1935) and Ellen Gates Starr (1859–1940) are credited with bringing the settlement house movement to the United States after visiting Toynbee Hall in 1888. They returned to Chicago and launched Hull House in 1889. Subsequently, settlement houses were established near Amherst College, Andover Theological Seminary, Union Theological Seminary, and in other locales during the late nineteenth and early twentieth century, numbering over 400 by 1910.[61] College settlement houses sponsored lectures and hosted art exhibits, musical concerts, daycare, kindergartens, mother's clubs, and English classes rather than focusing on charity

---

59. Davis, *Spearheads for Reform*, 6–7, 13.

60. Himmelfarb, *Poverty and Compassion*, 240.

61. Davis, *Spearheads for Reform*; McGerr, *Fierce Discontent*, 100. The settlement house movement was spurred on by Vida Dutton Scudder (1861–1954) who co-founded and led the College Settlements Association (CSA). In the 1930s, Fr. Paul Hanly Furfey (1896–1992) used a settlement house approach with Catholic University of America students to launch a social reform journey of university and community engagement. See Rademacher, *Paul Hanly Furfey*.

work. Although some were not explicitly religious, settlement houses had Christian origins and a clear civic mission. Some were sponsored by Christian congregations, particularly Anglican, Congregationalist, Presbyterian, and Methodist churches.[62]

In addition to sponsoring settlements, Protestant churches also opened their facilities to neighborhoods and organized a variety of programs. This so-called "institutional church movement" began in New York City and was an alternative to congregations dying or escaping urban blight. Social gospeler Josiah Strong explains:

> The institutional church . . . adapts itself to changed conditions. It finds that the people living around it have no opportunity to take a bath; it therefore furnishes bathing facilities. It sees that the people have little or no healthful social life; it accordingly opens attractive social rooms, and organizes clubs for men, women, boys, and girls. The people know little of legitimate amusement; the church therefore provides it. They are ignorant of household economy; the church establishes its cooking-schools, its sewing-classes, and the like. In their homes the people have few books and papers; in the church they find a free reading-room and library. The homes afford no opportunity for intellectual cultivation; the church opens evening schools and provides lecture courses.[63]

Settlements and the institutional church movement constituted a critique of charity as they attempted to remedy a structural cause of poverty (i.e., a lack of education) rather than merely providing alms. They also focused on the working class rather than the abject poor.[64] The median age of settlement workers was twenty-five. Most were single, and nearly all had attended college.[65] Settlement workers campaigned against child labor; developed playgrounds, parks, and gyms; encouraged industrial education and hands-on skills; advocated for school nurses and lunchrooms, housing reform, city planning, recreation centers, and clubhouses; preserved

---

62. Himmelfarb, *Poverty and Compassion*, 237. Settlement house participants shared ideas at national conferences and formed the National Federation of Settlements in 1911 to promote and improve settlement efforts. Over time, they expanded into local community development poverty awareness and advocacy. The settlement movement faced challenges and declined after World War I, but the federation continued operating, was renamed the United Neighborhood Centers of America, and today is the Alliance for Strong Families and Communities.

63. Strong, *Religious Movements*, 46–47.

64. Davis, *Spearheads for Reform*, 18.

65. Davis, *Spearheads for Reform*, 33.

immigrant customs by encouraging pageants, folk festivals, and handicrafts exhibits; promoted communication between labor and management; and defended organized labor. Many participants appreciated and affirmed the settlement house and institutional church movements. Less evident overall, however, was whether either yielded significant structural change in community poverty or justice.

HEALTHCARE

The tragic demands of the U.S. Civil War required advancements in health care logistics and facilities. Around the same time, discoveries of germ theory, anesthesia, and a host of other medical discoveries helped usher in modern, Western medicine. Heath care became increasingly professionalized. Physician licensure laws were passed in 1873 and medical education became more refined, beginning with the establishment of research-based medical schools such as the Johns Hopkins School of Medicine, financed in 1893 from the estate of Quaker businessman and philanthropist, Johns Hopkins (1795–1873). Anesthesia, antiseptics, X-rays, and vaccines came into widespread use. Nursing rose in prominence as well, quickened by the notoriety of Florence Nightingale (1820–1910) who cast an image of a calm and competent, spiritually focused caregiver.[66]

Although Catholics were a minority in most parts of the United States (in 1850, only 5 percent of the U.S. population was Catholic, compared with a Protestant population of 30 percent),[67] Catholic sisters had been active in caring for the poor and sick in North America for over a century.[68] Suspicions swirled around Catholics, however, whose loyalty to a hierarchy in Rome seemed discordant with American democracy. Rumors and conspiracy theories spread about convents kidnapping girls, Catholic nurses brainwashing patients, child abuse in Catholic orphanages, and "Romanist" plots to overthrow the U.S.[69]

Catholic (as well as Jewish and African American) doctors often had difficulty gaining staff privileges at elite private hospitals, and Catholic patients feared they might not be allowed last rites or would be pressed

---

66. Levin, "Bold Vision."

67. Finke and Stark, "Turning Pews into People," 189–90.

68. The service of Catholic sisters in the Civil War is memorialized in the Nuns of the Battlefield monument, located in Washington, DC. It memorializes more than six hundred nuns who provided medical care to northern and southern soldiers.

69. McGuinness, *Called to Serve*; Nordstrom, *Danger on the Doorstep*.

to convert to Protestantism in a moment of weakness.[70] This turned most Catholic compassion toward the millions of Irish, Polish, German, Italian, and other Catholic immigrants arriving on eastern shores and settling across northern states and provinces.

Religious women (especially the Irish) established hospitals to ensure adequate care and protect the faith and ethnic identity of Catholics. Catherine McAuley (1778–1841) founded the Sisters of Mercy and established dozens of hospitals in the United States, primarily serving the poor.[71] Frances Xavier Cabrini (1850–1917) continued extending Christian charity by establishing over sixty health, educational, and other institutions, many of which served Italian immigrants and children. "By 1885," Charles Rosenberg writes, "the Catholic community had opened 154 hospitals throughout the United States, more than had existed in the United States *in toto* in the late 1860s."[72] By 1930, over 600 Catholic hospitals existed in the United States.[73]

Protestants did their part as well, founding hospitals to respond to the needs of a growing population. Caught up in the excitement of modern medicine, they were inspired by past servants from their traditions and propelled by a social gospel vision of the future. Most early Protestant hospitals were founded by denominations that had experience in institutional care and access to funding. Lutherans, Episcopalians, and Presbyterians established many early institutions.

In 1849, Lutheran pastor William Passavant (1821–1894) established the Pittsburgh Infirmary, the first Protestant hospital in the United States, after visiting the Lutheran *diakonia* motherhouse in Kaiserswerth, Germany. The infirmary included housing for orphans as well as the ill and was designed as a training hub for deaconesses throughout North America.[74] Although the *diakonia* movement developed gradually in North America, deaconesses eventually served in German and Norwegian Lutheran hospitals in Philadelphia, Brooklyn, Minneapolis, Chicago, Saint Paul, Omaha, and elsewhere.[75] Pietistic denominations, such as today's Evangelical

---

70. Starr, *Social Transformation of American Medicine*, 173.

71. Catholic nurses, such as St. Elizabeth Hesselblad (1870–1957), cared for thousands.

72. Rosenberg, *Care of Strangers*, 240.

73. Johnson, *Social Work of the Churches*, 69. One hospital that grew out of a partnership between a surgeon and his two physician sons and a Franciscan convent of schoolteachers who went to help those injured by a tornado that had ravaged their small Minnesota town. That partnership, forged in 1889 with the Sisters of St. Francis, remains active today in the Mayo Clinic.

74. Fritschel, *One Hundred Years*, 17–20.

75. In 1899, 197 Lutheran deaconesses were serving in the United States. The number peaked in 1938 at 437 (Nelson, *Lutherans in North America*, 299–300). Anglican and Methodist deaconesses served as well. Numbered among these servants of

Covenant Church, similarly served their members and others in need
[**Swedish Covenanters**].

Swedish Covenanters

Shortly after establishing a church in Chicago in 1885, Swedish pietists
set about caring for Swedish immigrants in need, particularly those
suffering from cholera. In 1886, they established the Home of Mercy
in a three-story building that provided medical and indigent care on
the first floor, support for the aged on the second, and operated an orphanage on the third. The home expanded its medical care and eventually developed into Swedish Covenant Hospital in 1921. Influenced
by the eighteenth-century pietist movement, covenanters maintained
an allegiance to a living and active faith.[76]

Methodists were active as well among Protestants building hospitals.
Their first as Methodist Hospital in Brooklyn, opened in 1887. It was followed by other hospitals in urban areas, including Christ Hospital in Cincinnati (1889) which was staffed by graduates from any of the six Methodist
deaconess training institutions in the United States. Methodists also contributed to medical training among African Americans [**Meharry Medical
College**].

Meharry Medical College

An unlikely pair of Methodist doctors—one who had served in the
Confederate Army and his student who had served in the Union
Army—felt called to educate medical practitioners in Nashville—a
moderately-sized U.S. city with the highest mortality rate at the time.
Poverty among freed slaves led to disease and death, and Drs. William
Sneed (1835–1907) and George Hubbard (1841–1924) committed
to launch a school that would train young black men and women in

the twentieth-century deaconess movement in the United States are Elisabeth Fedde
(1850–1921) and Harriet Bedell (1875–1969).

76. Olsson, *Quality of Mercy*. ECC's Covenant Retirement Communities grew to
become one of the largest retirement housing providers in the United States.

medicine. With funding from the Freedman's Aid Society and support from Methodists, Congregationalists, and five Indiana brother farmers, Meharry Medical College opened in 1876.

Philanthropists often provided initial funding for hospitals and medical schools, and local church members supported the effort through fundraising and volunteerism. According to Kenneth Rowe,

> Hospital sponsors and their local churches organized charity balls, oyster suppers, fairs and other fund-raisers, while women made jams and jellies, rolled bandages, provided linens and flowers, and visited and cheered the patients. These activities had the double value of raising money and fostering group solidarity. Participation in hospital work defined and ratified social structures in the community while creating a visible beneficent upper class with its own continuing institutions.[77]

With most health care occurring at home [**Epidemic!**], hospitals served two populations: the indigent and the severely ill. Because the well-to-do were mixed into the latter category, a divide began to become apparent, with publicly funded hospitals providing a place of respite and recovery for the indigent and better-funded religious hospitals focusing on diagnosis and cure. The latter were more likely to employ progressive techniques and offer moral and spiritual support.

Critics warned against hospitals furthering pauperism, so most hospitals—Catholic and Protestant—charged patients a weekly rate that was slightly above the average cost of a boarding room. Additionally, donors pressed hospitals to become self-sufficient. As population growth increased demand, hospital administrators responded by decreasing the four-week average length of stay and increasing patient fees. Moral and spiritual health became more challenging to deliver given the shorter stays, and charges made "poor care" a more tenuous descriptor of some religious hospitals.[78] Hospital systems that intentionally served the poor were challenged to navigate the narrow strait between their calling and financial solvency.

---

77. Rowe, "Temples of Healing," 56.
78. Rowe, "Temples of Healing," 56–57.

Epidemic!

Since ancient times, plagues, epidemics, and pandemics have brought fear and death.[79] Bubonic plague, diphtheria, yellow fever, cholera, HIV/AIDS, Ebola, SARS, and many other diseases have presented individual Christians with needs. In 1873, cholera began spreading through Nashville.[80] Church of Christ minister David Lipscomb (1831–1917) traveled in his buggy from his rural home to the city interior to transport Dominican sisters to houses of the sick, and to visit African Americans who were ill at home.[81] Lipscomb asked his fellow members, "what would Christ have done" and "what did he do in the person of his representatives here?"[82] Lipscomb wrote:

> The religion of our Savior was intended to make us like Christ, not only in our labor of love—of our self sacrifice for the good of others, but also in raising us above a timid, quaking fear of death. . . . The rich often think that they cannot condescend to do the work of nursing and caring for the poor. It is degrading. It is hard I know, just precisely as hard as it is to enter the kingdom of heaven, not a whit more difficult to do the one than the other.[83]

---

79. For a brief survey of Christian responses to plagues, see Barnes, "Plagues."

80. Three large waves of cholera in the U.S. preceded this outbreak. See Rosenberg, *Cholera Years*. Outbreaks occurred globally. Caterina Dominici (1829–1894) is an example of one who responded courageously in the London outbreak of 1854, just as Pierre Toussaint (1766–1853) did earlier in New York City.

81. Catholic sisters were essential caregivers of cholera victims in each cholera wave in the U.S. See Rosenberg, *The Cholera Years*; Watson, "Sisters of Charity."

82. Consistently in epidemics, some clergy call people to repentance, seeing disease as punishment from God. Calls for service is another common clerical response.

83. Lipscomb, "Cholera," 651.

Fig. 5.3. David Lipscomb in Nashville cholera epidemic, 1873.

THE HOLINESS MOVEMENT AND THE SOCIAL GOSPEL

Two nineteenth-century Protestant theologies shaped thinking about compassion. One was the holiness movement and the other, the social gospel.[84] Of the former, Timothy L. Smith writes, "The quest for perfection joined with compassion for poor and needy sinners and a rebirth of millennial expectation to make popular Protestantism a mighty social force long before the slavery conflict erupted into war."[85] For those influenced by the nineteenth-century Wesleyan holiness movement, compassion often was practiced in tandem with evangelism and was expressed in advocacy and in organized, church-based, charitable outreaches of benevolence, temperance, and education. Some embraced perfectionist politics [**Timbuctoo**]. Wesleyans, according to Robert Black and Keith Drury, "saw social reform as nothing more or less than applied holiness, holiness in action."[86]

84. Catholic social teaching impacted Roman Catholics. It will be introduced in chapter 6.

85. Smith, *Revivalism and Social Reform*, 149.

86. Black and Drury, *Story of the Wesleyan Church*, 55; Evans, "History and Theology"; Roberts, "Nazarenes and Social Ministry"; Watson, *Pursuing Social Holiness*.

Timbuctoo

In the 1840s, wealthy abolitionist Gerrit Smith (1797–1874) divided 120,000 acres of his vast land holdings in northern New York into 40 acre lots to cede to 3,000 black New Yorkers. Smith's stated intent was that with the land, residents could become self-sufficient through farming and could meet the minimum asset requirement to vote.

Presbyterian minister Rev. Henry Highland Garnet supported the effort, saying, "I believe it is God's design that every man shall have a home. The complete reign of gospel principles will introduce a perfect system of agrarianism."[87] Smith embraced perfectionist politics which attempted to meld political and religious convictions.

Smith's generosity notwithstanding, most of the farms failed. Cash-poor settlers struggled to pay land tax and the Civil War disrupted families. Within a few years, Smith's land titles went to the auction block, eventually forming Adirondack National Park.

On both sides of the Mason-Dixon Line, pastors addressed moral issues. Northern ministers preached against slavery while southerners railed against greed. Owen Lovejoy (1811–1864) and the American Missionary Association (AMA) founded over one hundred anti-slavery churches.[88] Most Christians, however, remained detached, unable to imagine a "biracial kingdom of God;" supporting neither black Christians nor white agitators and focusing on spiritual rather than political salvation. As Ben Wright argues, Christians thus both inspired and limited abolition.[89] After the war broke out, Christians from the north and south aided the wounded. Abolitionists assisted runaway slaves through the underground railroad and YMCA members formed the United States Christian Commission to relay supplies and spiritual support to Union Army troops.

In the smoldering ashes of the Civil War, the need for spiritual and social reconstruction was palpable. Injustice, poverty, and oppression were evident, particularly in northern cities. With faith in the gospel and confidence from the Enlightenment, progressive Protestants began holding up

87. Garnet, *North Star* (Troy, N.Y.) quoted in "Dreaming of Timbuctoo."

88. Startup, *Root of All Evil.* After the war, the AMA assisted in founding eleven colleges, including Clark Atlanta, Fisk, and Howard.

89. Wright, *Bonds of Salvation.*

Jesus' ethical teachings as a window to a society that was falling short of a Christian vision for *shalom*.[90]

Theologians and pastors provided a compelling biblical and theological rationale for building the kingdom of God on earth. The movement was multivocal, with some advocating for evangelism and direct aid to the masses, such as Josiah Strong (1847–1916); gradual social reform, such as advocated by Washington Gladden (1836–1918); and sweeping radical, structural changes, such as advanced by Episcopal priest and Christian socialist W. D. P. Bliss (1856–1926).[91] Many white social gospel advocates held paternalistic views toward African Americans, but black clerics and theologians offered their own contributions to the movement—especially Booker T. Washington (1856–1915) and W. E. B. Du Bois (1868–1963).[92]

Popular histories often stress the differences between progressive and conservative Protestants regarding the social gospel. It's interesting to note what both groups shared, as well. As mentioned earlier, progressives and conservatives both pursued social reforms, just on different issues. Both also affirmed Christianity as the answer to human need, albeit with different emphases. As Matthew Bowman writes, "The social gospelers modeled the ideal Christian society upon that of the biblical patriarchs, one in which no distinction between the secular and sacred existed and sanctification guided the Christian's actions in the economy as well as in personal morality."[93] Similarly, Nancy Christie and Michael Gauvreau assert that,

> Just as nineteenth-century clergymen viewed historical theology as the means of preserving the tenets of evangelicals from the incursions of modern science and philosophy, twentieth-century Protestant ministers saw in the exaltation by the social services of the practical day-to-day experience of the individual, which made religion accessible to ordinary men and women, the greatest safeguard of Christianity in a society increasingly characterized by the rivalry of opposing classes.[94]

Prominent among social gospel theologians, and demonstrating the conservative-progressive overlap, was a German Baptist named Walter

---

90. The U.S. Progressive Era (1896–1916) overlapped the social gospel and, in sweeping reforms, took on economic, political, and human challenges.

91. Wogaman, *Christian Ethics*.

92. For a description of four streams of the social gospel movement among black theologians, see Dorrien, *New Abolition* and *Breaking White Supremacy*.

93. Bowman, "Sin, Spirituality, and Primitivism," 95; also, Abraham, "From Revivalism to Socialism," 167–8; Wacker, "Holy Spirit."

94. Christie and Gauvreau, *Full-Orbed Christianity*, xii.

Rauschenbusch (1861–1918). As a young professor at Rochester Theological Seminary in upstate New York, Rauschenbusch attempted to unite and mobilize various strands of the movement with a compelling theology and a prophetic call to the church. Commitment to the gospel seemed relatively strong in the United States compared with Europe, yet social ills seemed to be tolerated rather than addressed. Rauschenbusch and others could not reconcile curable poverty and oppression with the kingdom of God.

Fig. 5.4. Walter Rauschenbusch.

Rather than appealing for a state church or declaring the United States as a "Christian" nation, Rauschenbusch emphasized that ethical policies and practices were the correct agenda: "To put a stop to child labor in our country would be a more effective way of doing homage to his sovereignty than any business of words and names."[95] He also argued that although capitalism was a very efficient allocation system, and principled people worked within it, placing ownership and control in the hands of a few made it inevitably destructive to the common good. Rauschenbusch encouraged each follower of Christ to "comprehend the sinfulness of our economic system and

95. Rauschenbusch, *Christianizing the Social Order*, 124.

to realize his own responsibility for it," pressing toward some form of economic democracy—whether socialism or trade unionism.[96]

Rauschenbusch viewed individualistic piety as a truncated gospel, limiting the enabling of the kingdom of God on earth. Rauschenbusch asked, "What would Jesus do?" to transform institutions [**WWJD?**]. Rauschenbusch was not abandoning personal moral regeneration but rather, like antebellum Holiness preachers, was attempting to apply it. Toward the end of *Christianizing the Social Order*, Rauschenbusch wrote,

> We do not want to substitute social activities for religion. If the Church comes to lean on social preachings and doings as a crutch because its religion has become paralytic, may the Lord have mercy on us all! We do not want less religion; we want more; but it must be a religion that gets its orientation from the Kingdom of God. To concentrate our efforts on personal salvation, as orthodoxy has done, or on soul culture, as liberalism has done, comes close to refined selfishness. . . . Seek ye first the Kingdom of God and God's righteousness, and the salvation of your souls will be added to you.[97]

WWJD?

The question "What would Jesus do?" is commonly associated with the novel, *In His Steps*, authored by Charles Sheldon (1857–1946). Sheldon wrote the book in 1896 and read a chapter each Sunday evening to his home congregation, Central Congregational Church, in Topeka, Kansas. The chapters were well received, printed in a Chicago newspaper, and eventually published as a novel.

In the book, Rev. Henry Maxwell is preparing a sermon on 1 Peter 2:21: "For to this you have been called, because Christ also suffered for you, leaving you an example, so that you should follow in his steps." Rev. Maxwell's sermon preparation was interrupted by an unemployed man (a printer displaced by modern technology) who knocked on the pastor's door. Rev. Maxwell was kind but had little to offer. The man shows up elsewhere in town and receives a similar lack of response.

96. Rauschenbusch, *Christianizing the Social Order*, 323, 357. Business leaders did not always see the gaps in justice that theologians railed against; see Heidebrecht, *Faith and Economic Practice*, 243.

97. Rauschenbusch, *Christianizing the Social Order*, 464–65.

After an exceptional church service and sermon on Sunday, the congregation heard a voice from the back—it was the unemployed man who had met several of the members during the week. He walked to the front of the church and asked to say a few words. In his soliloquy, he tells the congregation that he had been looking for work in town for three days but had not received any assistance. He asks the congregation whether what they call following Jesus is the same thing as what Jesus taught on the subject. The man said, "Somehow I get puzzled when I see so many Christians living in luxury and singing, 'Jesus, I my cross have taken, All to leave and follow Thee,' and remember how my wife died in a tenement in New York City, gasping for air and asking God to take the little girl too." He continued,

> It seems to me there's an awful lot of trouble in the world that somehow wouldn't exist if all the people who sing such songs went and lived them out. I suppose I don't understand. But what would Jesus do? Is that what you mean by following His steps? It seems to me sometimes as if the people in the city churches had good clothes and nice houses to live in, and money to spend for luxuries, and could go away on summer vacations and all that, while the people outside of the churches, thousands of them, I mean, die in tenements and walk the streets for jobs, and never have a piano or a picture in the house, and grow up in misery and drunkenness and sin.[98]

Mid-sentence, the man collapses toward the communion table. He spends the week recuperating but dies the next Sunday morning. Rev. Maxwell and the congregation are shaken. The following week, Rev. Maxwell encourages the congregation to ask, "What would Jesus do?" when they face a dilemma, taken from the rich ruler who came to Jesus and asked, "What must I do to inherit eternal life?" (Luke 18:18).

Over the next year, the question slowly turns the members's focus from themselves toward the community. At the end of the book, Rev. Maxwell climbs into his pulpit and encourages his congregants:

> The Christianity that attempts to suffer by proxy is not the Christianity of Christ. Each individual Christian, business man, citizen, needs to follow in His steps along the path of personal

98. Sheldon, *In His Steps*, 14, 15.

sacrifice to Him. There is not a different path today from that of Jesus' own times. It is the same path.[99]

Perhaps ironically, Rev. Maxwell did not call on people to ask, "What would Jesus do?" But after the sermon, a band of parishioners gathers around him and commit to do exactly that from that day forward.

In His Steps is one of the best-selling books of all time. Although inspired by the social gospel, its application at the individual level made it widely appealing. It spoke to both progressives and conservatives.[100]

Among progressives, the social gospel won traction. The Federal Council of the Churches of Christ in America was established in 1908 in part to coordinate efforts among denominations to address social injustices.[101] Many progressive Protestants generally were supportive but denominational leaders held varying views which lead to intra-denominational debates. Some supported socialism and others feared it; some advocated for labor unions as a brake on monopolies while others disparaged that they were given to violence and sought power; some held to traditional causes of social problems, such as intemperance and extravagance; a few supported pacifism; many wished to reconnect the masses with Christianity and support human dignity.

Social Christianity increasingly leavened preaching, liturgy, and hymns, modifying or reimagining doctrinal emphases [**Where Cross the Crowded Ways**]. Although a stronger view than most would proffer, Quaker and Harvard Divinity School professor Henry Cadbury (1883–1974) wrote, "We can no longer, therefore, separate social work from religion . . . . It is part of religion. Child labor laws may be more edifying than all the creeds. A living wage may lead to eternal life. Some votes speak louder than prayers."[102]

Where Cross the Crowded Ways

Frank North (1850–1935), a minister in the Methodist Episcopal Church, served pastorates in New York and later served as president of the Federal Council of Churches. North's hymn, "O Master of the

---

99. Sheldon, *In His Steps*, 300.

100. Shore, "WWJD?"

101. Wogaman, *Christian Ethics*, 203.

102. Cadbury, "Social Servis [sic]." Quoted in Bacon, *Let This Life Speak*, 30.

Waking World," called Christians to global missions. Asked to write a
hymn on urban missions, North penned the words to "Where Cross the
Crowded Ways of Life" in 1905. It was this second hymn that gave voice
to millions of Christians yearning for the kingdom of God in World
War I and in the Great Depression. A portion of the hymn reads:[103]

> O Master, from the mountainside,
> make haste to heal these hearts of pain;
> among these restless throngs abide;
> O tread the city's streets again;
>
> Till all the world shall learn your love,
> and follow where your feet have trod;
> till glorious from your heaven above
> shall come the city of our God.

Around the turn of the century, American universities began adopt-
ing a German model of higher education which emphasized research
and discovery. Some Christian social scientists viewed their nascent disciplines as advancing the kingdom of God on earth, enabling the social
gospel [**Science and Progress**]. In academic arenas, the Enlightenment
and the American embrace of reason, individualism, and optimism fueled
a belief in the possibility of progress.[104]

Science and Progress

Protestant and Catholic social scientists believed their disciplines
could advance a more Christ-honoring society.[105]

103. Richard T. Ely observed a paucity of hymns addressing compassion and called
for more: "If the Church in her history has been full of love for man, it must be seen in
her hymns. Hearts welling up, filled to overflowing with love to our fellows, must seek
expression in song. Let the reader take any hymn-book he pleases and read hymn after
hymn, and seek for the hymns expressive of burning, all-consuming altruism. He will
not find them, though he will find any number which turn the heart in on itself and tend
to nourish a selfish, individualistic piety," Ely, *Social Aspects of Christianity*, 26–27.

104. For the impact of the Enlightenment on the social gospel, see Visser't Hooft,
Background, 102–125.

105. Hopkins credits Rev. Joseph Tuckerman as the first to apply social science in
a ministry addressing urban problems. He did so in Boston in 1826. See Hopkins, *Rise
of the Social Gospel*, 4.

Richard T. Ely (1854–1943), professor of economics at the University of Wisconsin and founder of the American Economic Association, argued that economics could help Christians understand how the exchange of goods could be modified to advance the kingdom of God. Ely viewed society as evolving through stages that would grow through the competition of capitalism and mature into Christian cooperation. Life-educated economist Henry George (1839–1897) advocated a single land tax, reasoning that it would provide for a nation's needs and be based on resources gifted from God.[106] Other economists were working to similar ends in melding biblical teachings to economic thought that would aid the world.[107]

At the University of Chicago, Albion Small (1854–1926) and Graham Taylor (1851–1938) were pioneering the emerging discipline of sociology. They believed that empirical and theoretical insights would be the tools to enable social betterment.[108] At Catholic University of America, John A. Ryan (1869–1945) and John O'Grady (1886–1966) were advocating social reform and living wages as they refined and expanded moral theology and sociology.

A minister and settlement house founder, Dana W. Bartlett (1860–1942), was an early leader in social work research, mentoring students from the University of Southern California and Occidental College in field research of tenement housing in Los Angeles. Bartlett's research informed the related field of city planning as well, where some envisioned prosperous cities whose pathways and parks would uplift morals. Although a civil rather than Christian initiative, the World's Columbian Exposition of 1893 propelled such a vision with breathtaking, classical white buildings of beauty and order (see Fig. 5.5)—a stark contrast to the urban squalor and unemployment that characterized Chicago at the time.[109]

As Housing Commission director for Los Angeles, Bartlett promoted a vision of the city that included single-family dwellings, parks and public baths, residential and commercial zoning, and accessible beaches

106. Nicklason, "Henry George: Social Gospeller [sic]"; Plowright, "Political Economy and Christian Polity."

107. Pioneering economists integrating biblical teachings included John Bates Clark (1847–1938); Simon Patten (1852–1922); and John R. Commons (1862–1945), the so-called spiritual father of Social Security.

108. Reed, "Alliance for Progress"; Swatos, "Faith of the Fathers."

109. Badger, *Great American Fair*, 94.

and mountains. John Nolen (1869–1937) seemed similarly inspired by postmillennial possibilities as he produced comprehensive plans for 28 U.S. cities, including Seattle, San Diego, Savannah, and Madison, Wisconsin.[110] As summarized by Charles Mulford Robinson (1869–1917), an evangelist for the City Beautiful movement, "As when the heavens rolled away and St. John beheld the new Jerusalem, so a vision of a new London, a new Washington, Chicago, or New York breaks with the morning's sunshine upon the degradation, discomfort, and baseness of modern city life. There are born a new dream and a new hope."[111]

Fig. 5.5. World's Columbian Exposition, 1893.

It was not only theologians and academics who fomented support for the social gospel. Heath Carter argues that Christian laborers played a significant role in protesting the wake of inequality, injustice, and poverty left by Gilded Age capitalism. Decrying the influence of money and power, often with biblical references, pro-union workers agitated through speeches and protests and, Carter argues, effectively moved some clergy away from attributing poverty to moral failings and toward more critical stands of

110. Hise and Deverell, *Eden by Design*, 12; Mackintosh and Forsberg, "'Co-Agent of the Millennium.'" Also see McCabe, "Building the Planning Consensus."

111. Robinson, *Modern Civic Art*, 4.

American economy and society. Priests and pastors were troubled as well about whether the working class would be lost to the church. Social Christianity provided an avenue for addressing both of these concerns.[112]

Some Congregationalists, Presbyterians, and Episcopalians found the social gospel to be appealing because it allowed Christianity to be modernized. It extracted the ethical teachings of Jesus from Scripture while downplaying myth and miracle, and it allowed the natural and social sciences to inform means and methods. But for many conservatives, the social gospel represented the Tower of Babel: it deemphasized Jesus' divinity, miracles, and resurrection and elevated the ability of people in righting society. With its stripping of mystery and miracle, and the seeming radical nature of labor agitation, the social gospel epitomized a threat to the Christian mission for many conservatives, rather than its extension. Social Christianity became a lightning rod that repelled progressive and conservative Protestants.[113]

Progressives emphasized social justice and humanitarianism, while conservatives stressed individual regeneration and privileged matters of the spirit over the body.[114] Although both engaged in advocacy in the early twentieth century, many conservatives temporarily retreated from political activism following failed attempts to curb alcohol sales and evolution in schools.[115] Both progressives and conservatives engaged in domestic and overseas missions, but the former embraced humanitarian needs and the latter emphasized winning souls.[116]

Prohibition

Following the U.S. Civil War and into the early twentieth century, Protestants and some Catholics worked hard to end liquor sales. Many

---

112. Carter, *Union Made*, 4–7, 73–96. Not all Christians, of course, supported unions; nor did all clergy support capitalism, for a variety of reasons. Carter argues, however, that many clergy were aligned with industrialists. Cf. Heidebrecht, *Faith and Economic Practice*, 148–165.

113. Prior to its appearance in North America, Scottish theologians debated social gospel notions. See McKay, *Kirk and the Kingdom*.

114. Hopkins, *Rise of the Social Gospel*, 16.

115. Rogers, "Religious Advocacy."

116. The division occurred unevenly. Among Lutherans, for example, missions of charity were dominant over social justice for all Lutheran fellowships. The Salvation Army, Wesleyan Church, American Baptists, and Brethren churches historically blended conservative theology with social care. Conservatives embracing divine healing often addressed ailments as an opportunity to demonstrate God's love and power. On Lutherans, see Black, "Word of God."

progressives and conservatives agreed that alcohol was injurious. For social gospelers, prohibition represented social reform; for conservatives, it was a hindrance to holiness. Through speeches, rallies, tracts, and lobbying, advocates cajoled citizens and pressed lawmakers and regulators to end alcohol trafficking.

Numerous voluntary societies and denominational agencies were established to aid the cause. The Methodist Episcopal Church and other denominations supported the Women's Christian Temperance Union (WCTU), the Anti-Saloon League, and other advocacy networks. State legislative victories culminated with the eighteenth amendment to the U.S. Constitution being passed in 1920. After it became obvious that prohibition did not end slums and crime, and was not working as social policy, the amendment was repealed by the twenty-first amendment in 1933.

For conservatives, benevolence occasionally was paired with evangelism to achieve individual spiritual regeneration. Urban rescue missions—such as those launched by David Nasmith (1799–1839) in Glasgow, Charles Garrett (1823–1900) in Liverpool, and Jerry McAuley (1839–1884) in New York City—invited individuals to come to Jesus.[117] When hymnwriter Fanny J. Crosby (1820–1915) volunteered in a rescue mission in Springfield, Massachusetts, in the early 1900s, one can only imagine that the lyrics from her hymn "Rescue the Perishing" stirred in her heart:

> Rescue the perishing, care for the dying,
> snatch them in pity from sin and the grave;
> weep o'er the erring one, lift up the fallen,
> tell them of Jesus the mighty to save.
>
> Rescue the perishing,
> care for the dying;
> Jesus is merciful,
> Jesus will save.[118]

---

117. Nasmith also founded the YMCA. McAuley founded the International Union of Gospel Missions, which is now called Citygate Network. See Smith-Rosenberg, *Religion and the Rise of the American City*; Standing, "Charles Garrett"; White, *Slaying the Dragon*, 72–74.

118. Crosby, "Rescue the Perishing."

Conservatives shared generously with others at home and abroad during the Great Depression, claiming that only those things that were given away were preserved.[119] But many conservative Protestants made benevolence and social action instrumental rather than terminal actions.

In the twentieth century, advocates for the social gospel met their match in pastor and theologian Reinhold Niebuhr (1892–1971), who argued forcefully and prolifically that the kingdom of God could not be achieved on earth. Institutions tended to seek their own interests rather than those of others; they could not be reformed like individuals could be. Niebuhr argued that compassionate service was at the heart of Christianity and that it would always be needed in a broken society.[120] His realism in accepting that some things cannot be changed is expressed in his popular serenity prayer: "God, give us grace to accept with serenity the things that cannot be changed, courage to change the things that should be changed, and the wisdom to distinguish the one from the other."[121]

SCIENTIFIC CHARITY

A final, more fleeting and more extreme contribution of thought during this era was scientific charity. Confidence in progressivism and science led some Christian and secular scientists and philanthropists to explore how science might advance social welfare through bureaucratization and sterilization.[122] Oscar C. McCulloch (1843–1891), a Congregationalist minister, was deeply concerned about the poor and became interested in rooting out pauperism due to genetics rather than choice. He sought to differentiate the worthy poor, who deserved support, from lazy paupers, who were disposed to take advantage of the system and resist change. McCulloch's investigations led him to eugenics and the idea that poverty was a predisposition passed genetically from one generation to the next.[123]

While not a Christian initiative per se, Christians inclined toward some forms of biological evolution viewed eugenics as a progressive application of science and a possible means of addressing addiction and pauperism. If those genetically inclined toward poverty could be identified, they could be sterilized and their genetic line ended. Indiana, Connecticut, and other U.S.

---

119. Curtis, "God Is Not Affected," 579–89.

120. Niebuhr, *Moral Man and Immoral Society*; Niebuhr, *Nature and Destiny of Man*.

121. Sifton, *Serenity Prayer*, 277.

122. For insights into the bureaucratization of the Society of St. Vincent de Paul, see Shok, "Organized Almsgiving."

123. Ruswick, *Almost Worthy*, 35–69.

states adopted forced sterilization laws based on eugenic research. Efforts were made to educate and enroll people in eugenics programs in the United States and elsewhere, resulting in around sixty-five thousand Americans being sterilized before the law was changed.[124]

Harry H. Laughlin (1880–1943) and Charles Davenport (1866–1944) were leading advocates for forced sterilization to prevent those predestined for chronic poverty from becoming a burden on society. Both were reared as Christians, but it appeared to be their scientific training rather than their theology that propelled them. McCulloch, the pioneer of eugenics, eventually migrated away from genetic causes of impoverishment and embraced public health, sociology, and economics as offering superior insights into poverty, disease, and unemployment. The poor, he concluded, were like everyone else.[125]

SUMMING UP

During the eighteenth and nineteenth centuries, Christians saw visions of the kingdom of God on earth and sought to coax them into reality with newly discovered natural and social sciences, employing modern civic and religious institutions. Compassion was expressed through direct service, such as in *diakonia*, the Salvation Army, and the Red Cross, and in institutional reform in prisons, housing, health care, and politics. We also saw an expansion of civil society; it existed previously (recall Roman associations and medieval confraternities) but mushroomed in the grassroots of British and U.S. society. We also witnessed the coordination and efficiency challenges of innumerable sectarian initiatives, and we saw attempts at collaboration (such as with the FCC). Innovations diffused across some organizations while others labored in relative isolation.

In the nineteenth and early twentieth centuries, many U.S. Protestant denominations divided along the Mason–Dixon line, increasing the number of religious bodies in an already divided Protestant field. Each conceptualized and organized its compassionate efforts domestically and abroad. Many, but certainly not all, pursued progress paternalistically.

Despite the whirring of institutions during the era of salvation and service, social change occurred slowly. Yet, the impact of this era remains alive in the present-day in both ideas and institutions. Initiatives continue expanding in the twentieth century, diverging into sectors emphasizing justice, humanitarianism, and the grassroots efforts of mutual aid and community development.

124. Bruinius, *Better for All the World*.
125. Ruswick, *Almost Worthy*, 201.

CONTEMPORARY

WE CLOSE OUR SURVEY with three passes through the twentieth and twenty-first centuries, sorting themes into the overlapping categories of liberation and justice, peace and humanitarianism, and mutual aid and community development.

In liberation and justice, Catholic and mainline Protestants play leading roles, influenced by Catholic social teaching, liberation theology, and the social gospel. To narrow the abundant applications we might explore, I limit applications to initiatives in labor and commerce.

Peace churches are early and enduring leaders in peace and humanitarianism, joined by progressive Christians in World War II and a flood of conservatives, after the war. The engagement of the latter narrowed the breach among Protestants over modernism and the social gospel.

In mutual aid and community development, Anabaptists and Latter-day Saints offer models that accentuate self-reliance and communitarianism. These join lively experiments in incarnational mission, intentional community, and community development. Some of the themes and actors we will encounter are given in the table that follows.

Chapter	Century	Era	Themes	Actors
6	Twentieth to Twenty-First	Liberation and Justice	The social gospel, Christian internationalism, industrial missions, Catholic social teaching, distributism, political and public theology, liberation and black theology, Orthodoxy, Catholic Worker movement, worker-priests, labor unions, woman's exchanges, fair and alternative trade, vocational training, advocacy, business as mission	Harry Ward, Lucy Randolph Mason, Gustavo Gutiérrez, Óscar Romero, Tom Skinner, Martin Luther King Jr., Georgy Gapon, Léon Harmel, Walter Ciszek, Peter Maurin, Dorothy Day, Toyohiko Kagawa, Edna Ruth Byler, John Cort
7	Twentieth to Twenty-First	Peace and Humanitarianism	Para-church agencies, faith-healing, peace churches, animal sponsorship, integral mission, Lausanne Movement, child sponsorship, dependency, CARE, congregational aid	*Christian Herald*, Heifer Project, A. B. Simpson, Aimee Semple McPherson, Church World Service, F. H. Henry, John R. W. Stott, Bob Pierce, Kyung-Chik Han, Samuel Escobar, René Padilla, Norman Borlaug
8	Twentieth to Twenty-First	Mutual Aid and Community Development	Beloved community, mutual aid, simple living, intentional community, auxiliary, fraternal, and mission organizations, economic cooperation, incarnational mission, community development	Jacob Hutter, Joseph Smith, Brigham Young, Clarence Jordan, Gordon Cosby, Jean Vanier, Rutba House, Epworth League, Fr. Michael McGivney, Penn-Craft, Chiara Lubich, Mondragón cooperatives, Viv Grigg, John Perkins

Compassion themes and actors in the contemporary era.

6

Liberation and Justice

TATTERED FLAGS OF CHRISTIAN liberation adorn the twentieth and twenty-first centuries. Loyal to a revolutionary Jesus, Christians take on suffrage, the criminal justice system, and political and religious freedom.[1] They protest war, promote environmental justice, welcome refugees and asylees, support human rights, and march for civil rights.[2] Christians demonstrate, provide sanctuary, and accept blows.[3] Behind it all, it is Jesus who ushers in justice, and God who promises,

> I am about to do a new thing;
> now it springs forth, do you not perceive it? (Isa 43:19a)

But Christians also rally to oppose these same causes, and an even larger crowd of believers remain ambivalent or uncommitted on the sidelines.

Those who join the fight for justice often are disturbed by oppressive power. They understand the widespread, devastating impact of legal,

1. Social gospelers advocated for collectivist structures in the name of justice. But Christians also have staunchly defended freedom from communism, such as Lin Zhao (1932–1968) who protested against Mao Zedong and the Chinese Communist Party, wrote many letters in her own blood, and was martyred. See Xi, *Blood Letters*.

2. A wonderful survey of progressive evangelicals is provided by Swartz, *Moral Minority*. Histories of select social engagements are available, such as Cameron's *Send Them Here* which recounts the leading role of Catholics, Protestants, and Jews in crafting resettlement policies and welcoming refugees after WWII.

3. Demonstration and sanctuary appear among various times and groups. Examples include García, *Father Luis Olivares*; Shearer, *Daily Demonstrators*.

economic, social, and political systems and how compassion can be channeled to liberate millions by reforming and resisting systems. As Martin Luther King Jr. (1929–1968) said at New York City's Riverside Church in 1967,

> A true revolution of values will soon cause us to question the
> fairness and justice of many of our past and present policies. On
> the one hand we are called to play the Good Samaritan on life's
> roadside, but that will be only an initial act. One day we must
> come to see that the whole Jericho Road must be transformed so
> that men and women will not be constantly beaten and robbed
> as they make their journey on life's highway. True compassion
> is more than flinging a coin to a beggar. It comes to see that an
> edifice which produces beggars needs restructuring.[4]

Christian dissenters are diverse in cause and personality. With a little
imagination, we can feel the passion and witness the courage of disciples
who "deny themselves and take up their cross daily" and are "persecuted for
righteousness' sake" (Luke 9:23; Matt 5:10). We begin with three contributions of thought. First, we consider the continued flow of the social gospel
into the twentieth century, mostly promoted by progressive Protestants. We
then consider Catholic social teaching and liberation and black theology.
Third, I introduce political and public theology. Following these introductions, we explore a single sector—labor and economics—with the hope that
it represents dynamics found in other sectors. We proceed chronologically,
migrating across geographies of space and faith.

THE PROTESTANT DIVISION

Through the early years of the twentieth century, the social gospel continued to shape the thinking and activities of progressive Protestant denominations.[5] Thirty-one progressive U.S. denominations formed the Federal
Council of the Churches of Christ in America (FCC) partly to promote and
coordinate their social efforts. In 1908, the FCC issued *The Social Creed of
the Churches*, crafted by Methodist minister, Harry F. Ward, Jr. (1873–1966),
to lay out the principles and positions guiding its member denominations in
social action [**Harry Ward**]. An expanded 1912 version contained sixteen
commitments, including:

---

4. King, "Beyond Vietnam." King's pivotal address was written by Vincent Harding,
an African-American Mennonite who became the first director of the King Memorial
Center in Atlanta.

5. For the context in brief, see Compton, *End of Empathy*, 25–40.

- The abolition of child-labor.

- The protection of the worker from dangerous machinery, occupational disease, injuries, and mortality.

- The right of employees and employers alike to organize and for adequate means of conciliation and arbitration in industrial disputes.

- The release of employment one day in seven.

- A living wage as a minimum in every industry, and for the highest wage that each industry can afford.[6]

Animated by the social gospel, Teddy Roosevelt ran for president on a similar Progressive Party platform. His acceptance speech at the 1912 Chicago convention was titled "A Confession of Faith." Social progress seemed within reach as the clouds of World War I (WWI) gathered in the distance.

Harry Ward

After graduating with a bachelor's degree in political science from Northwestern University, English-born Harry Ward took a position with the Northwestern settlement house. His strong political advocacy clashed with other leaders. He took a up pastorates with Methodist Episcopal congregations working with laborers and promoting the social gospel. Spurred on by his experiences with laborers and stirred by the writings of Karl Marx, Ward co-founded the Methodist Federation for Social Service (MFSS) in 1907. Ward served as a professor of Social Service at the Boston University School of Theology and later, as a professor of Christian ethics at Union Theological Seminary. He co-founded the American Civil Liberties Union (ACLU) but resigned when they barred communists.

In *The New Social Order*, Ward attempted to predict the reconstruction of western society toward human unity. He described a world transformed in WWI that would demand a new order, averting the exploitation of low-income nations and embracing collectivism. As Ward wrote, "the final result of Christian compassion is not the survival of the unfit but the removal of the causes of unfitness . . . ."[7] Ward

6. Ward, *Social Creed of the Churches*, 7.
7. Ward, *New Social Order*, 91.

viewed the regeneration of society as a natural next stage of Christian development which he referred to as "social evangelism":

> It now remains . . . to direct the forces of evangelism toward every part of the social order that remains unregenerate, to accomplish absolutely the Christian family, the Christian state, the Christians industry, and through these the Christian social order. *To put the dynamic of God's life into all the activities of man, to bring the social passion to a consciousness of its spiritual nature, to tie the social program to the eternities and fill it with the power of an endless life—this is the compelling task of the Church.*[8]

Progressive Protestant business leaders responded to social gospel sermons and writings in a variety of ways. Some infused their companies with the highest standards of integrity and generously donated to good causes. Others took a more instrumental view, believing that worker well-being affected product quality. Some of these became pioneers of "welfare work," which offered workers libraries, gardens, Sunday schools, company picnics, insurance plans, recreation centers, rest rooms, cafeterias, and retirement homes. Still others held to the myth of the self-made man, believing that material success was in reach for any honest person who worked hard.[9] Some corporate leaders were exacting and autocratic and viewed their calling as that of steward and taskmaster.

Counted among these diverse and notable Protestant corporate leaders in the United States were John Wanamaker (1838–1922), founder of Wanamaker's department store in Philadelphia; H. J. Heinz (1844–1919), of the H. J. Heinz Company; and Henry Parsons Crowell (1855–1944), autocrat and founder of the Quaker Oats Company and funder of Moody Bible Institute.[10] Christian leaders elsewhere, such as S. Homma, the Ishikawa family, and others in Japan, led similar efforts in Christianizing factory labor

---

8. Ward, *Social Evangelism*, 24. In "From Revivalism to Socialism," Abraham critiques Ward's social evangelism: "he is mistaken to think that we can make an easy conceptual shift from the regeneration of the individual to the regeneration of society; he is profoundly uncritical of the theory of social change that captures his allegiance; he has virtually no ecclesiology; he is working with a hopefully reduced account of Christianity; and he is far too conservative in his analysis of evangelistic method" (p. 177).

9. Paul Henry Heidebrecht writes, "Their image of the virtuous man was the individual who through disciplined labor and personal integrity achieved material success and the acclamation of his fellows": Heidebrecht, *Faith and Economic Practice*, 204.

10. Day, *Christian in Big Business*; Kirk, *Wanamaker's Temple*; Petrick, "Purity as Life."

practices. Following the sentence ending with "labor practices."[11] Leaders such as these advanced social good through institutions, philanthropy, influence, planning, and policy. Gatherings such as the Conference on Christian Politics, Economics, and Citizenship (COPEC) held in Birmingham, UK in 1924, inspired hundreds around the globe to engage in "Christian social work." Youth picked up the baton as well, linking hands with global neighbors [**Christian Internationalism**].

Christian Internationalism

Christian internationalism was an internationally focused first cousin of the social gospel. In the ashes of WWI, Christian youth from a variety of Protestant denominations embraced a "combination of pacifism, interracial reconciliation, and a vision of global unity that emerged from mission ideals."[12] If the United States refused to act Christianly by joining the League of Nations or accepting Asian immigrants (via the Oriental Exclusion Act of 1924), what reason would any non-Christian have to consider the faith?

U.S. President Calvin Coolidge opened the Foreign Missions Convention of 1925, "with an address urging missionaries to carry the best of Christianity to other cultures and to counteract the evils of western civilization by bringing back to America the best of other cultures."[13] Missions was less about taking the gospel from a "Christian" nation to a heathen one, and more about living the gospel in ways that brought about the kingdom of God.

Christian internationalism spawned church- and mission society-sponsored social initiatives, including school construction, enhancing agricultural production, and sponsoring settlement houses. The aim of the movement was to embrace world unity through Christian-inspired friendship and social betterment. Some efforts were imperialistic, but the impulse of the movement was to appreciate local cultures and thus appreciate the necessary contextualization of the Christian gospel.

11. Iglehart, *Century of Protestant Christianity*, 201–2.

12. Robert, "First Globalization," 52. Also, Thompson, *For God and Globe*.

13. Robert, "First Globalization," 52.

Most conservatives in the twentieth century were repelled by the social gospel. They chose to emphasize the individual rather than pin their
hopes on grand social designs. As people of the soil and the revival, they
stressed conversion, personal responsibility, and self-help. Many conservatives subscribed to a dispensational view of time, seeing this world as lost
and a better one on the horizon ushered in by Jesus. In the meantime, they
emphasized a routine of conversion, endurance, and heavenly rest as a salve
for suffering and injustice [**Industrial Missions**]. Occasionally, the social
gospel veered into conservative Protestantism—such as Lucy Randolph Mason's (1882–1959) successful campaign to get Southern Baptists to affirm
the right to organize and engage in collective bargaining. But few of these
efforts gathered momentum.

Industrial Missions

Hundreds of chaplains in nineteenth- and twentieth-century Britain
served in industrial missions and attempted to connect laborers with
Anglican, Methodist, Baptist, and Presbyterian churches. Paid and
volunteer chaplains made rounds in factories, ministering to family
needs, reconciling workers and managers, giving theological talks,
counseling, and nurturing fellowship. Christian laborers served as
missionaries, identifying needs among coworkers and facilitating the
efforts of chaplains.[14] Industrial missions were established in Germany, Scotland, England, Australia, Japan, and elsewhere.[15] Over time,
chaplains gravitated toward addressing structural issues and local
economic development as part of their efforts to aid workers.

After World War II (WWII), industrial missions were established
in manufacturing and extractive industries around cities such as Boston and Detroit. Chaplains from multiple denominations collaborated
in ministering to workers facing the alienating anomie of modern
industrial society. Most offered conversation about religion and work,

14. Torry, *Bridgebuilders*.

15. Bell, "Whose Side Are They On?"; Johnston and McFarland, "'Out in the Open'";
McFarland and Johnston, "Faith in the Factory"; Michelson, "The Role of Workplace
Chaplains"; Poethig, "Toward Worldwide Industrial Mission"; Symanowski, *The Chris-
tian Witness*; Todd, "Mission and Justice." Industrial missions with holistic social and
spiritual aims were pursued in Japan in the 1920s as urban areas and the church grew.
See Iglehart, *Century of Protestant Christianity*, 185.

facilitated fellowship, and provided pastoral care, rather than focusing on structural injustice.

Christian hymns reinforced the emphasis on hard work and heavenly reward, and this did not go unnoticed by critics.[16] Labor protest hymns and revolutionary anthems occasionally parodied familiar hymns. F. B. Brechler's "The Preacher and the Slave," which was popularized by labor activist and songwriter Joe Hill,[17] borrowed the tune of the beloved hymn "There's a Land that is Fairer than Day," a portion of which reads:

> Long-haired preachers come out every night,
> Try to tell you what's wrong and what's right;
> But when asked how 'bout something to eat,
> They will answer in voices so sweet:
>
> You will eat, bye and bye,
> In that glorious land above the sky;
> Work and pray, live on hay,
> You'll get pie in the sky when you die.
> And you'll eat in the sweet bye and bye.[18]

Joe Hill's parody accused Protestants of allowing transcendence to excuse them from addressing structural injustice, much like Jesus' condemnation of the Pharisees and scribes who believed that offering assets to God released them from caring for their parents in times of need or failing to tend to weightier themes in the law (Mark 7:9–13; Matt 23:23). Unlike most Protestants or Catholics, Hill's answer was anarchy and communism.[19] Some Christians, however, were keenly interested in bringing about social change.

---

16. Lynn et al., "Harmonizing Work."

17. Other labor parodies of hymns include "There Is Power in a Union," sung to "There Is Power in the Blood"; "Stand Up! Ye Workers," sung to "Stand Up for Jesus"; "Christians at War," sung to "Onward, Christian Soldiers"; "Dump the Bosses Off Your Back," sung to "Take It to the Lord in Prayer"; and "John Golden and the Lawrence Strike," sung to "A Little Talk with Jesus." All advocated for unionization and collectivism while implicating Christian injustice or passivity. See *Songs of the Workers*.

18. Hill, "Preacher and the Slave."

19. Some conservative Protestants would take up communism seriously throughout the twentieth century and particularly after WWII. See "Shooting Star of Conservatism."

CATHOLIC SOCIAL TEACHING

Returning to Europe and resetting the clock to the waning years of the
nineteenth century, we find the continent in social, political, and economic
upheaval. Rome felt the need to respond. With its heritage in systematic
theology and philosophy and a seat at the table with emperors, the Roman
Catholic Church had long been in a position to help envision a just society.
The church also had the advantage of issuing authoritative doctrine. In the
turmoil of nineteenth-century Europe, a special collection of writing called
Catholic social teaching (CST) started to form. In these documents, popes
and bishops applied enduring Christian teachings to contemporary social,
economic, moral, and political matters, thereby providing a Christian inter-
pretative lens on society.[20] Sometimes called "the church's best kept secret,"
CST offers a running commentary of church teachings on global social conditions and addresses multiple aspects of human and social relationships.

The CST corpus consists of papal encyclicals and pastoral letters from
bishops that are hammered out in ecclesial and theological conversation.
Because its aim is to bring enduring principles to contemporary issues,
Catholic social teaching reflects both the timeless and the timely. Opposing
positions sometimes find inspiration in a single document (see Table 6.1).

20. Although not as extensive as CST, some Protestant denominations have dis-
tilled social teachings as well. For examples, see Hood, *Social Teachings in the Episcopal
Church*; Russian Orthodox Church, "Basis of the Social Concept"; Evangelical Lutheran
Church in America, *Social Statements* and *Social Messages*; United Methodist Church,
United Methodist Revised Social Principles. These teachings contrast with pronounce-
ments by the World Council of Churches (WCC), which generally are brief endorse-
ments or condemnations of specific social developments.

Latin Title	English Title[21]	Year Published	Source	Major Challenges Addressed	Major Ideas or Messages
Rerum Novarum	The Condition of Labor	1891	Pope Leo XIII	Industrialization, urbanization, poverty	Focus is made on "family wage" and workers's rights.
Quadrag-esimo Anno	After Forty Years, or The Reconstruction of the Social Order	1931	Pope Pius XI	Great Depression, communism, fascist dictatorships	Subsidiarity is to be a guide to government interventions.
Mater et Magistra	Christian-ity and Social Progress	1961	Pope John XXIII	Technological advances	There is a need for global justice between rich and poor nations.
Pacem in Terris	Peace on Earth	1963	Pope John XXIII	Arms race, the threat of nuclear war	A philosophy of human rights and social responsibili-ties is needed.
Gaudium et Spes	Pastoral Constitution on the Church in the Modern World	1965	Second Vatican Council	How the church is to relate to contemporary society	The church must scrutinize "signs of the times."
Dignitatis Humanae	On the Declaration on Religious Freedom	1965	Second Vatican Council	How do we understand free-dom, truth, and the relationship between church and state?	We are free to seek what is true and good.
Populorum Progressio	On the De-velopment of Peoples	1967	Pope Paul VI	Widening gap between rich and poor nations	"Development is a new word for peace."
Octogesima Adveniens	A Call to Action	1971	Pope Paul VI	Urbanization marginalizing vast multitudes	Lay Catholics must focus on political action to combat injustices.
Justitia in Mundo	Justice in the World	1971	Synod of Bishops	Structural injustices and oppression inspire liberation movements	"Justice . . . is a constitutive dimension of the preaching of the Gospel."

21. English titles of CST documents are not always literal translations of the formal Latin titles.

Latin Title	English Title[21]	Year Published	Source	Major Challenges Addressed	Major Ideas or Messages
Evangelii Nuntiandi	Evangelization in the Modern World	1975	Pope Paul VI	Cultural problems of atheism, secularism, consumerism	The salvation promised by Jesus offers liberation from all oppression.
Laborem Exercens	On Human Work	1981	Pope John Paul II	Capitalism's and communism's treatment of workers as mere instruments of production	Work is the key to "the social question" and to human dignity.
Sollicitudo Rei Socialis	On Social Concern	1987	Pope John Paul II	Persistent underdevelopment, division of world and blocs	"Structures of sin" are responsible for global injustices.
Centesimus Annus	The Hundredth Year	1991	Pope John Paul II	Collapse of communism in Eastern Europe	Combat consumerism and greed in the new "knowledge economy."
Deus Caritas Est	God Is Love	2005	Pope Benedict XVI	Charitable activity	The lay faithful have a direct duty to work toward the common good.
Caritas in Veritate	Charity in Truth	2009	Pope Benedict XVI	Global financial and ecological crisis	Focus on the economy of gift and ethical renewal.
Evangelii Gaudium	The Joy of the Gospel	2013	Pope Francis	Evangelization	The proclamation of the Gospel to the poor is a form of charity.
Laudato Si	On Care for Our Common Home	2015	Pope Francis	Ecological crisis and climate change	Climate is a common good to be protected.
Fratelli Tutti	Fraternity and Social Friendship	2020	Pope Francis	Human dignity and fraternity	There should be no borders in how we respect and care for one another.

Table 6.1. Selected Catholic social teaching documents.[22]

22. Adapted with permission from Massaro, *Living Justice*, 34–35.

Thomas Massaro identifies nine themes woven through CST: the dignity of every person and human rights; solidarity, the common good, and participation; family life; subsidiarity and the role of government; property ownership in modern society; the dignity of work, rights of workers, and support for labor unions; colonialism and economic development; peace and disarmament; and an option for the poor and vulnerable.[23] Some might add care for God's creation as a tenth. Within these themes, CST affirms the dignity and rights of persons and favors the "common good" or social conditions that nurture human development for all; expresses concern about the abuses of capitalism, socialism, and communism toward humans and the earth; elevates the poor (a "preferential option for the poor"); views compassion as Christian witness; encourages decision making at the lowest possible level; and calls for Christians and parishes to engage in acts of justice and charity.[24] It is out of CST that many Catholic initiatives find their social justice rudder and their keel.

In the 1930s, CST inspired an alternative to capitalism called distributism. In response to the Great Depression, many ideas were advanced to correct the social upheaval created by the boom and bust cycles inherent in capitalism. Catholic thinkers Hilaire Belloc (1870–1953), G. K. Chesterton (1874–1936), and others promoted a notion where land and assets would be dispersed among people, creating an economy of thousands of small firms. Labor rights and fair wages would be ensured and although gains from economic consolidation would be limited, the owner-manager structure of firms would incentivize human and asset development.[25]

LIBERATION AND BLACK THEOLOGY

A second significant source of Catholic thought on justice is liberation theology. Although the letters of Latin American bishops are included in CST, liberation theology branched out beyond official church teaching. It was suspect and sometimes sanctioned by the Vatican, accused of being influenced by Marxist thought.[26]

---

23. Massaro, *Living Justice*, 79–119.

24. For an integrated view of themes, see Pontifical Council for Justice and Peace, *Compendium of the Social Doctrine*.

25. This small-scale approach to the economy fit the thinking of E. F. Schumacher who promoted similar ideas in his best-selling 1973 book, *Small is Beautiful*. Toward the end of his life, Schumacher converted to Catholicism. Schumacher, *Small Is Beautiful*.

26. For an introduction, see Palazzi, "Hope and the Kingdom."

In the 1960s and 1970s, Latin American theologians began viewing theology from the perspective of the poor—powerless, oppressed, exiled non-persons constituting the majority of the world's population. Theologians questioned the way theology had been constructed. They began reconsidering how God had worked through history and what Jesus had said and done in the Gospel accounts. The response was not merely a theology of suffering or a message of eschatological endurance, but a revolutionary gospel that rebuked oppressors and sided with the exploited, calling for unjust social structures to be resisted so the kingdom of God could be realized [The Kingdom of God].

The Kingdom of God

The kingdom of God is central to liberation theology and to other compassionate initiatives through history. It is a concept given to varying interpretations, reflecting diverse assumptions about God, the church, and all humanity. Kingdom of God conceptualizations flowered in multiple ways during the twentieth century.[27]

Some view the kingdom of God as occurring gradually when a society inches toward justice, kindness, and humility with God (Mic 6:8). This progression is imagined as occurring through accumulating acts of compassion and justice that radiate through society, eventually tipping the balance toward the good; or, it might occur through virtuous advocacy and leadership that advances just policies and affects the masses; or, it might occur inwardly, through individual formation and sanctification.

Others view the kingdom of God as taking a more defensive stance, holding firm and shining its light in a dark world. Creation will groan in the not-yet (Rom 8:18–25) until Jesus returns, when God will bring redemption and judgment. For now, the Christian's task is to endure hardship and persecution, caring for orphans and widows and remaining unstained by the world (Jas 1:27).

---

27. A particularly interesting debate of these views occurred among Scottish theologians in the previous century: McKay, *Kirk and the Kingdom*. Later, in North America, a widely influential treatise on the kingdom of God was Richard Niebuhr's, *Christ and Culture*.

A multitude of other nuanced views exists, some of which we might imagine in a stylized conversation among twentieth-century thinkers:

"Can you not see that Christians could help usher in the kingdom of God?" implores Walter Rauschenbusch. "If only those at the helm of social and economic structures would work for justice, our land would shine brightly with the gospel."

"I agree," asserts Leo Tolstoy, "but you needn't be in a high position to make a difference. You'll find the kingdom of God resides within each person. We must all nonviolently resist evil institutions that assail the gospel."

"Humans have tried utopia, and it always fails because it idolizes technology," inserts Jacques Ellul. "When the masses came to Jesus in the wilderness, he did not give them a home or food security; he offered only himself—Jesus is the kingdom of God, not some human-crafted city."

"The precise problem is that people can be moral but institutions cannot. They are flawed by self-interest and self-preservation. They cannot be born again," asserts Reinhold Niebuhr.

Karl Barth chimes in. "It's not really a matter of what we do or don't do. Only God can bring the kingdom. God will act. Our role is to wait faithfully."

"Yet God created the whole world—it's all God's and we have a mandate to influence it for justice," says Abraham Kuyper. "To stand by denies God's sovereignty and call in our lives. You might as well sing, 'Sit down, oh men of God, / His kingdom he will bring. / Whenever it may please his will, / You cannot do a thing.'"[28]

"It seems to me you are talking about the kingdom in terms of power," asserts Gustavo Gutiérrez. "Take a fresh look at Jesus, and you will see that God walks among the poor and seeks justice. The gospel liberates and, if we are his disciples, we must denounce the established order, which oppresses with power."

"How you get there matters indeed," inserts John Howard Yoder. "The gospel is unavoidably political and the appropriate Christian posture is cross-shaped."

28. William P. Merrill parodied the hymn, "Rise Up, O Men of God," in 1911, as quoted in Atkinson, *Prelude to Peace*, 169.

"Yes, but don't forget that the wealthy and the powerful need lib-
erating too—the kingdom of God reconciles rich and poor in Christ,"
affirms Jürgen Moltmann.
These and others through the centuries have offered insights on
what it means to pray "Your kingdom come. Your will be done on earth
as it is in heaven" (Matt 6:10).

Theologians such as Peruvian Gustavo Gutiérrez (b. 1928) began seeing the gospel through the eyes of the poor hearing its call to liberate people
from political, social, and economic oppression. Gutiérrez's A *Theology of
Liberation* opened the eyes of many to this fresh vision of the good news.
Over time, Ignacio Ellacuría (1930–1989), Leonardo Boff (b. 1938), Jon
Sobrino (b. 1938), and others added their voices. When Catholic bishops
met in Medellín, Colombia, in 1968 and in Puebla, Mexico, in 1979, they
asserted that Jesus wished to liberate the poor from hunger, poverty, and
ignorance—conditions brought about through the sin of oppression—and
that the gospel demanded political and social transformation to achieve
justice and peace. Society was in desperate need of conversion, but it would
not occur through a top-down social gospel. Instead, it required bottom-up
transformation, through resistance and revolution.

In some parts of Latin America, the Philippines, and elsewhere, small
groups of Catholics met together to study the Bible and spur one another
on in grassroots efforts for social justice [**Base Communities**]. Pastors held
varying views of liberation theology. Some, such as Nicaraguan Fr. Uriel
Molina Oliú (b. 1932), supported revolution and were critical of the church
for not taking a stronger stand. Priests generally took the side of the poor
and stood for justice. Some were subject to violence, most famously, Óscar Romero (1917–1980), whom some have called the father of liberation
theology. After his appointment as an archbishop in El Salvador, Romero
transformed into a bold representative for social justice.[29] Two weeks before
being assassinated, he said in an interview,

> I have frequently been threatened with death. I must say that, as
> a Christian, I do not believe in death but in the resurrection . . . .
> As a pastor, I am bound by a divine commitment to give my life

---

29. For biographical and theological insights, see *Brockman, Romero*; Colón-Emeric, *Óscar Romero's Theological Vision*; Romero, *Voice of the Voiceless*.

for those whom I love, and that includes all Salvadorans, even those who are going to kill me.[30]

Base Communities

Basic ecclesial communities, or *comunidades eclesiales de base* (CEBs), began developing in the late 1950s in Spain and France, prior to the emergence of liberation theology. CEBs were small groups of Catholics who would regularly gather to read and study the Bible and encourage one another to engage in acts of social justice.[31] Energized in regions of political oppression, CEBs helped the church function through underground meetings. They spread through developing countries and were prolific in parts of Central America, Brazil, and the Philippines.

BECs often were viewed with suspicion by those in political power. At times they were subjected to violence. As an example, Felipe (1931–1983) and María Barreda (1933–1983) of Nicaragua were abducted with other farmers while picking coffee beans. They were tortured and killed.[32] Around the same time, in communist Hungary, Fr. György Bulányi (1919–2010) encouraged cells of youth and adults to gather to pray and to encourage one another to serve the poor and practice pacifism.

While liberation theology was circulating in Latin America, Martin Luther King Jr. and other black Christian leaders and theologians, including James H. Cone (1938–1983) and later, Dwight N. Hopkins (b. 1953), focused on the American black experience of oppression and injustice.[33] Rooted in abolitionist tradition, many African Americans in the twentieth century resonated with the call for liberation and justice posed by social

30. Quoted in Brockman, *Romero*, 248.

31. For an example of CEBs, their work and parish links, see Gómez and Wright, "Bonds of Suffering, Bonds of Hope" Julia, "Beyond Basic Ecclesial Communities."

32. Cabestrero, *No los Separó la Muerte*.

33. Although they affirmed many of the views of white progressives and conservatives, black theologians frequently were marginalized from social gospel conversations. Dorrien, *Soul in Society*; Trimiew, "Social Gospel Movement." Later, womanist approaches offered additional insights to liberation. See Kirk-Duggan, "Womanist Theology."

gospel progressives and liberation theologians, but they generally favored the theology of Protestant conservatives.[34]

The inconsistencies between Christian moral theology and the actions of white Christians had long been recognized by Frederick Douglass, W. E. B. Du Bois, and countless other African Americans.[35] In the 1960s, Tom Skinner (1942–1994) chastised white Christians for their inconsistencies:

> And what about this man who claims that Jesus Christ is the answer? Heart tinged with emotion, he packs his bags and takes the next boat to Africa, to reach the black man with the Gospel. He spends millions of dollars to reach that black man. He crosses the Atlantic and Pacific Oceans, he flies, he goes through all kinds of sacrifices; he'll contract malaria; he'll get shot; he'll lose his own children in order to go to the mission field to reach the black man in Africa with the Gospel. But he won't cross the street. He won't spend sixty cents to go to the other side of town to reach a group of people with the same black skin, where there is no language barrier. . . . There is virtually no attempt to reach this vast number of black Americans who feel hopeless, frustrated, and want a way out.[36]

The spiritual-physical wedge that divided white Protestants in the twentieth century did not materialize in black theology, which often emphasized lifting up the black community.[37] Social justice and evangelism comfortably coexisted for many black Protestants who served their communities and

34. This combination was evident in the U. S. civil rights movement among African American denominations such as the Christian Methodist Episcopal Church and the Church of God in Christ. See Butler, *Women in the Church*; Chism, *Saints in the Struggle*; Sommerville, *An Ex-colored Church*; White, *Rise to Respectability*.

35. At the end of his autobiography, Frederick Douglass wrote of the antebellum American South: "What I have said respecting and against religion, I mean strictly to apply to the slaveholding religion of this land, and with no possible reference to Christianity proper; for, between the Christianity of this land, and the Christianity of Christ, I recognize the widest possible difference—so wide, that to receive the one as good, pure, and holy, is of necessity to reject the other as bad, corrupt, and wicked" (Douglass, *Narrative of the Life*, 150). In 1969, attendees at the National Black Economic Development Conference issued a "Black Manifesto" for restorative justice, in which they demanded $500 million in reparations from white churches and synagogues for economic injustices committed against African-Americans.

36. Skinner, *Black and Free*, 45–46.

37. Unruh and Sider, *Saving Souls*. Highlighted earlier, CST provided a foundation for social action as well. The City of St. Jude in Alabama offers one example. Fr. Harold Purcell (1881-1952) led an effort to offer education and health-care to African Americans beginning in 1934, hosting the first fully integrated hospital in the southeastern United States. In 1965, the City offered shelter to marchers walking from Selma to Montgomery. See Coffman, *Build Me a City*.

engaged in holistic mission in Africa.[38] Sharing in suffering and community betterment became themes for many in African American churches.
Women were particularly active in attempting to address economic and human need in the United States and abroad.[39]

Also distinctive was the willingness to network with other churches
in coalitions, such as in Operation Breadbasket, sponsored by the Southern
Christian Leadership Conference.[40] The twelve-year initiative (1962–1974)
advocated for job desegregation and black-owned businesses.[41] According
to Allison Calhoun-Brown, "In large part because racism and segregation
prohibited blacks from developing or participating in American mainstream institutions outside the church, the church became the medium for
all of civil society."[42] Finally, and particularly pronounced in the spirituality of Martin Luther King Jr., in much black theology, was an emphasis on
nonviolence in social change [**Nonviolence**].

Nonviolence and Peace

In advocating for civil rights, Martin Luther King Jr. encouraged a path
of love rather than violence. In the 1963 Birmingham, Alabama direct
action campaign, King asked participants to pledge themselves to
nonviolence via the following commitment. Note King's interweaving
of spirituality and practical theology in liberation and justice:

I hereby pledge myself—my person and body—to the nonviolent
movement. Therefore, I will keep the following Ten Commandments:

1. Meditate daily on the teachings and life of Jesus.

2. Remember always that the nonviolent movement
   in Birmingham seeks justice and reconciliation, not
   victory.

3. Walk and talk in the manner of love, for God is love.

4. Pray daily to be used by God in order that all men
   might be free.

38. Gilkes, "Until My Change Comes"; Hill, *A Higher Mission.*
39. Collier-Thomas, *Jesus, Jobs, and Justice.*
40. Gilkes, "Until My Change Comes."
41. Beltramini, "SCLC Operation Breadbasket."
42. Calhoun-Brown, "While Marching to Zion."

5. Sacrifice personal wishes in order that all men might be free.

6. Observe with both friend and foe the ordinary rules of courtesy.

7. Seek to perform regular service for others and for the world.

8. Refrain from the violence of fist, tongue, or heart.

9. Strive to be in good spiritual and bodily health.

10. Follow the directions of the movement and of the captain on a demonstration.[43]

Nonviolence has been a core commitment of several peace efforts led by Christians, including the Fellowship of Reconciliation (FoR) founded in 1914 to protest war; Pax Christi International, founded in France in 1945, broadly advocating for peace; the Southern Christian Leadership Conference, founded in 1957 and led by Martin Luther King Jr.; and the Plowshares movement (1980) led by Daniel (1921–2016) and Philip Berrigan (1923–2002), Catholic priests and brothers who protested nuclear arms.[44]

An Orthodox Flare

The liberation of labor was being attempted in Russia as well as in Europe, Latin America, and the United States. Theologians within the Russian Orthodox Church occasionally criticized social or labor oppression, but the seminaries and the church were shackled to the state and the party line.[45] Fr. John of Kronstadt (1829–1908), Grigory Petrov (1866–1925), and Fr. Georgy Gapon (1870–1906) appealed to the Tsarist government to return to orthodoxy and provide better working conditions for laborers. Under

---

43. Washington, *A Testament of Hope*, 537.

44. Wilcox, *Uncommon Martyrs*.

45. Benz, *The Eastern Orthodox Church*, 153. Priests in Greek Catholic and Russian Orthodox traditions who opposed Soviet control often served parishioners in underground churches within the Soviet Union. Some were banished. The role of prominent martyrs and suffering in the Greek Catholic Church are discussed by Halemba, "Suffering for and Against the Church."

threat, Petrov fled to Bulgaria and advocated for Christian socialism, but Gapon remained in St. Petersburg.

In 1905, on what later would be called the "Bloody Sunday" of the first Russian Revolution, Gapon marched with 150,000 workers and their families to the Narva Triumphal Arch in St. Petersburg (see Fig. 6.1). Singing hymns and carrying icons and crosses, workers were met by armed soldiers, who opened fire. Gapon escaped but later died under suspect circumstances at the age of thirty-six. Bloody Sunday was the beginning of two years of social upheaval and eventually ushered in the October Manifesto, which led to an overthrow of Tsarist Russia. Some historians compare Gapon's effort to a Russian version of the social gospel, but it also reflected a subterranean movement among seminarians who saw their priestly calling as including a prophetic voice for the masses—a foreshadowing of liberation theology.[46]

Fig. 6.1. Fr. Gapon leading workers in St. Petersburg, 1905.

46. Hedda, *His Kingdom Come*; Kenworthy, "Orthodoxy and the Social Gospel."

POLITICAL AND PUBLIC THEOLOGY

Protestant interest in politics and civil society emerged in the late twentieth century in two intersecting streams of political theology and public theology, shaped by scholars such as Johann Baptist Metz (1928–2019), Martin Marty (b. 1928), Robert N. Bellah (1927–2013), Peter L. Berger (1929–2017), and Stanley Hauerwas (b. 1940). More recently, Kathryn Tanner (b. 1957) and Joerg Rieger (b. 1963) have helped shape these conversations. These scholars connect a suffering God with a suffering world, and they call institutions and individuals alike to seek cruciform justice.

Two examples illustrate theologically-influenced voices for political justice in the late twentieth century. The first was the U.S. Sanctuary Movement of the 1980s. With parallels to the underground railroad, over two hundred North American Catholic and Protestant congregations sought out refugees fleeing military oppression in El Salvador and protected them in homes or within the walls of the church. Church leaders created loose networks of contacts and support, and several denominations supported the effort. Many Christians remained ambivalent or opposed to the effort and ultimately the U.S. government took legal action against the movement's representatives. But those willing to provide sanctuary to the alien remains an impulse and expression of social resistance that continues to resurface.[47]

A second example was the Jubilee 2000 movement. Coinciding with the Great Jubilee of the Catholic Church, which focused on God's mercy, Christians (mostly evangelicals mobilized by Tearfund, a faith-based humanitarian organization headquartered in the United Kingdom) joined with secular partners beginning in 1995 to advocate for debt relief for heavily indebted low-income countries. Countries in the Global South had borrowed money to get through skyrocketed gas prices in 1973. As interest rates climbed, debt loads became so large that the countries could never repay them. Debt payments drained governmental funds from countries where basic needs were unmet. Jubilee 2000 appeals, musical events, and protests swayed U.K. and U.S. governments to write off debts to qualifying nations.

We now turn to consider several practical expressions of liberation and justice theologies applied to economics, labor, and commerce. Our timeline will restart seeing that several of these movements paralleled one another. We begin with the Catholic worker movement.

---

47. For a historical and legal review, see Pirie, "Origins of a Political Trial."

THE CATHOLIC WORKER MOVEMENT

In the United States, amid the depths of the Great Depression, Catholic convert Dorothy Day (1897–1980) began inspiring people to reconsider the gospel of Jesus for the unemployed. The Catholic Worker movement attempted a "radical renewal of Catholicism and the social order," advocating voluntary poverty in solidarity with the poor.[48] From a small office in New York City, Peter Maurin (1877–1949) and Day called displaced workers to the liturgy and teachings of the church and urged the church to address oppressive market and political structures.[49]

Maurin was a French immigrant and idealist. Day was an astute observer of society. Together, they rejected the materialism of both capitalism and socialism, preferring a third way rooted in human dignity and community. They favored a communitarian and personalist approach that emphasized the dignity of people, who all reflected the *imago Dei*.

Day edited the *Catholic Worker*, a paper that advocated for social justice, nonviolence, and seeing Jesus among the poor—a message that the paper's prints of Quaker Fritz Eichenberg's (1901–1990) woodcuts often powerfully conveyed (see Fig. i.1). Refusing to cower to the power brokers of government, church, or commerce, Day spoke prophetically against structures that bypassed or harmed the poor.[50] Catholic worker houses spread across the United States, welcoming the poor and the unemployed. Catholic worker farms invited any to join in returning to the land to labor together.

WORKER-PRIESTS

The Catholic Church in nineteenth-century France was viewed by many as aligned with the upper classes and traditional politics, siding with the monarchy rather than with democratic revolutionaries. Frédéric Ozanam (1813–1853), founder of the Society of Saint Vincent de Paul, had appealed for the church to embrace democratic political structures because they gave voice to the people, but traditional interests prevailed, anti-clericalism grew, and many of the French proletariat abandoned the church. Some, such as Léon Harmel (1829–1915) [**Léon Harmel**], attempted reforms. They may have softened but they did not alter the direction of society away from the church.

---

48. Zwick and Zwick, *Catholic Worker Movement*.

49. For biographies, see Day, *Peter Maurin*; Loughery and Randolph, *Dorothy Day*.

50. Day, "Why Write About Strife and Violence?"

Léon Harmel

After becoming patron of his family's wool and cotton spinning mill in France, Léon Harmel, a dedicated Catholic, endeavored to accelerate his father's efforts to shape a factory based on Christian teachings. Between 1861 and 1875, Harmel assembled a core of dedicated Catholic employees in associations who encouraged their fellow workers to strengthen their commitment to the church. He constructed a chapel on the factory grounds and arranged for daily mass to be celebrated. With renewed faith, workers established savings banks and mutual aid societies to benefit the workforce. Harmel established livable wages to support a family, shortened the working day, set up a factory council for democratic oversight, welcomed a Christian union, funded worker pilgrimages to Rome, encouraged Catholic worker circles, invited chaplains to the factory floor, provided free education for youth and work and pensions for the aged. Harmel's efforts and friendship with Pope Leo XIII influenced the content of *Rerum Novarum*.[51]

Catholic priests elsewhere in Europe called for the support of laborers subject to industrialization.[52] The church opened the door to social, and in particular, labor reforms when Pope Leo XIII issued *Rerum Novarum* in 1891. Publication of this foundational CST document was accompanied by a flurry of efforts by the church to connect with workers—small experiments with credit clubs, insurance societies, pastoral care, and the like. But many workers saw little need for the church, and the divide between the masses and the church grew while Catholic advocates argued each side.

During WWII, German occupiers in France denied pastoral care to workers in munition factories. Bishops responded by selecting twenty-five priests (from two hundred volunteers) to take factory jobs so they secretly could minister to the French workers. It was in the Nazi factories and concentration camps that priests and workers rekindled a solidarity, often with the priest experiencing moments of existential crisis as he lived the life of a worker or convict. These represented just a few of the priests attempting to pastor others during the war while awaiting liberation [**Prison Pastors**].

51. Coffey, *Léon Harmel*.

52. For example, Adolph Kolping (1813–1865) advocated for workers in Germany. See Festing, *Adolph Kolping*.

Prison Pastors

Many priests and pastors served valiantly in WWII prisons, work camps, and concentration camps, and in communist prisons before, during, and after the war.[53] The long list includes Fr. Victor Dillard (1897–1945), who volunteered as a clandestine electrician and served workers and priests in German work camps; Fr. Bernhard Lichtenberg (1875–1943), who prayed for the Jews from his pulpit and encouraged his parishioners to choose solidarity over self-preservation; Fr. Maximilian Kolbe (1894–1941), who took the place of another prisoner condemned to death in Auschwitz; Fr. Engelmar Unzeitig (1911–1945) who became known as the "angel of Dachau"; Klymentiy Sheptytsky (1869–1951); Fr. Henryk Malak (1912–1987); Protestant Richard Wurmbrand (1909–2001), who endured years of torture and isolation; and hundreds of others.[54] Describing his time as a prisoner in Lubianka, where he spent four years before being transferred to Siberian work camps, Fr. Walter Ciszek (1904–1984) recalled,

> I learned to purify my prayer and remove from it the elements of self-seeking. I learned to pray for my interrogators, not so they would see things my way or come to the truth so that my ordeal would end, but because they, too, were children of God and human beings in need of his blessing and his daily grace. I learned to stop asking for more bread for myself, and instead to offer up my sufferings, the pains of hunger that I felt, for the many others in the world and in Russia at that time who were enduring similar agony and even greater suffering. I tried very hard not to worry about what tomorrow would bring, what I should eat, or what I should wear, but rather to seek the kingdom of God and his justice, his will for me and for all mankind.[55]

Ciszek became discouraged at times but he focused on God's will and God's ability to sustain him. He and other priests heard confession, celebrated mass, held retreats, encouraged others, and endured. These

---

53. Some died on the way to prison but protested openly against Nazi acts. Bernhard Lichtenberg (1875–1943) is one of these witnesses.

54. For a sampling, see Gaydosh, *Bernhard Lichtenberg*; Hoffmann, *Who Will Kill You*; Malak, *Shavelings in Death Camps*.

55. Ciszek and Flaherty, *He Leadeth Me*, 56.

prison pastors did not attempt to overthrow unjust structures and were in no position to do so, but they served valiantly within them.[56]

After WWII, concerned about growing numbers of unchurched working-class parishioners and class antagonisms, the Catholic Church attempted to connect once again with workers by having priests offer homilies and celebrate mass in train stations and movie theatres. It quickly became apparent that such a shallow outreach was inadequate. A closer relationship would be required to relate to workers.[57] In 1943, French priests received permission to apply for jobs in the factories, keeping their identities mostly quiet from management and revealing them to coworkers only when it yielded pastoral benefit. It was important that the priests were not funded externally, so they could not be accused of being a puppet of a wealthy benefactor or of benefiting from an economic safety net.

The worker-priests not only lived and worked with others, but they had freedom and discretion, and their alliances were tested when strikes, demonstrations, and Communist Party enlistments occurred. Many came to see the world through the eyes of the workers. They migrated toward leftist politics, joined labor unions and agitated for labor reforms. Several joined the Communist Party. With complaints from Catholic company managers and owners reaching the ears of bishops, and with the priests increasingly diverging from Vatican views, they were recalled from the factories.

The experience was successful in that it cautioned once again that a gap existed between the church and the masses. One worker-priest, Henri Perrin (1914–1954), provided reflections on his experiences:

> The priest must live among his people again, live familiarly with them, sharing their sufferings and joys, and not in a retirement which people attribute to pride. How could this deep gulf have come between us when after all our Lord wanted shepherds among his flocks, fishers of men, leaders of his people, not officials at desks.[58]

The outcome of the worker-priest experiment reminded observers that the church could lose touch with people and that only incarnational living could close the gap. But it was the priests alone who took the view of the

---

56. Less known are the fourteen Salvation Army missionaries who were detained for over two years in Japanese internment camps in Singapore during the war.

57. This section is influenced by Siefer, *Church and Industrial Society*, 18–104.

58. Perrin, quoted in Siefer, *Church and Industrial Society*, 44.

workers, not the church as a whole. As Gregor Siefer says, "The ghetto wall which had previously separated the 'Church' and the 'World' had not been broken down. Instead it had been pushed into the middle of the church, and now separated Right and Left, conservatives and progressives, parish clergy and worker-priests of the one Church."[59] The French church continued, partially divided by some advocating liberation and others staying the course.

CATHOLICS AND LABOR UNIONS

Another example of the Christian pursuit of liberation and justice are the efforts of Catholics to support the right to unionize. The Archbishop of Baltimore, James Gibbons (1834–1921), witnessed Catholics suffering as industry expanded in the eastern United States, and he took up their cause. Gibbons appealed to Pope Leo XIII to sanction labor union membership and the Pope responded in *Rerum Novarum* by supporting fair wages, safe working conditions, and the right of association. Frs. John A. Ryan and John O'Grady argued that Catholic moral theology supported just wages and human rights in the marketplace.

Catholic labor unions were founded in Europe, Latin America, and Africa throughout the twentieth century, including the World Confederation of Labor in The Hague (1920–2006) and Solidarity in Poland (1980), but relatively few religious unions formed in the United States.[60] Still, Catholic social teaching supported the right to organize, and with parishioners working in factories and fields, priests took up the cause of supporting justice. With minimal labor and antitrust law, U.S. businesses provided fertile soil in which unions could grow. Priests and workers found inspiration in two early social encyclicals, Pope Leo XIII's 1891 *Rerum Novarum* and Pope Pius XI's 1931 *Quadragesimo Anno*, both of which criticized unrestrained capitalism and supported the rights of labor.

In 1938, John Cort (1913–2006) founded the Association of Catholic Trade Unionists (ACTU) to bring virtue to unions. The intent was to educate Catholic union members (and their unions) about CST to enable Christian virtue to inform principles and actions and forestall the growth of communism.[61] Over the next two decades, more than 150 Catholic labor schools were established to teach CST to workers and relay the skills and knowledge required for organizing and operating a labor union with

---

59. Siefer, *Church and Industrial Society*, 9.

60. Many Catholics were involved in unions in the nineteenth century, including constituting much of the membership of the Knights of Labor and other union bodies.

61. Lubienecki, "Catholic Labor Education."

Christian virtue. With increasing numbers of Catholics moving into the middle class, the need for labor education declined in the 1960s. Secular universities developed extension programs, such as the School of Industrial and Labor Relations at Cornell University, that incorporated many of the elements of the Catholic labor schools while omitting the religious content.

Priests and Catholic laypersons, such as César Chávez (1927–1993) and Dolores Huerta (b. 1930) with their rallying cry *"¡Sí, Se Puede!"* ("Yes, We Can!"), supported and furthered labor organizing (see Fig. 6.2).[62] In so doing, they helped Catholics and non-Catholics explore a "third way" between capitalism and communism, a more humane capitalism that supported human dignity and rights. Catholics were not alone in advocating for a more just treatment of labor and economy [**Toyohiko Kagawa**], but they were prominent in leading the cause in the United States.

Fig. 6.2. Fr. John "Jack" O'Malley arrested during United Farm Workers demonstration, 1970.

62. Baker, *Go to the Worker.*

Toyohiko Kagawa

Orphaned as a youth, Toyohiko Kagawa (1888–1960) was educated by Presbyterian missionaries in Kobe, Japan. After postgraduate training at Princeton Theological Seminary, Kagawa returned to Kobe. He moved into a slum where he lived for many years and wrote research reports, novels, and poetry about the lives and living conditions of people in poverty. To advance human wellbeing, Kagawa advocated for labor unions, producer cooperatives, and the right to vote for men and women. He believed Christianity resonated with these causes and that they offered alternatives to capitalism, fascism, and authoritarianism. Kagawa inspired over one hundred rural gospel schools to be established, promoting participatory rural improvement and evangelism. Missionaries joined Kagawa in encouraging churches to improve social conditions and extend benevolence.[63] He was arrested for speaking out and for participating in labor strikes, which he did frequently. Kagawa wrote over one hundred fiction and non-fiction books and often has been described as the Japanese Gandhi.[64]

JUST BUSINESS

After WWII, journalists, returning soldiers, and Protestant and Catholic missionaries shared news of hunger and devastation across war-torn Europe and in the "third world." In the 1960s and 1970s, social unrest and riots tore through U.S. cities, exposing fissures over racial injustice and war. Christians responded in a range of ways—including by supporting the status quo. But many were stirred into action, and some took up the cause of workers. Most did not attempt to remediate the economic system but focused on the lack of market access as a source of injustice. Their response often was to clear obstacles to access and build individual capacities so all

---

63. Ingehart, *Century of Protestant Christianity*, 158–9, 185, 203. Hundreds of staff worked with the Omni Mission and YMCA in rural areas. The Baptist Misaki Kaikan, the first institutional church in Japan, was described in the first two decades of the twentieth century as the "busiest beehive of religious industry in Japan" (p. 159), extending a variety of social programs for Tokyo residents.

64. Schildgen, *Toyohiko Kagawa*.

could gain from the benefit of markets [**Woman's Exchange Movement and Appalachian Crafts**].

Woman's Exchange Movement and Appalachian Crafts

Dated to 1832, woman's exchanges were shops that allowed women bakers, seamstresses, and artisans a place to sell their wares on consignment and earn an income in a time when most women were restricted from business. Initially designed for well-to-do women, exchanges were expanded to women of any status who wished to make or sell homemade goods. A combination of self-help and women's liberation, woman's exchanges allowed women artisans and managers an opportunity to employ their skills in entrepreneurship and commerce. According to Kathleen Waters Sander, about seventy-two exchanges were established in U.S. cities during the nineteenth century, and many remained in operation in and beyond the twentieth century.[65]

In rural Appalachia, what eventually became the Highland Craft Guild provided an outlet for impoverished artisans. Presbyterian missionary Frances Goodrich (1856–1944), arrived in the 1890s from New England to "bring about what's missing." She urged local weavers to adjust their standards to those of northern markets. Others joined over time to enhance, preserve, and market southern crafts.[66]

Fair trade was an example of a market-utilizing justice initiative. Advocating for structural change and enhanced access, fair-trade castigated capitalism but saw value in markets. Some of its advocates subscribed to economic dependency theory, which placed the blame for global poverty at the feet of an unfair economic system, one that oppresses the poor to make others wealthy and then recycles charity with expectations of praise. Such a system was viewed as paternalistic and pernicious. But if markets respected the interests of the buyer and seller, if they allotted voice and wages fairly, they could work for the good of all. As Chris Sugden writes, fair trade was "a response of practical compassion often rooted in a Christian worldview that refuses to accept that in the market the only categories are winners and losers."[67]

65. This section relies heavily on Sander, *Business of Charity*.

66. For a history in her own words, see Goodrich, *Mountain Homespun*.

67. Sugden, "Fair Trade as Christian Mission," 9. A much broader proposal of

Fair trade cropped up in several places around the same time, facilitating the trade of commodities such as chocolate and coffee, and artisan goods. SERRV (Sales Exchange for Refugee Rehabilitation and Vocation) was one of the first organizations to emerge in post-WWII Italy. Church of the Brethren relief workers brought handicrafts back to the United States and discovered plentiful interest in the goods. Importing them connected an artisan without a market to supportive buyers willing to pay higher prices. Around 50 percent of the sales price was returned to the artisan. SERRV encouraged the creation of high-quality goods reflecting local cultures. In working with SERRV, artisans augmented their business skills.[68] Although Christians of many denominations purchased SERRV goods, Church of the Brethren customers often faced the uncomfortable dilemma of living simply versus purchasing nonessential goods.[69]

Self-Help Crafts was another early alternative trade organization. It began when Edna Ruth Byler (1904–1976) traveled to Puerto Rico and noticed the fine needlework of women who had a limited market for their goods. Byler purchased several items and brought them back to Akron, Pennsylvania, to sell. Eventually, the Mennonite Central Committee (MCC) supported Byler, and she traveled and acquired goods from multiple countries. The organization she began is known as Ten Thousand Villages, today. Other Christian artisan importers followed, such as Eternal Threads, founded by Linda Egle.

In Europe, Traidcraft began promoting fair trade in 1980 and grew to be a British leader in fair trade imports as well as an early leader in social accounting, publishing views from multiple global stakeholders regarding its performance. In 1988, Francisco Van der Hoff Boersma (b. 1939), a Dutch missionary to Latin America, launched Fairtrade, the first labeling initiative for fair trade products.[70] Certification addressed a variety of issues including fair credit and wages and the sustainable sourcing of natural materials.

Another approach to just business was to provide technical and vocational training for youth or adults. Goodwill Industries International is likely the best known among North American job training programs. Founded in 1902 by Methodist minister Edgar J. Helms (1863–1942), Goodwill offered employment for individuals with special needs. Other Christian job training programs offer a hand up through "welfare to work" programs. These included Focus: HOPE in Detroit, founded by Fr. William Cunningham

---

noncompetitive trade is offered in Tanner, *Economy of Grace*.

68. Kreider, *Cup of Cold Water*, 98, 100.

69. Thompson and Thompson, *Beyond Our Means*, 115.

70. Hoff Boersma, *Manifesto of the Poor*.

(1930–1997) and Eleanor Josaitis (1931–2011) to enhance racial unity and justice while training workers for jobs in automotive manufacturing. Homeboy Industries in Los Angeles is another well-known enterprise. Founded by Fr. Greg Boyle (b. 1954), Homeboy offers life and job training for former gang members. Added to these are a host of faith-based job and life training initiatives such as FaithWorks, founded by Joyce Dalzell in Abilene, Texas, and Christ Kitchen, founded by Jan Martinez in Spokane, Washington.[71]

Finally, an assortment of Christian business development initiatives emerged or were adopted during the last quarter of the twentieth century, their intent being to extend economic justice through enhanced entrepreneurial services. At the micro level, business development services and microcredit via loans and savings groups became popular among Christians. Faith-based nonprofits such as Opportunity International, Partners Worldwide, HOPE International, and the Chalmers Center offered a portfolio of capital, business or savings group training, or mentoring. Value chain and market systems development approaches were used by large faith-based development organizations, such as World Vision, to enhance the ability of women and smallholders to participate in agricultural markets.

Business as Mission (BAM) focused on launching small and medium-size enterprises in developing economies. Utilizing diverse forms and business models, BAM companies offered local employment in an enterprise that witnessed to Christ.[72] Generally smaller employment programs were designed to build capacity and restore dignity for individuals seeking a path out of poverty, sex work, domestic abuse, incarceration, racial injustice, or other opportunity-limiting situations. Many of these were attached to FBOs. Eden, a faith-based organization in Thailand, is one example.

These various approaches—from fair trade to enterprise development—represent a variety of postures regarding capitalism, from antagonistic to agnostic to embracing. As such, they hinted at the diversity of economic and theological ideologies held by the Christians who created them.[73]

---

71. "Focus: HOPE"; "Homeboy Industries."

72. Gort and Tunehag, *BAM Global Movement*. For historical examples, see Iglehart, *Century of Protestant Christianity*, 201. For a critical perspective, see Bronkema and Brown, "Business as Mission."

73. An assortment of Christian influences on modern working-class labor and economic justice is provided in Cantwell et al.'s lively volume, *Pew and the Picket Line*.

CONTRIBUTIONS IN OTHER SECTORS

The civil rights movement enveloped labor as well as political, educational, housing, and other rights. The gathering of hundreds of thousands in Washington, DC, where Martin Luther King Jr. delivered his "I Have a Dream" speech was the 1963 March on Washington for Jobs and Freedom. Dr. King delivered his "I've Been to the Mountaintop" speech in Memphis in support of the 1968 Memphis Sanitation Workers strike.

In the waning years of the twentieth century and spilling over into the twenty-first, several prominent activists, writers, and speakers prodded their fellow Christians to be transformed by the radical gospel and advocate for a variety of social justice causes. The list is long but it includes pioneers such as Unitarian minister, John Haynes Holmes (1879–1964) who co-founded the American Civil Liberties Union (ACLU) and the National Association for the Advancement of Colored People (NAACP); Norman Thomas (1884–1968), Presbyterian minister and socialist candidate for U.S. president; labor, nonviolence, and civil rights advocate, A. J. Muste (1885–1967); Edwin T. Dahlberg (1892–1986), an American Baptist peace activist; theologian, pastor, and civil rights leader, Howard Thurman (1899–1981); Gordon Cosby (1917–2013) and the Church of the Saviour; Lucius Walker (1930–2010), American Baptist advocate for Cuba; Desmond Tutu (b. 1931), Anglican Archbishop of Cape Town; Tony Campolo (b. 1935); Ron Sider (b. 1939) and Evangelicals for Social Action; Jim Wallis (b. 1948) and Sojourners; Ched Myers (b. 1955); Bryan Stevenson (b. 1959) and the Equal Justice Initiative; Gary Haugen (b. 1963) and International Justice Mission; and Shane Claiborne (b. 1975). Each of these has stirred people toward simple living, peacemaking, jubilee, and advocacy for the oppressed [**Advocacy**]. Catholic advocates of justice are diverse and numerous, and include, Chiara Lubich (1920–2008) and the Focolare Movement; Thea Bowman (1937–1990); Helen Prejean (b. 1939); Betty Williams (1943–2020); and Mairead Maguire (b. 1944).

Advocacy

Some have argued that the Bible emphasizes individual conversion rather than social and political change. Jesus, after all, said that his kingdom was "not of this world" (John 18:36), and Paul instructed slaves to be obedient (Eph 6:5–6; Col 3:22–24) and the Thessalonians to "aspire to live quietly, to mind your own affairs" (1 Thess 4:11a). But several biblical and historical examples testify to the faithful representing righteous causes to rulers. Consider, for example, the actions of Esther, Mordecai, Amos, Jeremiah, and Moses.

John Howard Yoder (1927–1997) argued that Christian discipleship cannot help but be political. Justice demands it. Yet many Christians remain wary about advocacy. Stephen Offutt and his colleagues appeal to all Christians to consider "transformational advocacy," which they define as

> intentional acts of witness by the body of Christ that hold people and institutions accountable for creating, implementing, and sustaining just and good policies and practices geared toward the flourishing of society. Transformational advocacy challenges injustice and obstacles to human flourishing at whatever level it is practiced by humbly engaging with people who can address the wrong, trusting God's Spirit to change all those involved as well as the institutions themselves.[74]

Offutt and his colleagues describe advocacy not as wielding power or mere problem solving but as "building relationships, envisioning new realities, and working together to foster the kind of change that emanates from the Lordship of Jesus Christ."[75]

The story of "ambulance drivers versus bridge builders" is a classic illustration of advocacy as an act of charity. It is taken from Ron Sider's influential book *Rich Christians in an Age of Hunger*:

> A group of devout Christians once lived in a small village at the foot of a mountain. A winding, slippery road with hairpin curves and steep precipices without guard rails wound its way up one side of the mountain and down the other. There were frequent fatal accidents. Deeply saddened by the injured people who were pulled from the wrecked cars, the Christians in the village's three churches decided to act. They pooled their resources and purchased an ambulance. Over the years, they saved many lives although some victims remained crippled for life.
>
> Then one day a visitor came to town. Puzzled, he asked why they did not close the road over the mountain and build a tunnel instead. Startled at first, the ambulance volunteers quickly pointed out that this approach, although technically quite possible, was not realistic or advisable. After all, the narrow mountain road had been there for a long time. Besides, the mayor of the

---

74. Offutt et al., *Advocating for Justice*, 11–12.
75. Offutt et al., *Advocating for Justice*, 116.

town would bitterly oppose the idea. He owned a large restaurant and service station halfway up the mountain.

The visitor was shocked that the mayor's economic interests mattered more to these Christians than the many human casualties. Somewhat hesitantly, he suggested that perhaps the churches ought to speak to the mayor. Perhaps they should even elect a different mayor if he proved stubborn and unconcerned. Now the Christians were shocked.

With rising indignation and righteous conviction they informed the young radical that the church dare not become involved in politics. The church is called to preach the gospel and give a cup of cold water, they said. Its mission is not to dabble in worldly things like social and political structures.

Perplexed and bitter, the visitor left. As he wandered out of the village, one question churned round and round in his muddled mind. Is it really more spiritual, he wondered, to operate the ambulances which pick up the bloody victims of destructive social structures than to try to change the social structures themselves?[76]

Today, on the basis of Christian faith, denominations, churches, and individual Christians have advocated for a variety of social, economic, and political issues, including, public education, capital punishment, welfare policy, abortion, child labor, fair trade, human and civil rights, labor organizing, food aid, war, housing, refugees, justice for farm workers, apartheid, foreign debt, and human trafficking. The Confessing Church defied Nazi fascism, and William Wilberforce (1780–1825) and abolitionists fought for an end to slavery in the British Empire. Numerous faith-based NGOs emphasize advocacy, including, Bread for the World, Pax Christi International, and Sojourners.

It is not difficult to recall occasions where Christians did not advocate for justice; when they were ambivalent, confused, overwhelmed, or lethargic. Their responses can be uneven or even oppositional to other Christians.[77] Christians hold a variety of views on complex issues and it can be challenging to discern whether one is hindering or furthering righteousness

76. Sider, *Rich Christians*, 2005, 219–20.

77. Recent historical examples include differences over the U.S. civil rights movement, war and conflict, famine, abortion, urban poverty and violence, mass incarceration, LGBTQ rights, and immigration legislation.

and justice by one's action or inaction. In these contexts, the vast reservoir of Scripture and Christian examples, teachings, and community continue to instruct, calling Christians to high standards of virtue and justice.

CLOSING INSIGHTS

This chapter spotlighted three foundational theologies for liberation and justice—namely, the social gospel, Catholic social teaching, and political and public theology. Additionally, we considered several pioneers and revolutionaries especially in the areas of labor and commerce. As we've journeyed, it is difficult to miss the fact that Christians often champion opposing viewpoints. As we conclude, I'd like to consider a few reasons why this might be the case.

First, it is clear that Christians can grow insensitive to injustice. When this occurs, the potency of the church weakens. This was apparent in the French church, when well-to-do Christians and the working class divided; between black and white social gospelers; between Latin American Catholics and the universal church; and between Protestants and the racially and economically oppressed. Losing touch with the vulnerable is a constant possibility if one is not a participant. The depth of the breech goes unrecognized until one awakes to the voices and experiences of others. Often, emissaries of the poor are prophetic individuals and organizations that do not compromise in speaking truth to power and that, with fire and sacrifice, attempt to change hearts, minds, and lives. History indicates that, often, these appeals are unheard or unheeded and change is slow, suggesting that, in the end, prophets must leave hearts and lives up to people and to God.

Second, the development of opposing positions can be attributed, at least in part, to ideology. Ideology represents an individual's composite of (often tacit) beliefs, attitudes, assumptions, and values, continually shaped by discourse and institutions. An ideology need not be congruent to be compelling. Frequently, contradictory beliefs cohere comfortably in what appears to be a uniform lens on the world, even though it is not.[78] For Christians, ideology should be open to the pulsating gospel; Scripture, tradition, and witness prevent beliefs from becoming bad faith. The faith may have been "once for all entrusted to the saints" (Jude 3), but that same teaching tells Christians they are disciples and pilgrims, learning and growing in humility. Placing oneself in regular proximity to God and to vulnerability typically exposes inconsistencies in ideology. This is why so many

---

78. Two of many examples of enigmatic religious ideology and social issues are Jones, *White Too Long*; Griffith, *God's Law and Order*.

reformers advocate for prayer and spiritual disciplines to accompany social action: they provide refreshment for the fight but also ensure a just cause, and because injustice is spiritual as well as physical. Ideology is inescapable, not unchangeable.

Finally, the twentieth century was marked by the contest of individuals versus institutions. Two world wars, a global depression, and the realism of Reinhold Niebuhr undermined confidence in the notion that institutions could deliver the social gospel. In the 1960s, Peter Berger advocated that Christians break free from them.[79] But political scientist John Compton has argued that individual convictions seldom compel action; rather, most people take their cues from, are stirred by, and are mobilized by institutions.[80] Neither individuals nor structures are perfect, but both can provoke us to love and good deeds (Heb 10:24–25). Institutions and organizations play a role in stimulating views and actions of compassion or judgment.[81]

Christian advocates for liberation and justice compel us not to fear and in responding to the radical call of Jesus, to recognize that the gospel is not neutral politically, and that "we must live our philosophy," as Jesuit tradition advocates. We are to seek the radical call of righteousness, "trusting God's Spirit to change all those involved as well as the institutions themselves," as transformational advocacy suggests.[82] As David Kirk writes in *Quotations from Chairman Jesus*, "Christianity is a matter of seeking the fullest life—which means knowing how to die, so as to be reborn in a way which liberates."[83]

79. Berger, *Noise of Solemn Assemblies.*

80. Compton, *End of Empathy.*

81. To see how the common good can be pursued in organizations, see Alford and Naughton, *Managing as if Faith Mattered*, 70–96.

82. Offutt et al., *Advocating for Justice*, 11–12.

83. Kirk, *Quotations from Chairman Jesus*, 16.

7

Peace and Humanitarianism

OUR SECOND PASS THROUGH the twentieth century takes up the theme of peace and humanitarianism. At the dawning of the century, two relatively quiet developments were under way: networks of Catholic and Protestant hospitals continued delivering medical care, and a few Christian denominations distributed generally modest amounts of charity for famine, education, and medical care through missionaries and young para-church agencies. Most early humanitarian initiatives were small, quiet, and sectarian. Several new waves of influence would bring change, however.

In England and in the United States, divine healing brought physical and spiritual renewal, and presaged the growth of Pentecostalism. Before World War II, North American pacifist Christians prepared for the front lines of service and Protestants embraced a composite of humanitarianism and nationalism, preparing them to respond to global need. After the war, peace churches went into the fray first, and evangelicals were stirred to action as they witnessed reports of suffering and starvation from journalists and evangelists.

Evangelism and service continued to come under scrutiny by conservatives, but by the close of the century, Christian humanitarianism among all branches of the faith had grown to an unprecedented scale. In short, WWII served as a watershed, with international development preparation preceding it and expanded mobilization following it. This chapter focuses on international humanitarianism, with an occasional nod to domestic peace and humanitarian labors, and it concludes with a spotlight on a single sector: food security.

COORDINATING AID

While Christian congregations and individual believers extended benevolence for local needs, global social need prompted a new level of organized effort. One of these needs was to support the waves of immigrants that flowed into the United States between 1850 and 1930. Many arrived with ties to a denomination. With the arrival of millions of German, Irish, and Italian Catholics, dozens of Catholic social institutions and efforts sprang up. Catholic Charities was established in 1910 to serve as a network and advocate for care. Nearly a decade later, the National Catholic War Council (NCWC) was created, later renamed the National Catholic Welfare Conference. The council addressed issues related to World War I, including facilitating aid for U.S. soldiers and European refugees.[1] The NCWC evolved into today's United States Conference of Catholic Bishops (USCCB). Of course, Christians would have to be energized to aid one another, and worship was just one of the notions of how that occurred [**Liturgy**].

Liturgy

Fr. Virgil Michel (1890–1938) was an advocate for social justice, rural life, and education. Inspiring each to its fullness, he believed, was worship. Michel's biographer wrote that Michel perceived "that a properly worshipping people, realizing that oneness in The Mystical Christ and actively contacting the living realities of the liturgy, could in time transform a whole society."[2] Michel believed that social reforms were ineffectual if they were not animated by the spirit of the Gospels. Liturgy conveyed that spirit and would transform worshippers to love God and others through catechesis, beauty, and mystery. As individuals formed in the gospel, they would bring about a more just society.

---

1. The NCWC provided a foundation for foreign aid that was expanded by John F. Kennedy, the first Catholic U.S. president. See Fitzpatrick-Behrens, "Catholic Roots of U.S. Foreign Assistance."

2. Marx, *Virgil Michel*, 36.

For Lutherans, social services were important but secondary to preaching the gospel. Benevolence was delegated to the congregational level, but pastors encouraged congregations to launch health, education, and poverty alleviation initiatives to address immigrants in need.[3] Associated Lutheran Charities, a tiny grassroots organization, was formed in 1901 to network Lutheran efforts.[4] Despite a proliferation of agencies, doctrinal differences impeded cooperation and delayed the establishment of Lutheran Services in America at the end of the century in 1997.[5] Lutheran World Relief formed mid-century, however, as a mechanism to respond to starving Lutherans in Europe.

These and parallel efforts represented largely sectarian aid—a denomination assisting its domestic and/or international members in need. Following WWII, dozens of these organizations were founded around shared belief or ethnicity (Table. 7.1). But other para-church agencies had a different origin and focus. Peace churches (Mennonites, Brethren, Quakers, and, in larger numbers in the UK, Christadelphians) organized early, having done so previously in Europe and seeking an alternative to military service in the United States. Some in progressive denominations, such as Methodists and Episcopalians, anticipated the wartime need for refugee assistance and mobilized people and resources to respond. After the war, evangelicals responded to images and reports of destruction and starvation relayed by missionaries and journalists.[6] But we're getting ahead of the story, which begins in the early decades of the century with evangelical journalism [**Louis Klopsch and the *Christian Herald***] and the appeals and labors of pacifists.

3. Lueking, *Century of Caring*; Svebakken and Bacon, "Dreams, Disappointments, Achievements."

4. Svebakken and Bacon, "Dreams, Disappointments, Achievements."

5. Gunz, "Delicate Dance."

6. In many cases, denominations collected and distributed funds prior to establishing para-church agencies and NGOs. Frequently, denominations were motivated to establish official organizations so they could have legal status and operate with enhanced freedom.

Organization	Denomination	Headquarters	Founded
Catholic Charities	Catholic	Alexandria, Virginia	1910
American Friends Service Committee (AFSC)	Quaker	Philadelphia, Pennsylvania	1917
Mennonite Central Committee (MCC)	Mennonite	Akron, Pennsylvania	1920
United Methodist Committee on Relief (UMCOR)	Methodist	Atlanta, Georgia	1940
Episcopal Relief and Development	Episcopal	New York, New York	1940
Catholic Relief Services (CRS)	Catholic	Baltimore, Maryland	1943
World Relief	Evangelical	Baltimore, Maryland	1944
Lutheran World Relief	Lutheran	Baltimore, Maryland	1945
Church World Service (CWS)	Mainline	Elkhart, Indiana	1946
Adventist Development and Relief Agency International (ADRA)	Adventist	Silver Spring, Maryland	1956
World Renew	Reformed	Grand Rapids, Michigan	1962
Tearfund	Evangelical	London, UK	1968
Compassion and Mercy Associates (CAMA)	Christian and Missionary Alliance	Colorado Springs, Colorado	1972
Nazarene Compassionate Ministries	Nazarene	Lenexa, Kansas	1984
International Orthodox Christian Charities (IOCC)	Orthodox	Baltimore, Maryland	1992
Latter-day Saint Charities	LDS	Salt Lake City, Utah	1996
Lutheran Services in America	Lutheran	Washington, DC	1997

Table 7.1. A sampling of church-related social service agencies.

Louis Klopsch and the Christian Herald

From the sixteenth century, missionaries had been active globally, periodically returning with reports and artifacts from distant lands. As the United States grew in population and wealth and as photography and media enabled widespread communication of human need conditions seemed ripe to spur on global sensitivities.[7]

---

7. Heather Curtis provides a fascinating history of Klopsch and the *Christian Herald* in Curtis, *Holy Humanitarians*. This insert is based on her scholarship.

In 1899, Louis Klopsch (1852–1910) and Reformed Church pastor Thomas De Witt Talmage made plans to produce an American version of the *Christian Herald*, a popular British newspaper. Klopsch's sensationalist approach to journalism spread the news of need, and he invited progressive and conservative believers to unite around the common cause of responding to domestic and global need. In a little more than a decade, the *Christian Herald* reached a peak circulation of nearly half a million subscribers. Klopsch raised millions of dollars to ship food and aid from American Christians to famine and disaster victims in Russia, India, Turkey, Japan, Italy, Mexico, and elsewhere.

Historian Heather Curtis argues that Klopsch advanced the idea that the United States was the "almoner to the world," divinely ordained by God to intervene in global affairs with moral imperialism. This manifestation of American triumphalism was suffused with racial ideology. American imperialism was driven by the notion that God had given white Americans the responsibility to civilize and Christianize their "little brown brothers" around the world who were viewed as incapable of ruling or taking care of themselves. They needed white American civilization to bring order out of chaos.[8]

Missionaries objected to Klopsch's portrayal of global people as helpless, ignorant, passive recipients of generous American aid. Instead they were partners respected for their knowledge, abilities, and dignity. Klopsch's mobilization of Christians for global aid primed global sensitivities but also jaundiced them. In 1895, Klopsch purchased the Bowery Mission in New York City, spurring on domestic aid. In 1901, he printed the first red-letter edition of the New Testament, with Jesus' words rubricated.

8. Stanley, *Nation in the Making*, 164.

Fig. 7.2. *Christian Herald* highlighting famine in Finland, 1903.

YOUR FAITH HAS MADE YOU WELL

In late nineteenth-century England and in the United States, faith healing emerged as an alternative to sanctified suffering and modern medicine.[9] Traveling from Europe to North America, the teaching and experience of miraculous healing fit with Wesleyan entire sanctification and with God's

9. Catholic tradition has long embraced healing by divine grace and miracles at shrines and via the intercession of saints. The faith healing movement among Protestants, however, signified a change in belief and practice and injected new theological understanding and teaching. For background, see Robinson's *Divine Healing* trilogy.

abundant grace in Reformed theology. Methodists, Baptists, Episcopalians, Adventists, and others embraced divine healing in faith, creating a seedbed for early Pentecostal fellowships.

Among the many prominent ministers who participated in healing were Charles Cullis (1833–1892), A. B. Simpson (1843–1919), and R. Kelso Carter (1849–1928) of the Christian and Missionary Alliance, and Aimee Semple McPherson (1890–1944), founder of the Foursquare Church. Several of these preached the "full gospel" or "fourfold gospel" of Jesus as savior, sanctifier, healer, and coming king. Healings occurred in faith homes, in pastoral prayer, and through mass gatherings and media. Alternate views of health and healing emerged during the century as well in Christian Science, promoted by Mary Baker Eddy (1821–1910), and the New Thought movement whose Unity Church was founded by Charles (1854–1948) and Myrtle Fillmore (1845–1931).[10]

For some, being restored in health by divine grace was linked to entire sanctification, wherein one was energized to live a sinless life focused on evangelizing and serving others. Higher Life theology nudged Christians to join social reform organizations such as the Young Men's Christian Association (YMCA) and the Women's Christian Temperance Union (WCTU) in a kind of conservative parallel to the social gospel, and it encouraged global evangelism as an act of sharing God's compassion for all.

Most social charity efforts in the movement focused on humanitarianism rather than ameliorating structural sin, but some benevolent outreaches involved massive mobilizations. For example, Aimee Semple McPherson's Angelus Temple, the largest Christian congregation in the world in the early twentieth century, provided relief for Japanese and Germans following WWI and a commissary, complete with a soup kitchen, an employment office, showers, medical and dental care, a laundry, and a dispensary, served over 2,000 meals per day and aided documented and undocumented Los Angeles residents in the 1920s and 1930s.[11]

Why were some healed and others were not? What role did faith play in healing? What healing was authentic and which practitioners, spurious? And what is "healing" and "sickness" and where do they fit among Christian doctrines? The movement overflowed with questions. Heather Curtis concludes that, in the end, advocates and practitioners learned to sit comfortably within the ambiguity and paradox of faith healing, content to praise the

---

10. Christian Science differs from faith healing in that disease is viewed as a mistaken idea, a mental apparition. The New Thought movement grows from metaphysical roots but differs from Christian Science on several doctrinal points.

11. Sutton, *Aimee Semple McPherson*, 188–96.

compassion of Jesus, the Great Physician.[12] Some denominations, such as the Church of God (Anderson), reversed their anti-medical teaching and, among some, divine healing receded.[13]

DOMESTIC HUMANITARIANISM

Early in the twentieth century, Christian congregations in the United States addressed a variety of social services and needs in urban and rural areas. Often, they cared through informal channels, person-to-person, but they also collaborated through faith-based organizations (FBOs) such as the YMCA and YWCA.[14] As the U.S. government increased its spending in the 1930s through the New Deal to assist the masses affected by the Great Depression, churches reduced their charitable spending.[15] This same process occurred in reverse following welfare reform in 1996: churches increased their charitable spending when the government reduced services.[16] But "crowd-out" was not the only relationship of church and state in charity. Often, secular, religious, and governmental entities performed different roles, and, occasionally, they collaborated.[17]

In contrast to the hesitancy of Protestants who were wary of supporting the unworthy poor and who blamed the poor for their destitution, some historians argue that Catholics tended to view poverty with encompassing acceptance, advocating for the rights and needs of all poor. Maureen Fitzgerald argues that Irish Catholic nuns were resolute in their advocacy for the poor in New York City, and that their advocacy and network of voluntary relief organizations, established in the late nineteenth and early twentieth centuries, prompted the establishment of public welfare structures.[18]

PACIFISTS ON THE FRONT LINES

As the clouds of the first world war gathered, Quakers, Mennonites, Brethren, Christadelphians, and a scattering of hundreds across other

12. Heather Curtis provides an excellent history of late nineteenth-century faith healing. This section relies heavily on her scholarship. See Curtis, *Faith and the Great Physician*, 7–8, 14.

13. Stephens, *Who Healeth All Thy Diseases*.

14. For a review, see Johnson, *Social Work of the Churches*.

15. Gruber and Hungerman, "Faith-Based Charity."

16. Hungerman, "Are Church and State Substitutes?"

17. For a proposal of collaboration, see Cnaan et al, *Newer Deal*.

18 Fitzgerald, *Habits of Compassion*.

denominations applied for exemption from military service.[19] They appealed to the U.S. government to serve without weapons or uniform: "We are united in expressing our love for our country and our desire to serve her loyally. We offer our service to the Government of the United States in any constructive work in which we can serve humanity."[20] Despite their offer, the inquiry seemed seditious to many, and no provision was made to exempt non-combatants. While church leaders awaited action, drafted pacifists were jailed rather than exempted. Some died in prison due to the harsh treatment they received as traitors.

As the war continued, Quakers established the American Friends Service Committee (AFSC) in 1917, in hope that the conscientious objector (CO) status eventually would be affirmed and they would be able to supply volunteers to the Red Cross.[21] As everyone waited for a response on the CO question, a few peace church members found other ways to serve. Herbert Hoover (1874–1964), an American Quaker financier living in London, was asked to organize food aid for Belgians who were starving due to German occupation. Hoover was successful, and his mobilization of food fed eleven million Belgians, plus others in France and China. Subsequently, Hoover was asked to head up the U.S. Food Administration and the American Relief Administration. In 1928, he was elected the thirty-first president of the United States.

When WWI ended, COs remained unrecognized by the U.S. government. The AFSC was poised, however, to volunteer in post-war relief and rebuilding and provided some of the first relief workers to walk into devastated Europe. Margaret Hope Bacon describes their efforts:

> AFSC workers helped to erect prefabricated houses, to assist in the development of cooperative stores, and to reestablish agriculture. A series of army dumps were turned over to the Quakers for the salvage of useful materials, among them rifle butts, which were literally turned into plowshares. The French government provided the Quakers with groups of German prisoners to assist with this work. Rather than accept free labor, members of the unit kept track of the hours the prisoners put

19. Some denominations had committees devoted to winning military exemption for conscientious objectors. The Northern Baptist Convention was one example. See Brodhead, "Baptists Further Social Gospel."

20. Bacon, *Let This Life Speak*, 38.

21. Numerous Mennonite service and relief organizations were formed between 1918 and 1950, with the Mennonite Central Committee (MCC) being launched in 1920. Mennonite organizations cooperated with the AFSC on several initiatives.

in and later gave the appropriate amount of money as a gift to their families.[22]

The compassion and care shown by volunteers was appreciated throughout war-torn regions in Europe, Asia, and the Middle East (see Fig. 7.3). Brethren served in the Spanish Civil War as well, introducing an innovative approach to sustainable food security [**Heifer Project**].

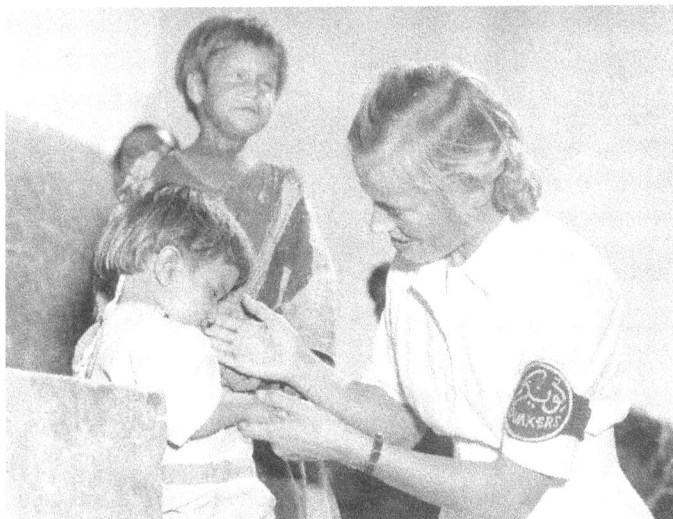

Fig. 7.3. AFSC nurse treating Palestinian boy.

Heifer Project

During the Spanish Civil War (1936–1939), Brethren Service and AFSC volunteers supplied powdered milk for infants. But even when watered down, the supplies were insufficient to feed hungry babies in Spain. Authorities made the painful decision to ration the distribution and provide milk only to the healthiest babies. In 1938, Brethren visionary Dan West (1893–1971) floated the idea of sending live cows to Spain. Some farmers did not think the notion was feasible, and some supporters did not like the idea that cows would go to both sides of the conflict. But a decision was made to try.

22. Bacon, *Let This Life Speak*, 50.

WWII erupted before the cows could be shipped, but as soon as the war ended, Goshen City Church of the Brethren donated three cows, named Faith, Hope, and Charity. The program was called the Heifer Project Committee, and it became a nonprofit in 1953. Keith Kreider summarizes what happened next:

> From the beginning the project believed it was more practical to send bred heifers overseas than to send calves or milk cows. Moreover, West conceived of a unique idea that became an indispensable feature of the project. Remembering that "it is more blessed to give than to receive," West developed the requirement that each recipient of a heifer would, in turn, donate the first female offspring to another qualified family. That family, in turn, would do the same, and the gift would continue to benefit more people.[23]

Hundreds of heifers were donated by farmers. When war prevented shipments, cows went to others in need—to sharecroppers in the United States and to households in Mexico and Puerto Rico. The effort was featured in *Time* magazine.

Later, the United Nations Relief and Rehabilitation Administration (UNRRA) collaborated with Brethren Service to ship Brown Swiss bulls to Greece to establish a breeding program. UNRRA paid for the transport while Brethren Service provided the labor.[24] With six million dairy animals destroyed in WWII, UNRRA announced that it would be providing seven ships to carry the milk cows to Europe. Thousands of cowboys hitchhiked or rode trains to board the ships and accompany horses, goats, chicks, and cows to Poland, Greece, Korea, Japan, Ecuador, Bolivia, Haiti, Ethiopia, and elsewhere. Sometimes, they were the first to arrive after a disaster. Animals were selected based on the local culture and included horses, goats, chickens, honeybees, yaks, buffalo, and several other species. Eventually, Heifer Project International was formed, and programs added training and environmental programming to ensure continued health for the animals and the land.

23. Kreider, *Cup of Cold Water*, 132.
24. Thompson and Thompson, *Beyond Our Means*, 103.

Fig. 7.4. Family in Greece receiving a Heifer Project cow.

AFSC volunteers were still working diligently in several European countries when WWII broke out. Some volunteers remained in place and others were recalled, but the needs eventually eclipsed those of the Great War. Peace churches continued to appeal to the U.S. government for CO status, and in 1940, the U.S. Selective Training and Service Act was passed, providing options for alternative service. Unfortunately, the act did not exempt COs from harassment and stigma. During the war, the U.S. Civilian Public Service (CPS) program assigned approximately twelve thousand COs to former New Deal Civilian Conservation Corps camps in the United States, where they implemented soil conservation and forestry projects, worked as smokejumpers, built dams, labored on farms, and worked as mental hospital attendants. Some were subjects in experiments testing the impact of starvation, hydration, climate, and disease on mental health. CPS workers were unpaid and restricted from serving outside the United States.[25] During WWII, men and women from 231 denominations served as CPS'ers. Most were from peace churches, but they also included Lutherans, Jehovah's Witnesses, Baptists, members of Churches of Christ, and others. Morale was low, and much of the service seemed meaningless.

People were displaced throughout the world due to war and famines created by the destruction of farms and agricultural supply chains. Added to refugee needs were those of German and Italian prisoners of war (POWs) and interned Japanese Americans. Along with Quakers, Brethren were also active

25. Mennonite Central Committee, "Civilian Public Service Story."

in Europe, providing relief supplies and serving in prisoner-of-war camps in Britain, France, Belgium, the Netherlands, and Italy.[26] Prisoners were protected by the Geneva Convention of 1929, and the Red Cross and YMCA were charged with their care: the Red Cross handled legal and health needs, and the YMCA was responsible for prisoners's spiritual and cultural welfare.

Approximately 350,000 Germans and tens of thousands of Italians were held in prisoner-of-war camps in Great Britain during WWII. Brethren staff often were the only non-military personnel allowed to visit the prisoners. Leaders helped facilitate educational programs and musical and athletic events. During the war, eight thousand Italian prisoners earned their high school diploma in English by passing a Cambridge examination.

For soldiers blinded in the war, the German war office provided a teacher for the blind, along with braille classes and course materials. Two Brethren volunteers ran a program to prepare German prisoners interested in youth or pastoral work following the war. Six hundred elementary school teachers were trained along with 130 Protestant and Catholic prisoners who received basic theological training, 125 prepared for youth work, and 200 readied for university study. Kenneth Kreider writes,

> These efforts to provide assistance by people whom they had pictured as enemies caused many German soldiers to re-evaluate what they had been taught about Americans. . . . [G]etting to know these captured soldiers as individuals rather than as part of a stereotyped "enemy" also led to changed attitudes on the part of those administering the camps.[27]
>
> In addition to direct aid, Christians of a variety of backgrounds provided shelter and protection, and at times, advocacy, such as in the Confessing Church, mentioned earlier [Hiding Places].

Hiding Places

Although some Christians were directly or indirectly complicit in persecuting Jews in WWII, other Christians are remembered for hiding or providing passage or false identities to Jews. Their stories are a few of the lights of compassion in a great darkness. Numbered among those providing protection were Betsie (1885–1944) and Corrie ten

26. Unless otherwise noted, the material in this section on Brethren is from Kreider, *Cup of Cold Water*, 61–100.

27. Kreider, *Cup of Cold Water*, 68.

Boom (1892–1983), Sára Salkaházi (1899–1944), Odoardo Focherini (1907–1944), Oskar Schindler (1908–1974), and others, some of whom have been recognized with the Israeli honorific title, "Righteous Among the Nations."

When WWII ended, Quakers, Mennonites, and Brethren ramped up their relief efforts. The needs were immense, and the logistics of managing personnel, supplies, and sites were incredibly complex. Multitudes of people were despondent, particularly the Germans.

In Carrara, Italy, Brethren volunteers responded by organizing the *Circolo O.K.* (O.K. Circle), a club for 360 children, many of whom were on the street or not in school. They offered a full-day program including education and training in hygiene plus meals, crafts, music, drama, and a store in which students could spend points earned through chores.

In the United States, an estimated eight thousand AFSC volunteers sorted blankets, food, and clothing and shipped them to facilities in Washington, DC; Chicago; New York City; and Detroit while also supporting refugees in the United States. Brethren set up collection and shipping centers in Maryland, Indiana, and California. According to Kreider,

> Supplies flooded in faster than the local post office could handle the volume of materials. Piles of packages accumulated on the sidewalk. The gymnasium at the service center was piled to the ceiling, and boxcars were rented from the railroad to serve as temporary warehouses. Volunteers were solicited from churches within three or four hours' driving distance . . . to process materials for shipment overseas.[28]

For their service, the AFSC and the U.K. Friends Service Council were jointly recognized with a Nobel Peace Prize in 1947. The award money went to purchase streptomycin to combat an outbreak of tuberculosis in Russia.[29] Many COs who had served in CPS camps chose to continue their service after the war. They joined organizations such as AFSC, Brethren Service, Mennonite Central Committee, Church World Service, Heifer Project International, and CARE.[30]

In 1952, during the Korean War, President Truman approved alternative service volunteers to serve internationally. A Mennonite Central

28. Kreider, *Cup of Cold Water*, 82.
29. Bacon, *Let This Life Speak*, 162.
30. Mennonite Central Committee, "American Friends Service Committee in Gaza."

Committee effort called "Pax" took Mennonites to more than forty countries as an alternative to carrying arms in Korea.[31]

CARE AND CHURCH WORLD SERVICE

In 1945, an opportunity arose for a private organization to distribute eight
million government food rations and other supplies. A diverse coalition
of twenty-two religious, labor, civic, and other entities banded together to
orchestrate the response in the Cooperative for American Remittances to
Europe or CARE. The idea was that Americans could send a "CARE package" to specific recipients in need in post-war Europe and Japan. CARE's
complex membership and structure yielded a sputtering start. Seventh-day
Adventists objected to cigarettes being included. Religious and secular entities squabbled about church-state relations. Yet, as Michael Barnett writes,
"After months of worries that CARE might be a losing venture, it became
an overnight sensation" due to a portfolio of marketing successes.[32] CARE
represented the early entrance of large, secular international development
non-governmental organizations (NGOs).

In 1946, the Federal Council of Churches (FCC) created the Church
World Service (CWS) to support and coordinate proliferating relief efforts
from its members.[33] At the time, CWS was the largest private organization
in the United States devoted to global relief. During its first year of activity,
CWS distributed nearly $9 million of in-kind goods and funds, largely to
war-torn regions.

In 1947, the Christian Rural Overseas Program (CROP) was established to coordinate the collection and distribution of materials to refugees
in the United States and abroad. Food, clothing, hygiene, and medical supplies were distributed with the support of seventy-five denominations and
service agencies that collaborated between 1944 and 1979. The program
gave sewing projects to congregations and five-gallon buckets for collecting
fat to make soap, yielding as much as forty tons of fat per year. Farmers
contributed food or funds from their "Lord's Acre" [The Lord's Acre].

31. Redekop, *Pax Story*.

32. Barnett, *Empire of Humanity*, 115.

33. The FCC had organized a variety of relief efforts previous to the CWS, including
efforts to rebuild churches destroyed in WWI (1918), collaboration in the European
Central Bureau for Interchurch Relief (1922), establishing a Committee on Foreign
Relief Appeals in the Churches (1939), and creating a Church Committee for Relief in
Asia (1944), among others.

The Lord's Acre

The concept of farmers donating the crops or income from an acre of land to the church traces back in recent times (perhaps inspired by Jewish law; see Lev 23:22) to a Baptist church in Bluffton, Georgia, that was highlighted in *Time* magazine in 1924. The church was offered as an example among many congregations whose members agreed to set aside a "Lord's Acre" or "Friendship Acre," whose produce or earnings would be devoted to aid. CWS promoted this program through its CROP initiative. Some farmers designated a cow, hog, or hen for relief, and workers designated the first hour's wages of each week.[34] The *Time* article highlighted an added benefit: "Acres planted for God have produced more abundant crops and have been miraculously free from the boll weevil, potato bug, army worm and other enemies of God's people."[35] Since 1969, urbanites and those without a farm participate by gathering sponsorships for a "CROP Hunger Walk." Participants collect pledges and walk up to ten miles to offset global hunger.[36]

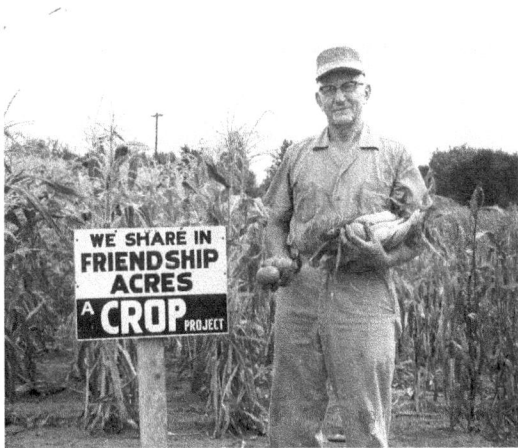

Fig. 7.5. The Lord's acre.

34. Kreider, *Cup of Cold Water*, 96.
35. "Religion: Lord's Acre."
36. Kreider, *Cup of Cold Water*, 97.

Despite the massive shipments, food shortages endured. The Dutch government offered to pay transportation costs if more wheat could be harvested and shared. Brethren and CWS worked together to fill thirty-one train boxcars with wheat donated by Christian farmers across the Midwest and nineteen boxcars of flour from Kansas Mennonites. A subsequent national "Friendship Train" was organized, amassing 270 boxcars of commodities as a gift from the American people to Europeans. Starting with twelve boxcars in Los Angeles, the train traveled through the Midwest, adding cars as it wound its way to the port of New York and then on to France and Italy. Banners and signs hung on the boxcars indicating the names of the farmers and companies that had filled them. Each package was accompanied by a message: "All races and creeds make up the vast melting pot of America, and in a democratic and Christian spirit of good will toward men, we, the American people, have worked together to bring this food to your doorsteps, hoping that it will tide you over until your own fields are again rich and abundant with crops."[37] The people of France sent a "Merci Train" in return, bearing forty-nine carloads of gifts—one car for each of the forty-eight U.S. states plus the District of Columbia.

In 1974, Arthur Simon (b. 1930) and a dozen colleagues founded Bread for the World, an organization advocating for food security in the United States and around the globe. David Beckmann (b. 1948) lead Bread for two decades prior to Eugene Cho taking the helm.[38]

DIVIDED AND INTEGRAL MISSION

While peace churches were busy serving, progressive and conservative Protestants were pursuing compassion in ways that were slowly drawing closer to one another.[39] After WWI broke out, a *Christian Century* editorial stated, "The saddest hearts in the world were the social thinkers and workers."[40] Much of their steady progress toward a more just society seemed to lie in ruin. Equally transformative was the realization that the narrow beam of Jesus as a moral exemplar was inadequate to support a sturdy and enduring

37. Scheele, "Friendship Train of 1947."

38. Simon, *Rising of Bread for the World*.

39. Historical accounts that focus on theological debates tend to stylize the breach between progressive and conservative Protestants. Compassion viewed at the level of lived religion resulted in a much more complex and blended account.

40. The editors attempted to accentuate the positive: "The war has brought the social point of view to even clearer definition in the minds of men than ever before." But many could not see the silver lining ("War and the Social Gospel," 5, 6).

Christian society. Abundant, strong theological scaffolding was being ignored, and some progressives thought it needed to be restored.

Voices from Africa appealed to progressives to invest in evangelism
and church growth and not only community development. In 1972, Gudina
Tumsa (1929–1979), an influential theologian with the Ethiopian Evangelical Church Mekane Yesus, appealed to the Lutheran World Fellowship for
the funding and flexibility to address spiritual as well as physical needs,
rather than tightly programmed aid that followed the funding priorities of
the Global North. Tumsa wrote that:

> In our view, a one-sided material development is not only self-
> deceiving, in the sense that man needs more than that but it
> is also a threat to the very values that make life meaningful, if
> carried out without due attention to a simultaneous provision
> to meet spiritual needs. . . . We believe that an integral human
> development, where the spiritual and material needs are seen
> together, is the only right approach to the development question
> in our society.

Among conservatives, suppression of social care sidelined much of the
teaching and ministry of Jesus. As Richard Stearns (b. 1951), president of
World Vision, said many years later, the absence of a public and transforming relationship with society constituted "the hole in our gospel."[41]

Throughout the twentieth century, social gospel advocates and conservatives volleyed verbal missiles at one another in sermons and writings, but
many theologians and pastors took practical steps toward a more holistic
vision of the gospel as early as the 1930s. William Temple (1881–1944),
archbishop of Canterbury from 1942 to 1944, emphasized service in society
but also charitable treatment of one another as a witness to the gospel.[42]
Carl F. H. Henry (1913–2003), of Fuller Theological Seminary, argued in
The Uneasy Conscience of Modern Fundamentalism (1947) that conservatives had overreacted in rejecting social action and care: evangelicals should
remain steadfast in their biblicism and not put too much hope in political
activism, but they must recognize and respond to the social implications of
the gospel.[43]

Billy Graham lent his support to a series of meetings that became
known as the Lausanne Movement, wherein evangelicals attempted to re-
energize global missions.[44] Diverse ideas were advanced in 1974, including

41. Stearns, *Hole in Our Gospel*, 2.

42. Dackson, "Anglicanism and Social Theology."

43. Henry, *Uneasy Conscience*. For context, see Swartz, *Moral Minority*, 13–25.

44. Parallel developments occurred within the WCC, summarized by Hookway and

liberationist views by Samuel Escobar (1934–2021) and René Padilla (b. 1932), and the notion of unreached people groups by Ralph D. Winter. Both garnered strong support as well as opposition. Respected Anglican priest John R. W. Stott (1921–2011) helped mollify the division in crafting the *Lausanne Covenant*, which laid out fifteen commitments addressing issues such as the universality of Christ, the nature of the Bible and work of the Holy Spirit, and social responsibility. A portion of the *Lausanne Covenant* reads,

> We express penitence both for our neglect and for having sometimes regarded evangelism and social concern as mutually exclusive. Although reconciliation with other people is not reconciliation with God, nor is social action evangelism, nor is political liberation salvation, nevertheless we affirm that evangelism and socio-political involvement are both part of our Christian duty. For both are necessary expressions of our doctrines of God and man, our love for our neighbor and our obedience to Jesus Christ.[45]

Despite the call for social justice, the *Lausanne Covenant* largely postponed the divide between mostly Anglo, North American delegates and delegates from South America.[46]

Impatient with the lack of progress on social issues, Evangelical leaders, mostly from the Global South, agreed at the 1980 Lausanne meeting in Pattaya, Thailand to assemble within future Lausanne meetings to advance the conversation on justice and social action. Debates continued, and a fuller statement was issued from a joint consultation of the Lausanne Committee for World Evangelization and the World Evangelical Fellowship, which met in Grand Rapids, Michigan, in 1982. In 1987, some of the leaders who had met separately within Lausanne formalized a separate organization called the International Fellowship of Evangelical Mission Theologians (INFEMIT). They established the Oxford Centre for Mission Studies (OCMS), Regnum Books International, and *Transformation: An International Journal of Holistic Mission Studies* to advance the boundaries of holistic mission.

In 2001, leaders from Christian organizations in fifty countries met in Oxford, England, to draft the *Micah Declaration on Integral Mission*, which attempted to further dovetail verbal proclamation and social engagement.[47]

Francis, *From Inter-Church Aid to Jubilee*; Slack, *Hope in the Desert*.

45. Lausanne Movement, "Lausanne Covenant." For context, see Birdsall, "Conflict and Collaboration"; Swartz, *Facing West*, 97–131.

46. Kidd, *Who is an Evangelical*, 107–8.

47. Micah Network, "Micah Network Declaration on Integral Mission."

What originally was an effort to integrate proselytization and service had been refined over time to be seen as a whole—as integral—rather than as two halves. Yet, westerners struggled with not breaking the whole into components. Debates and definitions of *integral, holistic,* and *transformational mission* continued, and not all Christians who engaged in humanitarian efforts viewed mission as integral.[48] Additionally, debates among theologians often did not parallel the views of congregants. Nevertheless, these various efforts provided theological and practical resources for Christians who were inclined to address compassion holistically.[49]

Adding to the healing of the evangelism-social responsibility breach in the late twentieth century were the writings of various academics and practitioners advocating for a gospel that included humanitarianism. These included theologians such as Ron Sider, practitioners such as Jayakumar Christian (b. 1954), and sociologists such as Tony Campolo and David O. Moberg (b. 1922). As Moberg wrote in 1977, "To omit social concern from the stewardship responsibilities of living the Christian life is just as much a process of selectively cutting out portions of the Bible as is the omission of evangelistic concern for the conversion of individuals."[50]

A final catalyst accelerating social engagement by Christians, and particularly conservatives, was the eruption of need and attention to injustice brought in the decades after WWII, paired with a booming economy. The nightly news of post-war famines and destruction, and the stories and images brought back by world-traveling evangelists such as Bob Pierce (1914–1978), co-founder of World Vision [**Kyung-Chik Han**] and founder of Samaritan's Purse, prompted a wave of responses by church members to come to the aid of those in need [**Child Sponsorship**].

Kyung-Chik Han

The stylized American version of World Vision's founding focused on evangelist Bob Pierce and the emotional response of evangelicals to

---

48. As an example of the latter, the International Mission Board of the Southern Baptist Convention states that "all human needs projects are intentionally designed to allow workers to share the Gospel, make disciples and start churches": International Mission Board, "Meeting Human Needs."

49. Jared Bok argues that Lausanne did not significantly nudge FBOs toward more holistic programming. Many were already there when Lausanne occurred. See Bok, "Distinction through Religious Activism," 311.

50. Moberg, *Great Reversal;* Sider, *Rich Christians.* Quotation from Moberg, *Wholistic Christianity,* 106.

global need following World War II. David Swartz completes the historical record by describing the efforts of World Vision's co-founder, Kyung-Chik Han (1902–2000), who served as a translator for Pierce during his Korean tour in 1950.[51]

After studying at Princeton Theological Seminary, Han returned home to Pyongyang (now North), Korea to pastor a congregation. First under Japanese occupation and then Russian, Han experienced considerable resistance. In 1945, with a warrant issued for his arrest, Han fled south and crossed the 38th parallel. He was distraught by the masses of Korean refugees in need and responded by gathering a small congregation and organizing social assistance. By the time Bob Pierce had arrived, Han had organized dozens of relief operations, widow's homes, and orphanages, and he was equipped to launch another with Pierce. Over time, Han played a role in over 100 humanitarian organizations. Youngnak Presbyterian Church, the congregation he founded in Seoul in 1945 and pastored until 1973, was the largest Presbyterian church in the world at the time of his retirement.

Swartz concludes that in the popularized, white American version of the story, "Christian Americanism saved Korea and added social justice to its anticommunist arsenal."[52] Koreans indeed gained from American partnerships but Christian humanitarianism was flourishing among Koreans long before Pierce arrived thanks in no small part to the leadership of Kyung-Chik Han.

Child Sponsorship

In 1947, evangelist Bob Pierce was preaching to large crowds in, and many were expressing faith in Jesus Christ. As recounted by his daughter and Franklin Graham, CEO of Samaritan's Purse, Pierce spoke to a group of youth at school, challenging them to accept Jesus, abandon ancestor worship, and share their faith with their families. One young girl named Jade White did so and returned to school the next day beaten and cast out by her family. The missionary administrators of the school could not afford to accept another child under their care. Graham relays what happens next according to Pierce's account:

51. Swartz, *Facing West*, 35–62.
52. Swartz, *Facing West*, 38.

I stood there with that child in my arms. Tears were running down her cheeks. She was scared to death, so insecure she was shaking in my arms. She was heavy and my arms were getting tired. I was shaken to the core. . . . I had never been held accountable for any *consequences* of my message. Now here I was faced with "Is what I say *true*? Is there any responsibility involved?"[53]

Pierce handed the school administrator some money and promised additional aid. Eventually, World Vision adopted child sponsorship as a sustainable response.

Child sponsorships had been used since at least 1816 when the ABCFM adopted the method to support children in India and Ceylon, linking them with sponsors in the U.K. Organizations in the U.S., particularly China Children's Fund (today, ChildFund), adopted and popularized the approach after WWI, with Save the Children and Compassion International, following. World Vision adopted the method in 1954, further enabling individuals and families to connect with and sponsor a child in need.[54] In the 1970s, child sponsorship organizations changed from funneling support to orphanages and schools to sending it directly to families. By 2015, an estimated 9 million children were being supported through child sponsorship.[55]

Christian Development Writing

Several authors advanced Protestant efforts in global compassion. Mentioned in the last chapter was Ron Sider's *Rich Christians in an Age of Hunger*, published in 1977. This best-selling prophetic book awakened Christians to global need, to the challenge and use of affluence, and to the idea of a progressive tithe. In 1999, Bryant Myers (b. 1945), a Christian professional with World Vision, published *Walking with the Poor*.[56] Myers introduced readers to the idea that poverty represented social, religious, economic, and

53. Graham and Lockerbie, *Bob Pierce*, 74.

54. To a lesser degree, Catholic organizations adopted child sponsorships, Unbound being a notable exception.

55 For more on World Vision and Bob Pierce, see King, *God's Internationalists*; Pierce-Dunker, *Man of Vision*. For child sponsorship, see Kaell, *Christian Globalism at Home*, 5–8; King, *God's Internationalists*, 72–74.

56. Myers, *Walking with the Poor*.

political brokenness. He introduced Christians to professional international development discourse and transformed that discourse with Christian theology. His writing influenced Christian development advocates for decades. Missionary Jim Harries (b. 1964) tirelessly rang the alarm on the corrosive influence of money in missions, and David Maranz attempted to convince westerners that money and aid are laced with deep cultural meanings.[57]

Over the next decade, multiple books were published by Christian missionaries and missiologists promoting holistic mission. One standout among these books was Steve Corbett (b. 1957) and Brian Fikkert's (b. 1964) best-seller, *When Helping Hurts*. This book popularized the notion that it was possible to do harm when one meant to help but that with an informed approach, effective holistic poverty alleviation was possible. Corbett and Fikkert and the staff at the Chalmers Center, originally located within Covenant College, shared ideas similar to those written by Bryant Myers a decade earlier in more technical prose.

Corbett and Fikkert further introduced their readers to notions, such as, non-material poverty—that even the wealthy could be impoverished; poverty-alleviation as reconciling broken relationships; asset- rather than need-based, development; participatory assessment; the difference between relief, rehabilitation, and development, and the frequent misalignment of response to need. They asserted that it was possible to work together toward *shalom* while avoiding God complexes and shaming, but that new views of oneself, of others, and of poverty were needed.[58] Corbett and Fikkert encouraged a theologically-informed view of wealth and poverty, the local church as a central participant in poverty alleviation, improvements in short-term missions, and microcredit and savings groups. They, and several others, warned of creating dependency [**Dependency**].

Dependency

Protestant missionaries and missiologists in the nineteenth century were concerned about dependency in mission contexts, as were missionaries during the closing decades of the twentieth.[59] But they weren't always talking about the same idea. *Dependency*, it turns out, connoted different ideas to different people.

57. Harries, *Vulnerable Mission*; Maranz, *African Friends*.

58. Corbett and Fikkert, *When Helping Hurts*.

59. Robert Reese provides a history of dependency in Christian mission in *Roots and Remedies*.

One meaning was captured in what economists called, "the Samaritan's dilemma." This occured when assistance created a disincentive to self-sufficiency.[60] This might also be summarized in the counsel, "Don't do for others what they can do for themselves." Aid, it is argued, subverted self-reliance and created unhealthy dependency. The Christian gospel could become polluted with an opportunity for material gain, resulting in people becoming be disempowered. The result was weak and unsustainable institutions dependent upon external monetary support and direction. Glenn Schwartz (b. 1938) and Jim Harries warned of this concern in global missions and Robert Lupton (b. 1944) heralded the same in community development.[61] Some who favored neoclassical economics and eschewed protectionism resonated with this sentiment. Communities interested in developing had sufficient assets to propel their own self-determined future.

An overlapping but different angle was voiced by missionary to China and missions observer, Roland Allen (1868–1947). Allen advocated self-supporting, self-governing churches and he warned of the distorted advantage garnered by western missionaries in importing money and building institutions in church planting. In 1912, Allen wrote,

> we have preached the Gospel from the point of view of the wealthy man who casts a mite into the lap of a beggar . . . . We have done everything for them, but very little with them . . . . We have imagined ourselves to be, and we have acted so as to become, indispensable . . . . We have educated our converts to put us in the place of Christ.[62]

Allen spotlighted missionaries and mission agencies as sup planting capable local leaders and distorting the apostle Paul's simple and pure approach to gospel teaching. Allen laid the blame for dependency at the feet of missionaries, not the capable people.[63]

Although other views existed, a third perspective was one that advocated on behalf of dependency, arguing for *interdependency*.

60. Buchanan, "Samaritan's Dilemma."

61. Schwartz, *When Charity Destroys Dignity*; Lupton, *Toxic Charity*.

62. Allen, *Missionary Methods*, 189–190. For Allen's critique of finances and missions, see pages 70–86.

63. A distinctly different definition of dependency is used by heterodox economists who propose that western nations pursue policies that keep other nations in poverty so the Global North can benefit.

Benefitting from cultural critiques of self-sufficiency and independence as western concepts, and embracing the ancient and biblical view of gift, advocates of this view argued that Christians should live and act as a body. Inequality is allowed as long as individuals stewarded gifts for the common good. Lydia Boyd explains that "Although dependency is marked as morally problematical for donors, hierarchical relationships for Ugandans have long been considered socially productive, providing benefits for both the givers and receivers of aid."[64]

We come full circle in recognizing that Schwartz and others differentiated between healthy and unhealthy dependency. Independence and self-reliance were not the sole end goal, but rather, interdependence, supporting the common good.

Community development advocates (described in the next chapter) added principles and methods that reinforced self-determination. Despite their link to Christian mission, seminaries and faith-based universities in North America were spotty in developing academic programs in community and global development [**Education and Development**].

Education and Development

In the twentieth century, the United Kingdom boasted the highest national concentration of international development postgraduate programs. In the 1960s, colonial administrators returned to the U.K. from newly decolonized countries in Asia and Africa. To continue U.K. relations with the countries, the government expanded its global development activities and universities geared up their research and educational programs to supply research and postgraduate education.

For a variety of reasons, relatively few academic programs in peace, global health, and humanitarianism were developed in the United States. Rooted in the American Baptist Church, Eastern University was an exception and early leader in global development. Eastern Mennonite University led in peace-related studies. Other evangelical colleges and seminaries with strong traditions in missions, health, and/or social action, marshalled resources to offer training and

64. Boyd, "Circuits of Compassion," 522–23.

occasionally research; these included Calvin University, Fresno Pacific University, Loma Linda University, Messiah University, North Park Theological Seminary, Point Loma Nazarene University, and Wheaton College, among others.

A few Catholic universities added programs, most notably and recently, the Pulte Institute for Global Development at the University of Notre Dame. Other Christian educators in global development and community development were embedded in across large public and private universities, teaching and furthering research. These included Norman Borlaug (1914–2009), a Lutheran who is credited with initiating the Green Revolution and was awarded the Nobel Peace Prize in 1970 for innovative farming practices to increase crop yields; economist Bruce Wydick (b. 1954) at the University of San Francisco; economist Christopher Barrett (b. 1963) at Cornell University; and many others.

A different story surrounded the building of colleges, universities, and seminaries *for* development. Through the twentieth century, Christians opened higher education institutions around the world. Enrollments and the establishment of new universities, however, exploded in the late twentieth century, particularly in sub-Saharan Africa. Around 130 Christian universities were founded outside North America between 1990 and 2017: 58 in Africa, 30 in Latin America, 22 in Asia, 17 in Europe (mostly in the East), and 2 in Oceania.[65] Together, nearly 700 colleges and universities in sub-Saharan Africa enrolled a combined 5.2 million students in 2010. Many of these were faith-based, including Daystar University in Kenya, Northrise University in Zambia, Heritage Christian College in Ghana, and African Christian College in Eswatini.[66] NationsUniversity, headquartered in the United States, offered online degree programs in religious studies in many countries.

GLOBAL PEACE AND HUMANITARIANISM EXPANDS

WWII brought a sense of global awareness and need, and a prosperous United States with wealth to share. Funds from progressives flowed first,

65. Glanzer, "Growing on the Margins," 23–25.
66. Carpenter et al., *Christian Higher Education.*

during and after the war, and a second wave of conservative aid rose in the decades that followed. As recognized with CARE and CWS, coordination enhanced efficiencies in logistics and programming. Yet diverse constituents often slowed and complicated decision-making.

National humanitarian aid agencies, such as the United States Agency for International Development (USAID), the Canadian International Development Agency (CIDA), and dozens of others, welcomed responses to requests for proposals from large NGOs (some of them faith-based, such as World Vision and Catholic Relief Services) to implement development programs overseas.[67] These further networked through multilateral organizations, such as the Food and Agriculture Organization (FAO), the United Nations Children's Fund (UNICEF), and the World Health Organization (WHO).

Many medium-size FBOs decided to avoid government financing, in part, because programming was beyond their scale and to maintain direction over their programming.[68] Christians stirred to action launched thousands of micro-FBOs as well, ministering to needs on a small scale. Few of these cooperated with others or were aware of development advancements or activities beyond their immediate experience or practiced by NGOs utilizing government financing.[69]

Calls to contribute to relief efforts and engage in holistic mission lead several denominations to launch or expand their overseas charitable activity via para-church agencies. Among these were Adventist Development and Relief Agency International (ADRA), World Renew, Compassion and Mercy Associates (CAMA), and Nazarene Compassionate Ministries (see Table 7.1). Several denominations supported World Relief, the relief and development arm of the National Association of Evangelicals (NAE).

In 1992, the diverse family of Orthodox churches joined efforts to form the International Orthodox Christian Charities (IOCC). The IOCC serves

67. Regarding Canadian funding, Vander Zaag reports that Canadian faith-based NGOs received one-third of all funding to Canadian NGOs between 2005 and 2011: Vander Zaag, "Canadian Faith-Based Development." For data since 2005, see Vander Zaag, "Trends in CIDA Funding."

68. Several of these organizations banded together in 1978 to form what is now the Accord Network. Caritas Internationalis and CIDSE (Coopération Internationale pour le Développement et la Solidarité) perform a similar networking function for Catholic international aid agencies. Some members welcome government contracts.

69. Secular international development agencies generally ignored small and some medium-size FBOs, in part, because of their diminutive scale, but also because of an impression that a faith distinction lent itself to proselytization, conservative views on women's reproductive health, and favoritism toward Christian beneficiaries Paras, "Between Missions and Development."

as the official humanitarian agency of the thirteen Orthodox jurisdictions in the United States that form the Assembly of Canonical Orthodox Bishops of the United States of America. The IOCC provides relief to millions in need, particularly in regions where large numbers of Orthodox members reside.

The product of this activism was thousands of large and small humanitarian organizations, NGOs, and para-church agencies, serving and competing with one another. Numerous specialized sectors developed, including education, food security, medical care, business development through microfinance and microenterprise development, peacebuilding, disaster aid, housing, water, sanitation, and hygiene (WASH), creation care, refugee and migration support, and more. Congregations engaged with organizations of all sizes but many had only cursory knowledge of the humanitarian space or its actors. Para-church agencies and mission boards often found themselves competing with other humanitarian organizations in capturing the attention of their member congregations and parishes.

As the twentieth century neared an end, western governments and multilateral institutions began including faith-based organizations in conversation, recognizing the importance of religion in relief and development and the unique contribution of FBOs. The United Nations Population Fund (UNFPA) stated in a 2014 consultation that:

> Development actors, both faith-based and secular, must learn how to navigate the complex world of religion, rather than ignore or marginalize its significance. Secular development actors are cautioned against either ignoring the role of religion (in which case the development agenda loses a valuable interlocutor), or over-simplifying the complexities and ambiguities often found in such domains, particularly around contentious rights-related issues.[70]

Many small FBOs and congregations, however, continued to pursue development largely on their own [**Congregational Aid**]. Some denominations and churches were experiencing sizable membership declines and were trimming or slashing global and community mission budgets. Others focused on local interests. Community development seemed to be expanding (see chapter 8) as was the church in the Global South.

---

70. United Nations Population Fund, "Religion and Development, Post-2015," v.

Congregational Aid

By the early twenty-first century, Protestant congregations were partnering with large-, medium-, and small-size humanitarian organizations. Some of the most popular partners were Compassion International, World Vision, Samaritan's Purse, International Justice Mission (IJM), and Bread for the World.

A survey in 2015 indicated that most congregations included humanitarian activities in their missions programs.[71] Peace churches lead the way with more than two-thirds of their international activities engaging humanitarian elements. Progressive Protestants, such as Methodists, Reformed, Presbyterians, and Lutherans, and some Holiness groups, such as the Church of the Nazarene, Free Methodists, and the Wesleyan Church, continued their historic trajectories in social action as well, with around 60 percent of their mission efforts engaging holistic mission.

The most common sectors for churches to engage were with youth, health care, construction, and education. A substantial percentage of these activities focused on short-term mission (STM) wherein youth or professionals engaged built houses or churches, offered medical care, participated in relief following a disaster, or provided youth outreach activities.

A distinctive contribution of the Catholic Church was its emphasis on the social mission of the church at the parish and individual level. In 2015, the USCCB released *Communities of Salt and Light*, a document affirming the importance of linking liturgy and life, of individual choices and lifestyles, and parish identity and activity.[72] As Pope Benedict XVI stated in his encyclical *Deus Caritas Est* (*God Is Love*), "There is no ordering of the State so just that it can eliminate the need for a service of love."[73] He stated that "the Church has an indirect duty . . . to contribute to the purification of reason and to the reawakening of those moral forces without which just structures are neither established nor prove effective in the long run." The direct duty

---

71. Protestant findings reported in this section are based on Lynn, "Congregational Aid."

72. USCCB, "*Communities of Salt and Light.*"

73. Benedict XVI, *God Is Love*, 69.

to work toward a just ordering of society, however, is the role of the faithful.[74] For Catholics and other communions, it was in everyday life that the disciples of Jesus were to extend compassion.

Throughout the century, peace churches continued their commitment to peacemaking, peacebuilding. Christian International Peace Service (CHIPS), founded by Roy Calvocoressi (1930–2012), and Christian Peacemaker Teams (CPTs) are two faith-based organizations that focus on peace and conflict resolution. New efforts emerged among Christians in conflict-ridden zones including Musalaha in Jerusalem, Arab Baptist Theological Seminary in Beirut, Lebanon, and Bethlehem Bible College in Palestine.

Through the twentieth century, Catholics continued to serve faithfully, and some did with notoriety. Among these, Solanus Casey (1870–1957) received thousands seeking aid, Pio of Pietrelcina (1887–1968) mystically suffered with others, Riccardo Pampuri (1887–1930) cared for the wounded in WWI and the poor thereafter, and Teresa of Calcutta (1910–1997) and her Missionaries of Charity cared for the ill and dying. Thousands of religious and clerical servants taught in schools, fed the hungry, nursed the sick, advocated for the vulnerable, and cared for the poor.

The Second Vatican Council (1962–1965) restored the Catholic diaconate as an intermediate clerical order of men to assist bishops and priests. As ministers of mercy, the Order of Deacons was charged to "express the needs and desires of the Christian faithful, serve as a driving force for service among the people of God, and symbolize Christ the servant."[75] Subsequent to Vatican II, thousands of men stepped forward to be ordained as permanent deacons. Lay fraternities further peace and charity too, the Community of Sant'Egidio being a prime example. Over thirty thousand lay members globally devote themselves to "prayer, the poor, and peace." The community bathes daily service and peace advocacy in prayer.[76]

Specialized sectors of compassion and service developed within nations, including organizations focused on food security, such as Bread for the World, and disaster relief such as Convoy of Hope. Volunteers were mobilized for disaster and other needs by United Methodist Volunteers in Mission (UMVIM), Lutheran Disaster Response, Presbyterian Disaster Assistance, Southern Baptist Disaster Relief (SBDR), and other para-church

---

74. Benedict XVI, *God Is Love*, 71.

75. McKnight, *Understanding the Diaconate*, 203. Also see United States Conference of Catholic Bishops, *National Directory*.

76. Morozzo della Rocca, *Making Peace*.

arms. Ministries to the incarcerated [**Prison Ministries**] and a host of others in need were founded after World War II.

Prison Ministries

Just as Christians through the ages followed Jesus' instruction to visit prisoners (Matt 25:36), modern ministries developed to support and encourage offenders, former offenders, and their families. Because prison wardens and criminal justice overseers restrict outside services, prison ministries are often limited to encouragement, spiritual chaplaincy, and education.

Several organizations have been launched to provide these services. One of the earliest was Yokefollow Prison Ministry, inspired by D. Elton Trueblood (1900–1994). Trueblood was traveling by train in 1949 when he read afresh the words of Jesus inviting us to share his yoke (Mat 11:28–30). The words sunk deeply in Trueblood's thinking. He changed the speech he was preparing to deliver at his destination. When he arrived, he encouraged his audience to become a *yokefellow* with Christ, engaging in small groups of spiritual disciplines and service.

After delivering similar encouragement to an audience of federal prison chaplains in 1955, two chaplains returned home and started small groups ministering to offenders. Their ministries grew and ultimately merged into the national Yokefellowship Prison Ministry (YPM), joining other prison ministries.[77] Other prison ministries that developed during the twentieth century include Dismas Charities, founded by Fr. William Diersen (1925–2002), Prison Fellowship, founded by Chuck Colson (1931–2012), and the Equal Justice Initiative founded by Bryan Stevenson (b. 1959).

CONCLUSION

The divide between discipling and development that had characterized conservatives and progressives began to narrow.[78] By the beginning of the

---

77. For an account of the Yokefollow history, see Trueblood, *While it is Day*, 104–24.

78. Bok, "Distinction through Religious Activism," 311.

twenty-first century, half of large conservative Protestant congregations had returned to organized humanitarianism, repeating a mantra that popularly (and erroneously) was attributed to Francis of Assisi: "Preach the gospel at all times and if necessary, use words."[79] Protestants, Catholics, and Orthodox contributed collectively and individually to FBOs to further peace and humanitarianism. Twentieth-century global humanitarianism was propelled by several forces, but primarily, by war. The varied patterns represent a weaving of threads that intertwine but retain a character, unique to each. Included in the fabric are spiritual views of illness, poverty, and healing; global peace church activism; a few notable efforts at cooperation and hundreds of independent, sectarian and faith-based initiatives.

In the second half of the twentieth century, witnessed the gradual return of conservatives to humanitarianism. Peace and humanitarianism required strength and courage as well as compassion, evidenced by sharing crops, volunteering in war-torn regions, hiding the persecuted, and the tireless and non-heroic tending to the daily needs of others. Real aid required intention to start and commitment to endure. In contrast to the prophets of liberation and justice, humanitarian witnesses often lived lives of quiet service, unnoticed by most but often precious to a few. If we were to select one personification, Madeleine Delbrêl (1904–1964) might exemplify the group. Delbrêl was a twentieth-century lay missionary, sometimes compared with Dorothy Day. She walked the streets of Ivry-sur-Seine, France, as a Catholic and former atheist, reflecting about God in the world: "We, the ordinary people of the streets," she wrote, "believe with all our might that this street, this world, where God has placed us, is our place of holiness. . . . For us, the whole world is like a face-to-face meeting with the one whom we cannot escape."[80] Some twentieth-century humanitarian actors saw themselves as the almoners of the world. Others more accurately viewed themselves as engaged in a divine engagement.

79. Galli, *Francis of Assisi and His World.*
80. Delbrêl, *We, the Ordinary People,* 54–55.

8

Mutual Aid and Community Development

THE THIRD AND FINAL pass through the twentieth century picks up a sampling of colorful organizations that emphasized compassionate community. In mutual aid and intentional community, Christians cared for one another, mitigating harm, assessing need, and delivering aid, often in countercultural social arrangements. Forged in a cauldron of persecution and possibility, communities both separated from broader society and witnessed to them with the light of Christ [**Beloved Community**].

Beloved Community

Often, *community* refers to a local group of people—a neighborhood or small gathering of Christians. But larger visions are possible as well. Martin Luther King Jr., for example, referred to "beloved community" in ways similar to the kingdom of God. His vision of community was of a nation, knitted together in interdependently in unity, spiritually transformed by the gospel.[1] King's view recalls Jewish rabbinic teachings that describe all community members as accountable

1. Lee, *We Will Get to the Promised Land.*

236

for ensuring justice; each one tasked with protecting society's weakest members.[2]

For these disciples, community represented more than a channel through which compassion was delivered. Close relationships uniquely contoured and enabled compassion. As Charles Cummings said of his Trappist community life, "My way to holiness and to personal wholeness lies through and with my fellow travelers. I will be faithful to my vocation and will experience the living God because of them, not in spite of them."[3] In other words, it is through close, reciprocal relationships that one truly becomes compassionate. However, as Eberhard Arnold (1883–1935), the spiritual father to the Bruderhof, pleaded, the candlestick of Christ must remain at the center and not be displaced by idolizing community.[4]

Communities varied on several dimensions, including in how they practiced compassion within the community and how much weight they placed on compassion beyond it. In our survey, we begin with mutual aid among Anabaptists, Latter-day Saints, and a sampling of intentional communities and fraternal organizations. We then consider two models of economic cooperation rooted in Catholic social teaching: the Focolare Movement, which originated in Italy, and the producer cooperatives of Mondragón, Spain. We close the chapter by briefly considering incarnational mission and Christian community development.

MUTUAL AID

As we saw with the early church in Acts 2 and 4, Christians maintained private property but also pooled resources to care for one another. Through history, we witnessed instances of Christians following a similar pattern, intensifying during times of persecution and loss or when boundaries were drawn voluntarily to separate the community from mainstream society. Whether separated by choice or by force (and often both), Christians at times created micro-societies in which they could craft quite distinctive patterns of compassion. Few societies, however, were truly isolated. Communities reacted to mainstream society just as the early Christians copied

2. Cohen, *Justice in the City*.

3. Cummings, *Monastic Practices*, 142.

4. Baum, *Against the Wind*, 200.

and rejected Jewish and Roman traditions.[5] But beyond providing missing public goods, praying for society, or veering away from it, many twentieth-century Christian communities attempted to live into Jesus' declaration that mutual love would be the hallmark of his followers (John 13:35).

When comparing communal compassion with other social forms, it may be helpful to consider the *thickness* of community, as Kent Smith does. Smith identifies eight possible assets that communities can share. The more assets are shared, the thicker the community. His assets are: *purpose*, or a common mission or goal; *people* who share lives together; *place*, where individuals associate in built and natural environments; *production*, or the creation of collaborative, meaningful work; *process*, which governs communal discernment and decision making; the *preparation* of new members to mutually discern their fit in the community; *possessions*, or the sharing of material and financial resources; and *play*, or recreation together.[6] The expressions in this chapter opt for thicker community in contrast to generally thin alternatives.

Anabaptists

Anabaptists constitute a diverse mosaic of believers who esteem mutual aid and who sometimes divide over its practice. Most sixteenth-century German, Swiss, and Dutch communities did not dissolve private property (although some did [**Hutterites**]) but voluntarily provided for the needs of fellow believers. They shared money, food, clothing, and shelter with community members in need.[7] They also viewed themselves as called to accept God's will for their station in life, expressed in the concept of *Gelassenheit*. This acceptance might include the patient endurance of suffering, poverty, and an inferior position in the social hierarchy.

5. As an example of inspiration from mutual aid, abundant nineteenth- and early twentieth-century fraternal societies in North America enabled access to social services, health care, burial, and institutions such as orphanages and homes for the elderly that otherwise would have been beyond their reach. Many of these evaporated when governmental supports became available during and after the Great Depression: Beito, *From Mutual Aid to the Welfare State.*

6. Smith, "Ecosystems of Grace."

7. Swartley and Kraybill, *Building Communities of Compassion.*

Hutterites

Jacob Hutter (1500–1536) inspired his Hutterite followers to adopt a robust "community of goods" approach, sharing nearly all property in common.[8] Persecution followed Hutterites from Europe to Ukraine and on to North America, where they were imprisoned for their unwillingness to pay war taxes, buy war bonds, or serve in the military during World War I. Anti-German attitudes and opposition to communal property occurred as well. After WWI, many Hutterites migrated to the Canadian provinces of Alberta, Saskatchewan, and Manitoba, but some remained in South Dakota, Montana, and nearby states.

Traditional forms of Anabaptist mutual aid included pooling labor and resources to assist community members. These expressions were practiced by most but particularly characterized Old Order Mennonite, Hutterite, Amish, and other conservative groups who relied on family, community, and sometimes other colonies for various needs. Helping one another was practiced by launching young couples into farming, paying medical expenses for community members, sharing knowledge with the young via circular letters, rebuilding houses ravaged by fire, and the iconic raising of barns.[9]

More progressive Anabaptists developed larger, more formalized systems of mutual aid, amending the traditional view of *Gelassenheit*. Canadian Mennonites did this when they attempted to help Russian immigrants secure solid economic footing through formalized relief. Later, a charity fund was developed for suffering members during the Great Depression, a benefit association provided insurance, and a credit union provided debt capital.[10] Similar to other groups of the time, Anabaptists in the early twentieth century developed dozens of mutual aid societies that provided property, medical, and burial insurance.[11]

Mennonite Mutual Aid was established to provide transitional support for Civilian Public Service volunteers returning from WWII. Although these were likely closer to informal, reciprocal relief organizations than

8. For a comprehensive history of a community of goods approach, see Pitzer, *America's Communal Utopias*; Saxby, *Pilgrims of a Common Life*.

9. Gingrich and Lightman, "Striving Toward Self-Sufficiency."

10. Fretz, "Mutual Aid among Mennonites I"; Good, "Changing Patterns."

11. Fretz, "Mutual Aid among Mennonites II"; Nolt, "Fifty-Year Partners."

many bureaucratized, hierarchical organizations, traditional Anabaptist groups viewed this level of institutionalization as mimicking society and as a lack of faith in God and one another for support. Mennonite mutual aid continues today in numerous forms, including in the Corinthian Plan (based on 2 Cor 8:1–15; 9:6–15), which provides health insurance for Mennonite pastors and church workers.

Both traditional and progressive Anabaptists emphasized simple living [**Simple Living**]. A mutual aid or community of goods approach was not exempt from envy or pride or appropriate to remedy every need. It was a social organization form that, in its best expressions, was informed by compassion. Although it was organized in different ways, mutual aid distinguished Anabaptists and their desire to live into the kingdom of God. As summarized by the *Confession of Faith in a Mennonite Perspective*,

> Jesus proclaimed both the nearness of God's reign and its future realization, its healing and its judgment. In his life and teaching, he showed that God's reign included the poor, outcasts, the persecuted, those who were like children, and those with faith like a mustard seed. For this kingdom, God has appointed Jesus Christ as king and Lord. We believe that the church is called to live now according to the model of the future reign of God. Thus, we are given a foretaste of the kingdom that God will one day establish in full. The church is to be a spiritual, social, and economic reality, demonstrating now the justice, righteousness, love, and peace of the age to come. The church does this in obedience to its Lord and in anticipation that the kingdom of this world will become the kingdom of our Lord.[12]

Simple Living

Simple living has a long history and is fed by secular and religious tributaries. In North America, several Christian traditions affirmed forms of simplicity.[13] Simplicity at times represented a pietistic avoidance of worldly superfluities, a means of doing with less so one can share with others, a desire to free oneself from encumbered life, or other impulses. Many Christian fellowships—including the Shakers, Quakers, and Anabaptists—followed an ethos of simplicity.

---

12. *Confession of Faith*, 89–90.
13. For a historical survey, see Shi, *Simple Life*.

Thomas Dubay provides an intriguing list of possibilities of what might be called voluntary simplicity, gospel poverty, or simple living. Dubay asks, "Is it . . . ?":

- *Destitution*, wherein we give up all we possess as Jesus asks of his disciples (Luke 14:33)

- *A spirit of poverty*, an inner detachment and readiness to be separated from material things when love of neighbor requires it

- *Moderation*, living at an average level of income and consumption of those around us

- Being *available* to others and emphasizing relationships

- *Economy* or *frugality*—wearing used clothes, avoiding luxuries, and reducing expenses and consumption

- *Sharing with others*

- *Avoiding artificial security* provided by insurance, savings, and home ownership, relying upon God

- *Downplaying power*

- Living in a way that *witnesses* simplicity to others[14]

Dubay's list illustrates that several possible meanings can be (and have been) proffered for what constitutes simple living. Each finds expression in Christian history, and especially in mutual aid.

Latter-day Saints

The Church of Jesus Christ of Latter-day Saints (LDS) envisioned a comprehensive plan for addressing the needs of its members through mutual aid.[15] Like Anabaptists, congregations—wards or branches in LDS termi-

14. Thomas Dubay provides an examen and insights on these and other approaches to simple living. Dubay, *Happy Are You Poor*, 18–20.

15. Communal societies preceding the Mormon United Order included the Ephrata Cloister (1732–1934) of the Schwarzenau Brethren (German Baptists) in Ephrata, Pennsylvania, and the Moravian village of Bethlehem, Pennsylvania (1741–62). Both communities attempted to be self-sufficient and both cared for the poor in their midst. The Ephrata Cloister focused on cultivating interior pietism while Moravian

nology—played an essential role. But rather than growing organically from the community up, LDS mutual aid had the advantage of being inspired by divine revelation given to the prophet Joseph Smith (1805–1844), and confirmed to other men holding the priesthood. The revelations provided direction; the progression of time and humanity would be required to implement them.[16]

In LDS theology, spiritual and temporal matters blended. In 1830, Joseph learned of the ancient city of Enoch, where people were "of one heart and of one mind" and had "no poor among them" (Moses 7:18). The following year, in Kirtland, Ohio, Joseph received a revelation of how to live into those ideals. This revelation, which became known as "the law of consecration and stewardship," stipulated that members should deed or "consecrate" their property to the bishop, who would then allocate a "stewardship" portion back to sustain the individual or family. If the assets consecrated exceeded family needs, the excess would be redistributed as a stewardship to those with assets insufficient to enable them to be self-reliant.

Likewise, annual production that exceeded family needs was placed under the oversight of the local bishop in the bishop's storehouse.[17] Surplus produce could be distributed to any in need or could be sold to raise funds for temple construction or other local church or member needs, including business expansion. Consecration and stewardship provided a social and economic alternative to an individualistic society, promising to put all on an equal footing, provide for the poor, and cultivate cooperation, self-reliance, and growth.

Scriptures (Mosiah 4:13–30, 27:4, 29:32; 4 Nephi 1:3) and subsequent revelation reaffirmed an emphasis on self-reliance and communal equality, including an 1835 revelation that "it is not given that one man should possess that which is above another, wherefore the world lieth in sin" (D&C 49:20; also, D&C 78:6). Revelations requiring tithing from one's stewardship followed (D&C 119).

The establishment of a united order was attempted by Joseph in Ohio, Missouri, and Illinois, but church leaders and members were unable to implement the level of mutual aid desired due to the level of need and the

---

communalism was intended to further evangelism.

16. This section relies heavily on Arrington et al., *Building the City of God*; Barton, "Mormon Poor Relief"; Lucas and Woodworth, *Working toward Zion*; Mangum and Blumell, *Mormons' War on Poverty*. Also see *Daughters in My Kingdom*.

17. Having been created shortly after the establishment of the church in 1830, bishops's storehouses were familiar institutions. Originally, they were for storing free-will offerings.

reluctance on the part of some to cede assets to the bishops (similar to Acts 5:1–10). Church leaders were successful, however, in setting up a Relief Society in 1842, composed of adult sisters who were given a charge to save souls and relieve suffering.[18]

After arriving in Utah, Brigham Young (1801–1877) set about implementing a communal society and building a self-sufficient state called Deseret. Missionaries returning from England brought news of cooperatives that provided a possible path to independence, egalitarianism, and self-sufficiency. In the late 1860s, a system of coordinated cooperative stores was launched, exchanging goods with a central warehouse in Salt Lake City. Prices and profits could be regulated and ownership disbursed. Financing was raised by selling stock, and prices were kept low so poorer members could purchase a share and receive discounts and dividends. The institution was named Zion's Co-operative Mercantile Institution, or ZCMI. It has been called the first department store in the United States, but it fell short of creating a cooperative society.

In 1874, Young announced that the church would move further toward consecration and stewardship. The "united order" would be implemented. In Brother Brigham's vision, the united order would eliminate poverty, build self-sufficiency, and function like a "well ordered family." It would reach these goals through frugality, land sharing, and central board oversight. Each ward would establish a united order wherein saints would cede or lend assets and receive shares of stock for their capital and labor. If a family left the community, they could withdraw their stock and any credit amassed for their contributions of labor. A local board orchestrated labor, wages, agricultural production, trades, and economic development. Meals were envisioned as communal events. Although people slept in private rooms, life would occur in the larger community rather than in the nuclear family.

This attempt to live into the united order took root in southern Utah, first in St. George, and then scattered throughout the region in today's Utah, Arizona, Nevada, and a lone community in Mexico. Farming, sawmills, dairies, mines, and other cooperative enterprises were established. Orders were received with eager idealism by some and reticence by others. A few orders flourished—most famously in Orderville, a small town in southern Utah where committed members set out to live the united order completely. Directed by a board, communities attempted to reach self-sufficiency, growing their own food, sewing their own clothing, mining their own coal, cutting their own lumber, and providing their own medical

---

18. Relief Societies continue to operate in the LDS Church today and represent the largest women's organization in the world.

care and schooling. Excess commodities were brought to the bishop's storehouse (see the building on the right in Fig. 8.1) and distributed from a united order storefront.

Fig. 8.1. Ephraim United Order Mercantile Institution, located in Ephraim, Utah.

Disagreements plagued the experiment, however. Inequities in responsibility and contribution grew. The possibility of families exiting with large labor credits and shares created inequities in voice and threatened economic stability. Within five years of Young's death in 1877, many of the united orders were disbanded, but not before nearly four hundred colonies were established. The united order gave way to boards of trade that maximized cooperation in trade, enhanced the quality of products, smoothed supply and demand, and increased economic welfare. Finally, in the early twentieth century, church-owned businesses emerged, and the united order reverted to an eschatological anticipation.

Mormons continued to address poverty, however, with an emphasis on church-wide solidarity. When economic depression hit in the 1930s, many of Utah's farmers suffered. In 1936, Mormon leaders called on church members to tithe and donate the money that would have been spent on food during their monthly fasts, committing these funds to support vulnerable members. Once again, self-reliance was emphasized. Stakes (groups of wards) purchased farms and enterprises and operated as a kind of public works program. Cash, food, and clothing were given to the needy in exchange for a contribution of labor. More storehouses were built, and local church leaders and Relief Society members assigned labor and compensated needy workers with commodities in accord with their need, not their labor.

In this way, the system supported the poor and the church, while employing the idle. Church members could contribute labor on farms when they were healthy and could withdraw the benefit when they were older and unable to work. Those already aged could be remunerated with produce for doing church work.

The Church Welfare Program, as it was called, underscored the LDS motif of self-reliance. It continues today in supporting ongoing and emergency needs among Latter-day Saints and others in the community. Other notable mutual aid advancements include the Perpetual Education Fund (2001) (based on the pioneer Perpetual Immigration Fund) to help returned missionaries from developing countries gain an education and learn vocational skills, Self-Reliant Services (2009) which offers group-based curricula in employment, education, personal finance, and entrepreneurship, and Brigham Young University's Pathway Connect (2009) and PathwayWorldwide (2017) which enable affordable, online, collaborative education for thousands of youth and adults.

Like Catholic social teaching, the LDS united order and its related initiatives charted a course distinct from the surrounding economy and society, affirming self-reliance and community, initiative, and equality. Whereas Catholic social teaching included a greater emphasis on social, political, and economic structures, LDS teachings stressed individual education and self-reliance. As church president Gordon B. Hinckley said in establishing the Perpetual Education Fund, "Where there is widespread poverty among our people, we must do all we can to help them to lift themselves, to establish their lives upon a foundation of self-reliance that can come of training. Education is the key to opportunity."[19]

INTENTIONAL COMMUNITIES

Anabaptists and Mormons are not alone in living out the Christian faith in community. Intentional Christian communities represent another expression of people seeking a meaningful relationship with God and others through the sharing of assets. Hundreds of communities with monastic, utopian, or intentional inclinations provided a home for thousands of people in the twentieth century. These have included Shaker communities;

---

19. Hinckley, "The Perpetual Education Fund," 53. President Hinckley's words echo Young's in 1877: "Now the object is to improve the minds of the inhabitants of the earth, until we learn what we are here for, and become one before the Lord, that we may rejoice together and be equal": *Journal of Discourses*, May 27, 1877, 46.

Christian Fourierist phalanxes composed of Swedenborgians and others;[20] the Amana Colonies of Amana, Iowa; Bishop Hill Colony of Bishop Hill, Illinois; the Harmony Society of Harmony, Pennsylvania and New Harmony, Indiana; the American Colony in Jerusalem; Bruderhof communities scattered around the world; Reba Place Fellowship of Evanston, Illinois; the Sojourners Community of Washington, DC, from which Sojourners Ministries originated; Casa Adobe of Heredia, Costa Rica; and others.

These communities were and are quite diverse. The Christian Commonwealth Colony attempted to live out the social gospel in Georgia in the closing days of the nineteenth century, melding apostolic Christianity with modern-day communism.[21] Catholic Worker houses fit into this category, as do service-oriented religious institutes and societies, such as Missionaries of Charity, Franciscans, or the Congregation of the Oratory of St. Philip Neri, and informal Catholic communities, such as St. Benedict's Farm (Waelder, Texas). Faith-based settlement houses embraced community, as well. College communities have numbered in the dozens and include Chesterton House at Cornell University (Ithaca, New York), Vista House at Furman University (Greenville, South Carolina), and The Foundry at Wake Forest School of Divinity (Winston-Salem, North Carolina). Christian communities continue to be created, such as the Simple Way (Philadelphia, Pennsylvania) and Eden Center for Regenerative Culture (Abilene, Texas).[22] Intentional communities often cast a critical light on broader society while witnessing to the goodness of shared life and assets in community. As stated at the beginning of this chapter, it is not so much in spite of others but with others that community flourishes.

A turn toward community can occur for numerous reasons, including persecution from without or voluntary separation from mainstream society. Each community has its own story, catalysts, members, and habits. I will describe four briefly, each of which has a different charism for social compassion.

Church of the Saviour

The Church of the Saviour in Washington, DC, was launched and pastored by Gordon Cosby (1917–2013), a WWII chaplain who was committed to following the radical call of Jesus in serving the poor. Eschewing traditional meeting places and large inward-focused churches, the Church of the

20. Guarneri, *Utopian Alternative*, 168; Swank, *Unfettered Conscience*, 351–80.
21. Kallman, *Kingdom of God*.
22. Miller, *Quest for Utopia*.

Saviour began as a small, ecumenical, multiracial group of believers gathering in houses and restaurants, yet yielding considerable social impact.

Now a network of small churches in the Washington, DC area, the Church of the Saviour is characterized by several distinctives. Members believe everyone is called to some form of service, employing his or her God-given gifts. They operate more than two dozen ministries among the urban poor, offering transitional and long-term housing, adult education, job placement, day care, foster care, medical services, and more. Perhaps most distinctively, they emphasize an inward/outward journey of spiritual formation and renewal, combined with service.[23]

Koinonia Farm

A second example is Koinonia Farm, founded by Clarence Jordan (1912–1969) in Americus, Georgia.[24] While a student in the 1930s at Southern Baptist Theological Seminary (which Gordon Cosby also attended), Jordan developed a conviction that brotherhood (*koinonia*) represented Christian community, not racial discrimination and violence. Having earned a PhD in New Testament Greek and believing that Christianity should be earthy and practical, he published much of the New Testament in his folksy *Cotton Patch Gospel* paraphrase.

23. For a history, see O'Connor, *Servant Leaders.*

24. Preceding Jordan, Sherwood Eddy (1871–1963) established two cooperative farms in Mississippi that were interracial and committed to economic equality. These farms operated from 1939 TO 1956.

Fig. 8.2. Clarence Jordan, Koinonia Farm.

In 1949, he and a few friends with pacifist convictions bought a few acres of land in Americus and founded Koinonia Farm, an interracial community practicing a community of goods approach. Racial tensions in the 1950s led to the farm being boycotted; they could neither deposit money in a bank nor buy or sell within a hundred-mile radius. They were fired on by gunshot, and the Ku Klux Klan held meetings close to the farm. African Americans were reluctant to join and give up hard-earned private property. Friends of Koinonia formed and subsidized the farm's operation during these difficult days.

In 1963, Koinonia Farm members moved to a new organization structure that replaced a community of goods with family units responsible for various farm profit centers, including a mail-order business. Key in the new effort was the continuing idea of brotherhood with a vision of operating discipleship schools around the United States. Koinonia Partners was launched in 1968. In cooperation with Millard and Linda Fuller, a revolving loan fund was created to provide capital for low-income housing construction. This

fund became Habitat for Humanity, an international organization furthering decent and affordable housing.[25]

L'Arche

In 1964, inspired by Catholic social teaching and the realization that many
individuals with intellectual disabilities resided in large institutions, Jean
Vanier (1928–2019) cofounded L'Arche ("The Ark") in Trosly-Breuil, France.
In the L'Arche model, staff and clients live together in a small community of
care. The model has been replicated and today operates as an international
federation in approximately 150 locations across forty countries. Perhaps its
most notable staff member was author Henri Nouwen.

Many have written that L'Arche, as with other intentional communities,
cannot be appreciated as an organizational form, but must be experienced
in transforming relationships of mutual disability and insight.[26] In 1979,
Vanier wrote *Community and Growth*, which became a treasured guide of
wisdom for those learning about and living in intentional communities. In
the book, Vanier describes the mutually transforming nature of community:

> People who gather together to live the presence of Jesus among
> people in distress are . . . called not just to do things for them,
> or to see them as objects of charity, but rather to receive them
> as a source of life and of communion. These people come to-
> gether not just to liberate those in need, but also to be liberated
> by them; not just to heal their wounds but to be healed by them,
> not just to evangelise them but to be evangelised by them . . . .
> The poor teach us how to live the Gospel. That is why they are
> the treasures of the Church.[27]

Rutba House

In 2003 in Durham, North Carolina, Jonathan and Leah Wilson-Hartgrove
founded a new monastic community called Rutba House. The community
of about a dozen members occupies two houses and shares a common life
of prayer, meals, community, hospitality, and peacemaking. Practicing a
modified common goods approach, members work in a variety of jobs and
contribute between 30 and 40 percent of their income to the community.

25. K'Meyer, *Interracialism and Christian Community*.

26. Groppi, "L'Arche as an Experience of Encounter."

27. Vanier, *Community and Growth*, 95–96.

Rutba House members actively engage as members of the surrounding community. The affiliated School for Conversion offers community education to churches.

These intentional communities represent a small sampling of many contemporary, Christian communities with a social mission dotted around the globe.[28] They also demonstrate the variety of ways compassion is learned within community life and practiced in the surrounding community.

AUXILIARY, FRATERNAL, AND MISSION ORGANIZATIONS

Occasionally, associations drew members from one or more denominations for the purpose of banding and growing together while serving church members and the local community. Many of these are relatively thin communities, as measured by the number of assets identified by Kent Smith, and they may not focus exclusively on local grassroots initiatives. But they share some assets, and thus, we consider them here. Four examples drawn from the scores active during the twentieth century are the Epworth League, the Knights of Columbus, self-help organizations, and Youth With A Mission (YWAM).

Epworth League

Five organizations had been founded within the Methodist Episcopal Church in the late nineteenth century to engage and develop youth.[29] These united in Cleveland, Ohio in 1889 in the Epworth League. Unlike most of the previous organizations that emphasized Scripture and literary study, the Epworth League added missions and service to its activities.

Gathering interest around the same time as the deaconess movement, Epworth League members—which grew to 1.75 million in North America by 1900—engaged in "mercy and help" and "social service." Teaching youth to serve was imperative because Christianity was seen as a foundation for a well-functioning society. It also mobilized youth in the social gospel.

28. For others, see the Nurturing Communities Network (https://www.nurturing-communities.org), the Missional Wisdom Foundation (https://www.missionalwisdom.com), and the Foundation for Intentional Communities (https://www.ic.org).

29. Other youth organizations were created during the waning years of the nineteenth century and first third of the twentieth, including Baptist Young People's Unions, Catholic Youth Organizations, Christian Endeavor Societies (Wells, *Union Work*), the YMCA, and YWCA. Most or all included charitable service but youth development and/or evangelism typically were emphasized.

Speakers and a library on social service were recommended for each chapter. Youth surveyed communities for local needs in poverty, recreation, health, housing, labor, and government.[30] Divisions and mergers within the Methodist Episcopal Church and the passage of time led to a slow decline of the movement through the early twentieth century.

Knights of Columbus

In 1882, Blessed Fr. Michael J. McGivney (1852–1890) formed the Knights of Columbus (K of C) as a Catholic alternative to secret fraternal societies; a Catholic fraternity of men defending the church's place in society, and supporting immigrant families who had no safety net. The initial men who joined him chose the name "Columbus," for his reputation as a Catholic and as a patriot.

The K of C mobilized millions of Catholic men in local councils to support patriotic, Catholic, and social causes.[31] They advocated for Catholic public policies, opposed Catholic defamation, and provided employment, education, and welfare assistance to widows, orphans, soldiers, and veterans. Councils quickly spread through communities and on college campuses in the United States and beyond. Knights continue to be active today, boasting millions of members.

Self-Help Organizations

Religious conversion was the primary approach to alcoholism in the eighteenth- and early nineteenth-century.[32] Following the upending of prohibition, a different approach emerged among those who had no control over alcohol's tempestuous traffic, and that was self-help organizations. These organizations encouraged a shift in viewing addiction as a weakness, over which a person has moral and physical control, to viewing it as a disease. [33]Best known among these is Alcoholics Anonymous (AA), co-founded by Bill Wilson (Bill W.) and Dr. Robert Holbrook Smith (Dr. Bob) in 1935. AA

---

30. Brummitt, *Efficient Epworthian,"* 208–23.

31. The Knights of Columbus were active participants in getting the phrase "under God" added to the U.S. Pledge of Allegiance in 1954.

32. One initiative that combined a mutual aid approach with conversion was the Keswick Colony of Mercy founded by William Raws (1858–1910). Alcoholics lived and worked in community. See White, *Slaying the Dragon*, 75–76.

33. Influential in hospitalizing alcoholics and changing views about the nature of addiction, was the "angel of AA," Sr. Mary Ignatia (1889-1966): Darrah, *Sister Ignatia*.

was non-sectarian yet carried religious influences of what to do and not do from Bill W. and Dr. Bob's experience with the Oxford Group—an informal gathering of Christians attempting to recapture the evangelistic fervor of first-century Christianity.[34]

Several religious groups have been formed to assist those who are dealing with addictions. Unique to most of these organization is that a person seeks help for him or herself, rather than for another, and they do so with the support of mutual aid. Thousands of self-help groups exist for a variety of causes. Faith-based groups focused on alcohol and other addictions include Alcoholics Victorious, Mountain Movers, High Ground, Overcomers Outreach, Lion Tamers Anonymous, Celebrate Recovery, the Calix Society, and Ladies Victorious.[35]

Youth With A Mission

Loren Cunningham (b. 1935), the son and grandson of Assemblies of God pastors, co-founded Youth With A Mission (YWAM) with his wife, Darlene in 1960. They were young and inspired by a vision of youth engaging in mission efforts, globally. YWAM trained youth and placed them in domestic or international teams where they could share the gospel in word and deed.

Initially focused on evangelism, YWAM Discipleship Training School preparation and placements increasingly enveloped humanitarian service. The Cunninghams acquired a large ship which could be docked in various ports and offer mobile medical care. Eventually, this was spun off to become Mercy Ships. YWAM's University of the Nations offers academic degrees to prepare youth in Christian missions and holistic mission. Over 20,000 YWAM staff have served in more than 1,200 ministry locations.

The Epworth League, Knights of Columbus, Alcoholics Anonymous, and YWAM are international organizations. Imbedded communal expressions existed as well, such as in Quaker-sponsored community revitalization efforts during the New Deal [Penn-Craft].

Penn-Craft

Included in U.S. President Franklin D. Roosevelt's New Deal effort to stabilize and stimulate the U.S. economy was a plan to create one

34. Kurtz, *Not-God*, 9, 37–57.

35. For a comprehensive review of religious approaches to alcoholism, see White, *Slaying the Dragon*, 71–78.

hundred communities in depressed regions. Arthurdale, West Virginia, is perhaps best known, as it received Eleanor Roosevelt's sponsorship and attention. Quakers, Mennonites, and Brethren volunteered in Arthurdale and in several other planned communities.

In 1936, the American Friends Service Committee (AFSC) bought the 175-acre Isaiah Craft farm in Luzerne Township, a mining region in southwestern Pennsylvania. The following year, the AFSC launched a community called Penn-Craft. The United States Steel Corporation and United Mine Workers contributed nearly $100,000 as seed money, and a Harvard Business School professor took up residence to study the community's development. Unemployed miners who lived in the region came from different nationalities and ethnicities, and Penn-Craft offered employment options in agriculture or at Redstone Knitting Mill, a new sweater factory.[36]

Interested applicants had to prove themselves by clearing the land before they could apply for a mortgage. Prejudice was not tolerated, nor was alcohol. The work was hard, given that many were not experienced in house construction or masonry. Families helped each other to construct homes, the factory, a store, and other community improvements. Although affordable because of the sweat equity, houses came with mortgages. Self-sufficiency was the goal. Maintaining the local economy proved to be as difficult as homebuilding was. The AFSC disconnected, and slowly the community evolved into a historic site for passing tourists.

36. Barnes, *Centennial History*, 105–6.

Fig. 8.3. Penn-Craft community member and builder.

ECONOMIC COOPERATION

The Catholic tradition is accustomed to thinking about social and economic structures and has produced several innovative adaptations of economic thought. In general terms, the application of Catholic social teaching principles to the structure and practice of commercial firms furthers fair wages, trade, prices, labor policies, and conceptions of the social impact of companies.[37] However, some Catholic-inspired initiatives were directed toward alleviating poverty and furthering human and social development. I will highlight two of these initiatives: the Focolare Movement's Economy of Communion and the producer cooperatives of Mondragón, Spain.[38] Both were birthed during times of economic hardship, when large numbers of

37. Alford and Naughton, *Managing as if Faith Mattered.*
38. Although not developed here, the Antigonish Movement of the 1920s and following addressed economic development through community self-determination and conflict resolution. Fathers Jimmy Tompkins (1870–1953) and Moses Coady (1882–1959) viewed self-determination and cooperatives as answers to the poverty and the languishing economy of Maritime Canada. Community self-reliance and peacebuilding methods stimulated community development in Nova Scotia, New Brunswick, and beyond.

people were suffering and inclined to share as a practical solution to coping with scarce. Although Catholic advocates for capitalism and socialism exist, innovators often searched for a third path.

The heavy hand of WWII's social and economic devastation prompted a variety of responses affirming mutuality in European communities. Many combined resources out of practicality; few resources remained and no one was wealthy, so it made sense to combine what was left as a means of building community and economy. One such effort was the Focolare Movement, founded by Chiara Lubich (1920–2008) in Trent, Italy.[39] With personal belongings destroyed and friends killed, Lubich and a few of her neighbors decided to respond as they believed the gospel affirmed—they combined their goods and shared with one another much like the early church. An estimated three thousand individuals in northern Italy had followed their example by 1949. Today, the movement involves diverse initiatives designed to bring people together and share, to "promote a culture of giving" and support child adoption, ecumenical dialogue, and social and economic development. More than one million individuals are affiliated with the movement in Brazil, Germany, and other countries.[40]

At an individual level, many Focolare members live in intentional communities and share their incomes with one another. But their efforts have evolved into various organizational structures, including local Focolare centers and model towns. The Economy of Communion (EoC) is an approach to forming businesses with the poor in mind, sharing profits beyond those needed for operating the business, much like sharing on an individual level.

Through EoC start-ups, revenues are generated that can be shared, lifting all in the community. Profits are placed into three pots: one for those in need of life necessities such as medical expenses, food, shelter, employment assistance, and education; one to support the infrastructure of the culture of giving, such as supporting model towns; and one to retain profits for reinvestment in the enterprise.[41] Start-ups have been created in several industries, such as groceries, textiles, engineering, and medical services, and some exist in emerging business parks, such as the Lionello Business Park near Loppiano, Italy.

Another commercial innovation based on Catholic social thought is a system of producer cooperatives located in Mondragón, Spain. Launched after the Spanish Civil War and after the Basque people fell out of favor with

39. Gentilini, *Chiara Lubich*, 2020; Gold, *New Financial Horizons*.

40. Descriptions of current practices of EoC firms are available in Gallagher and Buckeye, *Structures of Grace*.

41. Gold, *New Financial Horizons*, 88–90.

Franco, a local Catholic priest, José María Arizmendiarrieta (1915–1976), turned his efforts to job creation in the economically depressed region. His seminary training had exposed him to Catholic social thought and to the idea of priests serving parishioners, which included mentoring and nurturing them according to papal encyclicals. This background encouraged him to look beyond capitalism and socialism and led him into considering a producer cooperative model based on the idea that humans are social beings who benefit from collaboration and mutual respect.

Fr. José María mentored a group of young disciples who launched a new consumer appliances company with a goal to "promote a social movement which subordinated capital to labour, founded in an egalitarian Christian ethic of community, and aiming to transform local society through co-operation."[42] Producer cooperatives were structured so workers owned company assets and were involved in the firm's governance. The Mondragón Corporation launched in 1955 with one consumer appliance manufacturer and expanded to more than 250 firms in manufacturing, finance, retail, and service companies. In recent years, the Catholic identity of the Mondragón Corporation has faded, but the history and witness, remain.

INCARNATIONAL MISSION

Regularly, Christians feel called to live among the poor. Inspired by Jesus' humbling himself in Philippians 2, they go alone or in small groups, but they go to participate in gospel poverty with a heart of compassion and service. Toyohiko Kagawa and the Catholic Worker movement are two exemplars described in chapter 6.

A person who inspired many in the late twentieth century to "go and do likewise" was Viv Grigg. Grigg's incarnational mission approach paired evangelism and economic development while living in solidarity among the poor, generally in cities of the Global South. Grigg's example inspired others, including, Craig and Nay Greenfield, founders of Alongsiders, an organization that pairs youth from churches in developing countries with nearby youth in need of a mentor. Through peer mentoring, Alongsiders nurtures holistic development among the next generation.[43] Similarly, individual Christians who have struck out to live with the poor include new monastics, community developers, Catholic Workers, and pastors who minister in inner-city neighborhoods, among others. The community is the

---

42. Molina and Walton, "Alternative Co-Operative Tradition," 231.

43. For a beautiful account of Craig and Nay's beginning journey, see Greenfield, *Urban Halo*.

emphasis in incarnational mission. As Soong-Chan Rah counsels "Western culture's excessive individualism leads to the failure to understand that the power of the church is not in a heroic Christian individual superstar, but in the community that is the body of Christ."[44]

COMMUNITY DEVELOPMENT

Our final highlight of community is the leavening of community development in local and global settings. This movement has several tributaries— some Christian and some from mainstream development.

After WWII, economists had few tools for understanding how economies developed. Initiatives were pursued that sponsored top-down modernization and large-scale infrastructure projects, such as hospitals and highways. Also in the mix, however, were bottom-up approaches that attempted to be sensitive to local culture. U.S. President Franklin D. Roosevelt had read and was influenced by *A Bell for Adano*, a Pulitzer Prize-winning novel by John Hersey about an American Army officer who helped a Sicilian village acquire a new town bell after fascists had melted the old one into weapons. Similarly, John F. Kennedy was affected by the novel *The Ugly American*, by William Lederer and Eugene Burdick, which was published chapter by chapter in the *Saturday Evening Post*. Both novels portrayed the importance of international economic development acknowledging culture and self-direction.[45] Although large-scale development continued, many grew to appreciate the appropriateness of local determination, experimentation, and a greater role for markets in poverty alleviation.

In the United States, interest in urban revitalization took root among some Christians. Efforts included addressing homelessness, housing, gentrification, business development, and other expressions of community development. John Perkins (b. 1930) cofounded the Christian Community Development Association (CCDA) which advocated for listening to and joining with the community in church-supported self-determination [**Christian Community Development Philosophy**].[46] Community development has included diverse models, including a reincarnation of the settlement house model from the early twentieth century.[47]

---

44. Rah, "Rethinking Incarnational Ministry," 33–4.

45. Immerwar, *Thinking Small*, 1–3.

46. For description and application of each principle, see Gordon and Perkins, *Making Neighborhoods Whole*.

47. Polson and Scales, "Good Neighbor House."

Christian Community Development Philosophy

The Christian Community Development Association advocates eight principles in implementing development:

RELOCATION: LIVING AMONG THE PEOPLE

Living out the gospel means desiring for one's neighbor and neighbor's family that which one desires for one's self and family. Living out the gospel means bettering the quality of other people's lives spiritually, physically, socially, and emotionally as one betters one's own. Living out the gospel means sharing in the suffering and pain of others.

RECONCILIATION: PEOPLE TO GOD

Reconciliation is at the heart of the gospel. Jesus said that the essence of Christianity could be summed up in two inseparable commandments: Love God, and love thy neighbor. (Mt 22:37–39) First, Christian Community Development is concerned with reconciling people to God and bringing them into a church fellowship where they can be discipled in their faith.

REDISTRIBUTION: JUST DISTRIBUTION OF RESOURCES

When men and women in the body of Christ are visibly present and living among the poor (relocation), and when people are intentionally loving their neighbor and their neighbor's family the way a person loves him or herself and family (reconciliation), the result is redistribution, or a just distribution of resources.

LEADERSHIP DEVELOPMENT

The primary goal of leadership development is to restore the stabilizing glue and fill the vacuum of moral, spiritual, and economic leadership that is so prevalent in poor communities by developing leaders. This is most effectively done by raising up Christian leaders from the community of need who will remain in the community to live and lead.

Listening to the Community

Often communities are developed by people outside of the community that bring in resources without taking into account the community itself. Christian Community Development is committed to listening to the community residents, and hearing their dreams, ideas and thoughts. This is often referred to as the "felt need" concept. Listening is most important, as the people of the community are the vested treasures of the future.

Church-Based

The community of God's people is uniquely capable of affirming the dignity of the poor and enabling them to meet their own needs. It is practically impossible to do effective wholistic ministry apart from the local church. A nurturing community of faith can best provide the thrusts of evangelism, discipleship, spiritual accountability, and relationships by which disciples grow in their walk with God.

Wholistic Approach

Oftentimes, many in ministry get passionate and involved in one area of need and think if they solve this particular problem that all else will be resolved. Christians, of course, often focus this area on a personal relationship with Jesus Christ. Of course, the most essential element to Christian Community Development is evangelism and discipleship. Yet solving problems with lasting solutions is more than evangelism and discipleship.

Empowerment

Empowering people as community developers meet their needs is an important element to Christian Community Development. How does a pastor ensure that people are able to help themselves after they have been helped? Oftentimes, Christian ministry, particularly in poor communities, creates dependency. This is no better than the federal government welfare program. The Bible teaches empowerment, not dependency.[48]

The notion that attempting to help others may actually hurt them can represent a variety of meanings. For some, it resurrects the spirits of social Darwinism and neoclassical economics, suggesting that aid invariably weakens rather than strengthens. Mainstream global development research, however, suggests that it may not be helping that hurts, but paternalism and colonialism—imposing on others rather than allowing self-determination.[49] There is more to the story than this single consideration but it is impossible to miss the observation stressed by community developers—that some approaches to compassion further oppress and some liberate and transform.

Sister Churches

We conclude with a final example that combines mutual aid and community development—the sister church movement, popular among some Catholic parishes and Lutheran churches. Two parishes or congregations learn from each other and partner in initiatives of interest to one or both congregations.[50] A 2003 Center for Applied Research in the Apostolate (CARA) report stated that "these relationships are, or become, partnerships of mutual support, so that both parishes benefit from the relationship as they become partners in solidarity."[51]

The sister church movement grew out of Global North/South exchanges among parishes and churches. A few stretched back to the 1960s but more were established in the 1980s and 1990s. Many of these relationships grew organically within parishes, often from the initiative of a single member. Many engaged relationships with Latin American and Caribbean congregational partners. Partnerships vary in their activities and, sometimes, pairs of partners disagree in their emphases.[52]

---

48. Christian Community Development Association, "CCD Philosophy." Reprinted with permission.

49. Early research on unconditional cash transfers through organizations such as Give Directly suggest they can be quite effective in alleviating poverty because they allow motivated individuals to apply aid where it is best leveraged.

50. Bakker, *Sister Churches*; Hefferan, *Twinning Faith and Development*.

51. Gautier and Perl, "Partnerships of Solidarity," 1.

52. Bakker, *Sister Churches*, 42–71.

CONCLUSION

Mutual aid and community development represent an enduring motif in Christian history. They embody the sparing and sharing of Jesus' earliest disciples and affirm the richness of growing and serving in Christ in community. Contrasts abound in mutual aid and community development. Self-reliance and interdependence often are symbiotic. A tendency to pull away from others and assert one's independence and ownership coexists with the tendency to seek equality, solidarity, and intimacy. Groups may critique or mourn broader society. Yet, mustering the energy for a hard-fought social experiment is a testimony to hope and possibility. A community approach may seek to avoid mainstream social relationships or restore them in novel ways. Mutual aid and a focus on community represents hope and unity as well as critique and separation.

In our sampling of twentieth-century examples, we find old and new expressions of community in every major branch of Christianity. Some, such as Anabaptists, Mormons, and Shakers, have deeply embedded communal forms in their history and polity, just as do intentional communities and auxiliary, fraternal, and mission organizations. Community development combines an enduring commitment to poverty alleviation and flourishing with a desire to join and participate with others. Mutual aid and community are not a panacea and are not easy. They require sacrifice and growth. They personify many of the motifs from previous eras including sacrifice, mobilization, and formation. Mutual aid and community development, however, uniquely accentuate the transformative nature of compassion through intertwined relationships, underscoring that we need one another.

Closing

Maria Skobtsova wrote, "Nonpossession should not be merely passive—they don't ask, so I don't give. Nonpossession should be active: a monk should seek where to place the gifts given him by God precisely for that end."[1] In our journey across two millennia, we have witnessed disciples of Christ actively attempting to place gifts in the hands of others through the offering and receiving of charity. Assuming compassion is a divinely enabled response to God's love, we also have seen God at work. We encountered ideas, actors, and institutions expressing compassion within their time and spilling over into successive generations. Many of these influences linger today. The detail and diversity of actors is endless, but tracing the roots of Christian service can be both instructive and deepening. I hope this has occurred for you along the journey.

THEMES

Each era we considered offered insights into compassion and charity. A few of these might be summarized as follows:

- *Formation and sacrifice.* When Christians desire to be like Jesus, they begin seeing him in others. They yearn for and trust the eventual justice of God. Disciples of Christ take joy in God's overwhelming gift economy, sharing freely with others because of all they have received. They also recognize a gift they owe in return includes suffering. A future reality shapes their present activity.

- *Contentment and simplicity.* How and what one gives and receives can stimulate virtue to grow or wither. Christians of means should voluntarily curb their consumption and share with others in an exchange of

1. Skobtsova, *Mother Maria Skobtsova*, 103.

262

mutual giving and receiving. The rich and the church provide the poor and the poor offer spiritual blessings for their benefaction.

- *Mobilization and participation.* Material life is imbued with spiritual meaning. Charity can become simony—a mechanical exchange of penance to win security with God. Temptation is ever present for stewards to resources from the most vulnerable. Listen to prophetic witnesses which often speak from an acquaintance with brokenness.

- *Reform and expansion.* Compassion is the fruit of salvation and an expectation of Christians. As a divinely-established institution, governments may coordinate some social goods, but Christians, by their very identity and character, are to show compassion to others. Work hard and live modestly as a steward. Authentic and inauthentic need will always be with you. Try to be compassionate because "There but for the grace of God, go I."[2]

- *Salvation and service.* The priesthood of all believers and the potential for human progress provide the means for aiding others. A marketplace of ideas and institutions yield innovation and competition, which can result in challenges in communicating and coordinating. Be aware of paternalism; eschew colonialism.

- *Liberation and justice.* Jesus' prediction of insensitivity to need (Matt 25:31–46) is prescient because many do not notice or want to notice injustice. The radical gospel of Jesus and the kingdom of God require courage and counter-cultural lifestyles. Ideologies of contrasting beliefs deserve constant examination in the light of Christ. Theology can provide insight and direction.

- *Peace and humanitarianism.* Although often characterized as daily service and kindnesses, many efforts of compassion require intentionality to begin and commitment to endure. Individuals and institutions may hinder or advance righteousness. Discipling and development belong together.

- *Mutual aid and community development.* Mutual aid and community teach us the deep, but not the easy rhythms of compassion, self-reliance, and interdependence.

Cutting across all of these eras and expressions of compassion are a variety of observations. I'd like to suggest four as a beginning. First, human, Christian compassion consistently draws inspiration and comfort from

---

2. Attributed to John Bradford (1510–1555), an English Reformer who was burned at the stake.

God. Philosopher John Hare said it this way: "there is a God who loves us enough both to demand a high standard from us and to help us meet it."[3] In a historical review, it is easy to focus on the actors; to spotlight people and exaggerate moral human capacity. It is clear that compassion shines from all of the human facets explored in the introduction, yet, Christian theology reminds us to recognize compassion's source. The mercies and gifts of God that project an upside-down kingdom in this world and beyond, animate Christian compassion.[4] When humans fail, divine hope and love offer a compassionate salve, comforting disappointment, tiredness, and failure.

A second observation is that it is difficult to miss the central role of *kenosis* in Christian compassion. In sickness and in health, for richer or poorer, Christians are called to follow Jesus, imitating Christ, relinquishing power and privilege, and affirming a preferential option for the poor. Seeing the gospel in darkness and brokenness calls us to trust God with eschatological hope. For much of history, the majority of Christians had little power and few possessions to relinquish. The same is true today for many Christians. Yet for all, the call to care and advocate is an invitation to deeper individual and communal formation in Christ.[5]

Third, the whole person is of interest in Christian compassion. Many initiatives have been launched by a variety of organizations and institutions to address material or spiritual wellbeing. Rooted in principles of flourishing, Christians engage issues at individual, community, and social levels addressing physical, social, and spiritual needs. In other words, they sense and respond to brokenness because of the love of God.

A final observation cutting across eras is that Christian laypersons not only practice compassion, they frequently reclaim it. While theologies, leaders, and charitable institutions attract attention in histories such as this one, most charity is extended by the masses of Christians through innumerable virtues, prayers, and acts. When ecclesial structures are derelict or deficient in attending to the poor, it often is confraternities, lay pietists, laborers, and nameless Christians who serve faithfully and quietly and bring about a corrective in direction.

---

3. Hare, *Moral Gap*, 275.

4. For a reminder of the radical, transforming invitation of God, see Rowe's *Christianity's Surprise*.

5. For a brief theological treatment, see chapter 3, authored by Derran Reese, in Lynn et al., *Development in Mission*.

EXCURSIONS

Although they are beyond our scope, several additional paths could be cut in exploring the compassion terrain. One might be to trace particular initiatives, approaches, or audiences, such as prison reform, economic justice, or service to widows. It often is enlightening and encouraging to realize that one stands on the shoulders of others who have labored toward familiar ends with similar and novel assumptions and approaches. Many of those chains are hinted at in this survey and breadcrumbs are offered in the footnotes and the index.

A similar project might be to delve into theologies that accompany compassion. We've not wandered far into the woods of Christology, Mariology, pneumatology, ecclesiology, soteriology, or theodicy, yet Christianity extends compassion through each of these vis-à-vis concepts such as new birth, hospitality, and hope, and experiences with meaning, coping, community, and end-time assurance.[6] Similarly, we might explore the spirituality of compassion or view it through the lens of Christian ethics. A deep, incisive analysis applying sociological, political, historical, or other lenses portend additional insights about interlaced church, government, and civil society dynamics. Many such analyses are available, and regularly, new ones appear and disrupt the settled dust of history.[7]

A reflective reading of historical witnesses may prompt personal insights. For example: Who has sacrificed, endured pain, or given to you? How do virtue and new birth contour your compassion? Is ideal compassion transactional, instrumental, or transformational? Is gift an obligation to repay or an interdependency to nurture? What is the kingdom of God and how and where is it manifest? How effective are compassionate institutions and how is that gauged? How are you challenging countercultural justice, offering the balm of peace and humanitarianism, or participating in the fellowship of mutual aid? What do you consider to be the roles of church and government, individuals and organizations, in providing compassion? These and other questions might have been prompted in a reflective reading of compassion.[8]

6. Considerable research has been devoted to the ways Christianity provides coping, meaning, grit, and hope. A modern sampling includes: Bryan et al., "Randomizing Religion"; Lybbert and Wydick. "Poverty, Aspirations, and the Economics of Hope"; Pargament et al., "The Religious Dimension of Coping"; Park, "Religious as a Meaning-Making Framework."

7. As Ukeachusim argues, social action and institutions can be propelled by self-interest, guilt, or ego just as they can by selflessness. See "Understanding Compassion," 374, 385–90.

8. To reflect more deeply and personally on compassion, see Nouwen et al.,

Finally, much of the compassion and caring that we have examined has been from seats of privilege and power: as if *we* were extending aid to others. Less frequently have we learned the deep contours of compassion from those enduring poverty and hardship. If vulnerability, adversity, and oppression are transformative, it is likely that giving is qualitatively different when it is offered by a poor widow who gives all rather than from one with abundance to spare (Luke 21:1–4). How is compassion refined when it involves sacrifice? When it is offered by one who is slapped or sued and yet returns kindness to the oppressor (Matt 5:38–42)? Thankfully, we have encountered some of these along our journey. As Stanisław Barańczak reminded us in "Never Really," quoted in the opening of this book, few of us have earned our full stripes when it comes to suffering or charity. We pray for ears to hear on our communal journey from those who have (Matt 13:15).

BOUNDARIES

As we conclude, it seems appropriate to return to two cairns I placed at the boundaries of this project. One was that we would not focus on occasions where Christian compassion was absent; where Christians were inattentive, passive, callous, and even vicious. Unfortunately, these events and developments also are plentiful.[9] More despicable, perhaps, are acts done in the name of charity and benevolence which bring harm and evil.[10] As Lauren Winner says, "because nothing created is untouched by the Fall, Christians should not be surprised when lovely and good, potentially gracious Christian gestures are damaged, or when human beings deploy those Christian gestures in the perpetuation of damage."[11] Followers of Jesus have promoted and been complicit in war, slavery, injustice, oppression, corruption, and other evils, sometimes against others and sometimes against themselves. We can learn from both laudable and shameful histories, and we need not shy away from either, for this surely would not be honest or compassionate.

Second, as we've journeyed, I have applied the label "Christian" generously. However, it often is difficult for observers or actors to tease apart the origin and influence of their actions. Certainly, not all actions taken in a

---

Compassion.

9. One source, among many, is Stanley, *Christianity in the Twentieth Century*, 150–171.

10. One example is ethnocentric motivations propelling the adoption of indigenous children. See Goodwin et al., "Reframing the Orphan Mandate."

11. Winner, *Dangers of Christian Practice*, 3.

predominantly Christian society are Christian. On this point, Yves Congar, an influential Catholic theologian of Vatican II, reminds us that

> Christianity has lived for a long time. It is overloaded with all kinds of contributions from the history it has passed through and affected by all kinds of human circumstances. It's not that we condemn things that we should rather try to understand and explain historically. But the real point is this: there are things which come from history that it would be foolish to try to absolutize by making them identical with Christianity. Human and historical forms, developed throughout history, are linked to Christianity without pertaining to its essential reality.[12]

Indeed, the historical record witnesses to a melding of human and divine agency in which Christians engage imperfectly. Perhaps even these occasions provide an opportunity for compassion, confession, and hope as we witness history. As Congar encourages, "Christianity, when it is true to itself, requires a relentless obligation to pay attention to religious reform."[13] One thing we can know for sure—ordinary trials and catastrophic suffering will continue (Mark 14:7). Misery will not be eradicated by human effort, but neither is it a fatalistic cause. Instead, human need provides an ever-present opportunity to experience, anticipate, and join the compassion of God [**A Prayer Attributed to Óscar Romero**].

A Prayer Attributed to Óscar Romero

The Kingdom is not only beyond our efforts, it is even beyond our vision.

We accomplish in our lifetime only a fraction of the magnificent enterprise that is God's work.

Nothing that we do is complete, which is another way of saying that the kingdom always lies beyond us.

No statement says all that could be said.

No prayer fully expresses our faith.

No confession brings perfection.

No program accomplishes the church's mission.

No set of strategic goals and objectives includes everything.

That is what we are about.

12. Congar, *True and False Reform*, 47.
13. Congar, *True and False Reform*, 47.

We plant the seeds that one day will grow.

We water the seeds already planted, knowing that they hold future promise.

We lay foundations that will need further development.

We provide yeast that produces the effects far beyond our capabilities.

We cannot do everything, and there is a sense of liberation realizing that.

This enables us to do something, and to do it well.

It may be incomplete, but it is a beginning, a step along the way, an opportunity for the Lord's grace to enter and do the rest.

We may never see the end results, but that is the difference between the master builder and the worker.

We are workers, not master builders; ministers, not messiahs.

We are prophets of a future not our own.

Amen.[14]

---

14. Quoted in Udovic, "Our Good Will," 76–77.

Further Reading

COMPREHENSIVE

Riccardi, Andrea. *To the Margins: Pope Francis and the Mission of the Church*. Maryknoll: Orbis, 2018.

ANTIQUE

Allen, Pauline, Wendy Mayer, and Bronwen Niel, eds. *Preaching Poverty in Late Antiquity: Perceptions and Realities*. Leipzig: Evangelische Verlagsanstalt, 2009.

Anderson, Gary A. *Charity: The Place of the Poor in the Biblical Tradition*. New Haven: Yale University Press, 2013.

Armitage, David J. *Theories of Poverty in the World of the New Testament*. Tübingen: Mohr Siebeck, 2016.

Ferngren, Gary B. *Medicine and Health Care in Early Christianity*. Baltimore: Johns Hopkins University Press, 2009.

Holman, Susan R., ed. *Wealth and Poverty in Early Church and Society*. Grand Rapids: Baker Academic, 2008.

Longenecker, Bruce W. *Remember the Poor: Paul, Poverty, and the Greco-Roman World*. Grand Rapids: Eerdmans, 2010.

Rhee, Helen. *Loving the Poor, Saving the Rich: Wealth, Poverty, and Early Christian Formation*. Grand Rapids: Baker Academic, 2012.

Richardson, K. C. *Early Christian Care for the Poor: An Alternative Subsistence Strategy under Roman Imperial Rule*. Eugene: Wipf & Stock, 2018.

Wessel, Susan. *Passion and Compassion in Early Christianity*. New York: Cambridge University Press, 2016.

MEDIEVAL

Brodman, James William. *Charity and Religion in Medieval Europe*. Washington, DC: Catholic University of America Press, 2009.

Brown, Peter. *Through the Eye of a Needle: Wealth, the Fall of Rome, and the Making of Christianity in the West, 350–550 AD*. Princeton: Princeton University Press, 2012.

Miller, Timothy S. *The Orphans of Byzantium: Child Welfare in the Christian Empire*. Washington, DC: Catholic University of America Press, 2003.

Watts, Edward J. *The Final Pagan Generation: Rome's Unexpected Path to Christianity*. Oakland: University of California Press, 2015.

MODERN

Curtis, Heather D. *Faith in the Great Physician: Suffering and Divine Healing in American Culture, 1860–1900*. Baltimore: Johns Hopkins University Press, 2007.

Himmelfarb, Gertrude. *Poverty and Compassion: The Moral Imagination of Late Victorians*. New York: Knopf, 1991.

Ruswick, Brent. *Almost Worthy: The Poor, Paupers, and the Science of Charity in America, 1877–1917*. Bloomington: Indiana University Press, 2013.

CONTEMPORARY

Barnett, Michael. *Empire of Humanity: A History of Humanitarianism*. Ithaca: Cornell University Press, 2011.

Curtis, Heather D. *Holy Humanitarians: American Evangelicals and Global Aid*. Cambridge, MA: Harvard University Press, 2018.

Curren, Charles E. *The Social Mission of the U.S. Catholic Church: A Theological Perspective*. Washington, DC: Georgetown University Press, 2011.

Gutiérrez, Gustavo. *A Theology of Liberation: History, Politics, and Salvation*. Maryknoll, NY: Orbis, 1973.

McKay, Johnston. *The Kirk and the Kingdom: A Century of Tension in Scottish Social Theology, 1830–1929*. Edinburgh: Edinburgh University Press, 2012.

Massaro, Thomas. *Living Justice: Catholic Social Teaching in Action*. Lanham, MD: Rowan & Littlefield, 2012.

Smith, Luther E., Jr. *Intimacy and Mission: Intentional Community as Crucible for Radical Discipleship*. Eugene, OR: Wipf & Stock, 1994.

Swartz, David R. *Facing West: American Evangelicals in an Age of World Christianity*. New York: Oxford University Press, 2020.

Swartz, David R. *Moral Minority: The Evangelical Left in an Age of Conservatism*. Philadelphia: University of Pennsylvania Press, 2012.

Bibliography

Abraham, William J. "From Revivalism to Socialism: The Impact of the Poor on Harry Ward." In *The Poor and the People Called Methodists, 1729–1999*, edited by Richard P. Heitzenrater, 161–80. Nashville: Kingswood.

Adams, Vincanne. *Markets of Sorrow, Labors of Faith: New Orleans in the Wake of Katrina*. Durham: Duke University Press, 2013.

Alford, Helen J., and Michael J. Naughton. *Managing as if Faith Mattered: Christian Social Principles in the Modern Organization*. Notre Dame: University of Notre Dame Press, 2001.

Allen, Pauline, and Edward Morgan. "Augustine on Poverty." In *Preaching Poverty in Late Antiquity: Perceptions and Realities*, edited by Pauline Allen et al., 119–70. Leipzig: Evangelische Verlagsanstalt, 2009.

Allen, Roland. *Missionary Methods: St. Paul's or Ours: A Study of the Church in the Four Provinces*. London: Robert Scott, 1912.

Alves, Abel Athouguia. "The Christian Social Organism and Social Welfare: The Case of Vives, Calvin and Loyola." *The Sixteenth Century Journal* 20 (1989) 3–22.

Ambrose. *Les Devoirs. Tome II, Livres II–III*. Edited by Maurice Testard. Vol. 1. Paris: Société d'édition "Les Belles Lettres," 1992.

Andersen, Thomas Barnebeck, et al. "Pre-Reformation Roots of the Protestant Ethic." *The Economic Journal* 127 (2017) 1756–93.

Anderson, Mark. "Mistranslations of Josephus and the Expansion of Public Charity in Late Antiquity." *Early Medieval Europe* 25 (2017) 139–61.

Andrews, Frances. *The Early Humiliati*. Cambridge: Cambridge University Press, 2000.

————. *The Other Friars: Carmelite, Augustinian, Sack and Pied Friars in the Middle Ages*. Woodbridge, UK: Boydell, 2006.

Aquinas, Thomas. *Summa Theologica*, 2nd, rev. ed. New York: Benziger, 1948.

Armitage, David J. *Theories of Poverty in the World of the New Testament*. Tübingen: Mohr Siebeck, 2016.

Arrington, Leonard J., et al. *Building the City of God: Community and Cooperation among the Mormons*. 2nd ed. Urbana: University of Illinois Press, 1992.

Arrizabalaga, Jon. "Poor Relief in Counter-Reformation Castile: An Overview." In *Health Care and Poor Relief in Counter-Reformation Europe*, edited by Ole Peter Grell et al., 151–76. London: Routledge, 1999.

Arsdall, Anne Van. *Medieval Herbal Remedies: The Old English Herbarium and Anglo-Saxon Medicine*. New York: Rutledge, 2002.

Atkinson, Henry Avery. *Prelude to Peace: A Realistic View of International Relations.* New York: Harper & Brothers, 1937.

Augsburger, David. *Dissident Discipleship: A Spirituality of Self-Surrender, Love of God, and Love of Neighbor.* Grand Rapids: Brazos, 2006.

Augustine of Hippo. *Expositions of the Psalms (1–32).* Translated by Maria Boulding. Vols. 15–20. Hyde Park, NY: New City, 2000.

———. *St. Augustine's City of God and Christian Doctrine.* Translated by J. F. Shaw. Vol. 2. Edinburgh: T & T Clark, 1886.

———. *The Works of Saint Augustine: A Translation for the 21st Century. Sermons (273–305A) on the Saints.* Edited by John E. Rotelle. Translated by Edmund Hill. Hyde Park, NY: New City, 1994.

Avramea, Anna. "Land and Sea Communications, Fourth–Fifteenth Centuries," 57–90. Washington, DC: Dumbarton Oaks, 2002.

Bacon, Margaret Hope. *Let This Life Speak: The Legacy of Henry Joel Cadbury.* Philadelphia: University of Pennsylvania Press, 1987.

Badger, R. Reid. *The Great American Fair: The World's Columbian Exposition and American Culture.* Chicago: Nelson Hall, 1979.

Baker, Kimball. *"Go to the Worker." America's Labor Apostles.* New ed. Milwaukee: Marquette University Press, 2010.

Bakker, Janel Kragt. *Sister Churches: American Congregations and Their Partners Abroad.* New York: Oxford University Press, 2014.

Balch, David L. "Attitudes toward Foreigners in 2 Maccabees, Eupolemus, Esther, Aristeas, and Luke-Acts." In *The Early Church in Its Context: Essays in Honor of Everett Ferguson,* edited by Abraham J. Malherbe et al., 22–47. Leiden: Brill, 1998.

Bantu, Vince L. *A Multitude of All Peoples: Engaging Ancient Christianity's Global Identity.* Downers Grove: IVP Academic, 2020.

Barańczak, Stanisław. *The Weight of the Body.* Evanston, IL: TriQuarterly/Northwestern University Press, 1989.

Barclay, John M. G. *Paul and the Gift.* Grand Rapids: Eerdmans, 2015.

Barnes, Andrew E. *The Social Dimension of Piety: Associative Life and Devotional Change in the Penitent Confraternities of Marseille (1499–1792).* Mahwah, NJ: Paulist, 1994.

Barnes, Gregory A. *A Centennial History of the American Friends Service Committee.* Philadelphia: Friends, 2016.

Barnes, Jonathan S. *Power and Partnership: A History of the Protestant Mission Movement.* Eugene, OR: Wipf & Stock, 2013.

Barnes, Peter. "Plagues throughout History and Some Christian Responses." *Reformed Theological Review* 79 (2020) 77–96.

Barnes, Timothy David. *Tertullian: A Historical and Literary Study.* Oxford: Clarendon, 1971.

Barnett, Michael. *Empire of Humanity: A History of Humanitarianism.* Ithaca: Cornell University Press, 2011.

Barth, Karl. *Church Dogmatics.* Edited by G. W. Bromiley and T. F. Torrence. Vol. III.2, §43–44. London: T & T Clark, 2009.

Barton, Betty L. "Mormon Poor Relief: A Social Welfare Interlude." *Brigham Young University Studies* 18 (1978) 66–88.

Basil. "Homily on Luke." In *Patrologiae Cursus Completus.* Edited by Jacques-Paul Migne. Paris: Migne, 1857.

———. *On Social Justice*. Translated by Paul S. Schroeder. Yonkers, NY: St. Vladimir's Seminary Press, 2009.

Bates, Matthew W. *Salvation by Allegiance Alone: Rethinking Faith, Works, and the Gospel of Jesus the King*. Grand Rapids: Baker Academic, 2017.

Batson, C. Daniel. "The Empathy-Altruism Hypothesis." In *The Oxford Handbook of Compassion Science*, edited by Emma M. Seppälä et al., 27–40, 2017.

Baum, Markus. *Against the Wind: Eberhard Arnold and the Bruderhof*. Farmington, PA: Plough, 1998.

Baynes, Norman H. "The Life of St. John the Almsgiver." In *Three Byzantine Saints: Contemporary Biographies of St. Daniel the Stylite, St. Theodore of Sykeon and St. John the Almsgiver*, translated by Elizabeth A. S. Dawes. Oxford: Basil Blackwell, 1948.

Beach, Alison I. *The Trauma of Monastic Reform: Community and Conflict in Twelfth-Century Germany*. Cambridge: Cambridge University Press, 2017.

Bebbington, David W. *Evangelicalism in Modern Britain: A History from the 1730s to the 1980s*. London: Unwin Hyman, 1989.

Becker, Sascha O., et al. "Causes and Consequences of the Protestant Reformation." *Explorations in Economic History* 62 (2016) 1–25.

Beed, Clive, and Cara Beed. "A Biblical Basis for Reducing Extreme Disparity in Property Ownership." *Evangelical Review of Theology* 39 (2015) 324–42.

Behr, John. "Learning through Experience: The Pedagogy of Suffering and Death of Irenaeus." In *Suffering and Evil in Early Christian Thought*. Grand Rapids: Baker Academic, 2016.

———. "Social and Historical Setting." In *Cambridge History of Early Christian Literature*, edited by Francis Young et al., 55–70. Cambridge: Cambridge University Press, 2004.

Bein, Steve. *Compassion and Moral Guidance*. Honolulu: University of Hawaii Press, 2013.

Beito, David T. *From Mutual Aid to the Welfare State: Fraternal Societies and Social Services, 1890–1967*. Chapel Hill: University of North Carolina Press, 2000.

Bell, Adrian R., and Richard S. Dale. "The Medieval Pilgrimage Business." *Enterprise & Society* 12 (2011) 601–27.

Bell, Emma. "Whose Side Are They on? Patterns of Religious Resource Mobilization in British Industrial Mission." *Management & Organizational History* 1 (2006) 331–47.

Belsito, Antonio. *The Constitutions of the Institute of Charity: Called to be Saints Together*. Mansfield, UK: Rosmini 2017.

Beltramini, Enrico. "SCLC Operation Breadbasket: From Economic Civil Rights to Black Economic Power." *Fire!!!* 2, no. 2 (2013) 5–47.

Benbassat, Naomi. "Reflective Function: A Move to the Level of Concern." *Theory & Psychology* 30 (2020) 657–73.

Benedict. *The Rule of St. Benedict*. Oxford: Blackwell, 1964.

Benedict XVI. *God Is Love: Deus Caritas Est, Encyclical Letter*. San Francisco: Ignatius, 2006.

Benz, Ernst. *The Eastern Orthodox Church: Its Thought and Life*. Garden City, NY: Anchor, 1963.

Berger, Peter L. *The Noise of Solemn Assemblies: Christian Commitment and the Religious Establishment in America*. New York: Doubleday, 1961.

Bieringer, Reimund. "Texts That Create a Future: The Function of Ancient Texts for Theology Today." In *Reading Patristic Texts on Social Ethics: Issues and Challenges for Twenty-First-Century Christian Social Thought*, edited by John Leemans et al., 3–29. Washington, DC: Catholic University of America Press, 2011.

Bevans, Stephen B., and Roger P. Schroeder. *Constants in Context: A Theology of Mission for Today*. Maryknoll, NY: Orbis, 2004.

Birdsall, S. Douglas. "Conflict and Collaboration: A Narrative History and Analysis of the Interface between the Lausanne Committee for World Evangelization, the World Evangelical Fellowship, the International Fellowship of Evangelical Mission Theologians (INFEMIT), and the AD 2000 Movement." PhD diss. Oxford Centre for Mission Studies / Middlesex University, 2012.

Black, Christopher F. Italian *Confraternities in the Sixteenth Century*. Cambridge: Cambridge University Press, 1989.

Black, Christopher F., and Pamela Gravestock, eds. *Early Modern Confraternities in Europe and the Americas: International and Interdisciplinary Perspectives*. Abingdon, UK: Ashgate, 2006.

Black, Robert, and Keith Drury. *The Story of the Wesleyan Church*. Indianapolis: Wesleyan, 2012.

Black, Roger H. "The Word of God and Social Responsibility in the Lutheran Church in the United States of America." PhD diss. Marquette University, 1997.

Blackburn, Robin. *The Making of New World Slavery: From the Baroque to the Modern, 1492–1800*. London: Verso, 2010.

Blanton, Thomas R., IV. *A Spiritual Economy: Gift Exchange in the Letters of Paul of Tarsus*. New Haven: Yale University Press, 2017.

Blowers, Paul M., ed. *Moral Formation and the Virtuous Life*. Minneapolis: Fortress, 2019.

———. *Visions and Faces of the Tragic: The Mimesis of Tragedy and the Folly of Salvation in Early Christian Literature*. Oxford: Oxford University Press, 2020.

Bok, Jared. "Distinction through Religious Activism: How Capital Shapes the Organizational Repertoires of Transnational Protestant Outreach." *Sociology of Religion* 81 (2020) 294–318.

Bowman, Matthew. "Sin, Spirituality, and Primitivism: The Theologies of the American Social Gospel, 1885–1917." *Religion and American Culture* 17 (2007) 95–126.

Boyd, Lydia. "Circuits of Compassion: The Affective Labor of Uganda's Christian Orphan Choirs." *African Studies Review* 63 (2020) 518–39.

Bridges, Lois Carlson. *Monganga Paul: The Congo Ministry and Martyrdom of Paul Carlson, M.D.* Chicago: Covenant, 2004.

Brockman, James R. *Romero: A Life*. Maryknoll, NY: Orbis, 1989.

Brodhead, Charles Daniel. "Baptists Further Social Gospel: Plan Balanced Program of Action and Education." *The Christian Century*, March 15, 1939.

Brodman, James William. *Charity and Religion in Medieval Europe*. Washington, DC: Catholic University of America Press, 2009.

———. *Charity and Welfare: Hospitals and the Poor in Medieval Catalonia*. Philadelphia: University of Pennsylvania Press, 1998.

Bronkema, David, and Christopher M. Brown. "Business as Mission through the Lens of Development." *Transformation* 26 (2009) 82–88.

Brown, Ayanna Sheree. "'That Peace Shall Always Dwell among Them and True Love Be Upheld': Charity, the Seven Works of Mercy, and Lay Fellowship in Late Medieval and Early Reformation England." PhD diss. University of Michigan, 2014.

Brown, Peter. *Poverty and Leadership in the Later Roman Empire.* Hanover, NH: University Press of New England, 2002.

———. *Through the Eye of a Needle: Wealth, the Fall of Rome, and the Making of Christianity in the West, 350–550 AD.* Princeton: Princeton University Press, 2012.

———. *Treasure in Heaven: The Holy Poor in Early Christianity.* Charlottesville: University of Virginia Press, 2016.

Browne, Stanley George, et al., eds., *Heralds of Health: The Saga of Christian Medical Initiatives.* London: Christian Medical Fellowship, 1985.

Bruinius, Harry. *Better for All the World: The Secret History of Forced Sterilization and America's Quest for Racial Purity.* New York: Vintage, 2006.

Brummitt, Dan B. *The Efficient Epworthian: Being the "Epworth League Methods."* Rev. ed. Cincinnati: Methodist Book Concern.

Bryan, Gharad, et al. "Randomizing Religion: The Impact of Protestant Evangelism on Economic Outcomes." *The Quarterly Journal of Economics* 136 (2021) 293–380.

Buchanan, James M. "The Samaritan's Dilemma." In *Altruism, Morality, and Economic Theory*, edited by Edmund S. Phelps, 71–86. New York: Russell Sage, 1975.

Buell, Denise Kimber. "'Be Not One Who Stretches Out Hands to Receive but Shuts Them When It Comes to Giving:' Envisioning Christian Charity When Both Donors and Recipients Are Poor." In *Wealth and Poverty in Early Church and Society*, edited by Susan R. Holman, 37–47. Grand Rapids: Baker Academic / Holy Cross Greek Orthodox School of Theology, 2008.

Buhrer, Eliza. "From Caritas to Charity: How Loving God Became Giving Alms." In *Poverty and Prosperity: In the Middle Ages and Renaissánce*, edited by Cynthia Kosso and Anne Scott, 113–28. Turnhout, Belgium: Brepols, 2012.

Burchill-Limb, K.-Y. "The Actuality of Augustine's Distinction between 'Uti' and 'Frui.'" *Augustiniana* 56 (2006) 183–97.

Burridge, Claire. "Incense in Medicine: An Early Medieval Perspective." *Early Medieval Europe* 28 (2020) 219–55.

Butler, Anthea. *Women in the Church of God in Christ: Making a Sanctified World.* Chapel Hill: University of North Carolina Press, 2007.

Cabestrero, Teófilo. *No los Separó la Muerte: Felipe y Mary Barreda, Esposos Cristianos que Dieron su Vida por Nicaragua.* Santander, Spain: Sal Terrae, 1985.

Cadbury, Henry J. "Social Servis [sic]: Spirit and Method of a Great Movement in the Christian Church." Henry J. Cadbury Papers, Haverford College, c. 1915.

Calhoun, Craig. "The Imperative to Reduce Suffering: Charity, Progress, and Emergencies in the Field of Humanitarian Action." In *Humanitarianism in Question: Politics, Power, Ethics*, edited by Michael Barnett and Thomas G. Weiss, 73–97. Ithaca: Cornell University Press, 2008.

Calhoun-Brown, Allison. "While Marching to Zion: Otherworldliness and Racial Empowerment in the Black Community." *Journal for the Scientific Study of Religion* 37 (1998) 427–39.

Calvi, Rossella, et al. "The Protestant Legacy: Missions, Gender, and Human Capital in India." *Journal of Human Resources*, in print.

Calvi, Rossella, and Federico G. Mantovanelli. "Long-term Effects of Access to Health Care: Medical Missions in Colonial India." *Journal of Development Economics*, 135 (2018) 285–303.

Calvin, John. *The Institutes of the Christian Religion*. Translated by Henry Beveridge. Edinburgh: Calvin Translation Society, 1846.

Cameron, Geoffrey. *Send Them Here: Religion, Politics, and Refugee Resettlement in North America*. Montreal: McGill-Queen's University Press, 2021.

Cameron, Rondo. *A Concise Economic History of the World: From Paleolithic Times to the Present*. 2nd ed. New York: Oxford University Press, 1993.

Cantwell, Christopher D., et al., eds. *The Pew and the Picket Line: Christianity and the American Working Class*. Urbana: University of Illinois Press, 2016.

Cardman, Francine. "Poverty and Wealth as Theater: John Chrysostom's Homilies on Lazarus and the Rich Man." In *Wealth and Poverty in Early Church and Society*, edited by Susan R. Holman. Grand Rapids: Baker Academic / Holy Cross Greek Orthodox School of Theology, 2008.

Carpenter, Joel, et al., eds. *Christian Higher Education: A Global Reconnaissance* Grand Rapids: Eerdmans, 2014.

Carson, Stephen C. "The Accommodation of Joseph and Mary in Bethlehem: *Kataluma* in Luke 2:7." *New Testament Studies* 56 (2010) 326–42.

Carter, Heath W. *Union Made: Working People and the Rise of Social Christianity in Chicago*. New York: Oxford University Press, 2015.

Castelló-Climent, et al. "Higher Education and Prosperity: From Catholic Missionaries to Luminosity in India," *The Economic Journal*, 128 (2018) 3039–75.

Catechism of the Catholic Church. 2nd ed. Washington, DC: United States Catholic Conference, 2000.

Cayley, David. *The Rivers North of the Future: The Testament of Ivan Illich as told to David Cayley*. Toronto: Anansi, 2005.

Chadwick, Henry. *The Early Church*. Revised. London: Penguin, 1993.

Chalmers, Thomas. *Political Economy in Connexion with the Moral State and Prospects of Society*. Vol. 2. Edinburgh: Sutherland and Knox, 1850.

———. *Political Economy in Connexion with the Moral State and Prospects of Society*. Vol. 1. Edinburgh: Thomas Constable, 1852.

Châtellier, Louis. *The Religion of the Poor: Rural Missions in Europe and the Formation of Modern Catholicism, C1500–C1800*. Translated by Brian Pearce. Cambridge: Cambridge University Press, 1997.

Chesterman, Clement C. *In the Service of Suffering: Phases of Medical Missionary Enterprise*. London: Cargate, 1940.

Childers, Jeff W. *Divining Gospel: Oracles of Biblical Interpretation in a Unique Syriac Manuscript of John*. Berlin: De Gruyter, 2020.

Chism, Jonathan. *Saints in the Struggle: Church of God in Christ Activists in the Memphis Civil Rights Movement, 1954–1968*. Lanham, MD: Lexington, 2019.

Chittister, Joan. *In Search of Belief*. Ligouri, MO: Ligouri/Triumph, 1999.

Chitty, Derwas James. *The Desert a City: An Introduction to the Study of Egyptian and Palestinian Monasticism Under the Christian Empire*. Crestwood, NY: St Vladimir's Seminary, 1977.

Christian Community Development Association. "CCD Philosophy," n.d. https://ccda.org/about/philosophy/.

Christie, Nancy and Michael Gauvreau. *Full-Orbed Christianity: The Protestant Churches and Social Welfare in Canada, 1900–1940.* Montreal: McGill-Queen's University Press, 1996.

Chrysostom, John. "Homily 1." In *Homilies on Paul's Letter to the Philippians.* Translated by Pauline Allen. Atlanta: Society of Biblical Literature, 2013.

———. "Homily 3." In *Homilies on Paul's Letter to the Philippians.* Translated by Pauline Allen. Atlanta: Society of Biblical Literature, 2013.

———. "Homily 7." In *Homilies on Paul's Letter to the Philippians.* Translated by Pauline Allen. Atlanta: Society of Biblical Literature, 2013.

———. "Homily 10: A Sermon on Almsgiving." In *Fathers of the Church: On Repentance and Almsgiving: A New Translation.* Translated by Gus George Christo, 96, 131–49. Washington, DC: Catholic University of America Press, 1989.

———. "Homily 11." In *Homilies on Paul's Letter to the Philippians.* Translated by Pauline Allen. Atlanta: Society of Biblical Literature, 2013.

Church of Sweden. *A Bishops' Letter about Diakonia. Bishops' Conference 2015.* Uppsala: Church of Sweden, 2015.

Ciszek, Walter J., and Daniel L Flaherty. *He Leadeth Me.* San Francisco: Ignatius, 1995.

Clark, Christopher, and Michael Ledger-Lomas. "The Protestant International." In *Religious Internationals in the Modern World: Globalization and Faith Communities since 1750,* edited by Abigail Green and Vincent Viaene, 23–52. New York: Palgrave Macmillan, 2012.

Clifton-Soderstrom, Michelle. "The Convergence Model of Pietist Ethics: Faith Active in Love (Gal. 5:6)." *Political Theology* 11 (2010) 490–506.

Cloninger, C. Robert, et al. *The Temperament and Character Inventory (TCI). A Guide to its Development and Use.* St. Louis: Center for Psychobiology of Personality, Washington University, 1994.

Clossey, Luke. *Salvation and Globalization in the Early Jesuit Missions.* Cambridge: Cambridge University Press, 2008.

Cnaan, Ram A., et al. *The Newer Deal: Social Work and Religion in Partnership.* New York: Columbia University Press, 1999.

Coffey, Joan L. *Léon Harmel: Entrepreneur as Catholic Social Reformer.* Notre Dame: University of Notre Dame Press, 2003.

Coffman, Mary Ruth. *Build Me a City: The Life of Father Harold Purcell, Founder of the City of St. Jude.* Montgomery, AL: Pioneer, 1984.

Cohen, Aryeh. *Justice in the City: An Argument from the Sources of Rabbinic Judaism.* Brookline, MA: Academic Studies, 2012.

Cohn, Samuel K., Jr. *Cultures of Plague: Medical Thinking at the End of the Renaissance.* New York: Oxford University Press, 2011.

Collier-Thomas, Bettye. *Jesus, Jobs, and Justice: African American Women and Religion.* Philadelphia: Temple University Press, 2010.

Collins, John J. *What are Biblical Values? What the Bible Says on Key Ethical Issues.* New Haven: Yale University Press, 2019.

Collins, John N. *Deacons and the Church: Making Connections Between Old and New.* Harrisburg, PA: Morehouse, 2002.

———. *Diakonia Studies: Critical Issues in Ministry.* New York: Oxford University Press, 2014.

Colón-Emeric, Edgardo. *Óscar Romero's Theological Vision: Liberation and the Transfiguration of the Poor.* Notre Dame: University of Notre Dame Press, 2018.

Compton, John W. *The End of Empathy: Why White Protestants Stopped Loving Their Neighbors.* New York: Oxford University Press, 2020.

Confession of Faith in a Mennonite Perspective. Harrisonburg, VA: Herald, 1995.

Congar, Yves. *True and False Reform in the Church.* Translated by Paul Philibert. Collegeville, MN: Liturgical, 2011.

Constantelos, Demetrios J. "Origins of Christian Diakonia: Christian Orthodox Philanthropy in Church History." Finland, n.d. www.ioce/orthodoxdiakonia/content/constatelospaper.pdf.

Cooper, Alan. *Bridges, Law and Power in Medieval England, 700–1400.* Woodbridge, UK: Boydell, 2006.

Corbett, Steve, and Brian Fikkert. *When Helping Hurts: How to Alleviate Poverty without Hurting the Poor. . .and Yourself.* Chicago: Moody, 2009.

Corke-Webster, James. "Emperors, Bishops, Art and Jurisprudence: The Transformation of Law in Eusebius of Caesarea." *Early Medieval Europe* 27 (2019) 12–34.

Cornick, David. *Letting God Be God: The Reformed Tradition.* Maryknoll, NY: Orbis, 2008.

Crosby, Fanny J. "Rescue the Perishing." Public domain, 1869. https://hymnary.org/text/rescue_the_perishing_care_for_the_dying.

Cummings, Charles. *Monastic Practices.* Kalamazoo, MI: Cistercian, 1986.

Curtis, Heather D. "Depicting Distant Suffering: Evangelicals and the Politics of Pictorial Humanitarianism in the Age of American Empire." *Material Religion: The Journal of Objects, Art and Belief* 8 (2012) 154–83.

———. *Faith in the Great Physician: Suffering and Divine Healing in American Culture, 1860–1900.* Baltimore: Johns Hopkins University Press, 2007.

———. "'God Is Not Affected by the Depression': Pentecostal Missions during the 1930s." *Church History* 80 (2011) 579–89.

———. *Holy Humanitarians: American Evangelicals and Global Aid.* Cambridge, MA: Harvard University Press, 2018.

Cyprian. "Morality." In *The Fathers of the Church,* edited by Roy J. Deferrari, translated by Mary Hannan Mahoney, 36, 195–221. Washington, DC: Catholic University of America Press, 1952.

Cyrus, Cynthia J. *The Scribes for Women's Convents in Late Medieval Germany.* Toronto: University of Toronto Press, 2009.

Dackson, Wendy. "Anglicanism and Social Theology." *Anglican Theological Review* 94 (2012) 615–37.

Daley, Brian. *The Hope of the Early Church: A Handbook of Patristic Eschatology.* Cambridge: Cambridge University Press, 1999.

Daley, Brian E. "Oration 14: On the Love of the Poor." In *Gregory of Nazianzus,* 75–97. London: Routledge, 2006.

Daniels, Marilyn. *Benedictine Roots in the Development of Deaf Education: Listening with the Heart.* Westport, CT: Bergin & Garvey, 1997.

Darrah, Mary C. *Sister Ignatia: Angel of Alcoholics Anonymous,* 2nd ed. Center City, MN: Hazelden Educational Services, 2001.

Daughters in My Kingdom: The History and Work of Relief Society. Salt Lake City: The Church of Jesus Christ of Latter-day Saints, 2017. https://www.churchofjesuschrist.org/study/manual/daughters-in-my-kingdom-the-history-and-work-of-relief-society/title-page?lang=eng.

Davidson, Ivor J. "Church Growth in the Early Church." In *Towards a Theology of Church Growth*, edited by David Goodhew, 145–68. Milton Park, UK: Routledge, 2016.

Davis, Adam J. "Preaching in Thirteenth-Century Hospitals." *Journal of Medieval History* 36 (2010) 72–89.

———. *The Medieval Economy of Salvation: Charity, Commerce, and the Rise of the Hospital*. Ithaca: Cornell University Press, 2019.

Davis, Allen F. *Spearheads for Reform: The Social Settlements and the Progressive Movement, 1890–1914*. New Brunswick: Rutgers University Press, 1994.

Davis, Mark H. Measuring Individual Differences in Empathy: Evidence for a Multidimensional Approach. *Journal of Personality and Social Psychology* 44 (1983) 113–26.

Day, Dorothy. *Peter Maurin: Apostle to the World*. Maryknoll, NY: Orbis, 2004.

———. "Why Write About Strife and Violence?" In *Dorothy Day Selected Writings: By Little and By Little*, edited by Robert Ellsberg, 62–63. Maryknoll, NY: Orbis, 1992.

Day, Richard Ellsworth. *A Christian in Big Business: The Biography of Henry Parsons Crowell, the Breakfast Table Autocrat*. Chicago: Moody Bible Institute, 1946.

Decker, Corrie, and Elisabeth McMahon. *The Idea of Development in Africa: A History*. Cambridge: Cambridge University Press, 2020.

Decker, John R. "Civic Charity, Civic Virtue: The Master of Alkmaar's 'Seven Works of Mercy.'" *The Sixteenth Century Journal* 41 (2010) 3–28.

Delaney, Paul. "Purgatory, Alms-Giving, and the Needs of the Dead." *Interdisciplinary Journal of Research on Religion* 16 (2020) 1–24.

Delbrêl, Madeleine. *We, the Ordinary People of the Streets*. Translated by David Louis Schindler Jr. and Charles F. Mann. Grand Rapids: Eerdmans, 2000.

Demacopoulos, George E. *Gregory the Great: Ascetic, Pastor, and First Man of Rome*. South Bend, IN: University of Notre Dame Press, 2015.

Demoustier, Adrien. "The First Companions and the Poor." *Studies in the Spirituality of Jesuits* 21 (1989) 4–20.

Dennis, James S. *Christian Missions and Social Progress: A Sociological Study of Foreign Missions*. Vol. 2. New York: Fleming H. Revell, 1899.

Deressa, Samuel Yonas, and Sarah Hinlicky Wilson, eds., *The Life, Works, and Witness of Tsehay Tolessa and Gudina Tumsa, the Ethiopian Bonhoeffer*. Minneapolis: Fortress, 2017.

deSilva, David A. *Honor, Patronage, Kinship and Purity: Unlocking New Testament Culture*. Downers Grove, IL: InterVarsity, 2000.

Devine, Edward Thomas. *The Practice of Charity: Individual, Associated, and Organized*. New York: Lentilhon, 1907.

Dey, Hendrik W. "Diaconiae, Xenodochia, Hospitalia and Monasteries: 'Social Security' and the Meaning of Monasticism in Early Medieval Rome." *Early Medieval Europe* 16 (2008) 398–422.

Dictionary of African Christian Biography. https://dacb.org.

Disch, Lisa Jane. *Hannah Arendt and the Limits of Philosophy*. Ithaca: Cornell University Press, 1994.

Doleac, Miles. "Triclinium Pauperum: Poverty, Charity and the Papacy in the Time of Gregory the Great." Ph.D., Tulane University, 2013.

Donahue, John R. "Companions on a Journey: The Bible and Catholic Social Teaching." In *Scripture and Social Justice: Catholic and Ecumenical Essays*, edited by Anathea

E. Portier-Young and Gregory E. Sterling, 1–22. Lanham, MD: Lexington/Fortress Academic, 2018.

Dorrien, Gary. *Breaking White Supremacy: Martin Luther King Jr. and the Black Social Gospel*. New Haven: Yale University Press, 2019.

———. *Soul in Society: The Making and Renewal of Social Christianity*. Minneapolis: Fortress, 1999.

———. *The New Abolition: W. E. B. Du Bois and the Black Social Gospel*. New Haven: Yale University Press, 2015.

Douglass, Frederick. *Narrative of the Life of Frederick Douglass*. New York: Chartwell Books, 2015.

Downs, David J. *Alms: Charity, Reward, and Atonement and Early Christianity*. Waco: Baylor University Press, 2016.

Doyno, Mary Harvey. *The Lay Saint: Charity and Charismatic Authority in Medieval Italy, 1150–1350*. Ithaca: Cornell University Press, 2019.

"Dreaming of Timbuctoo." Exhibit at the John Brown Farm State Historic Site, North Elba, NY, 2019.

Drummond, Henry. *The Lowell Lectures on the Ascent of Man*. 12th ed. New York: James Pott, 1902.

Dubay, Thomas. *Happy Are You Poor: The Simple Life and Spiritual Freedom*. San Francisco: Ignatius, 1981.

Dunn, Geoffrey D. "Why Care for the Poor? The Role of Almsgiving in Jerome's Asceticism." *Zeitschrift Für Antikes Christentum / Journal of Ancient Christianity* 18 (2014) 283–301.

Eckhart, Meister. *Meister Eckhart: Sermons and Treatises*, vol. 2. Translated by Maurice O'Connell Walshe. Shaftesbury: Element, 1987.

Ehrman, Bart D. *The Apostolic Fathers. Epistle of Barnabas, Papias and Quadratus, Epistle to Diognetus, The Shepherd of Hermas*. Cambridge, MA: Harvard University Press, 2003.

Eire, Carlos M. N. *Reformations: The Early Modern World, 1450–1650*. New Haven: Yale University Press.

Eklund, Rebekah. "Blessed Are the Image-Bearers: Gregory of Nyssa and the Beatitudes." *Anglican Theological Review* 99 (2017) 729–40.

Elliott, Neil. "Political Theology and the New Testament." In *T & T Clark Handbook of Political Theology*, edited by Rubén Rosario Rodríguez, 61–74. London: T & T Clark, 2020.

Elson, Peter R. "A Short History of Voluntary Sector-Government Relations in Canada." *The Philanthropist* 21 (2009) 36–74.

Ely, Richard T. *Social Aspects of Christianity: And Other Essays*. New and Enlarged. New York: Thomas Y. Crowell, 1889.

Endres, David J. "American Crusade: Catholic Youth in the World Mission Movement from World War I through Vatican II," 1–2. Eugene, OR: Pickwick, 2010.

Evangelical Lutheran Church in America, *Social Statements* and *Social Messages*. https://elca.org/Faith/Faith-and-Society.

Evans, Christopher H. "History and Theology in the American Methodist Social Gospel: The Public/Private Split Revisited." *Wesleyan Theological Journal* 35 (2000) 159–79.

281

Evans Grubbs, Judith. "Infant Exposure and Infanticide." In *The Oxford Handbook of Childhood and Education in the Classical World*. New York: Oxford University Press, 2013.

Farmer, Sharon A. *Surviving Poverty in Medieval Paris: Gender, Ideology, and the Daily Lives of the Poor*. Ithaca: Cornell University Press, 2005.

Fehler, Timothy G. *Poor Relief and Protestantism: The Evolution of Social Welfare in Sixteenth-Century Emden*. Abingdon, UK: Ashgate, 1999.

Ferguson, Everett. *Early Christians Speak: Faith and Life in the First Three Centuries*. 3rd. ed. Abilene, TX: Abilene Christian University Press, 1999.

————. *The Early Church at Work and Worship*. Vol. 2. Eugene, OR: Cascade, 2014.

Ferngren, Gary B. *Medicine and Health Care in Early Christianity*. Baltimore: Johns Hopkins University Press, 2009.

Festing, Heinrich. *Adolph Kolping und sein Werk: Ein Überblick über Leben und Wirken des großen Sozialreformers sowie über die Entwicklung seines Werkes bis heute*. Freiburg: Herder, 1983.

Fikkert, Brian, and Kelly M. Kapic. *Becoming Whole: Why the Opposite of Poverty isn't the American Dream*. Chicago: Moody, 2019.

Finke, Roger, and Rodney Stark. "Turning Pews into People: Estimating 19th Century Church Membership." *Journal for the Scientific Study of Religion* 25 (1986) 180–92.

Firey, Abigail. "'For I Was Hungry and You Fed Me': Social Justice and Economic Thought in the Latin Patristic and Medieval Christian Traditions." In *Ancient and Medieval Economic Ideas and Concepts of Social Justice*. Leiden: Brill, 1998.

Fitzgerald, Maureen. *Habits of Compassion: Irish Catholic Nuns and the Origins of New York's Welfare System, 1830–1920*. Urbana: University of Illinois Press, 2006.

Fitzpatrick-Behrens, Susan. "The Catholic Roots of U.S. Foreign Assistance: From Good Neighbors to Allies for Progress." *U.S. Catholic Historian* 37 (2019) 123–45.

Fletcher, Richard. *The Barbarian Conversion: From Paganism to Christianity*. New York: Henry Holt, 1997.

Florovsky, Georges. *The Eastern Fathers of the Fourth Century*. Translated by Catherine Edmunds. Vol. 7. Vaduz, Liechtenstein: Büchervertriebsanstalt, 1987.

"Focus: HOPE." Accessed November 5, 2019. https://www.focushope.edu/.

Francis I. *Apostolic Exhortation Evangelii Gaudium*. Vatican, 2013. http://www.vatican.va/content/francesco/en/apost_exhortations/documents/papa-francesco_esortazione-ap_20131124_evangelii-gaudium.html.

Francis. *Misericordiae Vultus: Bull of Indiction of the Extraordinary Jubilee of Mercy*. Rome: Libreria Editrice Vaticana.

Fraser, Derek. *The Evolution of the British Welfare State*. 4th ed. Houndmills, UK: Palgrave Macmillan, 2009.

Freire, Paulo. *Pedagogy of the Oppressed*. Translated by Myra Bergman Ramos. New York: Herder and Herder, 1970.

French, Katherine L. *The Good Women of the Parish: Gender and Religion After the Black Death*. Philadelphia: University of Pennsylvania Press, 2008.

Fretz, J. Winfield. "Mutual Aid among Mennonites I: Mennonite Principles as a Preface to the Subject of Mutual Aid." *Mennonite Quarterly Review* 13 (1939) 28–58.

————. "Mutual Aid among Mennonites II: Mutual Aid Activities in a Single Mennonite Community." *Mennonite Quarterly Review* 13 (1939) 187–209.

Frey, Sylvia R., and Betty Wood. *Come Shouting to Zion: African American Protestantism in the American South and British Caribbean to 1830*. Chapel Hill: University of North Carolina Press, 1998.

Friesen, Stephen J. "Injustice or God's Will? Early Christian Explanations of Poverty." In *Wealth and Poverty in Early Church and Society*, 17–36. Grand Rapids: Baker Academic / Holy Cross Orthodox, 2008.

Fritschel, Herman L. *One Hundred Years of Deaconess Service, 1849–1949*. Milwaukee: Lutheran Deaconess Motherhouse, 1949.

Fuechtmann, Thomas G. "'There Is Great Charity, But . . .': Vincent de Paul and the Organization of Charity." *Vincentian Heritage Journal* 26 (2005) 43–63.

Gallagher, John, and Jeanne Buckeye. *Structures of Grace: The Business Practices of the Economy of Communion*. Hyde Park, NY: New City, 2014.

Galler, Jayson S. "A Sham, Pretense, and Hypocrisy? Poverty in The Book of Concord of 1580." In *Poverty and Prosperity: In the Middle Ages and Renaissance*, edited by Cynthia Kosso and Anne Scott, 55–74. Turnhout, Belgium: Brepols, 2012.

Galli, Mark. *Francis of Assisi and His World*. Downers Grove, IL: InterVarsity, 2002.

García, Mario T. *Father Luis Olivares, a Biography: Faith Politics and the Origins of the Sanctuary Movement in Los Angeles*. Chapel Hill: University of North Carolina Press, 2018.

Gardner, Gregg E. "Care for the Poor and the Origins of Charity in Early Rabbinic Literature." In *Wealth and Poverty in Jewish Tradition*, edited by Leonard J. Greenspoon, 13–32. West Lafayette: Purdue University Press, 2015.

———. *The Origins of Organized Charity in Rabbinic Judaism*. New York: Cambridge University Press, 2015.

Gariepy, Henry. *Christianity in Action: The International History of the Salvation Army*. Grand Rapids: Eerdmans, 2009.

Gautier, Mary L., and Paul Perl. *Partnerships of Solidarity with the Church in Latin America and the Caribbean*. Washington, DC: Center for Applied Research in the Apostolate, 2003.

Gavrilyuk, Paul L. "An Overview of Patristic Theodicies." In *Suffering and Evil in Early Christian Thought*. Edited by Nonna Verna Harrison and David G. Hunter. Grand Rapids: Baker Academic, 2016.

Gaydosh, Brenda L. *Bernhard Lichtenberg: Roman Catholic Priest and Martyr of the Nazi Regime*. Lanham, MD: Lexington, 2017.

Gecser, Ottó. "Doctors and Preachers against the Plague: Attitudes toward Disease in Late Medieval Plague Tracts and Plague Sermons." In *The Sacred and the Secular in Medieval Healing: Sites, Objects, and Texts*, edited by Barbara S. Bowers and Linda Migl Keyser, 78–102. London: Routledge, 2016.

———. "Giovanni of Capestrano on the Plague and the Doctors." *Franciscan Studies* 75 (2017) 27–47.

Geernaert, Donna. "Church as Koinonia/Church as Sacrament." In *One, Holy, Catholic and Apostolic: Ecumenical Perspectives on the 1991 Canberra Statement on Unity, Faith and Order Paper No. 163*, edited by Tamara Grdzelidze, 62–77. Geneva: WCC, 1993.

Gentilini, Maurizio. *Chiara Lubich: Prophet of Unity*. Hyde Park, NY: New City, 2020.

Gilkes, Cheryl Townsend. "'Until My Change Comes': In the African-American Baptist Tradition." In *Faith and Social Ministry: Ten Christian Perspectives*, edited by James D. Davidson et al., 179–204. Chicago: Loyola University Press, 1990.

Gilleard, Chris. "Old Age in Byzantine Society." *Ageing & Society* 27 (2007) 623–42.

Gingrich, Luann Good, and Ernie Lightman. "Striving Toward Self-Sufficiency: A Qualitative Study of Mutual Aid in an Old Order Mennonite Community." *Family Relations* 55 (2006) 175–89.

Glanzer, Perry L., "Growing on the Margins: Global Christian Higher Education," *International Higher Education*, no. 88 (2017) 23–25.

Goetz, Jennifer L., et al. "Compassion: An Evolutionary Analysis and Empirical Review." *Psychological Bulletin* 136 (2010) 351–74.

Gold, Lorna. *New Financial Horizons: The Emergence of an Economy of Communion.* Hyde Park, NY: New City, 2010.

Gonzalez, Michael J. "Flights of Fancy: Using the Historical Imagination to Understand the Franciscan Missionaries of California." *Franciscan Studies* 77 (2019) 231–44.

Good, E. Reginald. "Changing Patterns of Mutual Aid in Ontario, 1864–1994." In *Building Communities of Compassion: Mennonite Mutual Aid in Theory and Practice*, edited by Willard M. Swartley and Donald B. Kraybill, 171–91. Scottdale, PA: Herald, 1998.

Goodrich, Frances Louisa. *Mountain Homespun.* Knoxville: University of Tennessee Press, 2010.

Goodwin, Bonni, et al. "Reframing the Orphan Mandate." *Social Work & Christianity* 47(3) (2020) 33–49.

Gordon, Wayne, and John M. Perkins. *Making Neighborhoods Whole: A Handbook for Christian Community Development.* Downers Grove, IL: InterVarsity, 2013.

Gorman, Michael J. *Becoming the Gospel: Paul, Participation, and Mission.* Grand Rapids: Eerdmans, 2015.

———. *Inhabiting the Cruciform God: Kenosis, Justification, and Theosis in Paul's Narrative Soteriology.* Grand Rapids: Eerdmans, 2009.

Gort, Gea, and Mats Tunehag. *BAM Global Movement: Business as Mission, Concepts and Stories.* Peabody, MA: Hendrickson, 2018.

Goulding, Gill. "Celebrating Grace in and through the Sacrament of Their Own Lives—Listening to the Urban Marginalised." *New Blackfriars* 77, no. 900 (1996) 10–20.

Graham, Franklin, and Jeanette W. Lockerbie. *Bob Pierce: This One Thing I Do.* Waco, TX: Word, 1983

Greenfield, Craig. *The Urban Halo.* Milton Keynes, UK: Authentic, 2007.

Gregory the Great. *Moralia in Iob: The Books of the Morals of St. Gregory the Pope, or an Exposition on the Book of Blessed Job.* Vol. 2, Book 20. Lectionary Central, n.d. http://www.lectionarycentral.com/GregoryMoralia/Book20.html.

Gregory of Nazianzus. "On the Love of the Poor." In *Patrologia Graeca.* Edited by Jacques-Paul Migne, Vol. 35. Paris: J.-P. Migne, 1857.

Grieco, Holly J. "Pastoral Care, Inquisition, and Mendicancy in the Medieval Franciscan Order." In *The Origin, Development, and Refinement of Medieval Religious Mendicancies*, edited by Donald Prudlo, 117–55. Leiden: Brill, 2011.

Griffith, Aaron. *God's Law and Order: The Politics of Punishment in Evangelical America.* Cambridge, MA: Harvard University Press, 2020.

Griffiths, Fiona J. "The Cross and the Cura Monialium: Robert of Arbrissel, John the Evangelist, and the Pastoral Care of Women in the Age of Reform." *Speculum* 83 (2008) 303–30.

Grob, Gerald N. *The Mad Among Us: A History of the Care of America's Mentally Ill.* New York: Free Press, 1994.

Groppi, Tania. "L'Arche as an Experience of Encounter." In *The Practice of Human Development and Dignity*, edited by Paolo G. Carozza and Clements Sedmak, 285–302. Notre Dame: University of Notre Dame Press, 2020.

Grubbs, Larry. *Secular Missionaries: Americans and African Development in the 1960s.* Amherst: University of Massachusetts Press, 2009.

Gruber, Jonathan, and Daniel M. Hungerman. "Faith-Based Charity and Crowd-Out during the Great Depression." *Journal of Public Economics* 91 (2007) 1043–69.

Grundmann, Christoffer H. "Christ as Physician: The Ancient Christus Medicus Trope and Christian Medical Missions as Imitation of Christ." *Christian Journal for Global Health* 5(3) (2018) 3–11.

———. *Sent to Heal! Emergence and Development of Medical Missions.* Bangalore: Centre for Contemporary Christianity, 2014.

Grundmann, Herbert. *Religious Movements in the Middle Ages.* Translated by Steven Rowan. Notre Dame: University of Notre Dame Press, 1995.

Guarneri, Carl J. *The Utopian Alternative: Fourierism in Nineteenth-Century America.* Ithaca: Cornell University Press, 1991.

Gunz, Edward J. "A Delicate Dance: Identity Issues in a Religious Nonprofit Umbrella Organization." *Families in Society: The Journal of Contemporary Social Sciences* 89 (2008) 274–81.

Halemba, Agnieszka. "Suffering for and Against the Church. The Politics of Memory and Repression in the Mukachevo Greek Catholic Eparchy." *Religion, State & Society* 46 (2018) 123–38.

Hands, Arthur R. *Charities and Social Aid in Greece and Rome.* Ithaca: Cornell University Press, 1968.

Hare, John E. *The Moral Gap: Kantian Ethics, Human Limits, and God's Assistance.* Oxford: Oxford University Press, 1996.

Harries, Jim. *Vulnerable Mission: Insights into Christian Mission to Africa from a Position of Vulnerability.* Pasadena, CA: William Carey, 2011.

Hartnell, Jack. *Medieval Bodies: Life, Death and Art in the Middle Ages.* London: Profile, 2019.

Hartney, Aideen M. *John Chrysostom and the Transformation of the City.* Bristol, UK: Bristol Classical, 2004.

Hatlie, Peter. *The Monks and Monasteries of Constantinople, ca. 350–850.* Cambridge: Cambridge University Press, 2008.

Hauff, Adelheid M von. *Frauen Gestalten Diakonie.* Stuttgart: Kohlhammer, 2006.

Haukland, Linda. "Hans Nielsen Hauge: A Catalyst of Literacy in Norway." *Scandinavian Journal of History* 39 (2014) 539–59.

Hays, Christopher M. "Resumptions of Radicalism. Christian Wealth Ethics in the Second and Third Centuries." *Zeitschrift Für Die Neutestamentliche Wissenschaft Und Kunde Der Älteren Kirche* 102 (2011) 261–82.

———. "Slaughtering Stewards and Incarcerating Debtors: Coercing Charity in Luke 12:35–13:9." *Neotestamentica* 46 (2012) 41–60.

Hedda, Jennifer. *His Kingdom Come: Orthodox Pastorship and Social Activism in Revolutionary Russia.* Dekalb: Northern Illinois University Press, 2008.

Hefferan, Tara. *Twinning Faith and Development: Catholic Parish Partnering in the US and Haiti.* Bloomfield, CT: Kumarian, 2007.

Heidebrecht, Paul Henry. *Faith and Economic Practice: Protestant Businessmen in Chicago, 1900–1920.* New York: Garland, 1989.

Heine, Ronald E. "Articulating Identity." In *Cambridge History of Early Christian Literature*, edited by Francis Young et al., 200–31. Cambridge: Cambridge University Press, 2004.

Henry, Carl F. H. *The Uneasy Conscience of Modern Fundamentalism*. Grand Rapids: Eerdmans, 1947.

Heyne, Thomas. "Reconstructing the World's First Hospital: The Basiliad." *Hektoen International: A Journal of Medical Humanities*, Spring (2015).

Hill, Joe. "The Preacher and the Slave." In *Songs of the Workers: On the Road, in the Jungles and in the Shops*, 9th ed. Cleveland: I.W.W., 1916.

Hill, Kimberly D. *A Higher Mission: The Careers of Alonzo and Althea Brown Edmiston in Central Africa*. University Press of Kentucky, 2020.

Himmelfarb, Gertrude. *Poverty and Compassion: The Moral Imagination of the Late Victorians*. New York: Knopf, 1991.

Hinckley, Gordon B. "The Perpetual Education Fund." *Ensign*, May 2001.

Hise, Greg, and William Deverell. *Eden by Design: The 1930 Olmsted-Bartholomew Plan for the Los Angeles Region*. Berkeley: University of California Press, 2000.

Hoff Boersma, Francisco Van der. *Manifesto of the Poor*. East Meon, UK: Permanent, 2010.

Hoffmann, Bedrich. *And Who Will Kill You: The Chronicle of the Life and Sufferings of Priests in the Concentration Camps*. Translated by John L. Morkovsky. 4th ed. Poznan, Poland: Pallottinum, 1994.

Holman, Susan R. *The Hungry Are Dying: Beggars and Bishops in Roman Cappadocia*. New York: Oxford University Press, 2001.

Holmes, Augustine. *A Life Pleasing to God: The Spirituality of the Rules of St Basil*. 189. London: Darton, Longman & Todd, 2000.

"Homeboy Industries." Accessed November 5, 2019. https://homeboyindustries.org/.

Hood, Robert E. *Social Teachings in the Episcopal Church: A Source Book*. Ridgefield, CT: Morehouse, 1990.

Hookway, Esther, and Christopher Francis. *From Inter-Church Aid to Jubilee: A Brief History of Ecumenical Diakonia in the World Council of Churches*. Geneva: World Council of Churches, 2002.

Hoose, Adam L. "Orthopraxy and the Formation of the Early Waldensians and Franciscans, 1173–228." Ph.D., Saint Louis University, 2011.

Hopkins, Charles Howard. *The Rise of the Social Gospel in American Protestantism 1865–1915*. New Haven: Yale University Press, 1940.

Hopkins, Keith. "Christian Number and Its Implications." *Journal of Early Christian Studies* 6, no. 2 (1998) 185–226.

Hungerman, Daniel M. "Are Church and State Substitutes? Evidence from the 1996 Welfare Reform." *Journal of Public Economics* 89 (2005) 2245–67.

Huntsman, R. G., et al. "Twixt Candle and Lamp: The Contribution of Elizabeth Fry and the Institution of Nursing Sisters to Nursing Reform." *Medical History* 46 (2002) 351–80.

Hussain, Jamie. "Participating in Godliness: A Study of the Laws Concerning the Socially Marginalized in the Torah." *McMaster Journal of Theology and Ministry* 10 (2008) 101–39.

Husselbee, Lesley, and Paul Ballard. *Free Churches and Society: The Nonconformist Contribution to Social Welfare 1800–2010*. Bloomsbury, 2012.

Hutcherson, Caleb. "An Antidote to Christian Nationalism" Arab Baptist Theological Seminary. January 7, 2021. https://abtslebanon.org/2021/01/07/an-antidote-to-christian-nationalism-2/.

Iglehart, Charles E. *A Century of Protestant Christianity in Japan.* Rutland, VT: Tuttle, 1959.

Ignatius. *The Spiritual Exercises of St. Ignatius: Based on Studies in the Language of the Autograph.* Translated by Louis J Puhl. Chicago: Loyola University Press, 1951.

Immerwar, Daniel. *Thinking Small: The United States and the Lure of Community Development.* Cambridge, MA: Harvard University Press, 2015.

International Mission Board, Southern Baptist Convention. "Meeting Human Needs," n.d. https://www.imb.org/meeting-human-needs/.

Ireland, Jerry M. "A Missionary Theology of Compassion." In *For the Love of God: Principles and Practice of Compassion in Missions,* edited by Jerry M. Ireland, 19–41. Eugene, OR: Wipf & Stock, 2017.

Jarić, Snežana, et al. "Phytotherapy in Medieval Serbian Medicine According to the Pharmacological Manuscripts of the Chilandar Medical Codex (15–16th Centuries)." *Journal of Ethnopharmacology* 137 (2011) 601–19.

Jennings, Theodore W., Jr. *Good News to the Poor: John Wesley's Evangelical Economics.* Nashville: Abingdon, 1990.

Johnson, F. Ernest, ed. *The Social Work of the Churches: A Handbook of Information.* New York: Department of Research and Education of the Federal Council of the Churches of Christ in America, 1930.

Johnson, Todd M., and Sun Young Chung. "Tracking Global Christianity's Statistical Centre of Gravity, AD 33–AD 2100," *International Review of Mission* 93, no. 369 (2004) 166–81.

Johnson, Todd M., and Gina A. Zurlo, eds., *World Christian Database.* Leiden: Brill, 2020.

Johnston, Ronald, and Elaine McFarland. "'Out in the Open in a Threatening World': The Scottish Churches' Industrial Mission 1960–1980." *International Review of Social History* 55 (2010) 1–27.

Jones, Colin. "Perspectives on Poor Relief, Health Care and the Counter-Reformation in France." In *Health Care and Poor Relief in Counter-Reformation Europe,* edited by Ole Peter Grell et al., 201–14. London: Routledge, 1999.

Jones, Peter Murray. "Amulets and Charms." In *Medieval Christianity in Practice,* edited by Miri Rubin, 194–9. Princeton: Princeton University Press, 2009.

Jones, Robert P. *White Too Long: The Legacy of White Supremacy in American Christianity.* New York: Simon & Schuster, 2020.

Jongman, Willem M. "The Early Roman Empire: Consumption." In *The Cambridge Economic History of the Greco-Roman World,* edited by Walter Scheidel et al., 592–618. Cambridge: Cambridge University Press, 2007.

Julia, Norlan H. "Beyond Basic Ecclesial Communities (BECs): Challenges to the Reception of Communio Ecclesiology in Asia." *Landas* 26, 1 (2012) 127–38.

Julian of Norwich. *Revelations of Divine Love.* Grand Rapids: Christian Classics Ethereal Library, 2002.

Kaell, Hillary. *Christian Globalism at Home: Child Sponsorship in the United States.* Princeton: Princeton University Press, 2020.

Kallman, Theodore. *The Kingdom of God is at Hand: The Christian Commonwealth in Georgia, 1896–1901.* Athens: University of Georgia Press, 2021.

Karayannopoulos, Ioannes. "St. Basil's Social Activity: Principles and Praxis." In *Basil of Caesarea: Christian, Humanist, Ascetic: A Sixteen-Hundredth Anniversary Symposium, Part I*, edited by Paul Jonathan Fedwick, 375–91. Toronto: Pontifical Institute of Medieval Studies, 1981.

Keenan, James F. "Radicalizing the Comprehensiveness of Mercy: Christian Identity in Theological Ethics." In *Hope and Solidarity: Jon Sobrino's Challenge to Christian Theology*, edited by Stephen J. Pope, 187–200. Maryknoll, NY: Orbis, 2008.

Kempis, Thomas à. *The Imitation of Christ*. Translated by Leo Sherley-Price. New York: Penguin, 1952.

Kenworthy, Scott M. "Orthodoxy and the Social Gospel in Late-Imperial Russia." *Religion and Society in Central and Eastern Europe* 1 (2005) 1–29.

Kidd, Thomas S. *Who Is an Evangelical? The History of a Movement in Crisis*. New Haven: Yale University Press, 2019.

Kim, Daniel. "Explaining Early Christian Charity: A Psychosocial Theories Approach." *Interdisciplinary Journal of Research on Religion* 6 (2010) 1–21.

Kim, Sung Hae. "The Virtue of Holy Indifference: The Fruit of Saint Vincent de Paul's Spiritual Journey." *Vincentian Heritage Journal* 34 (2018) Iss. 2, Art. 3.

Kim, Sung-Ju, and Kou, Xiaonan. "Not All Empathy Is Equal: How Dispositional Empathy Affects Charitable Giving." *Journal of Nonprofit and Public Sector Marketing* 26 (2014) 312–34.

King, David P. *God's Internationalists: World Vision and the Age of Evangelical Humanitarianism*. Philadelphia: University of Pennsylvania Press, 2019.

King, John N. *Foxe's Book of Martyrs and Early Modern Print Culture*. Cambridge: Cambridge University Press, 2006.

King, Martin Luther, Jr. "Beyond Vietnam." Riverside Church, New York, April 4, 1967.

Kirk, David. *Quotations from Chairman Jesus*. Springfield, IL: Templegate, 1969.

Kirk, Nicole C. *Wanamaker's Temple: The Business of Religion in an Iconic Department Store*. New York: New York University Press, 2018.

Kirk-Duggan, Cheryl. "Womanist Theology as a Corrective to African American Theology." In *The Oxford Handbook of African American Theology*, 267–79. Edited by Anthony B. Pinn and Katie G. Cannon. Oxford: Oxford University Press, 2014.

Kitamori, Kazoh. *Theology of the Pain of God*. Richmond, VA: John Knox, 1965.

Klassen. *The Economics of Anabaptism*. The Hague Mouton, 1964.

Kleer, Richard A. "Final Causes in Adam Smith's Theory of Moral Sentiments." *Journal of the History of Philosophy* 33 (1995) 275–300.

Kleinschmidt, Harald. *People on the Move: Attitudes Toward and Perceptions of Migration in Medieval and Modern Europe*. Westport, CT: Praeger, 2003.

Klingshirn, William E. *Caesarius of Arles: The Making of a Christian Community in Late Antique Gaul*. Cambridge: Cambridge University Press, 2004.

K'Meyer, Tracy Elaine. *Interracialism and Christian Community in the Postwar South: The Story of Koinonia Farm*. Charlottesville: University of Virginia Press, 1997.

Koskenniemi, Erkki. *The Exposure of Infants Among Jews and Christians in Antiquity*. Sheffield, UK: Sheffield Phoenix, 2009.

Kraybill, Donald B. *The Upside-Down Kingdom*. 5th ed. Harisonburg, VA: Herald, 2011.

Kreider, Alan. *The Patient Ferment of the Early Church: The Improbable Rise of Christianity in the Roman Empire*. Grand Rapids: Baker Academic, 2016.

Kreider, J. Kenneth. *Cup of Cold Water: The Story of Brethren Service*. Elgin, IL: Brethren, 2001.

Kuenning, Paul P. *The Rise and Fall of American Lutheran Pietism: The Rejection of an Activist Heritage*. Macon, GA: Mercer University Press, 1988.

Kurtz, Ernest. *Not-God: A History of Alcoholics Anonymous*. Center City, MN: Hazelden Educational Services, 1979.

Laiou, Angeliki E. "Political History: An Outline," 9–28. Washington, DC: Dumbarton Oaks, 2002.

———. "The Human Resources," 47–55. Washington, DC: Dumbarton Oaks, 2002.

Lam, et al. "Empathy Training: Methods, Evaluation: Practices, and Validity." *Journal of MultiDisciplinary Evaluation* 7 (2011) 162–200.

Lambert, M. D. *Franciscan Poverty: The Doctrine of the Absolute Poverty of Christ and the Apostles in the Franciscan Order 1210-1323*. London: SPCK, 1961.

Lamberty, Kim. "The Art of Accompaniment." *Missiology: An International Review* 43 (2015) 324–38.

Lampe, Peter. *From Paul to Valentinus: Christians at Rome in the First Two Centuries*. Minneapolis: Fortress, 2003.

Lardos, Andreas, and Michael Heinrich. "Continuity and Change in Medicinal Plant Use: The Example of Monasteries on Cyprus and Historical Iatrosophia Texts." *Journal of Ethnopharmacology* 150 (2013) 202–14.

Lascaratos, J., et al. "Nursing Homes for the Old ('*Gerocomeia*') in Byzantium (324–1453 AD)." *Gerontology* 50 (2004) 113–7.

Lausanne Movement. "The Lausanne Covenant," n.d. http://www.lausanne.org/content/covenant/lausanne-covenant.

Lawrence, Louise J. *Sense and Stigma in the Gospels: Depictions of Sensory-Disabled Characters*. New York: Oxford University Press, 2013.

Lee, Alan Douglas. *Pagans and Christians in Late Antiquity: A Sourcebook*. Milton, UK: Routledge, 2015.

Lee, Hak Joon. *We Will Get to the Promised Land: Martin Luther King, Jr's. Communal-Political Spirituality*. Cleveland: Pilgrim, 2006.

Leemans, John, et al, eds. *Reading Patristic Texts on Social Ethics: Issues and Challenges for Twenty-First-Century Christian Social Thought*. Washington, DC: Catholic University of America Press, 2011.

Lev, Efraim, and Leigh Chipman. *Medical Prescriptions in the Cambridge Genizah Collections: Practical Medicine and Pharmacology in Medieval Egypt*. Cambridge Genizah Studies. Leiden: Brill, 2012.

Levin, Peter J. "Bold Vision: Catholic Sisters and the Creation of American Hospitals." *Journal of Community Health* 36 (2011) 343–7.

Liebeschuetz, J. H. W. G. *Ambrose and John Chrysostom: Clerics between Desert and Empire*. Oxford: Oxford University Press, 2011.

Lim, Kar Yong. "Generosity from Pauline Perspective: Insights from Paul's Letters to the Corinthians." *Evangelical Review of Theology* 37 (2013) 20–33.

Lindberg, Carter. "No Greater Service to God than Christian Love." In *Social Ministry in the Lutheran Tradition*, edited by Foster R. McCurley, 50–68. Minneapolis: Fortress, 2008.

Lipscomb, David. "The Cholera and the Christian Religion." *Gospel Advocate* 15 (July 17, 1873) 649–53.

Longenecker, Bruce W. *Remember the Poor: Paul, Poverty, and the Greco-Roman World*. Grand Rapids: Eerdmans, 2010.

López, Ariel G. "Shenoute of Atripe and the Uses of Poverty: Rural Patronage, Religious Conflict, and Monasticism in Late Antique Egypt." Berkeley: University of California Press, 2013.

Loughery, John, and Blythe Randolph. *Dorothy Day: Dissenting Voice of the American Century*. New York: Simon & Schuster, 2020.

Louth, Andrew. "The Cappadocians." In *Cambridge History of Early Christian Literature*, edited by Francis Young et al., 289–301. Cambridge: Cambridge University Press, 2004.

Lovejoy, Arthur O. "The Communism of Saint Ambrose." *Journal of the History of Ideas* 3 (1942) 458–68.

Lubienecki, Paul. "Catholic Labor Education and the Association of Catholic Trade Unionists: Instructing Workers to Christianize the Workplace." *Journal of Catholic Education* 18 (2015) 99–124.

Lucas, James W., and Warner P. Woodworth. *Working toward Zion: Principles of the United Order for the Modern World*. Salt Lake City: Aspen, 1996.

Lueking, F. Dean. *A Century of Caring: The Welfare Ministry among Missouri Synod Lutherans, 1868–1968*. St. Louis: Board of Social Ministry of the Lutheran Church-Missouri Synod, 1968.

Lupton, Robert D. *Toxic Charity: How Churches and Charities Hurt Those They Help (And How to Reverse It)*. New York: HarperCollins, 2011.

Luther, Martin. "A Treatise on Good Works, Together with the Letter of Dedication, 1520." In *Works of Martin Luther*. Edited by Henry Eyster Jacobs. Translated by W.A. Lambert, 1:173–231. Philadelphia: A. J. Holman, 1915.

Lybbert, Travis J., and Bruce Wydick. "Poverty, Aspirations, and the Economics of Hope." *Economic Development and Cultural Change*, 66 (2018) 709–53.

Lynn, Monty L. "Congregational Aid: North American Protestant Engagement in International Relief and Development." *Journal of Development Studies* 52 (2016) 965–85.

———, et al. *Development in Mission: A Guide for Transforming Global Poverty and Ourselves*. Abilene, TX: Abilene Christian University Press, 2021.

———, et al. "Harmonizing Work: Meaning and Meaning Making through Hymnody," Unpublished document, 2020.

Mackintosh, Phillip G., and Clyde R. Forsberg Jr. "'Co-Agent of the Millennium': City Planning and Christian Eschatology in the North American City, 1890–1920." *Annals of the Association of American Geographers* 103 (2013) 727–47.

MacMullen, Ramsay. "What Difference Did Christianity Make?" *Historia: Zeitschrift Für Alte Geschichte*, 35 (1986) 322–43.

Maddox, Randy L. "'Visit the Poor': John Wesley, the Poor, and the Sanctification of Believers." In *The Poor and the People Called Methodists, 1729–1999*, edited by Richard P. Heitzenrater, 59–81. Nashville: Kingswood.

Magdalino, Paul. "Medieval Constantinople: Built Environment and Urban Development," 529–37. Washington, DC: Dumbarton Oaks, 2002.

Malak, Henryk Maria. *Shavelings in Death Camps: A Polish Priest's Memoir of Imprisonment by the Nazis, 1939–1945*. Translated by Bozúenna J. Tucker and Thomas R. Tucker. Jefferson, NC: McFarland, 2012.

Mangum, Garth L., and Bruce D. Blumell. *The Mormons' War on Poverty: A History of LDS Welfare, 1830–1990*. Salt Lake City: University of Utah Press, 1993.

Maranz, David E. *African Friends and Money Matters: Observations from Africa*. Dallas: SIL International and International Museum of Cultures, 2001.

Marinis, Vasileios. *Death and the Afterlife in Byzantium: The Fate of the Soul in Theology, Liturgy, and Art*. New York: Cambridge University Press, 2017.

Markus, Robert A. "The Secular in Late Antiquity." In *Les Frontières Du Profane Dans L'Antiquité Tardive*, 1000–1009. Rome: École Française de Rome, 2010.

Marx, Paul. (1957). *Virgil Michel and the Liturgical Movement*. Collegeville, MN: Liturgical.

Massaro, Thomas. *Living Justice: Catholic Social Teaching in Action*. Lanham, MD: Rowman & Littlefield, 2012.

Matheny, Paul D. *Dogmatics and Ethics: The Theological Realism and Ethics of Barth's Church Dogmatics*. New York: Peter Lang, 1990.

Matthew the Poor, and Samuel Rubenson. *Sojourners: Monastic Letters and Spiritual Teachings from the Desert*. Translated by Monastery Monks from St Macarius. 1st revised. Cairo: St Macarius, 2019.

Matthiesen, Noomi, and Jacob Klitmøller. "Encountering the Stranger: Hannah Arendt and the Shortcomings of Empathy as a Moral Compass." *Theory and Psychology* 29 (2019) 182–99

Maxwell, Jaclyn L. *Christianization and Communication in Late Antiquity: John Chrysostom and His Congregation in Antioch*. Cambridge: Cambridge University Press, 2006.

Maxwell, Robbie. "'A Shooting Star of Conservatism': George S. Benson, the National Education Program and the 'Radical Right.'" *Journal of American Studies* 53 (2019) 372–400.

Mayer, Wendy. "John Chrysostom on Poverty." In *Preaching Poverty in Late Antiquity: Perceptions and Realities*, edited by Pauline Allen et al., 69–118. Leipzig: Evangelische Verlagsanstalt, 2009.

McCabe, Matthew P. "Building the Planning Consensus: The Plan of Chicago, Civic Boosterism, and Urban Reform in Chicago, 1893 to 1915." *American Journal of Economics and Sociology* 75 (2016) 116–48.

McClure, Jennifer M. "'Go and Do Likewise': Investigating Whether Involvement in Congregationally Sponsored Community Service Activities Predicts Prosocial Behavior." *Review of Religious Research* 59 (2017) 341–66.

———. "Introducing Jesus's Social Network: Support, Conflict, and Compassion." *Interdisciplinary Journal of Research on Religion* 12 (2016) 1–22.

McCormick, Michael. *Origins of the European Economy: Communications and Commerce AD 300–900*. Cambridge: Cambridge University Press, 2001.

McFarland, Elaine, and Ronnie Johnston. "Faith in the Factory: The Church of Scotland's Industrial Mission, 1942–58." *Historical Research* 83 (2010) 539–64.

McGerr, Michael. *A Fierce Discontent: The Rise and Fall of the Progressive Movement in America, 1870–1920*. New York: Oxford University Press, 2003.

McGlynn, Moyna. *Divine Judgement and Divine Benevolence in the Book of Wisdom*. Tübingen: Mohr Siebeck, 2001.

McGowen, Randall. "The Well-Ordered Prison, England, 1780–1865." In *The Oxford History of the Prison: The Practice of Punishment in Western Society*, edited by Norval Morris and David J. Rothman, 79–109. New York: Oxford University Press, 1995.

McGrath, Alister. "Theology, Eschatology and Church Growth." In *Towards a Theology of Church Growth*, edited by David Goodhew, 93–106. Abingdon, UK: Ashgate, 2015.

McGuinness, Margaret M. *Called to Serve: A History of Nuns in America*. New York: New York University Press, 2013.

McKay, Johnston. *The Kirk and the Kingdom: A Century of Tension in Scottish Social Theology, 1830–1929*. Edinburgh: Edinburgh University Press, 2012.

McKinley, Allan Scott. "The First Two Centuries of Saint Martin of Tours." *Early Medieval Europe* 14 (2006) 173–200.

McKnight, W. Shawn. *Understanding the Diaconate: Historical, Theological, and Sociological Foundations*. Washington, DC: Catholic University of America Press, 2018.

McNamer, Sarah. *Affective Meditation and the Invention of Medieval Compassion*. Philadelphia: University of Pennsylvania Press, 2010.

McNeil, Betty Ann. "Daughters of Charity: Courageous and Compassionate Civil War Nurses." *U.S. Catholic Historian* 31 (2013) 51–72.

Meier, Mischa. "The 'Justinianic Plague': The Economic Consequences of the Pandemic in the Eastern Roman Empire and its Cultural and Religious Effects." *Early Medieval Europe* 24 (2016) 267–92.

Mendes Drumond Braga, Isabel M. R. "Poor Relief in Counter-Reformation Portugal: The Case of the Misericórdias." In *Health Care and Poor Relief in Counter-Reformation Europe*, edited by Ole Peter Grell et al., translated by Christine Salazar, 201–14. London: Routledge, 1999.

Menning, Carol Bresnahan. *Charity and State in Late Renaissance Italy: The Monte Di Pieta of Florence*. Ithaca: Cornell University Press, 2019.

Mennonite Central Committee. "American Friends Service Committee in Gaza," n.d. http://civilianpublicservice.org/storycontinues/gaza.

———. "The Civilian Public Service Story," n.d. http://civilianpublicservice.org/.

Metz, Judith. "Sister Anthony O'Connell: Angel of the Orphan, the Sick, the Wounded, and the Outcast." *U.S. Catholic Historian* 35 (2017) 53–78.

Micah Network. "Micah Network Declaration on Integral Mission," September 27, 2001. http://www.micahnetwork.org/sites/default/files/doc/page/mn_integral_mission_declaration_en.pdf.

Michelson, Grant. "The Role of Workplace Chaplains in Industrial Relations: Evidence from Australia." *British Journal of Industrial Relations* 44 (2006) 677–96.

Miller, Timothy. *The Quest for Utopia in Twentieth-Century America*. Vol. 1. Syracuse: Syracuse University Press, 1998.

Mixson, James. "Observant Reform's Conceptual Frameworks between Principle and Practice." In *A Companion to Observant Reform in the Late Middle Ages and Beyond*, edited by James Mixson and Bert Roest, 60–84. Leiden: Brill, 2015.

Moberg, David O. *The Great Reversal: Evangelism and Social Concern*. Rev. Philadelphia: Lippincott, 1977.

———. *Wholistic Christianity: An Appeal for a Dynamic, Balanced Faith*. Elgin, IL: Brethren, 1985.

Molina, Fernando, and John K. Walton. "An Alternative Co-Operative Tradition: The Basque Co-Operatives of Mondragón." In *The Hidden Alternative: Co-Operative Values, Past, Present and Future*, edited by Anthony Webster et al., 226–50. Manchester: Manchester University Press, 2011.

Mollat, Michel. *The Poor in the Middle Ages: An Essay in Social History*. Translated by Arthur Goldhammer. New Haven: Yale University Press, 1986.

Montero, Roman A. *All Things in Common: The Economic Practices of the Early Christians*. Eugene, OR: Resource, 2017.

Montford, Angela. *Health, Sickness, Medicine and the Friars in the Thirteenth and Fourteenth Centuries*. Aldershot, UK: Routledge, 2004.

Morgan, Bonnie. *Ordinary Saints: Women, Work, and Faith in Newfoundland*. Montreal: McGill-Queen's University Press, 2019.

Morley, Neville. "The Poor in the City of Rome." In *Poverty in the Roman World*, edited by Margaret Atkins and Robin Osborne, 21–39. Cambridge: Cambridge University Press, 2006.

Morozzo della Rocca, Roberto. *Making Peace: The Role Played by the Community of Sant'Egidio in the International Arena*, 2nd ed. London: New City, 2013.

Morrisson, Cécile, and Jean-Pierre Sodini. "The Sixth-Century Economy." In *The Economic History of Byzantium*, edited by Angeliki E. Laiou, 171–220. Washington, DC: Dumbarton Oaks, 2002.

Moss, Candida R. *The Other Christs: Imitating Jesus in Ancient Christian Ideologies of Martyrdom*. New York: Oxford University Press, 2010.

Moulton, Phillips P. "John Woolman: Exemplar of Ethics." *Quaker History* 54 (1965) 81–93.

———, ed. *The Journal and Major Essays of John Woolman*. Richmond, IN: Friends United, 1989.

Mowbray, Donald. *Pain and Suffering in Medieval Theology: Academic Debates at the University of Paris in the Thirteenth Century*. Woodbridge, UK: Boydell, 2009.

Murdoch, Iris. *The Sovereignty of Good*. Abingdon, UK: Routledge & Kegan Paul, 1970.

Muzzarelli, Maria Giuseppina. "Pawn Broking between Theory and Practice in Observant Socio-Economic Thought." In *A Companion to Observant Reform in the Late Middle Ages and Beyond*, edited by James Mixson and Bert Roest, 204–29. Brill, 2015.

Myers, Bryant L. *Walking with the Poor: Principles and Practices of Transformational Development*. Maryknoll, NY: Orbis, 1999.

Nelson, Clifford E. *Lutherans in North America*. Minneapolis: Fortress, 1975.

Newfield, Timothy P. "Malaria and Malaria-like Disease in the Early Middle Ages." *Early Medieval Europe* 25 (2017) 251–300.

Nichols, Tom. "Secular Charity, Sacred Poverty: Picturing the Poor in Renaissance Venice." *Art History* 30 (2007) 139–69.

Nicklason, Fred. "Henry George: Social Gospeller." *American Quarterly* 22 (1970) 649–64.

Niebuhr, H. Richard. *Christ and Culture*. New York: HarperCollins, 2001.

Niebuhr, Reinhold. *Moral Man and Immoral Society: A Study in Ethics and Politics*. New York: Scribners, 1932.

———. *The Nature and Destiny of Man: A Christian Interpretation*. New York: Scribners, 1943.

Nolt, Steven M. "Fifty-Year Partners: Mennonite Mutual Aid and the Church." In *Building Communities of Compassion: Mennonite Mutual Aid in Theory and Practice*, edited by Willard M. Swartley and Donald B. Kraybill, 213–43. Scottdale, PA: Herald, 1998.

Nordstokke, Kjell. "The Study of Diakonia as an Academic Discipline." In *Diakonia as Christian Social Practice: An Introduction*, edited by Stephanie Dietrich et al., 46–61. Eugene, OR: Wipf & Stock, 2014.

Nordstrom, Justin. *Danger on the Doorstep: Anti-Catholicism and American Print Culture in the Progressive Era*. Notre Dame: University of Notre Dame Press, 2006.

Norman, Edward. *The Victorian Christian Socialists*. Cambridge: Cambridge University Press, 1987.

Nouwen, Henri J. M., et al. *Compassion: A Reflection on the Christian Life*. New York: Image, 1982.

Nussbaum, Martha. "Compassion: The Basic Social Emotion." *Social Philosophy and Policy* 13 (1996) 27–58.

Nygren, Anders. "Luther's Doctrine of the Two Kingdoms." *The Ecumenical Review* 1 (1949) 301–10.

O'Connor, Elizabeth. *Servant Leaders, Servant Structures*. Washington, DC: Servant Leadership School, 1991.

O'Donnell, Catherine. "'Many Customs and Manners': Transatlantic Influences in the Life and Work of Elizabeth Seton." *U.S. Catholic Historian* 36, no. 3 (2018) 29–50.

Oeltjen, Jarret C. "Pawnbroking: An Historical, Comparative Perspective." *Arizona Journal of International and Comparative Law* 8 (1991) 53–74.

Offutt, Stephen, et al. *Advocating for Justice: An Evangelical Vision for Transforming Systems and Structures*. Grand Rapids: Baker Academic, 2016.

Oliva, Marilyn. *The Convent and the Community in Late Medieval England: Female Monasteries in the Diocese of Norwich, 1350–1540*. Woodbridge, UK: Boydell, 1998.

Olson, Mancur. *The Logic of Collective Action: Public Goods and the Theory of Groups*. Cambridge, MA: Harvard University Press, 1971.

Olsson, Karl A. *Quality of Mercy: Swedish Covenant Hospital and Covenant Home: Seventy-fifth Anniversary 1886–1961*. Chicago: Swedish Covenant, 1961.

Osborne, Robin. "Introduction: Roman Poverty in Context." In *Poverty in the Roman World*, edited by Margaret Atkins and Robin Osborne, 1–20. Cambridge: Cambridge University Press, 2006.

Outka, Gene. *Agape: An Ethical Analysis*. New Haven: Yale University Press, 1977.

Ozment, Steven. *The Age of Reform, 1250–1550: An Intellectual and Religious History of Late Medieval and Reformation Europe*. New Haven, CT: Yale, 1980.

Palazzi, Félix. "Hope and the Kingdom of God: Christology and Eschatology in Latin American Liberation Theology." In *Hope and Solidarity: Jon Sobrino's Challenge to Christian Theology*, edited by Stephen J. Pope, 131–42. Maryknoll, NY: Orbis, 2008.

Paras, Andrea. "Between Missions and Development: Christian NGOs in the Canadian Development Sector." *Canadian Journal of Development Studies* 35 (2014) 439–57.

Pargament, Kenneth I., et al. "The Religious Dimension of Coping: Advances in Theory, Research, and Practice." In *Handbook of the Psychology of Religion and Spirituality*. 2nd ed. Edited by Raymond F. Paloutzian and Crystal L. Park, 560–79. New York: Guilford, 2013.

Park, Crystal L. "Religion as a Meaning-Making Framework in Coping with Life Stress." *Journal of Social Issues* 61 (2005) 707–29.

Parkin, Anneliese. "'You Do Him No Service': An Exploration of Pagan Almsgiving." In *Poverty in the Roman World*, edited by Margaret Atkins and Robin Osborne, 60–82. Cambridge: Cambridge University Press, 2006.

Patrich, Joseph. "Four Christian Objects from Caesarea Maritima." In *Studies in the Archaeology and History of Caesarea Maritima*, edited by Caput Judaeae and Metropolis Palaestinae, 249–58. Leiden: Brill, 2011.

Pattison, Bonnie L. *Poverty in the Theology of John Calvin.* Eugene, OR: Pickwick, 2006.

Peterson, Brian. "Being the Church in Philippi." *Horizons in Biblical Theology* 30 (2008) 163–78.

Peterson, Paul H., and Ronald W. Walker. "Brigham Young's Word of Wisdom Legacy." *Brigham Young University Studies* 42 (2003) 29–64.

Petrick, Gabriella M. "'Purity as Life': H.J. Heinz, Religious Sentiment, and the Beginning of the Industrial Diet." *History and Technology* 27 (2011) 37–64.

Pierce-Dunker, Marilee. *Man of Vision: The Candid, Compelling Story of Bob and Lorraine Pierce, Founders of World Vision and Samaritan's Purse.* Waynesboro, GA: Authentic, 2005.

Pirie, Sophie H. "The Origins of a Political Trial: The Sanctuary Movement and Political Justice." *Yale Journal of Law and the Humanities* 2 (1990) 381–416.

Pitzer, Donald E., ed. *America's Communal Utopias.* Chapel Hill: University of North Carolina Press, 1997.

Plowright, "Political Economy and Christian Polity: The Influence of Henry George in England Reassessed." *Victorian Studies* 30 (1987) 235–52.

Počivavšek, Marija. "Tradition of the Pharmacies of Celje." *Acta Medico-Historica Adriatica* 7 (2009) 237–52.

Poethig, Richard P. "Toward Worldwide Industrial Mission: The Presbyterian Story, 1945–1975." *American Presbyterians* 73 (1995) 35–47.

Polson, Edward, and Laine Scales. "Good Neighbor House: Reimagining Settlement Houses for 21st Century Communities." *Social Work & Christianity* 47(3) (2020) 100–22.

Pontifical Council for Justice and Peace. *Compendium of the Social Doctrine of the Church.* Washington, DC: United States Conference of Catholic Bishops, 2004.

Pope, Stephen J. *Human Evolution and Christian Ethics.* Cambridge: Cambridge University Press, 2007.

———. "Love in Contemporary Christian Ethics." *Journal of Religious Ethics* 23 (1995) 165–97.

Potts, E. Daniel. *British Baptist Missionaries in India, 1793–1837: The History of Serampore and its Missions.* Cambridge: Cambridge University Press, 1967.

Powell, Susan. *John Mirk's Festial.* Vol. 2. Oxford: Oxford University Press, 2011.

Presciutti, Diana Bullen. *Visual Cultures of Foundling Care in Renaissance Italy.* Abingdon: Ashgate, 2015.

The Proceedings of C.O.P.E.C. Being a Report on the Meetings of the Conference on Christian Politics, Economics, and Citizenship, held in Birmingham, April 5-12, 1924. London: Longmans, Green, 1924.

Prochaska, Frank. *Christianity and Social Service in Modern Britain: The Disinherited Spirit.* Oxford: Oxford University Press, 2006.

Prudlo, Donald S. "Mendicancy among the Early Saints of the Begging Orders." In *The Origin, Development, and Refinement of Medieval Religious Mendicancies*, edited by Donald Prudlo, 85–116. Leiden: Brill, 2011.

Pullan, Brian S. "Catholics, Protestants, and the Poor in Early Modern Europe." *Journal of Interdisciplinary History* 35 (2005) 441–56.

"Quakerism as an Experiment Station." *Friends Intelligencer*, September 18, 1915.

Quigley, William P. "Five Hundred Years of English Poor Laws, 1349–1834: Regulating the Working and Nonworking Poor." *Akron Law Review* 30 (1997/1996) 73–128.

Rademacher, Nicholas K. *Paul Hanly Furfey: Priest, Scientist, Social Reformer.* New York: Fordham University Press, 2017.

Rah, Soong-Chan. "Rethinking Incarnational Ministry." *CCDA Theological Journal* (2013) 31–37.

Ramelli, Ilaria L. E. *Social Justice and the Legitimacy of Slavery: The Role of Philosophical Asceticism from Ancient Judaism to Late Antiquity.* 1 edition. New York: Oxford University Press, 2017.

Rauschenbusch, Walter. *Christianizing the Social Order.* Waco: Baylor University Press, 2010.

Rebillard, Éric. *Christians and Their Many Identities in Late Antiquity, North Africa, 200–450 CE.* Ithaca: Cornell University Press, 2012.

———. *The Care of the Dead in Late Antiquity.* Ithaca: Cornell University Press, 2009.

Redekop, Calvin W. *The Pax Story: Service in the Name of Christ, 1951–1976.* Scotdale, PA: Pandora, 2001.

Reed, Jonathan L. "Instability in Jesus' Galilee: A Demographic Perspective." *Journal of Biblical Literature* 129 (2010) 343–65.

———. "Mortality, Morbidity, and Economics in Jesus' Galilee." In *Galilee in the Late Second Temple and Mishnaic Periods*, edited by David A. Fiensy and James Riley Strange, Vol. 1, 242–52. Minneapolis: Augsburg Fortress, 2014.

Reed, Myer S. "An Alliance for Progress: The Early Years of the Sociology of Religion in the United States." *Sociology of Religion* 42 (1981) 27–46.

Rees, B. R. *Pelagius: Life and Letters.* Woodbridge, UK: Boydell, 1998.

Reese, Robert. *Roots and Remedies of the Dependency Syndrome in World Missions.* Pasadena, CA: William Carey, 2010.

Reinhard, Wolfgang. *A Short History of Colonialism.* Manchester: Manchester University Press, 2011.

"Religion: Lord's Acre." *Time*, September 1, 1924.

Reumann, John H. *Stewardship and the Economy of God.* Eugene, OR: Wipf & Stock, 2014.

Rhee, Helen. *Early Christian Literature: Christ and Culture in the Second and Third Centuries.* London: Routledge, 2005.

———. *Loving the Poor, Saving the Rich: Wealth, Poverty and Early Christian Formation.* Grand Rapids: Baker Academic, 2012.

———. "Wealth, Poverty, and Eschatology: Pre-Constantine Christian Social Thought and the Hope for the World to Come." In *Reading Patristic Texts on Social Ethics: Issues and Challenges for Twenty-First-Century Christian Social Thought*, edited by John Leemans et al., 64–84. Washington, DC: Catholic University of America Press, 2011.

Richards, Jeffrey. *Consul of God: The Life and Times of Gregory the Great.* Abingdon, UK: Routledge, 2014.

———. *The Popes and the Papacy in the Early Middle Ages: 476–752.* Routledge, 2014.

Richmond, Vivienne. *Clothing the Poor in Nineteenth-Century England.* Cambridge: Cambridge University Press, 2013.

Richardson, K. C. *Early Christian Care for the Poor: An Alternative Subsistence Strategy under Roman Imperial Rule.* Eugene: Wipf & Stock, 2018.

Rigby, Cynthia. "Christian Life." In *The Cambridge Companion to Reformed Theology,* edited by Paul T. Nimmo and David A. S. Fergusson. Cambridge: Cambridge University Press, 2016.

Rivera-Pagán, Luis N. "The Political Praxis of Bartolomé de Las Casas." In *T & T Clark Handbook of Political Theology,* edited by Rubén Rosario Rodríguez, 131–44. London: T & T Clark, 2020.

Robert, Dana L. *Christian Mission: How Christianity Became a World Religion.* Chichester, UK: Wiley-Blackwell, 2009.

———. "The First Globalization: The Internationalization of the Protestant Missionary Movement Between the World Wars." *International Bulletin of Missionary Research* 26 (2002) 50–66.

———. "Introduction." In *Converting Colonialism: Visions and Realities in Mission History, 1706–1914,* edited by Dana Robert, 1–20. Grand Rapids: Eerdmans, 2008.

Roberts, Alexander, et al., eds. *The Epistle of Ignatius to the Smyrnaeans, Ante-Nicene Fathers.* Translated by Alexander Roberts and James Donaldson. Vol. 1. Buffalo, NY: Christian Literature, 1885.

Roberts, F. David. *The Social Conscience of the Early Victorians.* Stanford: Stanford University Press, 2002.

Roberts, Michael K. "Nazarenes and Social Ministry: A Holiness Tradition." In *Faith and Social Ministry: Ten Christian Perspectives,* edited by James D. Davidson et al., 157–78. Chicago: Loyola University Press, 1990.

Robinson, Charles Mulford. *Modern Civic Art or the City Made Beautiful.* 3rd ed. New York: G. P. Putnam's Sons, 1909.

Robinson, James. *Divine Healing: The Formative Years: 1830–1880: Theological Roots in the Transatlantic World: Theological Roots in the Transatlantic World.* Eugene, OR: Pickwick, 2011.

———. *Divine Healing: The Holiness-Pentecostal Transition Years, 1890–1906: Theological Transpositions in the Transatlantic World.* Eugene, OR: Pickwick, 2013.

———. *Divine Healing: The Years of Expansion, 1906–1930: Theological Variation in the Transatlantic World.* Eugene, OR: Pickwick, 2014.

Robinson, Jonathan. "Innocent IV, John XXII, and the Michaelists on Corporate Poverty." In *Poverty and Prosperity: In the Middle Ages and Renaissánce,* edited by Cynthia Kosso and Anne Scott, 197–224. Turnhout, Belgium: Brepols, 2012.

Rogers, Melissa. "Religious Advocacy by American Religious Institutions: A History." In *The Oxford Handbook of Church and State in the United States,* edited by Derek Davis, 99–138. New York: Oxford University Press, 2010.

Rollmann, Hans. *Labrador through Moravian Eyes: 250 Years of Art, Photographs and Records.* St. John's, NL: Special Celebrations Corporation of Newfoundland and Labrador, 2002.

Rollo-Koster, Joelle. "From Prostitutes to Brides of Christ: The Avignonese Repenties in the Late Middle Ages." *Journal of Medieval and Early Modern Studies* 32 (2002) 109–44.

Romero, Óscar. *Voice of the Voiceless.* Maryknoll, NY: Orbis, 1985.

Romero, Robert Chao. *Brown Church: Five Centuries of Latina/o Social Justice, Theology, and Identity.* Downers Grove: IVP Academic, 2020.

Rosenberg, Charles E. *The Care of Strangers: The Rise of America's Hospital System*. New York: Basic Books, 1987.

———. *The Cholera Years: The United States in 1832, 1849, and 1866*. Chicago: University of Chicago Press, 1987.

Roten, Johann. "Prayers of Saints to Mary." All About Mary. University of Dayton. https://udayton.edu/imri/mary/p/prayers-of-saints-to-mary.php.

Roth, Helena, et al. "Wood Economy in Early Roman Period Jerusalem." *Bulletin of the American Schools of Oriental Research* 382 (November 2019) 71–87.

Roth, John D. "Mutual Aid Among the Swiss Brethren, 1550–1750." In *Building Communities of Compassion: Mennonite Mutual Aid in Theory and Practice*, edited by Willard M. Swartley and Donald B. Kraybill, 119–43. Scotdale, PA: Herald, 1998.

Rowe, C. Kavin. *Christianity's Surprise: A Sure and Certain Hope*. Nashville: Abingdon, 2020.

Rowe, Kenneth E. "Temples of Healing: The Founding Era of Methodist Hospitals, 1880–1900." *Methodist History* 46 (2007) 47–57.

Rubin, J. "Printing and Protestants: An Empirical Test of the Role of Printing in the Reformation." *The Review of Economics and Statistics* 96 (2014) 270–86.

Russian Orthodox Church. "The Basis of the Social Concept." Accessed February 22, 2020. https://mospat.ru/en/documents/social-concepts/.

Ruswick, Brent. *Almost Worthy: The Poor, Paupers, and the Science of Charity in America, 1877–1917*. Bloomington: Indiana University Press, 2013.

Ruys, Juanita Feros. "An Alternative History of Medieval Empathy: The Scholastics and Compassio." *Emotions: History, Culture, Society* 2 (2018) 192–213.

Ryan, James D., ed. *The Spiritual Expansion of Medieval Latin Christendom: The Asian Missions*. Farnham, UK: Ashgate, 2013.

Rybolt, John E. "Vincent de Paul and the Galleys of France." *Vincentian Heritage Journal* 34 (2017) 1–22.

Saarinen, Aino I. L., et al. "The Relationship of Dispositional Compassion with Well-Being: A Study with a 15-year Prospective Follow-up." *The Journal of Positive Psychology* 15 (2020) 806–20.

Safley, Thomas Max. *The Reformation of Charity: The Secular and the Religious in Early Modern Poor Relief*. Boston: Brill Academic, 2003.

Salzman, Michele Renee. "From a Classical to a Christian City: Civic Euergetism and Charity in Late Antique Rome." *Studies in Late Antiquity* 1 (2017) 65–85.

Sander, Kathleen Waters. *The Business of Charity: The Woman's Exchange Movement, 1832–1900*. Urbana: University of Illinois Press, 1998.

Saxby, Trevor J. *Pilgrims of a Common Life: Christian Community of Goods through the Centuries*. Scotdale, PA: Herald, 1987.

Scheele, Dorothy R. "The Friendship Train of 1947," n.d. http://www.thefriendship train1947.org/index.htm.

Schildgen, Robert D. *Toyohiko Kagawa: An Apostle of Love and Social Justice*. Berkeley: Centenary, 1988.

Scheler, Max. *The Nature of Sympathy*. Translated by Peter Heath. Hamden, CT: Archon, 1954.

Schnabel, Eckhard J. "Persecution in the Early Christian Mission According to the Book of Acts." In *Rejection: God's Refugees in Biblical and Contemporary Perspective*, edited by Stanley E. Porter, 141–80. Eugene, OR: Pickwick, 2015.

Schumacher, E. F. *Small Is Beautiful: Economics as If People Mattered*. New York: Harper & Row, 1973.

Schwartz, Glenn J. *When Charity Destroys Dignity: Overcoming Unhealthy Dependency in the Christian Movement: A Compendium*. Lancaster, PA: World Mission, 2007.

Schweitzer, Albert. *Out of My Life and Thought: An Autobiography*. Translated by Antje Bultmann Lemke. Baltimore: Johns Hopkins University Press, 1990.

Scott, Anne M., ed. *Experiences of Charity, 1250–1650*. Farnham, UK: Ashgate, 2015.

Seccombe, David. "Was There Organized Charity in Jerusalem before the Christians?" *Journal of Theological Studies* 29 (1978) 140–3.

Segal, Elizabeth. *Social Empathy: The Art of Understanding Others*. New York: Columbia University Press, 2018.

Shaw, Ian F. "'This Way of Living': George Müller and the Ashley Down Orphanage." *Foundations: An International Journal of Evangelical Theology* 75 (2018) 73–92.

Shearer, Tobin Miller. *Daily Demonstrators: The Civil Rights Movement in Mennonite Homes and Sanctuaries*. Baltimore: Johns Hopkins University Press, 2010.

Sheldon, Charles M. *In His Steps*. Halifax, NS: British-American Book & Tract Society, 1897.

Shi, David E. *The Simple Life: Plain Living and High Thinking in American Culture*. New York: Oxford University Press, 1985.

Shinall, Myrick C., Jr. "The Social Condition of Lepers in the Gospels." *Journal of Biblical Literature* 137 (2018) 915–34.

Shok, Deborah S. "Organized Almsgiving: Scientific Charity and the Society of St. Vincent de Paul in Chicago, 1871-1918." *U.S. Catholic Historian* 16 (1998) 19-35.

Shore, Daniel. "WWJD? The Genealogy of a Syntactic Form." *Critical Inquiry* 37 (2010) 1–25.

Shuler, Eric. "Almsgiving and the Formation of Early Medieval Societies, A.D. 700–1025." Ph.D., University of Notre Dame, 2010.

———. "Caesarius of Arles and the Development of the Ecclesiastical Tithe: From a Theology of Almsgiving to Practiceal Obligations." *Traditio* 67 (2012) 43–69.

Sider, Ronald J. *Rich Christians in an Age of Hunger: A Biblical Study*. Downers Grove, IL: InterVarsity, 1977.

———. *Rich Christians in an Age of Hunger: Moving from Affluence to Generosity*. Nashville: Thomas Nelson, 2005.

Siefer, Gregor. *The Church and Industrial Society: A Survey of the Worker-Priest Movement and Its Implications for the Christian Mission*. Translated by Isabel McHugh and Florence McHugh. London: Darton, Longman and Todd, 1964.

Sifton, Elisabeth. *The Serenity Prayer: Faith and Politics in Times of Peace and War*. New York: Norton, 2003.

Simon, Arthur. *The Rising of Bread for the World: An Outcry of Citizens against Hunger*. New York: Paulist, 2009.

Skinner, Tom. *Black and Free*. Grand Rapids: Zondervan, 1968.

Skobtsova, Maria. *Mother Maria Skobtsova: Essential Writings*. Translated by Richard Pevear and Larissa Volokhonsky. Maryknoll, NY: Orbis, 2002.

Slack, Kenneth, ed. *Hope in the Desert. The Churches' United Response to Human Need, 1944-1984*. Geneva: World Council of Churches, 1986.

Smith, Adam. *The Theory of Moral Sentiments*. New York: Penguin, 2010.

Smith, P. Kent. "Ecosystems of Grace: An Old Vision for the New Church." *Missio Dei: A Journal of Missional Theology and Praxis* 7, Summer-Fall (2016).

Smith, Timothy L. *Revivalism and Social Reform: American Protestantism on the Eve of the Civil War.* Nashville: Abingdon, 1957.

Smith-Rosenberg, Carroll. *Religion and the Rise of the American City: The New York City Mission Movement, 1812–1870.* Ithaca: Cornell University Press, 1971.

Sneider, Matthew Thomas. "The Bonds of Charity: Charitable and Liturgical Obligations in Bolognese Testaments." In *Poverty and Prosperity: In the Middle Ages and Renaissánce,* edited by Cynthia Kosso and Anne Scott, 129–42. Turnhout, Belgium: Brepols, 2012.

Snyder, Arnold. "Anabaptist Spirituality and Economics." In *Anabaptist/Mennonite Faith and Economics,* edited by Calvin W. Redekop et al., 3–18. Lanham, MD: University Press of America, 1994.

Sobrino, Jon. *No Salvation Outside the Poor: Prophetic-Utopian Essays.* Maryknoll, NY: Orbis, 2008.

———. *The Principle of Mercy: Taking the Crucified People from the Cross.* Maryknoll, NY: Orbis, 1994.

———. "Spirituality and the Following of Jesus." In *Systematic Theology: Perspectives from Liberation Theology,* edited by Ignacio Ellacuría and Jon Sobrino, 677–701. Maryknoll, NY: Orbis, 1986.

———. *Where Is God?: Earthquake, Terrorism, Barbarity, and Hope.* Maryknoll, NY: Orbis, 2004.

Sommerville, Raymond R., Jr. *An Ex-colored Church: Social Activism in the CME Church, 1870–1970.* Macon, GA: Mercer University Press, 2004.

Songs of the Workers: On the Road, in the Jungles and in the Shops. 9th ed. Cleveland: I.W.W., 1916.

Sprunger, Mary S. "Dutch Mennonites and the Golden Age Economy: The Problem of Social Disparity in the Church." In *Anabaptist/Mennonite Faith and Economics,* edited by Calvin W. Redekop et al., 19–40. Lanham, MD: University Press of America, 1994.

Standing, Roger. "Charles Garrett and the Birth of the Wesleyan Central Mission Movement." *Wesley and Methodist Studies* 6 (2014) 89–123.

Stanley, Brian. "Christian Missions and the Enlightenment: A Reevaluation." In *Christian Missions and the Enlightenment,* edited by Brian Stanley, 1–21. Grand Rapids: Eerdmans, 2001.

———. *Christianity in the Twentieth Century: A World History.* Princeton: Princeton University Press, 2018.

Stanley, Peter W. *A Nation in the Making: The Philippines and the United States, 1899–1921.* Cambridge, MA: Harvard University Press, 1974.

Stark, Rodney. *The Rise of Christianity: A Sociologist Reconsiders History.* Princeton: Princeton University Press, 1996.

———. *The Triumph of Christianity: How the Jesus Movement Became the World's Largest Religion.* New York: HarperOne, 2011.

Starr, Chloë. *Chinese Theology: Text and Context.* New Haven: Yale University Press, 2016.

Starr, Paul. *The Social Transformation of American Medicine.* New York: Basic, 1982.

Startup, Kenneth Moore. *The Root of All Evil: Protestant Clergy and the Economic Mind of the Old South.* Athens: University of Georgia Press, 1997.

Stearns, Richard. *The Hole in Our Gospel: What Does God Expect of Us? The Answer That Changed My Life and Might Just Change the World.* Nashville: Thomas Nelson, 2009.

Stenning, Ronald E. *Church World Service: Fifty Years of Help and Hope.* New York: Friendship, 1996.

Stenschke, Christoph W. "Obstacles on All Sides: Paul's Collection for the Saints in Jerusalem, Part 1." *European Journal of Theology* 24 (2015) 19–32.

Stephens, Michael S. *Who Healeth All Thy Diseases: Health, Healing, and Holiness in the Church of God Reformation Movement.* Lanham, MD: Scarecrow, 2008.

Sterk, Andrea. *Renouncing the World Yet Leading the Church: The Monk-Bishop in Late Antiquity.* Cambridge, MA: Harvard University Press, 2004.

Stewart-Kroeker, Sarah. *Pilgrimage as Moral and Aesthetic Formation in Augustine's Thought.* Oxford: Oxford University Press, 2017.

Stoop, Patricia. "Fifteenth-Century Vernacular Sermons from the Augustinian Convent of Jericho in Brussels: Fifteenth-Century Vernacular Sermons from the Augustinian Convent of Jericho in Brussels." *Journal of Medieval Religious Cultures* 38 (2012) 211–32.

Straw, Carole. *Gregory the Great: Perfection in Imperfection.* Berkeley: University of California Press, 1988.

Strong, Josiah. *Religious Movements for Social Betterment.* New York: Baker and Taylor, 1900.

Stuber, Karsten. "Empathy." *International Encyclopedia of Ethics.* Wiley Online Library, 2020.

Sugden, Chris. "Fair Trade as Christian Mission." In *Markets, Fair Trade and the Kingdom of God,* edited by Peter Johnson and Chris Sugden, 5–24. Oxford: Regnum, 2001.

Sugirtharajah, R. S. *Jesus in Asia.* Cambridge, MA: Harvard University Press, 2018.

Sullivan, Loise. *Sister Rosalie Rendu: A Daughter of Charity on Fire with Love for the Poor.* Chicago: Vincentian Studies Institute, DePaul University, 2007.

Sutton, Matthew Avery. *Aimee Semple McPherson and the Resurrection of Christian America.* Cambridge, MA: Harvard University Press, 2007.

Svebakken, Gene L., and Paul Bacon. "Dreams, Disappointments, Achievements: The First 150 Years of Social Ministry." *Concordia Historical Institute Quarterly* 70 (1997) 204–16.

Swan, Laura. *The Forgotten Desert Mothers: Sayings, Lives, and Stories of Early Christian Women.* New York: Paulist, 2001.

Swank, Scott Trego. *The Unfettered Conscience: A Study of Sectarianism, Spiritualism, and Social Reform in the New Jerusalem Church, 1840–1870.* PhD diss. University of Pennsylvania, 1970.

Swartley, Willard M., and Donald B. Kraybill. *Building Communities of Compassion: Mennonite Mutual Aid in Theory and Practice.* Scottdale, PA: Herald, 1998.

Swartz, David R. *Facing West: American Evangelicals in an Age of World Christianity.* New York: Oxford University Press, 2020.

———. *Moral Minority: The Evangelical Left in an Age of Conservatism.* Philadelphia: University of Pennsylvania Press, 2012.

Swatos, William H. "The Faith of the Fathers: On the Christianity of Early American Sociology." *Sociology of Religion* 44 (1983) 33–52.

Swierenga, Robert P. *Elim: A Chicago Christian School and Life-training Center for the Disabled.* Grand Rapids: Eerdmans, 2005.

Symanowski, Horst. *The Christian Witness in an Industrial Society.* Translated by George H. Kehm. Philadelphia: Westminster, 1965.

Symeon the Theologian. *The Philokalia: The Complete Text.* Vol. 4. London: Faber & Faber, 1995.

Tabernee, William. "Eusebius' 'Theology of Persecution': As Seen in the Various Editions of his Church History." *Journal of Early Christian Studies* 5 (1997) 319–34.

Taliadoros, Jason. "Law, Theology, and Morality: Conceptions of the Rights to Relief of the Poor in the Twelfth and Thirteenth Centuries: Law, Theology, and Morality." *Journal of Religious History* 37 (2013) 474–93.

Tanner, Kathryn. *Economy of Grace.* Minneapolis: Fortress, 2005.

———. *The Politics of God: Christian Theologies and Social Justice.* Minneapolis: Augsburg Fortress, 1992.

Tappert, Theodore G. *The Book of Concord: The Confessions of the Evangelical Lutheran Church.* Philadelphia: Fortress, 1959.

Tellenbach, Gerd. *The Church in Western Europe from the Tenth to the Early Twelfth Century.* Translated by Timothy Reuter. Cambridge: Cambridge University Press, 1993.

Terpstra, Nicholas. *Lay Confraternities and Civic Religion in Renaissance Bologna.* Cambridge: Cambridge University Press, 1995.

Tertullian of Carthage. *Apology (Apologeticus).* In *Associations in the Greco-Roman World: A Sourcebook,* edited by Richard S. Ascough et al., 248–50. Waco: Baylor University Press, 2012.

Thomas, Gabrielle. "The Human Icon: Gregory of Nazianzus on Being an *imago Dei.*" *Scottish Journal of Theology* 72 (2019) 166–81.

Thompson, Augustine. "The Origins of Religious Mendicancy in Medieval Europe." In *The Origin, Development, and Refinement of Medieval Religious Mendicancies,* edited by Donald Prudlo, 3–30. Leiden: Brill, 2011.

Thompson, James W. *The Church According to Paul: Rediscovering the Community Conformed to Christ.* Grand Rapids: Baker Academic, 2014.

Thompson, Michael G. *For God and Globe: Christian Internationalism in the US between the Great War and the Cold War.* Ithaca Cornell University Press, 2015.

Thompson, R. Jan, and Roma Jo Thompson. *Beyond Our Means: How the Brethren Service Center Dared to Embrace the World.* Elgin, IL: Brethren, 2009.

Thurston, Bonnie Bowman. *The Widows: A Women's Ministry in the Early Church.* Philadelphia: Fortress, 1989.

Tierney, Brian. *Medieval Poor Law: A Sketch of Canonical Theory and Its Application in England.* Berkeley: University of California Press, 1959.

Todd, George. "Mission and Justice." *International Review of Mission* 65 (1976) 251–61.

Torjesen, Karen Jo. "Social and Historical Setting: Christianity as Culture Critique." In *Cambridge History of Early Christian Literature,* edited by Francis Young et al., 181–99. Cambridge: Cambridge University Press, 2004.

Torry, Malcolm. *Bridgebuilders: Workplace Chaplaincy–A History.* Norwich, UK: Canterbury, 2010.

Toynbee, Arnold. "*Progress and Poverty,*" A Criticism of Mr. Henry George: Being Two Lectures Delivered in St. Andrew's Hall, Newman Street, London.* London: Kegan Paul, Trench, 1884.

Tracy, Myles A. "Insurance and Theology: The Background and the Issues." *The Journal of Risk and Insurance* 33 (1966) 85–93.

Trimiew, Darryl M. "The Social Gospel Movement and the Question of Race." In *The Social Gospel Today*, edited by Christopher H. Evans, 27–37. Louisville: Westminster / John Knox, 2001.

Troeltsch, Ernst. *The Social Teaching of the Christian Churches.* Vol. 1. Translated by Olive Wyon. London: George Allen & Unwin, 1931.

Trueblood, Elton. *While it is Day: An Autobiography.* New York: Harper & Row, 1974.

Tucker, Ruth A., and Walter Lyfeld. *Daughters of the Church: Women and Ministry from New Testament Times to the Present.* Grand Rapids: Zondervan, 1987.

Twelftree, Graham H. *In the Name of Jesus: Exorcism among Early Christians.* Grand Rapids: Baker Academic, 2007.

Udovic, Edward. "'Our Good Will and Honest Efforts.' Vincentian Perspectives on Poverty Reduction Efforts." *Vincentian Heritage Journal* 28 (2008) 69–77.

———. "Pictures from the Past: Saint-Lazare as a Prison: 1792–1940." *Vincentian Heritage Journal* 28 (2008) 65–72.

Ukeachusim, Chidinma Precious, et al. "Understanding Compassion in the Gospel of Matthew (Matthew 14:13-21)." *Theology Today* 77 (2021) 372–92.

Umble, Jeni Hiett. "Mutual Aid among the Augsburg Anabaptists, 1526–1528." In *Building Communities of Compassion: Mennonite Mutual Aid in Theory and Practice*, edited by Willard M. Swartley and Donald B. Kraybill, 103–18. Scotdale, PA: Herald, 1998.

United Methodist Church. *United Methodist Revised Social Principles.* Washington, DC: Church & Society, United Methodist Church, 2020. https://www.umcjustice.org/who-we-are/the-revised-social-principles.

United Nations Human Rights. *The Rights of Vulnerable Children under the Age of Three: Ending Their Placement in Institutional Care.* Geneva: The Office of the High Commissioner for Human Rights, 2017.

United Nations Population Fund. *Religion and Development, Post-2015.* New York, 2014. https://www.unfpa.org/sites/default/files/pub-pdf/DONOR-UN-FBO%20May%202014.pdf.

United States Conference of Catholic Bishops. "Communities of Salt and Light: Reflections on the Social Mission of the Parish." USCCB, 2015. https://www.usccb.org/resources/communities-salt-and-light-reflections-social-mission-parish.

———. *National Directory for the Formation, Ministry, and Life of Permanent Deacons in the United States.* Washington, DC: USCCB, 2005.

Unruh, Heidi, and Ronald J. Sider. *Saving Souls, Serving Society: Understanding the Faith Factor in Church-Based Social Ministry.* New York: Oxford University Press, 2005.

Unterman, Jeremiah. *Justice for All: How the Jewish Bible Revolutionized Ethics.* Philadelphia: Jewish Publication Society, 2017.

Vander Zaag, Ray. "Canadian Faith-Based Development NGOs and CIDA Funding." *Canadian Journal of Development Studies* 34 (2013) 321–47.

———. "Trends in CIDA Funding to Canadian Religious Development NGOs: Analysing Conflicting Studies." *Canadian Journal of Development Studies* 35 (2014) 458–74.

Vanier, Jean. *Community and Growth.* Rev. New York: Paulist, 1979.

Venema, Janny. "Poverty and Charity in Seventeenth-Century Beverwijck / Albany, 1652–1700." *New York History* 80 (1999) 369–90.

Visser't Hooft, Willem A. *The Background of the Social Gospel in America*. St. Louis: Bethany, 1963.

Vives, Juan Luis. *Concerning the Relief of the Poor; or, Concerning Human Need; A Letter Addressed to the Senate of Bruges*. Translated by Margaret M. Sherwood. New York: New York School of Philanthropy, 1917.

Volder, Jan de. *The Spirit of Father Damien: The Leper Priest-A Saint for Our Times*. San Francisco: Ignatius, 2010.

Voltmer, Rita. "Political Preaching and a Design of Urban Reform: Johannes Geiler of Kaysersberg and Strasbourg." *Franciscan Studies* 71 (2013) 71–88.

Wacker, Grant. "The Holy Spirit and the Spirit of the Age in American Protestantism, 1880–1910." *The Journal of American History* 72 (1985) 45–62.

Waldenström, P. P. "Lord Jesus, Make Us Merciful Like You!" In *The Swedish Pietists: A Reader*, edited and translated by Mark Safstrom, 199–202. Eugene, OR: Wipf & Stock, 2015.

Walsh, Gerald G., and Francis L. Glimm, eds. *The Fathers of the Church. 1 Clement*. Washington, DC: Catholic University of America Press, 1947.

"The War and the Social Gospel." *The Christian Century*, December 27, 1917.

Ward, Harry F. *The New Social Order: Principles and Programs*. New York: Macmillan, 1920.

———. *The Social Creed of the Churches*. New York: Abingdon, 1914.

———. *Social Evangelism*. New York: Missionary Education Movement of the United States and Canada, 1915.

Ward, Haruko Nawata. *Women Religious Leaders in Japan's Christian Century, 1549–1650*. Surrey: Ashgate, 2009.

Warren, Michelle Ferrigno. *The Power of Proximity: Moving Beyond Awareness to Action*. Downers Grove, IL: InterVarsity, 2017.

Washington, James M., ed. *A Testament of Hope: The Essential Writings and Speeches of Martin Luther King Jr*. New York: HarperCollins, 1991.

Watson, Kevin M. *Pursuing Social Holiness: The Band Meeting in Wesley's Thought and Popular Methodist Practice*. New York: Oxford University Press, 2014.

Watson, William. "The Sisters of Charity, the 1832 Cholera Epidemic in Philadelphia and Duffy's Cut." *U.S. Catholic Historian* 27 (2009) 1–16.

Watts, Edward J. *The Final Pagan Generation: Rome's Unexpected Path to Christianity*. Oakland: University of California Press, 2015.

Weaver-Zercher, David L. *Martyrs Mirror: A Social History*. Baltimore: Johns Hopkins University Press, 2016.

Wells, Amos R. *Union Work: A Manual for Local, County, District, and State Christian Endeavor Societies*. Boston: United Society of Christian Endeavor, 1916.

Welp, Laura R., and Christina M. Brown. "Self-Compassion, Empathy, and Helping Intentions." *The Journal of Positive Psychology* 9 (2014) 54–65.

Wesley, John. "Sermon 98-On Visiting the Sick." *The Sermons of John Wesley*. Nampa, ID: Wesley Center for Applied Theology, 1999.

Wessel, Susan. *Passion and Compassion in Early Christianity*. New York: Cambridge University Press, 2016.

Wet, Chris L. de. *Preaching Bondage: John Chrysostom and the Discourse of Slavery in Early Christianity*. Berkeley: University of California Press, 2015.

White, Calvin, Jr. *Rise to Respectability: Race, Religion, and the Church of God in Christ.* Fayetteville: University of Arkansas Press, 2017.

White, W. C. *A Call to Medical Evangelism and Health Education: Being Selections from the Writings of Ellen G. White.* The Pacific Coast Conferences of the Seventh-day Adventists, c. 1933.

White, William C. *Slaying the Dragon: The History of Addiction Treatment and Recovery in America,* 2nd ed. Bloomington, IL: Chestnut Health Systems/Lighthouse Institute, 2014.

Wicks, Jared. "Applied Theology at the Deathbed: Luther and the Late-Medieval Tradition of the Ars Moriendi." *Gregorianum* 79 (1998) 345–68.

Wigg-Stevenson, Tyler. *The World Is Not Ours to Save: Finding the Freedom to Do Good.* Downer's Grove, IL: InterVarsity, 2013.

Wilcox, Fred A. *Uncommon Martyrs: The Berrigans, the Catholic Left, and the Plowshares Movement.* Reading, MA: Addison-Wesley, 1991.

Wilhelm, Mark Ottoni, and René Bekkers. "Helping Behavior, Dispositional Empathic Concern, and the Principle of Care." *Social Psychology Quarterly* 73 (2010) 11–32.

Wilson, Walter T. *The Sentences of Sextus.* Atlanta: Society of Biblical Literature, 2012.

Winner, Lauren F. *The Dangers of Christian Practice: On Wayward Gifts, Characteristic Damage, and Sin.* New Haven: Yale University Press, 2018.

Wogaman, J. Philip. *Christian Ethics: A Historical Introduction.* Louisville: Westminster / John Knox, 1993.

Wolf, Kenneth Baxter. *The Poverty of Riches: St. Francis of Assisi Reconsidered.* New York: Oxford University Press, 2005.

Wolfe, Greg. "Writing Poverty in Rome." In *Poverty in the Roman World,* edited by Margaret Atkins and Robin Osborne, 83–99. Cambridge: Cambridge University Press, 2006.

Wright, Ben. *Bonds of Salvation: How Christianity Inspired and Limited American Abolitionism.* Baton Rouge: Louisiana State University Press, 2020.

Xi, Lian. *Blood Letters: The Untold Story of Lin Zhao, a Martyr in Mao's China.* New York: Basic Books, 2018.

Yoder, Peter James. *Pietism and the Sacraments: The Life and Theology of August Hermann Francke.* State College: Pennsylvania State University Press, 2020.

Young, Brigham. "The Work of the Priesthood the Improvement of the Human Family—The Gospel More Than Morality, It Includes Redemption—Differences Between the Ideas of the Saints and the World—The Prophets in Regard to the Increase of Mineral Wealth—Teach the Children." *Journal of Discourses* 19 (May 27, 1877) 45–50.

Zika, Charles. "Compassion in Punishment: The Visual Evidence in Sixteenth-Century Depictions of Calvary." In *Cultural Shifts and Ritual Transformations in Reformation Europe: Essays in Honor of Susan C. Karant-Nunn,* edited by Victoria Christman and Marjorie Elizabeth Plummer, 251–83. Leiden: Brill, 2020.

Zwick, Mark, and Louise Zwick. *The Catholic Worker Movement: Intellectual and Spiritual Origins.* New York: Paulist, 2005.

Index of Historical Actors, Institutions, and Ideas